American Rococo, 1750-1775: Elegance in Ornament

American Rococo, 1750-1775: Elegance in Ornament

MORRISON H. HECKSCHER

———

LESLIE GREENE BOWMAN

THE METROPOLITAN MUSEUM OF ART

LOS ANGELES COUNTY MUSEUM OF ART

Distributed by Harry N. Abrams, Inc., New York

This book has been published in conjunction with the exhibition *American Rococo, 1750–1775: Elegance in Ornament,* held at The Metropolitan Museum of Art, New York, from 26 January to 17 May, and at the Los Angeles County Museum of Art from 5 July to 27 September 1992.

The exhibition is made possible by The Henry Luce Foundation, Inc., and the National Endowment for the Arts.

The exhibition was organized by The Metropolitan Museum of Art and the Los Angeles County Museum of Art.

Additional support for the exhibition in New York has been provided by The Real Estate Council of The Metropolitan Museum of Art.

Additional support for the exhibition in Los Angeles has been provided by the Robert and Nancy Daly Foundation.

The exhibition is also supported at the Metropolitan Museum by grants from Annette de la Renta, H. Richard Dietrich, Jr., Mr. and Mrs. Anthony L. Geller, Mr. and Mrs. Robert G. Goelet, Grace Foundation Inc., Mr. and Mrs. Robert A. Hut, Joullian & Co., Mr. and Mrs. George M. Kaufman, Mrs. Alexander O. Vietor, and Mr. and Mrs. Erving Wolf.

The book that accompanies the exhibition is made possible in part by a generous grant from the Luce Fund for Scholarship in American Art, a program of The Henry Luce Foundation, Inc. Additional funding was received from The William Cullen Bryant Fellows of The American Wing at the Metropolitan Museum, The Chipstone Foundation, Sotheby's, John L. Marion, and the American Decorative Arts Department of Christie's, New York.

John P. O'Neill, *Editor in Chief and General Manager of Publications*
Mary-Alice Rogers, *Editor, The William Cullen Bryant Fellows Publications, The American Wing*
Elizabeth Finger, *Designer*
Helga Lose, *Production*

Typeset by Craftsman Type Inc., Dayton, Ohio
Color reproduction by Reprocolor International s.r.l., Milan, Italy
Printed and bound by Arti Grafiche Motta, S.p.A., Milan, Italy

Library of Congress Cataloging-in-Publication Data

Heckscher, Morrison H.
American rococo, 1750–1775: elegance in ornament / Morrison H. Heckscher, Leslie Greene Bowman.
    p.   cm.
Includes bibliographical references and index.
ISBN 0-87099-630-4.—ISBN 0-87099-631-2 (pbk.).— ISBN 0-8109-6412-0 (Abrams)
1. Decoration and ornament, Rococo—United States—Exhibitions. 2. Decoration and ornament—United States—History—18th century—Exhibitions. I. Bowman, Leslie Greene. II. Title.
NK1403.5.H4 1992 745.4'4974'090330747471—dc20   91-29595
                                                            CIP

Cover-jacket: Slab table, Philadelphia, ca. 1770. The Metropolitan Museum of Art, John Stewart Kennedy Fund, 1918 (18.110.27)

Frontispiece: Coffee pot, ca. 1753, Philip Syng, Jr., Philadelphia. Philadelphia Museum of Art, Purchased: John D. McIlhenny Fund (66-20-1)

CONTENTS

FOREWORD   VII

PREFACE   VIII

ACKNOWLEDGMENTS   XI

LENDERS TO THE EXHIBITION   XV

———

The American Rococo   I

Architecture   17

Engravings   37

Silver   71

Furniture   133

Cast Iron, Glass, and Porcelain 219

———

NOTES   240

BIBLIOGRAPHY   257

EXHIBITION CHECKLIST   264

INDEX   276

PHOTOGRAPH CREDITS   288

FOREWORD

The rococo style was among the primary artistic contributions of the eighteenth century. Its manifestations throughout Europe have been comprehensively acknowledged and chronicled, but its influence in America, where it was probably the century's crowning design achievement (commonly referred to as the Chippendale style), has never been thoroughly examined. It was a lavish taste that found surprisingly fertile ground in the colonies, where affluent members of society, rejoicing in their hard-won prosperity, strove to adopt London fashions. Their success in so doing is richly demonstrated in the pages that follow and in the exhibition that this book accompanies.

We are especially pleased that *American Rococo, 1750–1775: Elegance in Ornament* should be jointly organized by our two institutions. The undertaking began with the desire of the Los Angeles County Museum of Art to mount an exhibition of American Chippendale furniture in a city where such objects have always been in short supply. With the realization that there had never been a comprehensive examination of the rococo style as it was practiced in the American colonies, and that such an exhibition might be of interest on the east coast as well as on the west, the Metropolitan Museum joined forces with Los Angeles.

This bicoastal venture results from the efforts of Morrison H. Heckscher, Curator, American Decorative Arts, at The Metropolitan Museum of Art, and Leslie Greene Bowman, Curator of Decorative Arts at the Los Angeles County Museum of Art. Such a partnership acknowledges the century of commitment to American decorative arts at The Metropolitan Museum of Art and the extraordinary growth of the Los Angeles County Museum of Art since its founding in 1913.

We take pleasure in extending our gratitude to a number of institutions and individuals for the generosity that made *American Rococo* possible, particularly The Henry Luce Foundation, Inc., whose gift toward the book in 1985 launched the undertaking and whose further contribution in 1991 materially aided the endeavor. Additional support for

the exhibition has been provided by the National Endowment for the Arts. At a crucial moment, members of the Visiting Committee of the Department of American Decorative Arts at the Metropolitan took up the cause of the project with handsome individual gifts. We are also obliged to the William Cullen Bryant Fellows of The American Wing of the Metropolitan Museum, whose editor, Mary-Alice Rogers, saw the book through to publication.

The presentation of the exhibition in New York is made possible in part by the financial assistance provided by The Real Estate Council of The Metropolitan Museum of Art. Additional support for the exhibition in New York has been provided by Annette de la Renta, H. Richard Dietrich, Jr., Mr. and Mrs. Anthony L. Geller, Mr. and Mrs. Robert G. Goelet, Grace Foundation Inc., Mr. and Mrs. Robert A. Hut, Joullian & Co., Mr. and Mrs. George M. Kaufman, Mrs. Alexander O. Vietor, and Mr. and Mrs. Erving Wolf. We are further obligated to the Robert and Nancy Daly Foundation for its contribution toward the production of the exhibition in Los Angeles.

We are indebted to the Luce Fund for Scholarship in American Art, a program of The Henry Luce Foundation, Inc., for providing a generous grant toward the publication of the book. Additional funding was received from The Chipstone Foundation, Sotheby's, John L. Marion, and the American Decorative Arts Department of Christie's, New York.

Museums have always depended for their very existence on the sponsorship of their friends and benefactors. That tangible outpouring of care and interest has never been more vital than it is in the world of today, nor have we ever had more reason to cherish it.

Philippe de Montebello, *Director*
The Metropolitan Museum of Art

Earl A. Powell III, *Director*
Los Angeles County Museum of Art

PREFACE

American Rococo, 1750–1775: Elegance in Ornament is a book about a style. In planning it and the exhibition it accompanies, the authors decided on two arbitrary restrictions: that the definition of rococo be limited to the ornamental aspect of the eighteenth-century style and that the works chosen for inclusion be limited to those of American manufacture. Obviously, however, there had to be some flexibility in the range of dates defined in the title. In addition, though a handful of English-made pieces are present to illustrate the essential English quality of the style as well as the manner of its transmission to America, we chose to concentrate not on the admixture of imported and native-made objects that was the reality of the furnishings of the colonial elite but on the best examples of domestic creativity, which we selected for their exceptional workmanship and aesthetic merit. As is always the case with a loan exhibition, because of conservation concerns, financial exigencies, and other practical limitations, we had to forgo certain objects we would otherwise have chosen.

The book does not purport to be a survey of the arts in America in the third quarter of the eighteenth century. Silver and furniture—in this country the two categories most congenial to rococo ornamentation—form the principal sections and are therefore discussed at greatest length. Among the avenues of artistic endeavor we excluded are American paintings (such as mid-century portraits by Blackburn and the young Copley) now generally considered to be of a rococo sensibility but having little, if anything, to do with rococo ornamentation. The inclusion of certain domestic neoclassical portraits is justified by their being enclosed in their original, luxuriously rococo frames. Unrepresented are some of the era's major regional schools, either because their output is not in the rococo mode (the famous baroque block-and-shell furniture of Newport, for instance) or

because their invocation of the style is so far removed from the English source as to constitute a totally different image (furniture by Eliphalet Chapin of Windsor, Connecticut—an idiosyncratic offshoot of Philadelphia design—immediately comes to mind).

Primarily, the book and the exhibition were conceived to address the fundamental question: Did the rococo style exist in colonial America? The relevance of that question became increasingly apparent through our long preparation by the omnipresent specter of John Henry Belter, whose fostering of the rococo-revival style in mid-nineteenth-century America is so widely recognized as to obfuscate the original rococo's flourishing on these shores. *Baroque & Rococo: Architecture & Decoration*, edited by Anthony Blunt (London, 1978), a major international survey of the dominant styles of the seventeenth and eighteenth centuries, never even mentions England's colonies in the New World. As authors, we owe a debt of inspiration to *Rococo: Art and Design in Hogarth's England*, an exhibition at the Victoria and Albert Museum, and its accompanying catalogue (London, 1984), which provided a cornucopic view of the style's presence in England; it is our aim to achieve something comparable for its presence in America.

The first chapter of the book, a summary of the European origins and the American manifestations of the rococo, concludes with a brief discussion of firearms, whose ornament consists equally of engraved metal and carved wood, and textiles, which are too few in number to warrant a separate study. The second chapter is devoted to architecture. Though little of it survives and only one example is contained in the exhibition, it provided the setting for the style's use in the other mediums and in itself served as a showplace for the carver's art. The rest of the book is arranged in chapters according to medium (paper; silver; wood; iron, glass, and ceramics), with the focus of the text on the style of an object and with matters of construction, condition, and provenance touched on only insofar as was deemed relevant.

Objects whose illustrations are identified by a number and a brief caption are part of the exhibition and are recorded in full in its checklist (pp. 264-75). The number appears in boldface type at that point in the text where the object is discussed at length, in a section set off by spaces, suggesting what would be an entry in a standard exhibition catalogue. Illustrations identified by a figure number are of objects that could not be included in the exhibition or of images that were added to the text for comparative purposes.

Dimensions are given in inches, to the nearest eighth of an inch, and in centimeters. Where only one dimension is given, it is the greatest; where there are two or three, unless otherwise noted, they are in order of height, width, and depth. For works on paper, the measurements are of the plate mark, if it exists, or of the image, if it does not. For objects of wood, the semicolon after the primary wood denotes that those that follow are secondary. The bibliography (pp. 257-63) contains not only all references employed in short form in the text and in the endnotes but also sources of general importance to any investigation of the American rococo.

Morrison H. Heckscher
Leslie Greene Bowman

ACKNOWLEDGMENTS

An exhibition of the scope and complexity of *American Rococo* is possible only with the combined efforts of countless people of diverse talents. We acknowledge the almost universal enthusiasm and cooperation with which we were greeted during our years of travel and research. Our first debt is to Philippe de Montebello and Earl A. Powell III, directors of The Metropolitan Museum of Art and the Los Angeles County Museum of Art, respectively, for their steadfast support, which made possible this joint venture of the two institutions.

At the Metropolitan, scores of individuals worked to make *American Rococo* happen. In the director's office we are particularly indebted to Mahrukh Tarapor and Martha Deese; in the development office, Emily Kernan Rafferty, Nina McN. Diefenbach, and Carol Ehler; for all registrarial details, John Buchanan and Nina S. Maruca; for exhibition design, David Harvey, for graphic design, Jill Hammerberg, and for lighting, Zach Zanolli; for the conservation of objects, John Canonico, Rudolf Colban, Sherry Doyal, Kathryn J. Gill, Hermes Knauer, William Louche, Dorothy Mahon, Mark Minor, Marjorie N. Shelley, Catherine Turton, Antoine M. Wilmering; for photography, Barbara Bridgers, Alexander Mikhailovich, Karin L. Willis, and Carmel Wilson. Assistance was also graciously provided by Colta Ives, David W. Kiehl, and Tom Rassieur of the Department of Prints and Photographs, and by Clare LeCorbeiller, Jessie McNab, and William Rieder of the Department of European Sculpture and Decorative Arts.

We are grateful to all our colleagues in the American Wing: John K. Howat, The Lawrence A. Fleischman Chairman of the Departments of American Art; curators Alice Cooney Frelinghuysen, Peter M. Kenny, Amelia Peck, Frances Gruber Safford, and especially Catherine Hoover Voorsanger; administrative assistants Ellin Rosenzweig and Seraphine Wu; departmental technicians Gary Burnett, Edward Di Farnecio, Sean Farrell, and Don E. Templeton.

We owe special thanks to the interns and volunteers who devoted their energies to various aspects of this project: Gordon Frey, Elizabeth J. Kannan, Florence Klein, Andrew J. Kronenberg, Jordana Pomeroy, Leslie Symington, and Carla Yanni.

At Los Angeles, we particularly appreciate the forbearance and support of members of the decorative arts department: Martin G. Chapman, Jeanette Hanisee, Roger E. Jones, Martha D. Lynn, Judy Anderson, and former department head Timothy Schroder, as well as department interns Deidre Cronenbold, Kathy Goddard, and Wendy Wasson. Research assistance was also provided by Eleanor Hartman, Anne Diederick, and other members of the library staff. For help with grants, contracts, and fund-raising, we thank Ronald B. Bratton, deputy director; Elizabeth H. Algermissen, assistant director; Julie A. Johnston, director of development, and her assistant, Tom Jacobson; and Mark Mitchell, budget manager. For their invaluable assistance with the exhibition in Los Angeles we acknowledge assistant director Arthur Owens and his staff members Mary Loughlin and William Stahl; head of exhibition programs John Passi, exhibition designer Bernard Kester, special events planning director Janis Dinwiddie and her staff; we also credit Steven N. Oliver for his photography. For exhibition installation we are obliged to Roma Allison, Lou Massad, Willie Williams, and their staffs; for registrarial assistance, Renee Montgomery and Chandra King; for conservation consultation, Pieter Meyers, Steve Cristin-Poucher, and Don Menveg; for travel arrangements, Janice Ellis and Feroza Vimadalal.

We are indebted to our colleagues at innumerable museums, libraries, and historical societies for making their collections accessible (and in many cases also facilitating loans), for assisting with research, and for providing illustrations. In particular, we salute the following individuals and their institutions: Albany Institute of History and Art:

Tammis K. Groft, Christine Robinson; American Antiquarian Society: Georgia B. Barnhill; The Art Institute of Chicago: Andora Morginson, Milo M. Naeve; The Baltimore Museum of Art: Wendy A. Cooper, William Voss Elder III, Deborah A. Federhen; Boston Marine Society: Harold F. Lynch; Boston Public Library: Sinclair Hitchings; The Brooklyn Museum: Kevin Stayton; The John Carter Brown Library: Susan L. Danforth, Norman Fiering; Burlington County Historical Society: Rhett Pernot; The Carnegie Museum of Art: Phillip M. Johnston; The Charleston Museum: Christopher T. Loeblein; The Chipstone Foundation: Luke Beckerdite; Sterling and Francine Clark Art Institute: Beth Carver Wees; Colonial Williamsburg: Wallace B. Gusler, Graham Hood, Ronald Hurst, Margaret Pritchard; Columbia University: Hollee Haswell, Herbert Mitchell; Connecticut Historical Society: Christopher P. Bickford; The Corning Museum of Glass: Dwight P. Lanmon, Jane S. Spillman; Department of State: Clement Conger, Mary Itsell, Gail Serfati; Dickinson College Library: Marie Booth Ferré, George Hing; The Dietrich American Foundation: Deborah McCracken Rebuck; Essex Institute: Robert Weis; First Troop Philadelphia City Cavalry: John C. Devereux; Fogg Art Museum: Louise Todd Ambler, Marjorie B. Cohn, Jane Montgomery; Henry Ford Museum & Greenfield Village: Michael J. Ettema; Genealogical Society of Pennsylvania: Antoinette J. Segraves; Gibbes Museum of Art: Angela D. Mack; Hershey Museum: Leslie A. Bellais, James McMahon; High Museum of Art: Donald C. Peirce; Historic Charleston Foundation: Jonathan H. Poston, J. Thomas Savage, Jr.; Historic Cherry Hill: Anne W. Ackerson; Historic Deerfield, Inc.: Amanda Merullo, Bruce Mosely, Janine Skerry, Philip Zea; The Historical Society of Pennsylvania: David Cassedy; Hopewell Furnace National Historic Site: Lee Boyle, Diane Cram; Independence National Historic Park: Karie Diethorn, Doris D. Fanelli;

Library Company of Philadelphia: John C. Van Horne; Marblehead Historical Society: Bette Hunt, Mary Parrish; Maryland Historical Society: Jennifer F. Goldsborough, Gregory Weidman; Moravian Historical Society: Susan M. Dreydoppel; Mount Vernon Ladies' Association of the Union: Christine Meadows; Museum of the City of New York: Deborah Dependahl Waters, Jan S. Ramirez; Museum of Early Southern Decorative Arts: John Bivins, Jr., Frank L. Horton, Madelyn Moeller, Bradford L. Rauschenberg, Margaret Vincent; Museum of Fine Arts, Boston: Ellenor Alcorn, Edward S. Cooke, Jr., Jonathan Fairbanks, Jeannine Falino, Rachael Monfredo, Jeffrey Munger, Janice Sorkow, Linda Thomas, John Woolf; Museum of Fine Arts, Houston: Michael K. Brown; National Trust for Historic Preservation: Jennifer Esler, Elizabeth M. Laurent, Frank E. Sanchis; The New Jersey Historical Society: Rosalind Libbey, Wilson E. O'Donnell; New Jersey State Museum: Suzanne Corlette Crilley, Susan Finkel; The New-York Historical Society: Timothy Anglin Burgard, Nina R. Gray, Holly Hotchner, Wendy Shadwell; The New York Public Library: Roberta Waddell; Philadelphia Museum of Art: Beatrice B. Garvan, Jack L. Lindsey, Nancy Quaile; Portland Museum of Art: Martha R. Severens; Rhode Island School of Design: Thomas S. Michie, Christopher P. Monkhouse, Franklin W. Robinson; The Society for the Preservation of New England Antiquities: Brock Jobe, Richard Nylander; State Museum of Pennsylvania: James Mitchell; Van Cortlandt House: Elizabeth B. Leckie; Virginia Museum of Fine Arts: William M. S. Rasmussen; Wadsworth Atheneum: William Hosley, Elizabeth Kornhauser; Winterthur Museum: Kenneth Ames, Burt Denker, Nancy G. Evans, Donald L. Fennimore, E. McSherry Fowble, Thomas A. Graves, Paul B. Hensley, Charles F. Hummel, Anizia Karmazyn, John Krill, Greg Landrey, Richard McKinstry, Katharine Martinez, Michael S. Podmaniczky, Ian M. G. Quimby, Cheryl Robertson,

Karol A. Schmiegel, Susan Swan, Neville Thompson, Robert F. Trent, Philip D. Zimmerman; Worcester Art Museum: Sally R. Freitag, Susan E. Strickler; Yale University Art Gallery: David L. Barquist, Diane Hart, Patricia E. Kane, Jules D. Prown.

Many individuals also deserve mention and thanks: Robert Barker, Henry L. P. Beckwith, jr., Philip H. Bradley, Alice Braunfeld, Christopher Burr, Margaret B. Caldwell and Carlo M. Florentino, Marian S. Carson, Mr. and Mrs. Robert A. Daly, William K. du Pont, Mr. and Mrs. Carlyle C. Eubank II, Martha Gandy Fales, JoAnn and Julian Ganz, Wendell D. Garrett, Robert George, William H. Guthman, Michael Hall, Kenneth Hawkins, Gregory A. Higginson, James P. Jenkins, Mr. and Mrs. William S. Kilroy, Joe Kindig III, Mr. and Mrs. Bernadotte P. Lester, Jr., Bernard Levy, S. Dean Levy, Arthur Liverant, Israel Liverant, Joseph H. McGee, Peter Manigault, Alan Miller, Ruth Miller, Mr. and Mrs. James L. Nugent, Jr., Max Palevsky, Arlene Palmer, Lloyd A. Pearson, Adolph and Beverley Placzek, D. J. Puffert, Richard H. Randall, Jr., Michael Rebic, Barbara Roberts, Alexandra W. Rollins, Albert Sack, Harold Sack, Robert Sack, Jeanne Sloane, Michael Snodin, Willman Spawn, Laura F. Sprague, Patricia A. Teter, Gilbert T. Vincent, Barbara and Gerald W. R. Ward.

At the Metropolitan Museum, we express our appreciation to members of the editorial department for the production of the book: John P. O'Neill, Editor in Chief and General Manager of Publications; Barbara Burn, Executive Editor; Teresa Egan, Managing Editor; Kendra Ho, proofreader; Susan Bradford, indexer; Steffie Kaplan, mechanicals artist; Peter Antony and especially Helga Lose, production associates.

Our greatest debts, however, are to Elizabeth Finger, for the timeless beauty of her book design; David Allison, for the fine and sensitive new photography for the book; and Frances Bretter, for her dedicated and meticulous assistance in all phases of the exhibition. Mary-Alice Rogers, master wordsmith, labored unstintingly to achieve whatever clarity and elegance are found in this volume. Our final acknowledgment is to our families and friends for their steadfast forbearance and encouragement.

Morrison H. Heckscher
Leslie Greene Bowman

LENDERS TO THE EXHIBITION

Albany Institute of History and Art

American Antiquarian Society

Avery Architectural and Fine Arts Library,
    Columbia University

Mrs. Graham John Barbey, Courtesy of the Maryland
    Historical Society

Birdsboro Community Memorial Center

Boston Marine Society

Mrs. Murray Braunfeld

David M., Nelson F., Peter R., and Robert W. Brinckerhoff,
    and their families

The Brooklyn Museum

The John Carter Brown Library at Brown University

Burlington County Historical Society

The Carnegie Museum of Art

The Charleston Museum

The Chipstone Foundation

Cliveden, a co-stewardship property of the National Trust
    for Historic Preservation

The Colonial Williamsburg Foundation

Connecticut Historical Society

The Corning Museum of Glass

The Richard Henry Dana family

Dickinson College

The Dietrich American Foundation

H. Richard Dietrich, Jr.

Diplomatic Reception Rooms, Department of State

William K. du Pont

George G. Meade Easby

Essex Institute

First Scots Presbyterian Church, Charleston

Gibbes Museum of Art

Harvard University Art Museums

Henry Ford Museum & Greenfield Village

Hershey Museum

High Museum of Art

Historic Cherry Hill

Historic Deerfield, Inc.

The Historical Society of Pennsylvania

Mr. and Mrs. George M. Kaufman

Joe Kindig III

Robert E. Lee Memorial Association, Inc.,
    Stratford Hall Plantation

Bernard and S. Dean Levy, Inc.

The Library Company of Philadelphia

Los Angeles County Museum of Art

Marblehead Historical Society

Mr. and Mrs. Frank A. Mauri

The Metropolitan Museum of Art

Moravian Historical Society

Museum of Art, Rhode Island School of Design

Museum of the City of New York

Museum of Early Southern Decorative Arts

Museum of Fine Arts, Boston

The National Society of Colonial Dames in the State of
    New York; Van Cortlandt House

The New Jersey Historical Society

New Jersey State Museum

The New-York Historical Society

The New York Public Library

Eric Noah

Mr. and Mrs. Edward J. Nusrala

Philadelphia Museum of Art

The State Museum of Pennsylvania

Philip Van Rensselaer Van Wyck

Wadsworth Atheneum

The Winterthur Library

Winterthur Museum

Erving and Joyce Wolf

Worcester Art Museum

Yale University Art Gallery

Private collectors (six)

THE AMERICAN ROCOCO

The word "rococo" was evidently first coined in 1796 or 1797 by Maurice Quaï, a pupil of Jacques-Louis David's, who used it as a pejorative description of the style associated with Louis XV.[1] Quaï was almost certainly corrupting the term "rocaille," one of the rococo's characteristic motifs. "Rocaille" was originally used to refer to the tortuous rockwork fabricated for artificial caves or grottoes, themselves evocative of aquatic fantasies, in the seventeenth-century pleasure gardens of the aristocracy. "Rococo" lost its negative connotation by the 1840s, and since that time has been used to name a style that during the first half of the eighteenth century permeated all branches of artistic endeavor in Europe, from the fine arts to the decorative, expressing a new, unconventional, and highly ornamental spirit of fantasy, elegance, and movement. In its departure from classical order and symmetry, the rococo scorned the rule and the compass in favor of embellishment that required skillful freehand rendering and an imagination that transcended the bounds of academic convention.

Tracing its origins to sources in Italian baroque designs, the rococo was nurtured to maturity in France in the 1730s, largely at the hand of the gifted designer Juste-Aurèle Meissonnier (1695-1750), architect, painter, sculptor, and silversmith, who from 1726 until his death was the official court designer to Louis XV.[2] Among the earliest French rococo manifestations are Meissonnier's designs of 1728 for a sculptural candlestick on which frolicking putti intertwine with spiraling scrollwork;[3] he went on to produce a wide range of other designs for architecture, sculpture, furniture, and silver in the rococo mode. His ornamental prints of architectural caprices amid surreal landscapes of fountains,

FIGURE 1.   Ornamental design, *Oeuvre de Juste-Aurèle Meissonnier* (Paris, ca. 1750), Plate D22. Engraving on paper, 4½ x 8 in. (11.4 x 20.3 cm.). The Metropolitan Museum of Art, Rogers Fund, 1918 (18.62.5)

Side chair (No. 147) after Chippendale design (No. 1)

shells, and rocaille (FIG. 1), attracting considerable attention and widely imitated, came to characterize the *genre pittoresque* (the French rococo). As one of his contemporaries observed, "Meissonnier began to destroy all the straight lines that were of the old usage . . . he invented contrasts, that is to say he banished symmetry."[4]

In England, traditionally dependent on French example in matters of taste, the adoption of the *genre pittoresque* was fostered by a substantial community of French Huguenot craftsmen who had come to live in London. They included many of the best metalsmiths, engravers, and woodworkers who fled their country after 1685, when Louis XIV revoked the Edict of Nantes, which had protected the rights of French Protestants. Collectively, whether recently arrived or of a succeeding generation, those émigrés not only transformed English design but also elevated standards of craftsmanship to new heights. Among the first exponents of the rococo style and the artisan who subsequently exercised great influence on English silver was Paul de Lamerie (1688-1751), a silversmith born in London of Huguenot extraction, whose oeuvre demonstrated rococo tendencies as early as 1731.[5] English engraving was similarly affected by the French draftsman and engraver Hubert Gravelot (1699-1773), who arrived in London in 1732 and whose influence extended well beyond his specialty. As a teacher at the Saint Martin's Lane Academy, then the chief school for English artists and one that became the nexus of training in rococo design, Gravelot introduced the rococo into all branches of English art. The academy and the other schools of drawing that took up the style were vital to its development, for they educated the draftsmen and the modelers who supplied patterns for carvers, engravers, silversmiths, and other artisans.

Two designers figured prominently in the distinctly English interpretation of rococo ornament that emerged in the 1740s: Matthias Lock and Henry Copland.[6] Lock (d. 1765) was a wood-carver who between 1744 and 1746 etched several suites of designs for carved furniture (frames and tables). He also published booklets of ornamental shields, or cartouches, and, about 1746, issued *The Principles of Ornament, or the Youth's Guide to Drawing of Foliage*, an instruction manual in drawing ragged-edged acanthus leaves, known in rococo parlance as raffles (FIG. 2). Copland (d. 1753) was an accomplished engraver who also published suites of ornamental prints. His sharp style of engraving and his asymmetrical and fantastic schemes, combining scrolls and rocaille with naturalistic flowers and grasses (FIG. 3), set the tone for succeeding English engraved ornament. In 1752, Lock and Copland issued jointly *A New Book of Ornaments with Twelve Leaves*. Their designs, which were often more inventive, energetic, and bizarre than French precedents,

FIGURE 2.   Title page, M. Lock, *The Principles of Ornament* (London, ca. 1746; reissue, ca. 1768). Engraving on paper, 3⅝ x 6 in. (9.2 x 15.2 cm.). The Metropolitan Museum of Art, Harris Brisbane Dick Fund, 1934 (34.90.2)

had a lasting influence on engravers and wood-carvers in England and in her colonies.

Lock and Copland represent the two crafts for which the rococo was particularly well suited: carving and engraving (though the two were almost never employed together). The style's ornamental nature made it immediately popular with the craftsmen who stood chiefly to gain from its adoption. Engravers were uniquely positioned to promote the rococo, not only in ornamental prints but also in pattern books and printed ephemera. The interpretation of engraved designs required the skilled ministrations of wood-carvers, metal engravers, and silver chasers. In addition to objects of silver, engravers embellished silvered brass faces on tall clocks, brass and silver mounts on firearms, and even, occasionally, pewter. Chasers hammered rococo designs into the surface of silver; carvers executed three-dimensional designs in architectural woodwork, furniture, and patterns for casting or molding such divergent materials as silver, iron, and porcelain. The rococo, more than any previous style, relied on specialized craftsmen to interpret correctly its demanding artistic vocabulary.

The publications of Lock and Copland were followed in the mid-1750s by a spate of other pattern books incorporating rococo ornament. *One Hundred and Fifty New Designs* (1758; 1761) by Thomas Johnson, a well-known carver, carried on Lock's championing of carved furniture. In 1762, he too published *A New Book of Ornaments*, though his was a suite of but six designs (see FIG. 48, p. 202). Other publications made the style available to cabinet- and chairmakers. Thomas Chippendale's *Gentleman and Cabinet-Maker's Director* (1754; 1755; 1762) and William Ince and John Mayhew's *Universal System of Houshold Furniture* (1762) were opulent folios aimed at noble clients. *Genteel Houshold Furniture in the Present Taste* (1760; 1762), by a "Society of Upholsterers," and Robert Manwaring's *Cabinet and Chair-Maker's Real Friend and Companion* (1765) were pocket-sized volumes intended for craftsmen, but their use soon extended beyond urban centers to the provinces and thence to the colonies.

Chippendale's *Director* requires special mention. The largest, most luxurious, and most famous of eighteenth-century furniture pattern books, *The Director* was probably the most broadly disseminated. (It was widely available in America, though its stylistic influence was strong only in Philadelphia.) With it Chippendale brilliantly promoted his cabinet shop in Saint Martin's Lane; with it he inadvertently, but indelibly, linked his name to English furniture in the rococo style. In the mid-nineteenth century, rococo engravings by Lock and others were indiscriminately attributed to him,[7] and, to this day, English and American rococo furniture is popularly called "Chippendale."

FIGURE 3. Design for a cartouche, H. Copland, *A New Book of Ornaments* (London, 1746; 2nd ed. ca. 1750). Engraving on paper, 6⅝ x 4¾ in. (16.8 x 12.1 cm.). The Metropolitan Museum of Art, Harris Brisbane Dick Fund, 1925 (25.20)

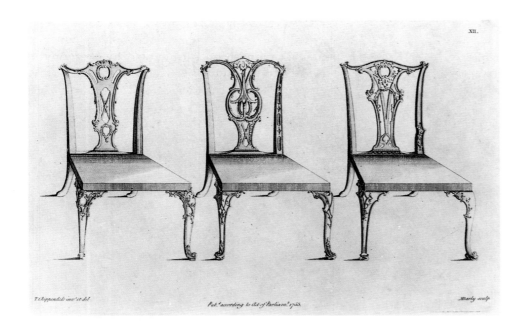

1

Designs for chairs, Thomas Chippendale
The Gentleman and Cabinet-Maker's Director
(London, 1754), Plate XII
Engraving on paper, 13½ x 8¾ in.
The Metropolitan Museum of Art

The Director offered the most complete codification of the English rococo taste in furniture. On the title page of the 1754 edition (see No. 6), the author presented three principal modes of design: Gothic, Chinese, and Modern. The Gothic, a wholly British contribution employing pointed arches, trefoils, quatrefoils, and applied and cluster columns (see Nos. 82, 150), was given impetus by Horace Walpole (1717-1797), who between 1747 and 1776 rebuilt in the Gothic style his famous villa, named Strawberry Hill, at Twickenham, Middlesex. The Chinese, with its pagodalike roofs, oriental figures, latticework, and pierced frets, was a rococo expression of chinoiserie, the Occident's long-running fascination with the mysterious East (see Nos. 51, 102). The third mode, the Modern, was Chippendale's designation for the French rococo, with its scrolls, shells, and rocaille, interpreted both in silver and furniture with sinuous cabriole legs, serpentine skirts, and elaborate foliate carving (see Nos. 88, 130). After the book's publication Chippendale found himself the target of criticism from other craftsmen, who claimed that his plates, "especially those after the Gothick and Chinese Manner," were "so many specious Drawings, impossible to be worked." In his preface to the edition of 1762, he hotly denied that charge.

The introduction of the rococo in England in the 1730s and 1740s coincided with the unprecedented expansion of a prosperous middle class and its concomitant need for fashionable possessions to proclaim and secure a new, worthy position in society. There were now two distinct strata of rococo patrons. The first was the nobility and landed gentry, who favored the style from its inception until the 1760s, when its novelty was upstaged by the newly fashionable neoclassicism introduced by Robert Adam. The second was the successful merchants and tradesmen of London and the larger provincial cities of Britain, who, once the rococo had become codified, embraced it until the late 1780s, when George Hepplewhite and Thomas Sheraton took up the Adam style and, through pattern books, made it accessible to the newly rich and respectable.

It is to that second group that one must look for parallels in the American experience. A New England historian came to the same conclusion as early as 1725, when he wrote: "[A] Gentleman from London would almost think himself at home at Boston when he observes the numbers of people, their Houses, their Furniture, their Tables, their Dress and Conversation, which perhaps, is as splendid and showy, as that of the most considerable Tradesmen in London."[8] At that level of patronage, there was no perceptible lag between the time a style became fashionable in London and in Boston (or Philadelphia).

The American adoption of the rococo focused almost exclusively on the style's ornamental motifs—shells and rocaille, scrollwork, acanthus leaves ("raffles"), and other flora and fauna, often in asymmetrical compositions. These were enthusiastically applied by many leading urban craftsmen to the architectural interiors, engravings, silver, furnishings, and accessories of cast iron, glass, and porcelain that are the subjects of this study. The earliest indications of the style occurred in silver and engraving in the 1740s and in furniture and architecture in the 1750s. Though largely supplanted by neoclassicism by 1790, isolated examples of high rococo date from that decade and even later, particularly in engraved glass (see No. 168) and Kentucky rifles (see Nos. 7, 9). American versions were patterned almost exclusively after British examples. A common culture, strong ties of kinship, and mercantile regulations that prohibited the American colonies from trading independently with other nations made that artistic dependence inevitable. About the only notable objects fashioned after Continental prototypes were firearms and glasswares made by German immigrants, primarily in Pennsylvania. Colonial interpretation of the style, while almost always readily recognizable as such, rarely strays far from the designs of the English model. The differences are in materials (secondary woods in furniture, for example), in sometimes improvisational construction techniques, and in the individual handling of ornament. Exceptions, where the basic design has been transformed into a uniquely American expression, include the famous Philadelphia high chest (see Nos. 136–138) and cast-iron stoves (see Nos. 160, 163). Once it leaves the colonial cities, rococo ornament takes on an engaging, if untutored, informality (see Nos. 19, 45, 57).

The rococo crossed the Atlantic by three principal means: engraved designs in printed ephemera and pattern books, imported objects, and immigrant artisans. Because the Saint Martin's Lane Academy in London had no American counterpart to foster the style, colonial interpreters were largely reliant on imported design sources. Probably the first harbingers of the new taste were ephemera in the form of bookplates, bill heads, trade cards, and commercial papers. An English bookplate was likely the origin of the armorial engraving that is the only rococo ornament on a teapot dated 1745 (see FIG. 28, p. 84)—the earliest documented appearance of the style in American silver. Some years later, Paul Revere modeled at least one of his trade cards directly from a London prototype (see Nos. 12, 13).

The influence of pattern books is relatively easy to trace. Booksellers' advertisements, listings of private and public libraries, and inventories of estates divulge the names of volumes available in America. The visual link is clearly demonstrated in the American objects that replicate or adapt designs from those sources. That said, exact copying was not particularly common. *The Director* was widely available, yet even in Philadelphia, site of its greatest influence, only one design was duplicated in toto: a scroll-footed chair (No. 147) based on Plate XII (**No. 1**) of the 1754 edition. When designs were faithfully followed, they were more likely to be single motifs arranged in fresh compositions. For exam-

ple, a Lock and Copland design for an elaborate chimneypiece (**No. 2**) contains a robed oriental figure within an architectural composition surmounted by a canopy of undulating rocaille. On the side plate of a cast-iron stove from Virginia (No. 162), the same figure is the central element, now standing behind a parapet of similar rocaille. Many of the London pattern books were reissued in 1768 in editions that had immediately visible effects in America; a spandrel design from Lock and Copland's *New Book of Ornaments*, for instance, is found in its entirety in a house built that same year (see FIG. 10, p. 24).

2
Design for a chimneypiece (detail)
M. Lock and H. Copland
A New Book of Ornaments (London, 1752)
Engraving on paper, 9⅞ x 7 in.
The Metropolitan Museum of Art

3
Design for a chimneypiece, Abraham Swan
The British Architect (London, 1745), Plate LI
Engraving on paper, 13¾ x 8½ in.
The Metropolitan Museum of Art

On 5 December 1774, John Norman (ca. 1748–1817), an engraver recently arrived from London, advertised "Proposals for Printing by subscription, the American edition of Swan's British Architect."[9] The volume, with sixty folio copper plates, was available the following June, published by Robert Bell, then Philadelphia's leading printer and bookseller. The first architectural book ever printed in America, it was a faithful copy of Abraham Swan's *British Architect: Or, the Builder's Treasury of Stair-Cases*, originally published in London in 1745 (when Lock and Copland were in their inventive prime) and reissued three times. Its popularity in the colonies (see pp. 18–21), where it was more influential on American architecture than Chippendale was on American furniture, undoubtedly inspired Norman's copy. The American edition was marketed to subscribers in advance, as such publications were in London. Norman's illustrations, which he traced onto his copper plates directly from pages in a London edition (**No. 3**), are sketchily rendered in reverse (**No. 4**) and printed on thinner paper; in executing them, he used an etcher's needle rather than an engraver's burin.

At the outbreak of the Revolution, Norman was at work on at least two other volumes of the same size and with the same number of illustrations as *The British Architect*. The first was Swan's *Collection of Designs in Architecture*, only ten plates of which were produced. The second was *The Gentleman and Cabinet-Maker's Assistant*. Of the latter, only the "Proposals" for its publication were ever printed (**No. 5**), bound into some copies of the Norman-Bell edition of *The British Architect*. The text of the proposals, dated 20 June 1775, bears more than a passing resemblance to the title page of the first edition of Chippendale's *Director* (**No. 6**). What was proposed was evidently a complete American Chippendale. Bell was to have been the publisher and the ingenious Philadelphia cabinetmaker John Folwell (d. 1786) was to have provided the designs. When the publication was interrupted by war, Folwell turned his hand to other vehicles of artistic expression, such as military flags (see FIG. 4, p. 14).

The rococo also arrived in the New World in the form of imported goods, whether specifically ordered by colonists for their own use or for resale. English wares, highly prized symbols of social position, played a major role in guiding American taste. Imported furniture and silver, along with tablewares, textiles, and paper hangings (wallpapers), were not at all uncommon in affluent households. The American-made objects that are the subjects of this book existed harmoniously with English counterparts in colonial homes and were undoubtedly judged on their similarity to London examples. The decision whether to purchase English or American goods was based not only on fashion but also on practical considerations. Anything ordered from England took from ten months to a year to arrive, and cost was an added factor. Benjamin Franklin, who prior to the Revolution spent much of his time in London as representative of the Pennsylvania Assembly and as spokesman for colonial rights, received a letter from his son William in October 1772 that illustrates how such choices were made:

> Captn. Williams brought over with him from England some Mahogany Chairs with Hair Bottoms, which cost him about 22s. Sterling a Piece, and 3s. Sterling a Piece for Matts, packing and Frieght to Philada. I wanted the Workmen here to make me a Dozen like them, but tho' Mahogany is considerably cheaper here than in England, I could not get anyone to undertake to make them under 55s. Currency a Piece, and they would probably not be so well finished. I shall therefore be obliged to you if you would send me a Dozen of such kind of Chairs, made in a fashionable Taste.... P.S. Since Writing the above, I have agreed with a Workman for the *Chairs*, so you need not send them.[10]

Despite a considerable trade in English furnishings and accessories, few English pieces survive with their American histories. Though that hampers direct linkage with American objects, a few identifiable relationships exist. Among them are Paul Revere's coffee pot for a Salem client, unmistakably influenced by an English pot of similar design already owned there (see Nos. 46, 47); an English chair, demonstrably the prototype for a Boston example (see Nos. 100, 101); and imported picture frames that inspired similarly carved American frames within the same set of family portraits (see Nos. 103, 104). While no specific English objects can be singled out as models, essays in American porcelain were unarguably patterned on imported wares with which they struggled to compete (see Nos. 169, 170).

The third means by which the rococo was introduced to America, and by far the most important, was the specialized immigrant artisans required to execute the ornamental intricacies of the style. The English guild system, with its rigorous apprenticeship, provided the necessary schooling in engraving and carving and in the chasing and piercing of silver, but instruction in those specialties was not readily come by in the colonies. In the 1750s and 1760s, a veritable wave of highly skilled and ambitious young craftsmen, most of them London trained, emigrated to America, drawn by the demand for their abilities and by opportunities for personal and social advancement.

Their effect on the colonial arts was analogous to that of the Huguenots' arriving in England nearly a century before: a dramatic improvement in stylistic consciousness and craftsmanship. The finest American rococo engravings came from the hands of English-trained engravers (see Nos. 21, 32), and the superior quality of Philadelphia rococo furniture

4

Design for a chimneypiece
John Norman, after Abraham Swan
The British Architect (Philadelphia, 1775), Plate LI
Engraving on paper, 13⅞ x 8⅛ in.
The Metropolitan Museum of Art

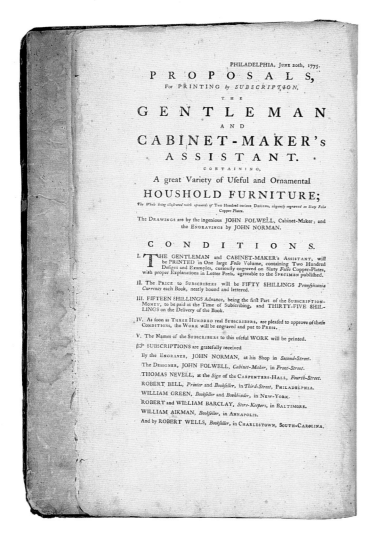

PHILADELPHIA, JUNE 20th, 1775.

PROPOSALS,

For PRINTING by SUBSCRIPTION,

THE

GENTLEMAN

AND

CABINET-MAKER's
ASSISTANT.

CONTAINING,

A great Variety of Useful and Ornamental

HOUSHOLD FURNITURE;

The Whole being illustrated with upwards of Two Hundred curious Designs, elegantly engraved on Sixty Folio Copper-Plates.

The DRAWINGS are by the ingenious JOHN FOLWELL, Cabinet-Maker; and the ENGRAVINGS by JOHN NORMAN.

CONDITIONS.

I. THE GENTLEMAN and CABINET-MAKER's ASSISTANT, will be PRINTED in One large Folio Volume, containing Two Hundred Designs and Examples, curiously engraved on Sixty Folio Copper-Plates, with proper Explanations in Letter Press, agreeable to the Specimen published.

II. The PRICE to Subscribers will be FIFTY SHILLINGS Pennsylvania Currency each Book, neatly bound and lettered.

III. FIFTEEN SHILLINGS Advance, being the first Part of the SUBSCRIPTION-MONEY, to be paid at the Time of Subscribing, and THIRTY-FIVE SHILLINGS on the Delivery of the Book.

IV. As soon as THREE HUNDRED real SUBSCRIBERS, are pleased to approve of these CONDITIONS, the WORK will be engraved and put to PRESS.

V. The Names of the SUBSCRIBERS to this useful WORK will be printed.

☞ SUBSCRIPTIONS are gratefully received

By the ENGRAVER, JOHN NORMAN, at his Shop in Second-Street.

The DESIGNER, JOHN FOLWELL, Cabinet-Maker, in Front-Street.

THOMAS NEVELL, at the Sign of the CARPENTERS-HALL, Fourth-Street.

ROBERT BELL, Printer and Bookseller, in Third-Street, PHILADELPHIA.

WILLIAM GREEN, Bookseller and Bookbinder, in NEW-YORK.

ROBERT and WILLIAM BARCLAY, Store-Keepers, in BALTIMORE.

WILLIAM AIKMAN, Bookseller, in ANNAPOLIS.

And by ROBERT WELLS, Bookseller, in CHARLESTOWN, SOUTH-CAROLINA.

THE

GENTLEMAN
AND
CABINET-MAKER's
DIRECTOR.

BEING A LARGE

COLLECTION

OF THE MOST

Elegant and Useful Designs of Houshold Furniture

IN THE

GOTHIC, CHINESE and MODERN TASTE:

Including a great Variety of

BOOK-CASES for Libraries or Private Rooms. COMMODES, LIBRARY and WRITING-TABLES, BUROES, BREAKFAST-TABLES, DRESSING and CHINA-TABLES, CHINA-CASES, HANGING-SHELVES, | TEA-CHESTS, TRAYS, FIRE-SCREENS, CHAIRS, SETTEES, SOPHA'S, BEDS, PRESSES and CLOATHS-CHESTS, PIER-GLASS SCONCES, SLAB FRAMES, BRACKETS, CANDLE-STANDS, CLOCK-CASES, FRETS,

AND OTHER

ORNAMENTS.

TO WHICH IS PREFIXED,

A Short EXPLANATION of the Five ORDERS of ARCHITECTURE, and RULES of PERSPECTIVE;

WITH

Proper DIRECTIONS for executing the most difficult Pieces, the Mouldings being exhibited at large, and the Dimensions of each DESIGN specified:

THE WHOLE COMPREHENDED IN

One Hundred and Sixty COPPER-PLATES, neatly Engraved,

Calculated to improve and refine the present TASTE, and suited to the Fancy and Circumstances of Persons in all Degrees of Life.

Dulcique animos novitate tenebo. OVID.
Ludentis speciem dabit & torquebitur. HOR.

BY

THOMAS CHIPPENDALE,
Of St. *MARTIN's-LANE,* CABINET-MAKER.

LONDON,

Printed for the AUTHOR, and sold at his House in St. MARTIN's-LANE, MDCCLIV. Also by T. OSBORNE, Bookseller, in Gray's-Inn; H. PIERS, Bookseller, in Holborn; R. SAYER, Printseller, in Fleetstreet; J. SWAN, near Northumberland-House, in the Strand. At EDINBURGH, by Messrs. HAMILTON and BALFOUR: And at DUBLIN, by Mr. JOHN SMITH, on the Blind-Quay.

5

Proposals for Printing by Subscription
The Gentleman and Cabinet-Maker's Assistant
(Philadelphia, 1775)
Printed paper, 16½ x 9½ in.
Avery Library, Columbia University

6

Thomas Chippendale
The Gentleman and Cabinet-Maker's Director
(London, 1754), title page
Printed paper, 17¼ x 11⅛ in.
The Metropolitan Museum of Art

is attributable to the numerous foreign cabinetmakers and carvers working in that city (see pp. 182-84). The identity and contributions of immigrant silversmiths are harder to trace, since most of them worked under an American master smith's mark, but their influence is apparent not only in high-rococo objects that would have demanded their participation but also in the various newspaper references to foreign-trained assistants working in the great urban centers (see pp. 74-78). Moreover, to launch industrial production of fine table glass and porcelain, entrepreneurs had to bring experienced workmen over from abroad (see pp. 229-34).

Craftsmen relied on the patronage of wealthy city dwellers who made it their business to keep current with London fashion. They included many of the most prominent families of each region: in New England, the Apthorps, Derbys, Faneuils, Hancocks, and Lees; in New York, the Beekmans, Cornells, Schuylers, Van Rensselaers, and Verplancks; in Philadelphia and neighboring Maryland, the Cadwaladers, Chews, Dickinsons, and Galloways. As a class, they were well educated and widely traveled, and they took great pride in the furnishing of their houses. In 1764, Benjamin Franklin began to build a new house in Philadelphia. The next year, from London, the busy diplomat attended to every detail of the interiors himself. In letters to his wife, Deborah, he bombarded her with questions and instructions: "Let me have the Breadth of the Pier, that I may get a handsome Glass for the Parlour."[11] And again, "The blue Mohair Stuff is for the Curtains of the Blue Chamber. The Fashion is to make one Curtain only for each Window."[12]

In the absence of banks and stock markets, real estate and household possessions (especially silver) were favored investments, representing a far larger percentage of total assets than would be customary today. When wealthy Philadelphian John Cadwalader went off to fight with the Revolutionary forces, he took care to secure the magnificent furnishings (see Nos. 153-156) of his Second Street house. Cadwalader acted through one of his friends, Jasper Yeates, of Lancaster, who was in Philadelphia at the time and who sent instructions to his wife by post: "Col. John Cadwalader has requested Leave of me to store a part of his most valuable Furniture in our House. If it should come up to you in my Absence, you will please to have it put up in the Garret & have the Room locked up."[13]

Only in and around the major cities were the necessary ingredients in place to cultivate the development of an American rococo style: designs, patrons, artisans, and materials. The most fertile areas of American rococo design were Boston, New York, Philadelphia, and Charleston, all seaports and all linked as closely (perhaps more closely) to London as to each other. Their adopting the rococo style was therefore a result more of their ties to England than to one another.

By the rococo era Boston was entering the twilight of her colonial dominance. Economic reversals and competition with New York and Philadelphia combined to arrest her growth, and though wealthy Boston merchants certainly did indulge in rococo excesses, the city's expression of the taste was as a whole the most conservative of the four urban centers. New York was the second largest colonial city and a Loyalist stronghold during the Revolution; when the British relinquished the city in 1783, a third of the population evacuated with them. A large percentage of New York's rococo creations were doubtless removed by departing Loyalists or destroyed in the disastrous fires that accompanied the occupation of the city. Nonetheless, surviving examples demonstrate a highly cosmopolitan rococo consciousness. Concurrently, Philadelphia was just reaching the apogee of her ascendancy and wealth. The largest city in the colonies, her prosperity and culture attracted immigrant craftsmen uniquely qualified to provide rococo ornament to her richest citizens. Predictably, the city became the Athens of America and the arbiter of the new style. Charleston, by virtue of her agricultural trade with Great Britain, was also thriving. The interiors of her houses exemplified the rococo fashion as much as those in Philadelphia, though Charlestonians were far more reliant on imported goods. The few surviving examples of locally made rococo furniture and silver nevertheless suggest that the city cultivated sophisticated domestic interpretations of the style.

The American rococo developed independently in each of the four cities, sometimes with a distinctive regional character. In engravings and silver, imported examples, mostly of standard forms, were widely available and highly influential on domestic designs; local interpretations are limited. Far less furniture, however, came into the country, and what did varied from city to city. In Boston, for example, where immigrant craftsmen were not welcomed, an isolated object was more likely to set a local style (see Nos. 100, 101). By contrast, Philadelphia, where London pattern books and foreign-trained artisans held sway, was far less impressed by English-made furnishings.

The development of the rococo style in America must be examined in the context of the political climate, since the fashion for the new taste coincided with a dramatic change in relations between England and her American colonies. The government's laissez-faire attitude throughout the first half of the eighteenth century, when such inconveniences as restrictive trading regulations were discreetly ignored, contributed to colonial prosperity and a sense of autonomy.

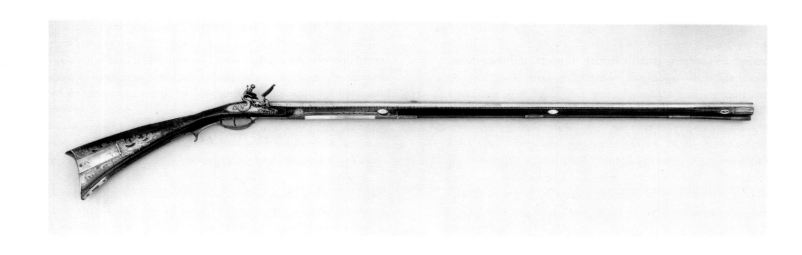

7

Flintlock rifle, 1812–20
Jacob Kuntz, Philadelphia
Maple, iron, brass, and silver,
L.: 59¼ in.
The Metropolitan Museum of Art

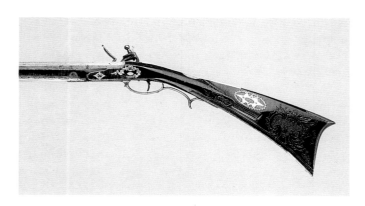

The French and Indian War (1754–63), during which British forces were employed in colonial defense at considerable expense to the English government, irrevocably altered those conditions. When the war ended, cabinet ministers in London sought to reestablish their authority and, by the imposition of tariffs, to extract revenue for payment of war debts.[14] What followed was a series of events that inexorably led the colonists to revolution. They ranged from the Sugar Act of 1764, which brought in train enlarged customs restrictions, to the Stamp Act of 1765, instituted to pay off war debts by taxing the commercial documents and publications of merchants and lawyers who vociferously opposed the act and forced its repeal, to the Townshend Acts, which in 1767 imposed duties on imported glass, lead, paint, paper, and tea, all, except for the last, British made. Those events served to stimulate domestic manufactures but also brought about the first regional nonimportation agreement, whereby a Boston town meeting determined not to purchase certain imported wares, including "Household Furniture, Wrought Plate of all Sorts, China Ware."[15] A groundswell of public support for the boycott of British goods persuaded an ever increasing circle of urban merchants into binding nonimportation agreements: in Boston and New York, in 1768–70; in Philadelphia, in 1769–70; and in Charleston, in 1769–71.

The agreements, which were anathema to merchants who relied on trade for their livelihood but a boon to local craftsmen competing with British imports, ignited efforts to establish a full panoply of domestic industries—what might be called a "Buy Colonial" campaign. In 1769, upholsterer Plunket Fleeson announced his "American Paper Hangings, Manufactured in Philadelphia, of all kinds and colours, not inferior to those generally imported; and as low in price."[16] That same year, in Manheim, Pennsylvania, Henry William Stiegel founded his American Flint Glass Manufactory (see p. 229); a year later, in Philadelphia, the partners Bonnin and Morris established their China Manufactory (see p. 234). In 1774, John Hewson of that city opened a "Calicoe Printing Manufactory," promising that "his work shall be equal in colour, and will stand washing, as well as any imported

from London or elsewhere, otherwise will require no pay."[17] Those efforts at factory production of luxury goods on which rococo decoration could be employed met with staggering reverses when the nonimportation agreements were repealed following the withdrawal of the duties imposed by the Townshend Acts—all except the duty on tea. The colonists reacted to that final outrage by staging the Boston Tea Party, and revolution was inevitable.

The war, with its sacrifices and privations, effectively arrested further development of the American rococo, though it did not signal the introduction of a replacement style. As securely dated examples imply, whatever ornamental goods were made in America during the war years must have been rococo (see Nos. 60, 93, 94). While there were sporadic expressions of rococo design after independence

8

Pair of flintlock pistols, 1812–20
Jacob Kuntz, Philadelphia
Maple, iron, brass, and silver,
L.: 14¼ in.
Private collection

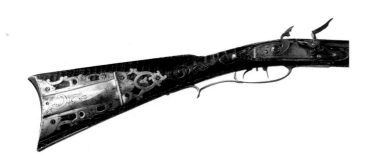

9

Flintlock rifle, ca. 1790
Simon Lauck, Winchester, Virginia
Maple, iron, brass, and silver,
L.: 60½ in.
Private collection

was achieved, the style had lost ten years to the Revolution; in the 1780s, with the establishment of a new country, the rococo gave way to neoclassicism.

During the glorious years of its reign, the rococo style, with its ornamental nature, was firmly aligned with the decorative arts. Its principal American expressions—architectural carving, engravings, silver, and furniture—are fully explored in the chapters that follow, as are domestic efforts to manufacture cast iron, glass, and porcelain. Other manifestations, while out of the mainstream (firearms, for example, or the now extremely rare examples of textiles), must not be overlooked, since they illustrate the rococo's pervasive nature.

Firearms represent both the arts of the engraver and carver, the only objects that do. The American flintlock, or long, rifle, better known today as the Kentucky rifle, was a distinctive form of weapon based on European hunting pieces. Examples were being manufactured in America by mid-century, but only after the Revolution was any attention given to their carved and engraved ornamentation. The majority of Kentuckys having rococo decoration were made in Pennsylvania between 1780 and 1820 by gunsmiths of German or Swiss descent, but others were produced in Virginia and the Carolinas.[18]

One of the Pennsylvania master gunsmiths was Jacob Kuntz (1780-1876). Born in Lehigh County, he probably served his apprenticeship in Philadelphia. Between 1799 and 1811 he practiced his craft in his native county; in 1812 he located in Philadelphia. A rifle representative of his best work (**No. 7**), signed "J. Kuntz" on top of the breech, has a curly maple stock ornamented with self-contained rococo motifs. The cheek, or left, side (see detail) has two cartouches flanking an engraved silver eight-pointed star. Though carved in low relief, basically symmetrical in design, and wrought from a hard, unyielding wood, they have a lively and expressive vigor. The lock, or right, side (see detail) is cut out with a patch box, used for storing wadding and other paraphernalia for loading the weapon. Its hinged brass cover with pierced and engraved side plates is a feature unique to American rifles, but the plates' scrolls, inhabited by eagles, lions, and human allusions, are an enchanting provincial echo of the European rococo.

American gunsmiths made pistols as well as rifles, though far less frequently. A pair of pistols (**No. 8**) by Kuntz are inscribed "Philada." and "J. Koons" (the latter, twice), a spelling that may have been Anglicized to suit the Philadelphia market. The original owner, however, was a German-American from Lehigh Township, Northampton

10

Arms of the Flower family, 1765
Elizabeth Flower, Philadelphia
Embroidery on silk, mahogany frame,
11½ x 12¾ in.
Collection of
Mr. and Mrs. Edward J. Nusrala

County, whose name, George Nagle, is engraved on each pistol. The pair must have been made in Philadelphia not long after the gunsmith moved there in 1812. The barrels are brass, the stocks are curly maple, and rococo ornament is limited to engraved brass and silver cornucopias above the triggers and engraved and chased silver mounts on the butts.

A rifle (**No. 9**) marked on the breech by Simon Lauck, of Winchester, Virginia, exhibits the same vocabulary of design motifs used by Kuntz, but in a lighter and more delicate and unified composition. On the cheek side of the stock, carved scrolls, shallow and sinuous, flow unimpeded into elegant silver-wire inlays encircling a silver star. On the lock side, the patch-box cover is engraved with equally delicate rococo patterns.

While no fine weaving industry existed in America for the production of rococo-patterned silks, a few domestic textiles are noteworthy for their rococo ornament. Needlework formed an important part of a young girl's education. Marriageable daughters in well-to-do families were expected to excel in fancy stitching as a means of impressing eligible suitors. Elizabeth Flower (1742-1781) completed an exquisitely embroidered silk needlework picture (**No. 10**) in 1765, at the age of twenty-three;[19] her sister, Ann, made a similar picture in 1763.[20] Elizabeth and Ann were the daughters of the Philadelphia joiner Enoch Flower (1705-1773) and his wife, Ann (b. 1711). Both sisters' pictures display the arms of the Flower family of Philadelphia in a lavish rococo surround probably copied directly from an armorial engraving, and both were worked in the most elegant needlework materials: silk thread, as well as gold and silver metallic threads, on cream silk moiré. The cipher of Elizabeth's initials at the base of the design was copied from *A New Book of Cyphers*, a book commonly referred to in the colonies.[21]

FIGURE 4.   *Standard of the Philadelphia Light Horse*, 1775,
John Folwell and James Claypoole, Philadelphia. Painting on silk,
33 x 40 in. (83.8 x 101.6 cm.). First Troop Philadelphia
City Cavalry

Another isolated survival of a superb American rococo textile is the large and impressive standard of the Philadelphia Light Horse troop (FIG. 4), dating from 1775, the finest American Revolutionary flag in existence. A standard, or "colors," served to identify a particular military unit.[22] The Revolutionary standards were generally of silk, which unfurled easily in a breeze, of a solid color painted or embroidered with appropriate symbols and emblems. The rococo part of the Light Horse standard is its central heraldic cartouche, strongly asymmetrical and composed of adjoining C-scrolls, which encloses a central golden knot tied of thirteen radiating ribbons, symbolizing the united colonies. The allegorical figures of Fame and America (the latter, an Indian with a liberty cap on a pole; see also Nos. 34, 55) flank the shield, with its crest of a horse's head over which the troop's initials are intertwined in rococo style. A scrolling motto ribbon below the central emblem is emblazoned with the phrase FOR THESE WE STRIVE.

The standard survives from a pair commissioned in 1775 for the mounted troop by its first commanding officer, Captain Abraham Markoe. The original bills for the two document Philadelphia designer John Folwell as the craftsman who was paid £1-15 for "Drawing & Designing the Coulours for the Light Horse" and James Claypoole, of the same city, as the artisan who earned £8 for "painting, gilding & silvering a Device, Union & Motto on 2 Colours for the Troop of Light Horse."[23] Besides being a rare instance of the rococo in American textiles, the standard, in its painted decoration, represents a type of rococo ornament, once common, that has been almost entirely lost. Similar rococo cartouches decorated ships, shop signs, carriages, and fire buckets. The accounts of John Cadwalader include an entry for a dozen fire buckets Claypoole painted in 1771, which were doubtless rococo in design.[24]

Between 1750 and 1775, the rococo was the dominant style in America. It is discernible as early as the mid-1740s and traces of it remain long after 1775. Patterned resolutely after English examples, the American rococo was virtually restricted to urban areas where patronage, craftsmanship, and prosperity permitted its flowering. As one would expect, Britain's major western colonies attempted to emulate London fashion as fully as possible. In this, they differed little from such other provincial satellites as Dublin or Edinburgh. Foreign craftsmen, English engravings, and imported furnishings fostered the style in the colonies. Nonimportation agreements briefly encouraged the manufacture of local products, but the style would undoubtedly have enjoyed fuller maturity throughout America if the imperial-colonial conflicts had been resolved peaceably.　　LGB, MHH

ARCHITECTURE

Though limited mainly to ornamental highlights within plain, classically conceived spaces, the rococo style in American architecture was a symbol of the affluence of the mercantile elite, Loyalist and patriot alike, during the prosperous decade and a half prior to the Revolution. Today, such architectural examples that remain are no less important. Because they are firmly rooted in time and place, they serve as benchmarks both for identifying regional rococo manifestations and individual artisans and for suggesting the effect of the style in its totality.

Architectural rococo, mostly the work of wood-carvers, was employed primarily on the fireplace—the sole source of heat in colonial days and a natural gathering place—to establish it as the visual focus of a room. There, carving was often executed on what were called trusses—either scrolls buttressing the sides of the fireplace or scrolled consoles supporting the mantel shelf. In the most ornate interiors, overdoor pediments echoed the overmantel. The use of carved brackets at the open end of each tread of a staircase was equally common. Rococo-carved ornament appeared in the spandrels of archways, especially in those separating entrance halls from stair halls, and in rooms where arched openings flanked fireplaces or windows.

In churches, columns and pilasters were frequently embellished with carved capitals that followed the time-honored designs of the classical orders (principally the Corinthian and the Composite), with rococo carving reserved for imparting visual interest to the altarpiece and the pulpit, the ecclesiastical elements to which the congregation's attention would naturally be drawn.

Not all architectural decoration in the rococo style was of carved wood. Stuccoists could give a similar effect in plaster, and upholsterers, whose activities ranged beyond the mere covering of furniture, could provide inexpensive imitations made of papier-mâché (paper pulp pressed in molds). Few examples of rococo-style wall decoration survive in stucco (plaster), but a number of plaster- or papier-mâché-ornamented ceilings remain intact—only a suggestion of what was an accepted feature of the parlors and entrance halls of the most fashionable houses of the Revolutionary era. Least well represented in twentieth-century survivals is the once-ubiquitous painted interior woodwork, usually grained and marbleized, though rococo ornament painted on paneling or plasterwork, known today in only one Virginia example, was probably not uncommon.

Another province of the upholsterer—one closely linked with papier-mâché decoration—was the selling and installing of paper hangings (as wallpaper was then called) often found in fine colonial interiors. Most of them had printed designs with a continuously repeated pattern, and most of them were imported. There were fledgling efforts to manufacture paper hangings in New York in 1756 and 1765, and in 1769, Plunket Fleeson offered "American Paper Hangings... Manufactured in Philadelphia," something the local firm of Ryves and Fletcher tried again six years later.[1] No domestic examples from the period are known. The paper of choice for the grandest houses of the rococo era and the epitome of the rococo taste came in sets of large-scale landscape paintings with trompe l'oeil carved frames, each set designed and hand painted in England to fit a particular room.

In American architecture, the full flowering of the rococo style occurred in the 1760s and early 1770s. Datable houses having rococo ornament are found in Cambridge, Massachusetts, from 1759; in New York City, from 1763; in Philadelphia, from 1764; and in Charleston, from 1767. Except for Cambridge, examples made well into the early

Chimney breast from the James Beekman house (No. 11)

1770s can be found in each of those urban centers. In the 1780s, after the Revolution, there was a late flurry of rococo architectural ornament north of Boston, notably in Portsmouth, New Hampshire, and Newburyport, Massachusetts.

In the mid-eighteenth century, a vast proliferation of publications spread the doctrine of architecture based on the classical orders throughout the English-speaking world. Whether elegant engraved folios addressed to noble English country-house builders or crudely printed handbooks carried by carpenters, the publications furnished advice on construction methods and on the makeup and proportioning of the classical elements; some even provided illustrations of architectural ornament. Many of the books were available in the American colonies,[2] where one in particular had a pronounced influence: *The British Architect: Or, the Builder's Treasury of Stair-Cases*, by Abraham Swan. First published in London in 1745, the book was reissued in 1750, in 1758, and in the mid-1760s. (American editions of Swan's treatise appeared in Philadelphia in 1775 and in Boston in 1794.) It was for sale by booksellers in Philadelphia and New York in 1760 and in Boston in 1763; it was also available in subscription libraries in Philadelphia. Two architects—Peter Harrison in New England and William Buckland in Virginia and Maryland—are known to have owned copies.[3] It was the first architectural tome to feature large-scale illustrations of rococo embellishment, including "Stair-Cases...With a great Variety of curious Ornaments" and "A great Variety of New and Curious Chimney-Pieces, in the most elegant and modern Taste,"[4] the two areas in which the new style was most often employed by American builders. Swan's patterns expressed the quintessential English application of rococo ornament onto a firmly classical framework; florid in decoration though they were, they never allowed the ornament to transcend the support to which it was attached. Despite their classicism, the designs in *The British Architect* have a distinctive character of their own. For example, the chimneypieces do not incorporate flanking pilasters or columns or the cornice of a room but are independent designs. The mantel and overmantel are composed of large-scale elements in the heavy, baroque treatment associated with the English architect William Kent and carved decoration in the full, florid rococo manner of Lock and Copland.

New England

A mere dozen examples of rococo architectural carving remain in all New England. That none are from Boston, the region's preeminent city, must reflect in part on the city's constant rebuilding, for a number of the largest houses survive from mid-century in Cambridge, across the Charles River. The John Vassall house, built on Brattle Street in 1759, contains the earliest known rococo-style ornament in New England architecture: lighthearted scrolled and leafage-carved spandrel panels in the southwest parlor. The Vassall house was quickly followed over the next two years by that of the Reverend East Apthorp, whose parlor retains its original carved chimneypiece (FIG. 5) with design elements faithfully borrowed from Swan's *British Architect*: the trusses supporting the mantel shelf from Plate XLVIII, the flanking overmantel trusses from Plate LIII.[5] The two houses, both clearly the work of the same craftsmen, sport front-door surrounds based on Plate XXXII in Batty Langley's *Treasury of Designs* (published in London in 1756 and readily available in Boston),[6] but with swags carved in the rococo style replacing the baroque ones of the engraving.

East Apthorp (1737–1816) was a devotee of fashionable English architectural design. A son of the immensely rich merchant and army contractor Charles Apthorp (1698–1758) of Boston, East was a distinguished student of religion and the classics at Jesus College, Cambridge University, between 1751 and 1758. On the death of his father, he came home to Massachusetts, his return coinciding with plans for establishing an Anglican church in Cambridge, in the shadow of Congregational Harvard College. Young Apthorp, who was appointed Christ Church's first rector, also sat on the church building committee that chose as architect the English-trained designer Peter Harrison (1716–1775). It has been suggested that Harrison, who owned copies of the Swan and Langley books, had a hand in the design of Apthorp's own house (which was of a magnificence remarked on by John Adams),[7] with rococo ornament

FIGURE 5.   *Parlor chimneypiece*, 1760–61, the East Apthorp house, Cambridge. Photograph, ca. 1890

FIGURE 6.   *Parlor chimneypiece*, ca. 1768, the Jeremiah Lee house, Marblehead. Photograph, 1891

that may have been executed by Edward Burbeck (1715–1785) and W. Austin, carvers for the church.[8]

There are a few examples of rococo architectural ornament by other artisans in the immediate environs of Boston,[9] but the Apthorp house carver must also have worked in Newburyport, near the present Massachusetts–New Hampshire border. Two chimneypieces from 8 Water Street, begun in 1783 for William Coombs (1736–1814), Newburyport's leading importer, have an unusual and distinctive feature also found in the chimneypiece of the Apthorp house parlor: beneath the overmantel, a carved cavetto molding extending at either end on which rest decorative side trusses.[10]

For the ultimate expression of the architectural rococo in Massachusetts, however, one must turn to the Lee house in Marblehead, about fifteen miles northeast of Boston. With its seven bays and three stories, it was probably the largest New England dwelling of its generation, and was completed in 1768 by the patriot merchant Jeremiah Lee (1721–1775), supposedly to the designs of his brother Samuel.[11] The house, remarkably well preserved inside and out, offers the twentieth-century visitor perhaps the most authentic possible experience of American rococo interiors. The architectural fittings are undisturbed. The walls on both floors of the main stair hall and in the two front chambers have their original paper hangings, painted to order in England, with

FIGURE 7. *Staircase*, ca. 1768, the Jeremiah Lee house, Marblehead. Photograph, 1891

landscapes in trompe l'oeil frames. Even the rococo cast-iron firebacks remain (see No. 157). As is the case throughout New England, the interiors owe a very clear debt to Swan's *British Architect*. In the fully paneled ground-floor parlor (FIG. 6), the moldings of the entablature are carved after Plate XI (the Corinthian order); the chimneypiece, with a full complement of trusses and swags, is an amalgam of Plates LI (No. 3) and LIII, and, in the hall, the stair brackets (FIG. 7) reproduce Plate XXXIII. The chimney breast, though its projection is too slight to set it off effectively from the surrounding wall, demonstrates unusually fine carved work.

Portsmouth, New Hampshire, at the mouth of the Piscataqua, was the major urban center north of Boston. Its architecture shows a certain independence within the New England idiom.[12] A number of great houses remaining from the period demonstrate that the rococo flourished in Portsmouth somewhat later than in Boston. The first of them is the massive frame dwelling built between 1760 and 1764 for the ship captain turned shipowner John Moffatt (1692–1786). The joiner was Michael Whidden III and the carver was Ebenezer Dearing (1730–1791) of nearby Kittery, Maine. In 1761, Dearing billed Moffatt for various ornamental carvings, including two chimneypieces (one possibly that of the drawing room, with its leaf-carved trusses and central panel) and the "17 Stare Brakets" that still grace the main staircase.[13] The acanthus-scrolled designs were almost certainly inspired by Swan, but lack the effervescence of his mature rococo style. The well-known Wentworth-Gardner house, built about 1760, is also handsomely fitted up and looks to be by the same craftsmen.

The Moffatt and the Wentworth-Gardner houses are exact contemporaries of the Vassall and Apthorp houses in Cambridge and, though their ornamental details generally lack that rococo spirit, are equally grand. The style in its full maturity did arrive in Portsmouth, but not until much later, with the John Langdon house, which was begun in 1783. Langdon (1746–1819), a merchant and politician, began to purchase the land for his house in 1775 and married in 1777. Then war intervened. Only in 1783 did the actual work begin, performed by the same craftsmen Moffatt had employed twenty years earlier. On 14 December 1785, Ebenezer Dearing and his son William were paid £169 for carving that must have included the magnificent chimneypieces in the north and the south parlors (FIG. 8) and the north parlor's spandrels and keystones.[14] By that time, the Dearings' style had evolved into a distinctive rendition of chimneypiece designs from Swan: large in scale, with bold carving in high relief, but with the trusses flattened out to create a vigorous abstract pattern exclusive to Portsmouth.[15]

FIGURE 8. *Parlor chimneypiece*, 1783–85, the John Langdon house, Portsmouth

New York

In the valley of the Hudson, up to Albany, there remains but a handful of examples of rococo architectural ornament, only three of which are intact in their original structures. The 1760s, the heyday of the style, saw the construction of many a grand house, including that of Charles Ward Apthorp (brother to East) in upper Manhattan (1764), the Morris–Jumel house, also in Manhattan (1765), and the Schuyler Mansion, in Albany (1761–64); the first demolished, the others remodeled and any rococo woodwork destroyed. Though James Beekman's Manhattan country house and Stephen Van Rensselaer's Albany manor house are also gone, fragments of them that survive are among the most splendid reminders of New York's rococo heritage. Only in the Philipse Manor house, in Yonkers; Van Cortlandt House, in the Bronx (the two manorial estates immediately north of Manhattan Island); and Saint Paul's Chapel, on Broadway, in lower Manhattan, can the rococo be seen in situ. The apogee of the New York rococo can be pinpointed to the mid-1760s by Saint Paul's, built between 1763 and 1767; the Beekman house, between 1763 and 1764; and the Van Rensselaer manor house, between 1765 and 1768. From what survives at those sites some sense of the very high-style and high-quality rococo interiors of colonial New York can still be gleaned.

The house at Philipse Manor, in the eighteenth century some fifteen miles above the city proper, has probably the earliest examples of the architectural rococo in New York. The original stone house was built by the first Frederick Philipse (1626–1702) in the 1680s. The two-story addition, which contains the "rococo" rooms, must have been built by Frederick Philipse III (1720–1786) sometime after 1751, when he inherited the property, and probably about 1756, when he married Elizabeth (Williams), widow of Anthony Rutgers.[16] (The weightiness of the carving suggests a time well before the mature rococo of the mid-1760s.) The two parlors have elaborate fireplace walls, each with a full clas-

FIGURE 9.   *Parlor chimneypiece*, ca. 1756, Philipse Manor house, Yonkers. Photograph, ca. 1910

sical order (engaged Ionic columns on that of the first floor, Doric pilasters on that of the second). The mantels are gone, but the overmantels have molded frames flanked by nearly identical trusses from which emerge luxuriant garlands of fruit and flowers.[17] The overmantel of the first-floor room (FIG. 9) has a heavy broken-scroll pediment and a tablet displaying a head of Diana the huntress; that of the second-floor room has an open pediment with a finial of three clustered feathers and a rocaille-carved frieze below. The three feathers, the symbol of the Prince of Wales, may refer here to Frederick (1707–1751), heir apparent to George II, who was an avid patron of art and design in the 1730s and 1740s.[18]

The first-floor room still has its rococo-enriched ceiling, one of the most elaborate from colonial America and the only one left in New York. The decoration—scrollwork inhabited by birds, animals, and profile portrait busts, all contained within a broad decorative outer band—has the characteristic disjointed look of papier-mâché ornament: the putting together of a lot of individually molded elements. Stylistically freer and more playful than the fireplace-wall woodwork, it looks to have been installed in the 1760s. Philipse's likely supplier was Roper Dawson, who advertised "Paper Hangings and in Figures, Bass Relievo [bas-relief] for Ceilings, &c" in the *New-York Gazette or the Weekly Post-Boy* of 3 June 1762.[19]

James Beekman built Mount Pleasant as a country estate at what is now the corner of Fifty-first Street and First Avenue in Manhattan, on property he acquired early in 1763 (see p. 155). The major surviving element of the house is the chimney breast given by Beekman's descendants to The New-York Historical Society in 1874 (**No. 11**; see also ill. opp. p. 17). Like those at the Philipse Manor house, it is dominated by a monumental and richly carved scroll-pedimented overmantel flanked by representations of a classical order, in this case fluted Doric pilasters resting directly on the mantel shelf. The carved rococo cartouche framing the family arms that once hung within the pediment, while probably contemporaneous with the chimneypiece, was not an integral part of the design. In striking contrast to these heavy architectural features is the thoroughly rococo carved ornament of the trusses and mantel frieze.[20] It consists of rocaille work, pierced and with parallel-gouged surfaces, and, at the middle of the frieze, a paddling dog flanked by strident swans—a touch of rococo whimsy in the manner of the engraved designs of the London carver Thomas Johnson.[21]

The building of the Van Rensselaer manor house, the greatest of the river valley houses of that time, was begun in 1765

11

Parlor chimney breast, New York, 1763–64
From Mount Pleasant, the James Beekman house
White pine, painted, H.: 115 in.
Installation photograph, 1964
The New-York Historical Society

FIGURE 10. *Entrance hall*, 1765-68, Van Rensselaer manor house, Albany, as installed at The Metropolitan Museum of Art

FIGURE 11. *Interior*, Saint Paul's Chapel, New York, 1764–66. Photograph, ca. 1900

and completed three years later by Stephen II (1742–1769; the eighth Van Rensselaer patroon), who married Catherine Livingston in 1764. Though the house was destroyed in 1893, the architectural woodwork and the paper hangings of the entrance hall were salvaged and ultimately reassembled at the Metropolitan Museum, where they represent the New York rococo architectural interior at its most complete (FIG. 10). The walls are laid out according to the Ionic order, as the pilasters on either side of the archway to the stair hall demonstrate. The plaster surfaces between dado and cornice, like those of the Lee house in Marblehead, are hung with hand-painted wallpapers made in London in 1768, which feature grisaille landscapes depicting the Four Seasons and scenes of classical ruins within trompe l'oeil carved rococo frames.[22] The spandrels of the archway, their scrolled foliage copied directly from a plate in Lock and Copland's *New Book of Ornaments*, which had just been reissued in Lon-

don,[23] exemplify New York rococo carving at its grandest. Only the ceiling is without ornament, and that was not the original intent. In 1768, Philip Livingston, Van Rensselaer's father-in-law, wrote to him: "I am told You Intend to gett Stucco work on the Ceiling of Your Hall which I would not advise You to do, a Plain Ceiling is now Esteemed the most Genteel."[24]

The only surviving public structure built with rococo ornamentation is Saint Paul's Chapel. The cornerstone was laid on 14 May 1764; the first service in the chapel was held on 30 October 1766. The hexagonal pulpit and sounding board, to the left of the altar (FIG. 11), have elaborately carved moldings that include an openwork rococo bolection, bows and swags, and vines growing around the square balusters of the pulpit stair. Even more loosely handled and more fully rococo in manner is the magnificent cartouche above the Palladian window behind the altar.

Pennsylvania

In the eighteenth century, architectural carving was probably more common in Philadelphia than in any other American city except possibly Charleston. The fair number of existing rococo examples show a period of great activity between about 1764 and 1772.[25] The local treatment of chimneypieces—a heavy tabernacle frame mounted on the wall several inches above a mantel shelf on trusses—can be found in Swan (Plates XLII-L) but is nowhere precisely copied. Most of that carving has been attributed to London artisans: Bernard and Jugiez, in Philadelphia by 1762, and Hercules Courtenay, in Philadelphia by 1765.[26]

The rococo style may have been introduced at Mount Pleasant, a magnificent stone country house overlooking the Schuylkill River just north of the city. Captain John Mac-Pherson, a Scot made rich through privateering in the late 1750s, bought the land and began the construction of the house in 1761. The account book of master builder Thomas Nevell documents the work over the next four years.[27] Rococo carving, confined to the chimneypiece in the first-floor parlor and to the chimneypiece and flanking cupboards of the upstairs drawing room (FIG. 12), is in the manner of Bernard and Jugiez. Both chimneypieces are of an oddly incomplete design. The overmantel frame has been so elongated that it rests not on a mantel shelf but directly on the scrolled trusses. In the upstairs room, however, the overmantel frame breaks out at the top into a broken-scroll pediment in which is centered a vibrant, flowing pierced shell, perhaps the earliest example of the full rococo in Philadelphia architecture.[28]

At Cliveden, in Germantown, six miles north of the city, the carvers of Mount Pleasant were employed to embellish the stone house begun in 1763 on the country estate of Benjamin Chew (1722–1810), a noted jurist and later chief justice of Pennsylvania. (The house remains intact and has much of its original furniture.) In 1766, Bernard and

FIGURE 12. *Chimneypiece*, 1761–65, upstairs drawing room, Mount Pleasant, the John MacPherson house, Philadelphia

FIGURE 13. *Parlor chimneypiece*, ca. 1765, from the Stamper–
Blackwell house, Philadelphia, as installed at Winterthur Museum

FIGURE 14. *Fireplace wall of ballroom*, 1769–70, the Samuel Powel house, Philadelphia, as installed at the Philadelphia Museum of Art

Jugiez received payment for two rocaille-carved trusses for the parlor chimneypiece and ten smaller, leaf-carved trusses for the overdoor pediments of the parlor and the entrance hall.[29] The chimneypiece design, the consoles supporting a mantel shelf, is now fully developed.[30]

The general design of the Cliveden chimneypiece and overdoors is repeated, but greatly enriched, in the parlor (now at Winterthur) from the Pine Street house thought to have been built in the early 1760s by the merchant and mayor of Philadelphia John Stamper and later owned by the Reverend Robert Blackwell. The room is the most elaborate of extant Philadelphia interiors (FIG. 13). On the chimneypiece (its ornament probably by Hercules Courtenay), the overmantel frame is surrounded by carved fronds and garlands; between the trusses that support the mantel shelf are three panels carved in landscape vignettes, the center one after a Thomas Johnson engraving of 1762.[31]

The final surviving monument to the rococo in Philadelphia architecture is a brick town house at 244 South Third Street. The original building was erected in 1765–66 by Charles Stedman (1713–1784), a Scots shipmaster turned merchant, and was purchased by Samuel Powel (1738–1793), heir to a great mercantile fortune and later a mayor of Philadelphia, after returning from his grand tour and five days before his marriage to Elizabeth Willing, in August 1769. Powel made massive alterations to the interior in the next two years.[32] He employed the city's best carvers— Bernard and Jugiez, Hercules Courtenay, and James Reynolds (see p. 184)—for architectural work that included

the ornament of the upstairs back parlor (now at the Metropolitan Museum) and that of the upstairs ballroom (now at the Philadelphia Museum of Art; FIG. 14), the latter notable for the leaf-and-scroll carving in the frieze after a plate in Swan's *Designs in Architecture* (London, 1757) and for the superb ornamental plaster ceiling by James Clow. In May 1770, Powel paid the Scottish-trained Clow, who had arrived in Philadelphia in 1763, £31 for "Stuccoing a ceiling."[33]

Powel was not the only owner to upgrade the interior of his town house in the early 1770s, but the other structures are now all gone. John Cadwalader, who bought a house on Second Street in 1769 and proceeded to gut and refit it (see p. 185), paid £362-9-7½ for architectural carving alone—a bravado display of colonial grandeur. Today, his furniture, the most elaborate ever made in Philadelphia, has been placed in Powel's grand ballroom (see ill. opp. p. 133) at the Philadelphia Museum of Art.

On occasion, the Philadelphia style of architecture spread south to Delaware and the Eastern Shore of Maryland. Swan's engraved designs were used at the Corbit house, begun in Odessa, Delaware, in 1772, but without the rococo carving.[34] Just the opposite occurred in two houses in Queen Annes County, Maryland. At Cloverfields, built for William Hensley, there is a chimneypiece with similarities to those at MacPherson's Mount Pleasant; at Chestertown, Thomas Ringgold, a merchant with close Philadelphia ties, had a parlor (now at the Baltimore Museum of Art) with elaborate overmantels and overdoors executed in a manner not unlike John Stamper's (see FIG. 13).[35]

The South

The colonial capital of Maryland, Annapolis, on the banks of the Chesapeake, emerged as a very prosperous city in the 1760s and 1770s. Many of the major houses from that time survive. Of some fourteen erected in the decade from 1765 to 1775, the first to parade rococo ornament was the residence James Brice built on a lot he inherited in 1766. Construction of the stately brick building was begun in 1767 and took five years to complete. The interiors are remarkable for their size, their massive, carved full entablatures, and their rococo chimneypieces. Though more than one carver's hand is apparent, the principal artisan was clearly the otherwise unknown William Bampton, whom Brice, in his journal for March 1770, credited with £40-0-1 for "finishing largest Room in my House the Carpenters and Joiners work & carving Chimney Piece."[36] He was surely referring to the first-floor northwest room and its chimneypiece (FIG. 15), whose somewhat naively carved trusses copy Swan's Plate LI.

The largest of the Annapolis houses, a three-story brick cube, was begun by Samuel Chase in 1769 and purchased unfinished by the patriot and public official Edward Lloyd IV (1744–1796) in 1771.[37] William Buckland (1735–1774), a joiner and designer from Richmond County, Virginia, moved to Annapolis in that year, apparently to work for Lloyd, bringing with him the London-trained carver Thomas Hall. Hall is attributed with the carving of the most elaborate room in the house, now the dining room, for which Lloyd paid Buckland £62-0-6 in 1772 and 1773.[38] The appliqués on the frieze of the overdoors (FIG. 16), though large in scale and broadly conceived, were probably inspired by stair-bracket designs in Swan, a book Buckland owned. Rawlings and Barnes, a pair of English stuccoists late from London, did more than £200 worth of work in the house, mostly neoclassical in style but including the decoration of the hall ceiling—a central rosette with delicate rococo surrounds. In March 1774, the land directly opposite Lloyd's house was purchased by Matthias Hammond, for whom

FIGURE 15. *Chimneypiece*, 1767–72, first-floor northwest room, the James Brice house, Annapolis. Photograph, ca. 1900

FIGURE 16. *Doorframe*, 1772–73, dining room, the Chase-Lloyd house, Annapolis. Photograph, ca. 1900

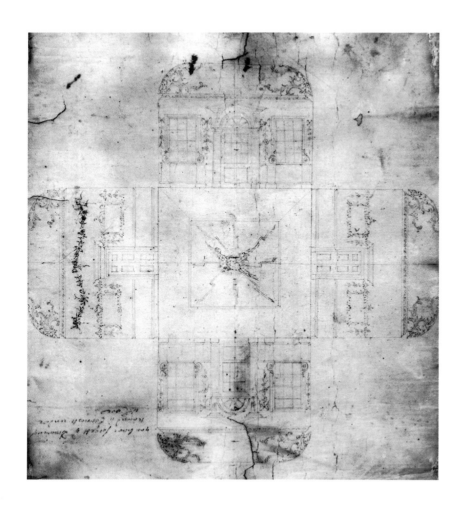

FIGURE 17. *Plan and elevations,* ca. 1764,
for entrance hall, Whitehall, the Horatio Sharpe
house, near Annapolis, 1764–69.
Pencil on paper, 15 x 19 in. (38.1 x 48.3 cm.).
Collection of Mr. and Mrs. Charles Scarlett, Jr.

FIGURE 18. *Entrance hall,* Whitehall, 1764–69

Buckland designed an elegant brick house with symmetrical wings. The richly carved chimneypieces and the door and window frames of the first-floor interiors, much in the manner of the Lloyd house dining room, have also been attributed to Thomas Hall.[39]

A few miles outside Annapolis, on the banks of the Severn, is Whitehall, a villa built by Maryland's colonial governor, Horatio Sharpe (1718–1790). The central block of the house, which was begun in 1764 and completed prior to 1769, contains a great entrance hall, or saloon. The room's decorative program is shown in an unsigned drawing (FIG. 17), a unique American counterpart of a common English architectural rendering, which includes a reflected ceiling plan and the four walls. The square chamber, nearly a cube, has a coved ceiling whose corners contain huge carved-wood rococo cartouches that frame masks representing the Four Winds. Centered in each wall is a door; on the front and rear walls are large windows with architraves terminating at the dado in carved scrolls; affixed to the side walls are mirrors; and the empty spaces on all four walls are filled with rococo garlands (FIG. 18). There is nothing else of quite this grandeur from colonial America. Buckland has been credited with Whitehall's ornamental trim.[40]

While there is probably a greater number of fine pre-Revolutionary houses in Virginia than in any other state, there is a paucity of architectural ornament in the rococo style. None exists even in Williamsburg, the colonial capital, though carvers there are known to have fabricated rococo furniture (see No. 123). Except for papier-mâché ornaments added about 1762 to the front-hall and drawing-room ceilings at Westover, built about 1731–35 by William Byrd (1674–1744) on the James River not far from Williamsburg,[41] there was no compelling fashion for the style in the Tidewater region. For the most part, one must look to the Northern Neck of Virginia, on the banks of the Potomac, for architectural rococo.

George Washington, who had acquired his estate at Mount Vernon in 1754, oversaw its first enlargement in 1757–59, years when he remodeled the West Parlor, probably installing the existing handsome chimneypiece, for which in 1757 he ordered the landscape painting that fits within the overmantel frame. The mantel and overmantel have carved friezes and flanking trusses—simplifications of Plates L and LIII in Swan—and Washington's family arms are displayed within a carved rococo cartouche. Years later, in 1775, during his second expansion of the house, he hired William Bernard Sears, who had worked previously in Virginia for Buckland, to carve a new mantel for his small dining room (FIG. 19). Instead of the usual white pine, the mantel is fashioned of walnut; the overmantel, of plaster. The whole

design has been faithfully copied from Swan's Plate L, but in a modest scale and by a heavy and somewhat labored hand. As Lund Washington, a cousin who was superintending the work at Mount Vernon for the general, candidly wrote to him: "I think you never intended such a one and must have been mistaken in the look of the draught of the chimney piece."[42]

FIGURE 19. *Chimneypiece*, 1775, small dining room, Mount Vernon

Between 1755 and 1759, Washington's neighbor the planter and, later, Revolutionary statesman George Mason (1725–1792) was building Gunston Hall, a small but exquisite Georgian house. In the entrance hall, the spandrels of the archway have *C*-scrolls with pierced rocaille mantels, and the drawing room and the dining room have elaborate carved moldings based on Swan's *Designs in Architecture*. The woodwork in the house was the responsibility of Buckland, whom Mason brought over from London for the occasion; the carving was by Sears, who is also thought to have come from England at Mason's request.[43] In this and in subsequent commissions, it was the efforts of those two men that account for much of the rococo in southern architecture.

Buckland's next important commission, in 1761–64, was for John Tayloe (1721–1779), who was building Mount Airy, a great stone house overlooking the Rappahannock River, a few miles south of the Potomac. The interiors burned in the nineteenth century, but many of the pictures and some of the furniture were saved. The most extraordinary of these pieces is an elaborate pier table (FIG. 20), which may be considered an extension of the interior architecture of the house.[44] Screws are used to secure the frame, and moldings are attached with exposed nails—techniques more commonly used by joiners than by cabinetmakers. The carving, its surface textured with shallow parallel lines, has the distinctive style of Sears's work at Gunston Hall. It is thus fair to conclude that Buckland and Sears designed and built the table as a piece of wall furniture, an integral part of the Mount Airy interior. The overall design is taken from a "Sideboard Table" in *The Director* (Plate LIX), a pattern having a pierced skirt and legs of such delicacy that Chippendale recommended using a wooden top. To support the weighty stone, the legs of the Mount Airy example were reinforced in the back, effectively blocking the pierced work, and the skirt was made solid and ornamented with the same guilloche pattern of overlapping circles found on window surrounds in the drawing room at Gunston Hall.

Midway between the Potomac and the Rappahannock rivers, not far from Fredericksburg, lies Marmion, a Fitzhugh family house built sometime around the middle of the eighteenth century. The walls of its best parlor (now at the Metropolitan Museum) are sheathed in paneling that was covered about 1770, probably when new, with the most extravagant painted decorative scheme of any colonial American room. The entablature, Ionic pilasters, and dado paneling are marbleized, and the large wall panels are embellished in an almost Continental manner with scrolls, swags, and imaginative rococo stands of fruit (FIG. 21). In the world of American painted decoration, it is without peer.[45]

FIGURE 20. *Mahogany pier table*, ca. 1765, made for Mount Airy, the John Tayloe house, Warsaw. Mahogany, 33 x 42½ x 25 in. (83.8 x 108 x 63.5 cm.)

FIGURE 21.   *Wall of parlor*, ca. 1770, from Marmion, the
John Fitzhugh house, near Fredericksburg, as installed at
The Metropolitan Museum of Art

FIGURE 22. *Parlor chimneypiece*, 1769–70,
the Humphrey Sommers house, Charleston.
Photograph, ca. 1890

In Charleston, South Carolina, architectural carving was particularly fashionable. The English artisan Henry Burnett supervised the execution of £1,000 worth of such decorative work at Saint Michael's Church between 1757 and 1760. While no record exists of what it looked like, some dozen examples of household interiors with ornamented woodwork do survive, the greatest concentration in any colonial American city. The vast majority of buildings having rococo architectural decoration were built between 1767 and 1772. Much of that work has been attributed to the carvers Thomas Woodin, who arrived from London in 1764 and died in 1774, and John Lord, who came from London in 1766 and stayed in Charleston for nine years.[46]

Among the grandest of those houses is that of Miles Brewton, 27 King Street, which was completed in 1769. It has a two-story entrance portico, a vast second-floor ballroom with a coved ceiling, and yard upon yard of elaborately carved moldings. One of the primary craftsmen on the job, and the only one now known by name, was Ezra Waite, who advertised on 22 August 1769 as a "Civil Architect, House-builder in general, and Carver, from London [who has] finished the architecture... and carved all the [tabernacle frames] in the four principal rooms... of Miles Brewton, Esquire's House."[47] The work is strong on carved moldings and geometric fretwork, characteristics of Charleston architectural ornament. Of all the Charleston chimneypieces in this style, that from the parlor of the Humphrey Sommers house, about 1769-70, is the fullest expression of the wood-carver's art (FIG. 22). A continuous cornice unites the overmantel frame and flanking pilasters in a composition reminiscent of designs in Robert Morris's *Architectural Remembrancer* (London, 1751).[48] On the mantel frieze and within the architrave of the overmantel of another chimneypiece—this one at the Daniel Heyward house—is figure-eight-patterned fretwork not unlike that found on much Charleston case furniture.[49] The cabinetmaker Thomas Elfe supplied builders with fretwork by the foot (forty-six feet in November 1772) and even the occasional "frett chimney piece."

Newspaper announcements of the period show that paper hangings from London were widely used in Charleston, though no examples remain in place. Papier-mâché ornament, however, survives in the ceiling of the downstairs parlor of the Miles Brewton house (FIG. 23). The various molded motifs—scrollwork, swags, and borders—are delicate in scale and arranged with much more order and taste than are other American examples (those at Philipse Manor, for instance). The ornament may be the work of John Blott, an upholsterer who arrived from London in 1764 and advertised in the *South Carolina Gazette* of 11 May 1765, "Machee

Ornaments for cielings, &, to imitate Stoco Work."[50] By far the supreme instance of rococo stucco work in Charleston is the decoration on the walls of a room in what is now the Colonel William Rhett house, 54 Hasell Street.[51] There, added to the overmantel and overdoors is large, bold scrollwork, rendered in a manner that can be compared with English or Irish work.

MHH

FIGURE 23. *Parlor ceiling*, ca. 1769, the Miles Brewton house, Charleston

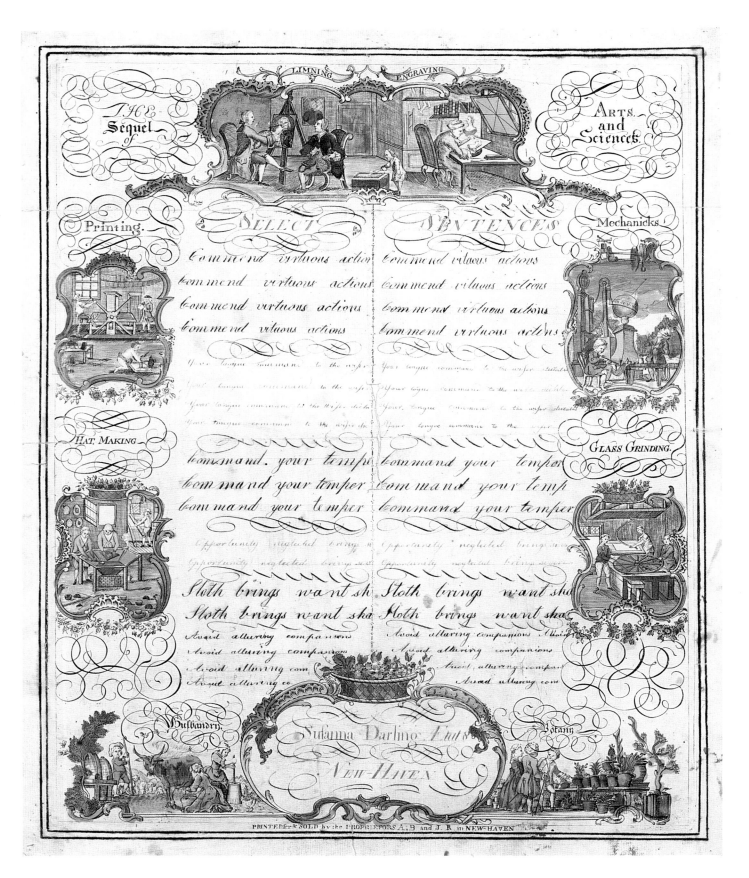

THE Sequel of

ARTS and Sciences.

LIMNING ENGRAVING

Printing. SELECT SENTENCES Mechanicks

Command virtuous actions — Command virtuous actions
Command virtuous actions — Command virtuous actions
Command virtuous actions — Command virtuous actions
Command virtuous actions — Command virtuous actions

Your tongue command to the wiser dictates — Your tongue command to the wiser dictates
Your tongue command to the wiser dictates — Your tongue command to the wiser dictates
Your tongue command to the wiser dictates — Your tongue command to the wiser dictates
Your tongue command to the wiser dictates — Your tongue command to the wiser dictates

HAT MAKING — GLASS GRINDING.

Command your temper — Command your temper
Command your temper — Command your temper
Command your temper — Command your temper

Opportunity neglected brings — Opportunity neglected brings
Opportunity neglected brings — Opportunity neglected brings

Sloth brings want sha — Sloth brings want sha
Sloth brings want sha — Sloth brings want sha

Avoid alluring companions — Avoid alluring companions
Avoid alluring companions — Avoid alluring companions
Avoid alluring com — Avoid alluring compa
Avoid alluring co — Avoid alluring com

Husbandry. Botany

Susanna Darling Aets
NEW-HAVEN

PRINTED & SOLD by the PROPRIETORS A. B. and J. R. in NEW-HAVEN

ENGRAVINGS

In eighteenth-century America, printed engravings provided the most widespread manifestation of rococo ornament. Bookplates, trade cards of all sorts, membership certificates and notifications, even the title cartouches of maps—all were influential in opening colonial eyes to the London fashion. They have rightly been called the ambassadors of the rococo style.[1]

Economic considerations played no small part in that phenomenon. Depending on its size, a copper plate could be elaborately engraved for an investment of as little as twelve shillings, with the cost of printing a hundred copies far less. Many American artisans and shopkeepers (who never could have afforded rococo-style silver or furniture for their own use) were therefore able to indulge in the fashionable English practice of owning elaborate business cards.[2] Such prints, or ephemera, are extraordinarily rare today, only occasionally preserved after having served their original, short-lived functions, perhaps as a bill head, a craftsman's label, or an invitation to a long-ago event.

Both in England and her colonies, designs for ephemera — mostly asymmetrical cartouches and variations on rectangular frames — were based on a relatively small number of prototypes. Rampant copying was the practice. The earliest dated English rococo trade card was made by Henry Copland in 1738. In 1746, he issued *A New Book of Ornaments* and Matthias Lock engraved *A Book of Shields*, two suites of fully rococo decoration, mostly cartouches, which initiated the development of the style.[3] In 1752, the two designers collaborated on another publication, titled *A New Book of Ornaments with Twelve Leaves*, which was the volume that first made popular a light and airy naturalism and a taste for fantasy and whimsy.[4]

As quickly as printed designs arrived from England, American engravers felt free to copy them, duplicating them virtually line for line on occasion, changing only the text or, in the case of bookplates, the armorial. For example, the elegant trade card (the date 1765 written on the reverse) of the London brass wiremaker Joseph Welch (**No. 12**) was the precise model for a card made by Paul Revere for the Boston hardware merchant William Breck (his copy marked 1770 on the reverse). It was also used for an all but identical card (**No. 13**) attributed to Revere, made for William Jackson, a Boston dry-goods merchant and prominent Tory, who pasted a copy on the back of a looking glass he imported and sold in 1770.[5] The impression illustrated here was used as a bill for a transaction of 28 August 1773, as inscribed on the reverse.

For printing on paper, the engraver cut the design in reverse on a copper plate. For each impression, or copy, required, he inked the plate, covered it with a sheet of paper, and ran it through a press.[6] For engraving on various scientific or measuring devices—clock dials of silvered brass, for example—and the ornamental mounts of firearms or other weapons, the design was not reversed but engraved as it was to be seen, as on objects of silver. It was therefore not uncommon for engravers to provide their services to silversmiths; alternatively, some silversmiths, most notably Paul Revere, were also expert engravers.

The main centers of engraving were Boston and Philadelphia. New York's practitioners, though less active, had close ties with their Philadelphia peers, and, late in the century, what might be considered a distinctive regional school of engravers flourished in central Connecticut. In Boston, the engravers whose work included fine rococo ornament were Thomas Johnston (his birthplace unknown) and Nathaniel Hurd and Paul Revere, both native born.

Their work was decorative but orderly, having symmetrical cartouches made up of scrolls, foliage, and other motifs

Writing certificate, attributed to Abel Buell (No. 36)

12

Trade card of Joseph Welch
London, 1760–65
Engraving on paper, 6⅝ x 5⅜ in.
The Metropolitan Museum of Art

13

Trade card of William Jackson
Attributed to Paul Revere, Boston, 1765–70
Engraving on paper, 7⅝ x 6¼ in.
American Antiquarian Society

of the rococo repertoire. Johnston (1708–1767) was active in Boston by 1726 and advertised his own shop in 1732.[7] In his trade card of that year, he described himself as a "Japaner" who did japanning, varnishing, drawing, gilding, painting, and engraving. He was also a housepainter, a sign painter, and an organ builder. His success can be measured by the substantial estate he had amassed at his death.[8] Of the more than thirty known engravings of his, four maps, two trade cards, and one bookplate include elements of rococo ornament. His first essay in the style seems to have been the title cartouche on a map he made in 1753. The painter John Greenwood, who was apprenticed to Johnston from about 1742 to 1745, later recalled that one of his tasks during that period was to engrave bookplates.[9]

Nathaniel Hurd (1730–1777) was born in Boston and trained in silversmithing by his father, the highly regarded craftsman Jacob Hurd (see p. 84). The younger Hurd never distinguished himself as a silversmith but excelled in engraving on both copper and silver. He is best known for his heraldic bookplates, forty of which are signed by him and fifteen more are attributed to him.[10] The source for the heraldic illustrations on at least twenty-eight of the fifty-five plates was John Guillim's *Display of Heraldry*, the sixth edition (London, 1724) "improved with large additions of many hundred coats of arms."[11] When Hurd's portrait was painted by John Singleton Copley about 1765, the subject was seated behind a table on which lay a copy of the heraldic manual.[12]

Boston-born Paul Revere (1735–1818) was trained as a

silversmith by his French immigrant father, Apollos Rivoire, and took over his shop in 1754, after Rivoire's death. Revere's career in engraving grew out of his silversmithing and remained secondary to it. His two volumes of Day Books, or ledgers (the first covering the years 1761–83; the second, 1784–97), document his business in both skills.[13] Though the books record only outstanding accounts and contain no mention of works paid for in cash on delivery or of projects he initiated himself, they document his production of the full range of printed ephemera, including Massachusetts currency and metal-cut illustrations for magazines and newspapers, many of which have been identified and show rococo influence. All told, Revere is associated with eleven bookplates and a like number of trade cards.[14] Though as an engraver he is best known for patriotic propaganda prints, especially his representation of the Boston Massacre, a number of his bookplates, trade cards, and certificates are accomplished examples of the rococo style.

In 1757, Revere married Sarah Orne (1736–1773) and after her death he married Rachel Walker (1745–1813); eleven children survived from the two marriages. As a patriot, Revere, who served briefly as a lieutenant in the French and Indian War (1754–63), is famous for his Revolutionary activities, especially the one immortalized in 1861 by Longfellow in *The Midnight Ride of Paul Revere*. Revere embarked on that ride on 18 April 1775 as messenger for the Massachusetts Committee of Correspondence. He was also a member of the Sons of Liberty and, from 1776 to 1779, lieutenant colonel of the Massachusetts State's Train of Artillery. A prominent Freemason, he belonged to three different lodges between 1760 and 1810 and was Grand Master of the Grand Lodge of Massachusetts from 1795 to 1797.[15]

In Philadelphia, the most famous engravers to work in the rococo style were James Turner, Henry Dawkins, and James Smither. All were English immigrants who had trained in the specialty. Their ornamental work, in the English manner seen in engravings by Lock, Copland, and Johnson, has a greater sense of movement, of asymmetry, than does that of the Boston engravers. Turner (active 1743–d. 1759) located first in that city, where his earliest known effort, a view of Boston Harbor, appeared in *The American Magazine* of 1743, and another of the same subject was published the following year.[16] Two years later, he advertised as a silversmith and engraver. His views of Boston Harbor probably attracted the attention of the magazine's Philadelphia distributor, Benjamin Franklin. Franklin arranged further commissions for Turner and may have been the cause of his moving to Philadelphia, where he had settled by 1754.[17] Franklin's influence provided Turner with his three major engraving commissions in the city—Lewis Evans's

map of the middle British colonies in 1755, Joshua Fisher's chart of Delaware Bay (No. 38) in 1756, and Nicholas Scull's map of the Province of Pennsylvania in 1758. Turner died of smallpox the next year.

Henry Dawkins (d. 1786) worked in New York as well as in Philadelphia.[18] The son of John Dawkins, a London bricklayer, he was apprenticed in 1749, after his father's death, to the London engraver James Wigley.[19] By 1754, he was in New York, where he engraved a bookplate (No. 18) for John Burnet. In 1755, Dawkins advertised that he had set up his own shop, "where he engraves in all sorts of mettals."[20] Shortly afterward, he moved to Philadelphia and there, in 1757, married Priscilla Wood. He worked briefly for Turner before announcing in January 1758 that he had opened his own business in neighboring premises:

> Henry Dawkins, Engraver from London, Who lately wrought with Mr. James Turner; having now, entered into business for himself...engraves all sorts of maps, Shopkeepers bills, bills of parcels, coats of Arms for gentlemens books, coats of Arms, cyphers and other devices on Plate likewise seals and mourning rings cut after the neatest manner and at the most reasonable rates.[21]

Dawkins returned to New York in 1774, on the eve of the Revolution. Though he was imprisoned for counterfeiting colonial bank notes in 1776, two years later found him engraving the first coat of arms for New York State and, in 1780, the new country's official currency. The last mention of him is in an advertisement of 3 May 1786 in Philadelphia's *Freeman's Journal* for the sale of "Eight elegantly engraved copper-plates, by Dawkins."[22]

James Smither (1741–1797) is thought to have trained in England as a maker and ornamenter of firearms.[23] The first notice of him in America was in the *Pennsylvania Chronicle* of 18 April 1768, where he announced that he performed "All Manner of Engraving in Gold, Silver, Copper, Steel, and all other Metals—Coats of Arms, and Seals, done in the neatest Manner. Likewise cuts Stamps, Brands, and metal Cuts for Printers, and ornamental Tools for Bookbinders. He also ornaments Guns and Pistols, both engraving and inlaying Silver, at the most Reasonable Rates."[24] He is known best for the spectacular rococo advertisements of the Philadelphians Benjamin Randolph and Robert Kennedy (Nos. 32, 33). In 1769, Smither advertised "Proposals for opening A Drawing School, Being a new institution in this city ...where young gentlemen and ladies shall be carefully instructed in that useful art."[25] He moved to New York in 1777, shortly before the Supreme Executive Council of Pennsylvania accused him of the crime also committed by Dawkins—counterfeiting currency.

Bookplates

The diminutive but elaborately engraved bookplate (what Dawkins called "coats of Arms for gentlemens books") is perhaps the best indication of the prestige of books and the value given to their ownership in colonial America. Pasted on the inside cover of a bound volume (see No. 21), a bookplate proudly identified its owner and issued a tacit warning to the would-be borrower. Although a few eighteenth-century libraries survive more or less intact, such as that of James Logan at the Library Company of Philadelphia and that of Isaac Norris at Dickinson College, Carlisle, Pennsylvania, and though there are listings of the contents of others in eighteenth-century inventories, only through bookplates can the large number of once-existing private and public libraries be identified. At the end of the nineteenth century, when it was fashionable to collect bookplates, the majority of American examples were removed from their housings and mounted in albums. Though disembodied, they still preserve the names of those Americans possessing enough volumes to warrant the commissioning of a personal label. Of bookplates assignable to the third quarter of the eighteenth century, the great preponderance are in the rococo style. Unlike any other form of printed ephemera of the time, most survive in multiple impressions.

Bookplates were always personalized with the owner's name or arms. Whether he was entitled to bear the latter, according to the College of Heralds in London, mattered not. Guillim's *Display of Heraldry* was the most popular source for the armorials. The decorative cartouches or mantlings chosen to surround the armorial shield were copied from stock English prototypes inspired in turn by the engravings Lock and Copland published in the 1740s and 1750s. In New England, Nathaniel Hurd, relying heavily on Guillim, played the leading role in bookplate design and production; in New York and Philadelphia, Dawkins probably came as close as anyone to filling that position. Before trained engravers were available in America, some bookish

colonists, such as James Logan, whose fully rococo bookplate must date well before his death, in 1751, had their bookplates engraved in England.[26]

Nathaniel Hurd specialized in the rendering of bookplates, three-quarters of them rococo in style, for Boston's elite.[27] The earliest dated American rococo bookplate (**No. 14**), engraved with the name of Thomas Dering (1720–1785) and the date 1749, was made by Hurd when he was only nineteen years old. The mantling, which he was to employ on a number of later bookplates, signaled the introduction of rococo-style engraved ornament to New England. The Dering family is generally associated with New York, but Thomas was born in Boston and moved to Shelter Island, off the eastern end of Long Island, New York, only in 1750. The arms (three stags' heads) are like those of the Deering family given in Guillim's *Display of Heraldry*.[28] The asymmetrical mantle of the bookplate is composed of *C*-scrolls with rocaille work framing the shield and spiky grasses and flowers projecting from either side; at the bottom, water pours from an opening in a shell.

The rococo-mantle design Hurd used for Thomas Dering was employed with only minor variations by Thomas Johnston on a bookplate with the arms of the Oliver family, featuring an outstretched arm grasping a grotesquely severed hand (**No. 15**). The design is placed low on the copper, leaving no room for the owner's name. The plate is said to have been used by Andrew Oliver (1706–1774), lieutenant governor of the Province of Massachusetts Bay.[29] That, however, is unlikely; another bookplate with the Oliver arms, attributed to Paul Revere, prominently displays Oliver's name.[30] The Johnston bookplate, one of four he signed, is his only one in the new style. The awkward attachment of the ribbon scroll on the design may be evidence that Johnston took Hurd's basic pattern and adapted it to accommodate the Oliver family motto.

Paul Revere's essays in rococo bookplate design consist of three signed plates and four others that have been attributed to him.[31] All have the same mantling and motto ribbon and are a slightly squatter, more symmetrical, and more coherent version of the Hurd and Johnston model.[32] The bookplate of Epes Sargent (1721–1779), the arms a chevron between three dolphins (**No. 16**), can be dated precisely. In an entry of 27 September 1764 in Revere's ledgers, Sargent is charged "To Engraving your Arms on a Copper Plate 0-12-0" and "To 150 Prints at 4s pr Hund. 0-6-0."[33] That proves how inexpensive bookplates were after the initial investment in the engraving.

14

Bookplate of Thomas Dering
Nathaniel Hurd, Boston, 1749
Engraving on paper, 2⅞ x 2½ in.
The Metropolitan Museum of Art

16

Bookplate of Epes Sargent
Paul Revere, Boston, 1764
Engraving on paper, 3¼ x 2½ in.
American Antiquarian Society

15

Bookplate with Oliver family arms
Thomas Johnston, Boston, 1755–65
Engraving on paper, 3⅞ x 3⅛ in.
American Antiquarian Society

17

Bookplate of Gardiner Chandler
Paul Revere, Boston, ca. 1765
Engraving on paper, 3⅜ x 2¾ in.
American Antiquarian Society

VIRESCIT VULNERE VIRTUS

John Burnet Esq.
New=York.

H. DAWKINS.   Sculp. 1754.

18

Bookplate of John Burnet
Henry Dawkins, New York, 1754
Engraving on paper, 3⅞ x 3 in.
The Metropolitan Museum of Art

The bookplate for Gardiner Chandler (1723–1782), a Boston merchant and Loyalist (**No. 17**), has mantling identical to that of Epes Sargent's. It differs somewhat, however, from the mantle that surrounds the identical Chandler family arms (three lions on a checkered ground) on a silver salver Revere supplied to Gardiner's sister Lucretia (see No. 71). Revere seems never to have used the bookplate mantle for any other purpose.

The earliest known American engraving by the prolific Henry Dawkins is a bookplate (**No. 18**) he made in 1754, during his brief stay in New York City, for John Burnet, a local attorney. The design is composed of a principal cartouche enclosing the Burnet arms (three holly leaves and a hunting horn) and a second, horizontal cartouche containing Burnet's name, the whole flanked by pairs of figures appearing in carefree musical pursuits. This is one of those rare occasions in American usage of the human allusions common in European rococo design. The double-cartouche arrangement was a well-known English ornamental design that Dawkins repeated in a number of other bookplates, but never again with the technical accomplishment of this example.

The double-cartouche design made its way up the Hudson and was the model for a copper plate (**No. 19**) engraved by the native-born Andrew Billings (1743–1808), of Poughkeepsie, New York. But how different from Dawkins's! While possessed of a naive charm, this is rendering by a hand untutored in the niceties of English copper-plate engraving. The bookplate, illustrated in a twentieth-century impression, was made for Philip Van Rensselaer (1747–1798), probably sometime between his marriage to Maria Sanders, in 1768, and the building of Cherry Hill, his country house on the outskirts of Albany, in 1786. The copper plate, still at Cherry Hill, bears testimony to the rapid transformation from the elegant and formal rococo of the city's specially trained artisans to the engaging linear patterns of the country copyist.

One of the few dated American bookplates in the rococo mode is that for IER, VN, RENSSELAER (**No. 20**), engraved by Elisha Gallaudet in 1761. The abbreviations probably refer to Jeremias (1738–1764), of that branch of the Van Rensselaer family then occupying the Lower Manor, on the east bank of the Hudson. The bookplate is of the standard asymmetrical-cartouche type, with the family's quartered arms (cross, battlement and stars, crowns, chevrons) in a design not unlike that Hurd used in New England (see No. 14). Gallaudet, born of Huguenot stock in New Rochelle, New York, about 1730, was locally trained. He married Jeanne

19

Plate for Philip Van Rensselaer bookplate
Andrew Billings, Poughkeepsie, 1768–86
Engraving on copper, 3⅞ x 2⅞ in.
Together with recent impression (above)
Historic Cherry Hill

20

Bookplate of Jeremias Van Rensselaer
Elisha Gallaudet, New York, 1761
Engraving on paper, 3½ x 2⅝ in.
Historic Cherry Hill

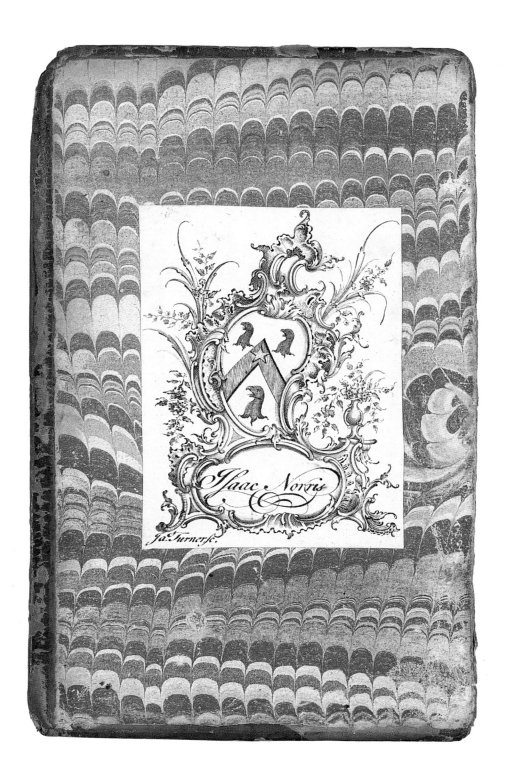

21

Bookplate of Isaac Norris
James Turner, Philadelphia, ca. 1757
Engraving on paper, 3⅛ x 2⅜ in.
On inside cover of book
Dickinson College

Dubois in 1755 and by 1759 was in New York City, when he was listed as a subscriber, along with "Mr. Furer [Fueter], Silversmith in French Church Street," to a series of engraved portraits.[34] In 1771, Gallaudet moved from Smith Street to the "Broad-Way near the Bowling Green," where he carried on his engraving business.[35] His Van Rensselaer bookplate illustrates a considerable competence, though no genius, in the technique of English engraved rococo ornament.

A small number of bookplates engraved in Philadelphia by Turner or Dawkins exhibit the writhing and energetic quality, the playful irrationality, of the engraved rococo designs Lock and Copland published in London. Turner, who as early as 1810 was described as "the best engraver which appeared in the colonies before the revolution,"[36] reached the apogee of his talent during his Philadelphia sojourn of five or six years before his death, in 1759. Among his finest work is a bookplate (**No. 21**), made for the bibliophile Isaac Norris, of the double-cartouche type: the upper part surrounding the Norris arms (chevron between three ravens' heads) is in Copland's spiky style (see FIG. 3, p. 3); the vase at the middle right was a motif much favored by Philadelphia carvers (see No. 160).

Norris (1701–1766) took over the family mercantile business at his father's death, in 1735, and in 1750 was elected to the first of several terms as Speaker of the Pennsylvania Assembly. A solid classical education and extensive travel abroad as a young man led him to increase manyfold the library he inherited from his father.[37] In November 1757, he began a catalogue of the books; that is likely the time he ordered his bookplate from Turner. The library descended to his daughter Mary, who married John Dickinson in 1770. In 1785, Dickinson gave some sixteen hundred of the volumes to what was to be named Dickinson College, at Carlisle, where they still remain. Some four hundred of them have the Turner bookplate, often pasted onto colorful marbled boards, an evocative reminder of a learned American's library.[38]

Among Dawkins's best rococo bookplates is the one he made for Francis Hopkinson (**No. 22**). The asymmetrical cartouche is enlivened by a fantastic hissing dragon set against a cloudy sky, the sort of caprice that is characteristic of Copland's work. Hopkinson (1737–1791) was born in Philadelphia and studied law under Benjamin Chew, attorney general of the Province of Pennsylvania. An author and accomplished musician, Hopkinson presumably gathered a sizable library. The bookplate, with the family arms (a chevron and three stars), was probably ordered sometime around his second marriage, to Ann Borden, in 1768. About 1773, he moved to Bordentown (named for his father-in-law), New Jersey, where he rapidly achieved political prominence. He was a signer of the Declaration of Independence from New Jersey.

22

Bookplate of Francis Hopkinson
Henry Dawkins, Philadelphia, ca. 1768
Engraving on paper, 3½ x 3 in.
American Antiquarian Society

Books, Metal Cuts, and Bookbindings

Books of sheet music reproduced by means of copper-plate engravings and with engraved title pages are among the few American imprints to have fashionable rococo ornament. A good example is James Lyon's *Urania, or A Choice Collection of Psalm-Tunes, Anthems, and Hymns* (**No. 23**). The volume was executed in Philadelphia in 1761 by the indefatigable Dawkins. A handsome cartouche, occasionally invaded by the lettering, fills the narrow horizontal space of the title page. *Urania* was one of some two dozen publications issued between 1760 and 1765 by William Bradford (1722–1791), who had learned the printing trade from Andrew Bradford, his uncle and the founder of the first newspaper in Pennsylvania. Music books like these were extremely popular. In Boston, between 1755 and 1766, Thomas Johnston engraved either three or four sets of such plates.[39] In 1764, Revere copied Dawkins's title page almost exactly for *A Collection of The best Psalm Tunes, in two, three, and four Parts,*[40] compiled by Josiah Flagg, an almost unprecedented case of Philadelphia engraving having influence in Boston.

Illustrations for eighteenth-century newspapers, broadsides, almanacs, and pamphlets were almost always metal cuts — that is, engravings on type-metal (a lead alloy) suitable for incorporation in pages of newsprint. The best documented of such work is a group of some twenty-two by Paul Revere, who in his ledger referred to the process as "Engraving a Leading plate for newspaper."[41] Revere's metal cuts never evince the aspiration to ornament of his engravings. Of all the metal-cut illustrations in the colonial press, only one can be said to aim for high rococo fashion: the advertisement (FIG. 24) of the New York drawing master and merchant Gerardus Duyckinck (1723–1797), which appeared in *The New-York Gazette and the Weekly Mercury* from 1767 to 1769. On Duyckinck's notice, dozens of rococo raffles and scrolls are linked together to create a mirrorlike frame — long and narrow to fit the shape of a newspaper column — in which to proclaim Duyckinck's wares.

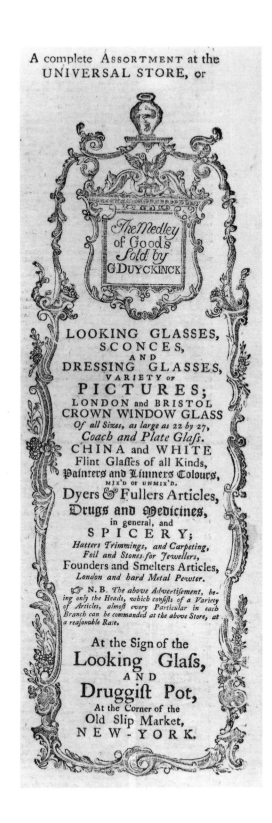

FIGURE 24. Advertisement of Gerardus Duyckinck, 1767–69, *The New-York Gazette and the Weekly Mercury.* Metal cut on paper, 9⅜ x 3 in. (23.9 x 7.6 cm.)

23

Title page of *Urania*
Henry Dawkins, Philadelphia, 1761
Engraving on paper, 4 x 8½ in.
American Antiquarian Society

Decorated boards on American bookbindings from the latter part of the eighteenth century are very rare, primarily because of a trend that began in the 1760s, with the increased availability of books, to shelve them upright, with their spines visible, rather than horizontally, with the edges of the pages exposed. (Isaac Norris made that shelving switch in 1764.)[42] Stored in the new way, the covers were not visible and there was no purpose in decorating them. The only exceptions were presentation volumes, often kept out on a table. Perhaps the sole American binder whose work ever really achieved a rococo sensibility was Robert Aitken (1735–1802). Trained in his native Scotland, he made a reconnaissance visit to Philadelphia in the summer of 1769. In May 1771, he settled there permanently with his family; a month later he set up his printing and bindery shop on Front Street. The waste book, or log, of that business, which dates from the shop's inception until 1802, details its success. In 1782, Aitken was described as "having the most taste of a printer of any man in [Philadelphia]."[43]

Aitken's great rococo achievement was the special binding of a number of copies of a popular Scottish work, *Lectures on Rhetoric and Belles Lettres*, by Hugh Blair. Aitken published the first American edition of the book in 1784, counting on good sales to make up for the money he had lost on the so-called Aitken Bible, an edition he had brought out in 1782. Of *Lectures on Rhetoric*, he said, "If the Literati are not blind to their own interest, [they] must purchase this work with great avidity."[44] Of the few existing copies of the thick paper edition, with its elaborately tooled leather bindings, one has a history of having been presented by an otherwise unidentified Gerardus Clarkson to his son in 1788, when the youth graduated from Nassau Hall. That provenance corresponds to a binding entry in the waste book, securing the binding's attribution.[45] On another copy (**No. 24**), said to have belonged to one Charles Thompson (Charles Thomson, first secretary of the Continental Congress?), the binding is of smooth red morocco, elaborately tooled in gold.[46] The spine has six panels, one with the title, BLAIR'S / LECTURES, each of the others with a central oval and a ribbon. The front and back covers have elaborate foliate borders decorated with a basket and columns and inhabited by parrots, phoenixes, and insects. Were the dies for these stamps among the ornamental tools for bookbinders Smither advertised in 1768? London bindings of the early 1770s display almost identical wildlife but are more precisely detailed.[47]

24

Back cover of *Lectures on Rhetoric and Belles Lettres*
Robert Aitken, Philadelphia, 1784
Red morocco, gold tooled, 10⅝ x 8⅝ in.
American Antiquarian Society

Trade Cards and Other Ephemera

In England and in her American colonies, engravers were called on to provide ornamental prints to be distributed in furtherance of individual businesses and the activities of various organizations. What had been an occasional venture in advertising in the 1730s and 1740s became a common practice by the 1760s, when a number of large and handsome rococo sheets engraved in the full London manner were produced in America.

The trade card (short for tradesman's card) usually consisted of an ornamental cartouche decked out with illustrations of the wares of the merchant or the shopkeeper and containing his name, address, and a description of his interests. They range in size from little larger than a bookplate to a full page. In 1774, two recently arrived London engravers—John Hutt in New York and John Norman in Philadelphia—used almost precisely the same language to advertise the variety of their commercial ephemera, which included shop bills, bills of exchange, bills of lading, bills of parcels.[48] Those distinctions no longer have much meaning, though some of the few examples that remain, mostly in unique impressions, have actual accounts written on them. Other popular uses of ornamentally engraved sheets were as certificates of membership or achievement in an organization and as invitations to, or notifications of, an organization's event. Revere's ledgers include numerous charges for engraving single plates, usually at a cost of between two and three pounds, and for printing between one hundred and two hundred impressions, at a cost of four to six shillings per hundred.

One of the earliest American rococo trade cards was engraved in 1757 by Thomas Johnston for Boston hardware merchant Lewis Deblois (**No. 25**). The phrase "Bot of Lewis Deblois" engraved by Johnston below the ornament shows the example to have actually been a bill head, the lower part of the sheet now removed. What is known about Deblois is

25

Trade card of Lewis Deblois
Thomas Johnston, Boston, 1757
Engraving on paper, 6⅜ x 7⅝ in.
Winterthur Library

gleaned from his advertisements in Boston newspapers. In 1751, he was in partnership with his brother Gilbert, an importer of brass and pewter; in September 1757, he was in partnership with a man named Wickham at the sign of the Golden Éagle. Before the end of the year, according to the trade card, Deblois was on his own at the Golden Eagle, in Dock Square; in April 1758, he advertised from there again. In January 1761, "lately returned from London," he opened a new store on King Street, where he sold paper hangings (wallpaper) and fabrics, as well as hardware.[49]

When he undertook to make Deblois's card, Johnston's only previous essays in the rococo had been unassuming title cartouches for four maps he engraved between 1753 and 1756.[50] The card shows him technically proficient but not fully comfortable with the style. Though the ornamental framework is perfectly symmetrical, except at the lower middle, there is an almost disconcerting imbalance about the design that results from the off-center placement of the text, which occasionally exceeds its bounds. The ruled line that forms an ineffective boundary around the design is contrary to the sense of freedom that is an essential element of the rococo.

Nathaniel Hurd, best known for his bookplates, also engraved a variety of business ephemera, including a furniture label for Benjamin Frothingham (FIG. 32, p. 136) and the highly ornamental order blank of the Nicholas Brown company of Providence, makers of spermaceti candles (**No. 26**). Scrollwork with emergent foliage and rocaille appears to be growing out of, and perhaps consuming, the straight, molded frame; within the small cartouche on top is a vignette of a whaling scene. The legend within the frame is given in English at the top and in French at the bottom. In the middle, flanking a representation of the mighty sperm whale, are spaces, apparently for denoting the number of candles of various sizes to the pound.

The Nicholas Brown company was established in 1762 in Providence, Rhode Island. One of the specialties of the firm's international trade was sperm-whale oil. As early as 1748, candles made from that oil had been described locally as "exceeding all others for Beauty, Sweetness of Scent when extinguished; Duration, being more than double Tallow Candles of equal size; Dimensions of Flame, nearly four Times more."[51] The company transformed the spermaceti candle business from a household activity to a factory setting and went on to monopolize the American market. Little wonder that they would go to Boston for a business card in the latest international style. About 1753, Hurd had engraved a comparable order blank for another candlemaker, Joseph Palmer, of Germantown, near Boston. On the Palmer

26

Trade card of Nicholas Brown & Company
Nathaniel Hurd, Boston, ca. 1762
Engraving on paper, 6¼ x 7⅞ in.
The John Carter Brown Library, Brown University

27

Trade card of Joseph Webb
Paul Revere, Boston, 1765
Engraving on paper, 7½ x 6 in.
American Antiquarian Society

28

Notification of meeting
Saint Peter's Lodge, Newburyport
Paul Revere, Boston, 1772
Engraving on paper, 7¾ x 6½ in.
American Antiquarian Society

example, the ornamental mantel had a rectilinear interior and was of a heavier and more static design.[52]

Paul Revere's ledgers record the engraving of some dozen shopkeeper's cards, or advertisements. The five that are known today clearly show that Revere's rococo ornamental style was fully matured by the mid-1760s. The most elaborate of them, that of Joseph Webb (**No. 27**), is recorded under the date 28 September 1765: "Mr Joseph Webb Dr settled / To Engraving a Copper Plate for Advertisements 3-0-0 / To 150 Advertisements Printing at 4-1 per Hdd 0-7-0."[53] The rococo cartouche is bestrewed with pots and kettles and other items of hardware that Webb purveyed at his store near Oliver's Dock, Boston. Though most of what he sold was utilitarian and plain, some of the ornamental iron chimneybacks for Jeremiah Lee's grand Marblehead house came from him and bear his name (see p. 220). Joseph

Webb (1734–1787), a merchant and ship chandler, was, like Revere, prominent as both a patriot and a Freemason. Note the use of Masonic emblems (a square, a compass) at the card's bottom.

Revere, who was probably the leading Freemason in all New England, made eight different engravings for various Masonic groups, two of which have the same mantling design as found on the Webb card.[54] The first, a printed notification for Saint Peter's Lodge in Newburyport (**No. 28**), is listed in his ledger entry of 15 September 1772: "Mr. Simon Greenleaf Newbury-port Dr / To Engraving a plate for Notification 2-8-0 / To 300 Prints 0-18-0."[55] Greenleaf was a charter member of the Lodge, which was formed that year. The copy shown was made out to an Enoch Pike in the Masonic year 5777 (1777). The second was done for one of two Saint Andrew's Lodges in Boston in 1784.[56]

The real eye-catcher among Revere's rococo ephemera is the certificate issued to those who attended the anatomical lectures and surgical demonstrations (for the latter, read dissections, not at first publicly condoned) of Dr. John Warren of Boston. In 1780, Warren sought to launch "an incipient medical school institution,"[57] an ambition that resulted three years later in the founding of the Harvard medical school, where Warren was professor of anatomy and surgery. The certificate, the cost of its engraving underwritten by a subscription in 1780, was given to students in Warren's private courses (1780–82) or, later, his university classes. Levi Bartlett (1763–1828), the recipient of this example (**No. 29**) on 8 June 1785, became a distinguished physician. On the certificate, Revere's scrolled frame is bolder and simpler than those of the 1760s, and his use of four large images—the head of the second-century Greek physician Galen, two hanging skeletons, and a dissection in progress—has a ghoulish effect. It was not for the faint of heart.[58]

Not much rococo ephemera remains from New York. Samuel Prince's furniture label, probably the work of a locally trained artisan who did not sign his name (FIG. 37, p. 154), has an ingenuous charm. The bill head engraved by John Hutt in 1771 for the upholsterer Richard Kip (FIG. 25) uses the outline of a bedstead (its canopy copied from *The Director*) in place of an ornamental cartouche. That made for the New York mathematical instrumentmaker Anthony Lamb (**No. 30**), one of the grandest of American advertising sheets, is the work of Henry Dawkins. Since no other rococo mantling by Dawkins has quite the overall coherence and competence demonstrated by this example, it must have been copied directly from one of many similar English cards. (That facility of Dawkins's was to lead him into temptation: as already noted, he was imprisoned in 1776 for counterfeiting.)

Lamb, born about 1703, was made a freeman of the City of New York in 1731 and advertised as a mathematical instrumentmaker in 1749 and again in 1753. Two years later, on 25 October 1755, it was announced in *The New-York Mercury* that "Henry Dawkins, engraver, who lately lived with Mr. Anthony Lamb, has now set up his [own] business."[59] Dawkins had come to New York about 1754 and was to move to Philadelphia by 1757; presumably, he executed the Lamb card while residing with Lamb and in his employ.

Another New York example of the full rococo style is the card of notification, or invitation, for meetings of the Hand-in-Hand Fire Company (**No. 31**). The engraving has been attributed to Dawkins,[60] which would mean that it too was executed prior to his departure for Philadelphia. Like the

29

Certificate of attendance
Dr. Warren's anatomical lectures
Paul Revere, Boston, 1780
Engraving on paper, 9¼ x 7⅝ in.
American Antiquarian Society

FIGURE 25. *Trade card of Richard Kip*, 1771. John Hutt, New York. Engraving on paper, 9 x 5⅞ in. (22.9 x 14.9 cm.). Rare Books and Manuscripts Division, The New York Public Library, Astor, Lenox, and Tilden Foundations

30

Trade card of Anthony Lamb
Henry Dawkins, New York, ca. 1755
Engraving on paper, 11 x 7½ in.
The New-York Historical Society

design of the bill head made for Lamb, this triple cartouche must have had its origins in an English prototype. The cityscape vignette, which cannot be identified with any site in New York, may also have been copied from an English print.

The recipient of this particular invitation, dated 3 March 1762, to a meeting at the City Arms tavern in the Broadway, was the self-styled earl of Sterling, born William Alexander (1726–1783) in New York, who was educated in the city and made an advantageous marriage with the governor's sister. During a sojourn in England between 1756 and 1761, he attempted unsuccessfully to assert his claim to the earldom of Stirling, a title he nevertheless assumed when he returned to New York.

Among a number of large London-style trade cards made in Philadelphia prior to the Revolution, two by James Smither stand out as spectacular representations of the American rococo. His advertisement for Benjamin Randolph (**No. 32**) was engraved in 1769 to coincide with the cabinetmaker's building of a new house and a shop named the Golden Eagle in Chestnut Street, between Third and Fourth streets (see p. 183)—the very block where Smither had settled on his arrival from London the previous year.[61] This celebrated image has an arrestingly asymmetrical cartouche liberally embellished with designs for furniture copied from various pattern books, including *The Director* and *Houshold Furniture*.[62] What distinguishes this from all other trade cards, both English and American, is its bizarre juxtapositions: an oversize eagle on a bedstead tester, a clock on a colonnade, and what is probably a clapboard wall with plain square windows over a masonry wall whose arched Gothic opening is marked "B.Rs Ware Room." Such irrationalities are an aspect of the English rococo seldom explored in America.

The advertisement Smither made for the printer and printseller Robert Kennedy (**No. 33**) is impressive for its grandeur of scale and looseness and informality of execution. The design owes a debt to the title page of Johnson's *One Hundred and Fifty New Designs* (1761), with which it shares the distinctive motif of a cluster of five balusters.[63] Kennedy opened a copper-plate printing shop in Philadelphia on Third Street in 1761; in 1767, while still at the same address, he branched out into selling prints. In December 1768 (the year Smither arrived in the city), Kennedy was in partnership with his brother Thomas, having just opened a separate "Print Shop, in Second-street near Chestnut-street."[64] Since the Smither advertisement gives an address at Second Street below Walnut and makes no mention of Thomas Kennedy, the brothers' partnership must have been dissolved and the

31

Invitation for the Hand-in-Hand Fire Company
Possibly by Henry Dawkins, New York, ca. 1755
Engraving on paper, 7⅞ x 6½ in.
The New York Public Library

Benj.ⁿ Randolph
Cabinet Maker
at the Golden Eagle in Chesnut Street
Between third and fourth Streets.
PHILADELPHIA,
Makes all Sorts of Cabinet & Chair work
Likewise Carving, Gilding &c Perform'd in the Chinese
and Modern Taste.

J. Smither, Sculp.ᵗ Philad.ᵃ

32

Trade card of Benjamin Randolph
James Smither, Philadelphia, 1769
Engraving on paper, 9 x 7 in.
The Library Company of Philadelphia

Robert Kennedy
at WEST'S HEAD
in Second Street below
Walnut Street
PHILAD.ª

Has for Sale,
a large and beautiful Collection of
PICTURES and PRINTS;
On the most interesting and pleasing Subjects;
Done from Capital Paintings, of the
Greatest Masters, that England, France,
or Italy, has ever produced; they are
Elegantly Framed, & Glazed.
He also makes and Gilds all
kinds of Picture & Family Frames;
pastes & varnishes MAPS & carrys on
the COPPER PLATE PRINTING,
as usual, in the neatest manner.
the favour & Encouragement of the
Public, shall be gratefully acknowledged.
& they may be assured that he will supply them with
the above Articles, on much lower terms than they can be
Imported; of equal Quality, he also sells Crown Glass,
of any size or Quantity, on the lowest terms.

33

Trade card of Robert Kennedy
James Smither, Philadelphia, ca. 1769
Engraving on paper, 10 x 7¼ in.
Winterthur Museum

34

Certificate of membership
New York Mechanick Society
Abraham Godwin, New York, 1786
Engraving on paper, 8½ x 11⅛ in.
Winterthur Museum

shop moved by the time the engraving was ordered. This example was originally mounted on the back of a print after Van Dyck's *Continence of Scipio*, engraved in London in 1766 and framed in Philadelphia by Robert Kennedy.[65]

Toward the end of the eighteenth century, more and more fraternal organizations were established by the important trades. The purposes were social (to instill a sense of common identity) and benevolent (to help the widows and impoverished families of the brethren). Large and handsomely engraved certificates of membership—what might be called "corporate trade cards"—reinforced the importance of belonging. Usually divided into a series of compartments and in a large format suitable for framing, they are among the grander American manifestations of the rococo style and among the last.

One of the earliest of the organizations was the New York Marine Society, established in 1766. Its certificate, printed in London, has a series of vignettes in the spaces surrounding the central cartouche[66] and must be the prototype for the first of its kind in America, that of the New York Mechanick Society (**No. 34**). Founded in 1785 by representatives of thirty-one different trades, the organization

was incorporated in 1792 as the General Society of Mechanics and Tradesmen. At a meeting on 2 August 1786, "A committee was appointed to wait on Mr. Godwin, and to engage him to engrave a plate for a certificate of membership, the design and price having been previously agreed upon."[67] Abraham Godwin (1763–1835), born in Paterson, New Jersey, apprenticed with Andrew Billings in Poughkeepsie, New York. His bill came to a total of £23-14-8. At the top, above a raised arm contained within a circle, is the motto "By Hammer & Hand, all Arts do stand." Around the central cartouche, with its inscription, are vignettes depicting workshops and allegorical landscapes (at the upper left, for example, America, in the guise of an Indian princess, welcomes representations of Liberty and Industry to her shores). This certificate, the society's seal affixed to it at the bottom, was made out to Seabury Champlin, the organization's 196th member, by Jonathan Post, chairman, on 3 June 1791.

The certificate of the Boston Marine Society (**No. 35**), engraved in 1789 by Joseph Callender, was clearly modeled after Godwin's design.[68] This copy was presented on 1 November 1792 to Peter Chardon Brooks, later a wealthy

Boston banker and politician. Callender (1751–1821) was a native Bostonian; other than this piece, most of the ephemera he produced were neoclassical in style. A separate Marine Society was established in Portland, Maine, in 1796.[69] In 1807, it got its own engraved certificate, fashioned closely after Callender's. So did the rococo-style design carry on into the nineteenth century.

What might almost be called a native school of engraving, which emphasized rococo ornamentation, emerged in central Connecticut during the 1760s. One of its first exponents was Abel Buell (1742–1832), born in Killingworth, who, before moving to New Haven in 1770, trained under his brother-in-law, the goldsmith Ebenezer Chittenden of Madison.[70] Buell engraved a diploma surrounded by a modest rococo mantle for Yale College about 1774. Probably about the same time, in association with James Rivington, a New York printer, he produced this splendid certificate (**No. 36**; see also ill. opp. p. 37) with its recondite title, "The Sequel of Arts and Sciences."[71] The sheet is bordered with rococo cartouches containing elaborately engraved vignettes of various endeavors: limning and engraving, "mechanicks," glass grinding, botany, husbandry, hat making, and printing, alternating with calligraphic titles. While skillfully executed, the designs are all taken from illustrations in English publications.[72] In this copy, its vignettes tinted in watercolor, the large central space is filled with "select sentences" penned by Susanna Darling, aged eight, of New Haven. Only two other copies are known, both dated 1793 and the work of Matthew Talcott 2nd of Norwich.[73]

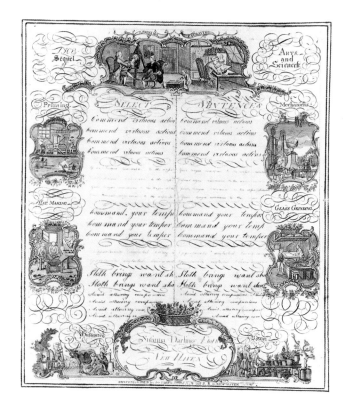

Maps

The largest and most impressive of eighteenth-century American engravings are city views, plans, and maps, on which the rococo plays only a subsidiary role, if any at all. Because they would compete with the scene depicted, large ornamental title cartouches seldom occur on views. On maps, however, they provide a focal point and much-needed visual interest; when there is enough space, rococo cartouches, similar in size and arrangement to the ornament of trade cards, often enclose titles, dedications, even subscription lists.

Since maps were essential tools in both commerce and war, the decade of the 1750s, which ushered in the French and Indian War, was one of great cartographic activity in America. Plans of interior lands, where there were rival claims between colonies as well as with the French, were urgently needed, as were reliable charts of the coast, for even the major shipping lanes were largely unplotted.

While maps and plans had to be prepared in America, their actual engraving and printing were more often than not done in England. "Engraved from the Original Drawing sent over from Philadelphia, in the possession of Carington Bowles" is how one London publisher inscribed his view of that city.[74] When a major topographical survey was engraved and printed on this side of the Atlantic, however, it was sure to be pirated and copied numerous times in London and on the Continent.

Though each of the four maps Thomas Johnston engraved in Boston in the 1750s has a modestly decorative rococo title cartouche, only in Philadelphia, over the next decade, were surveys lavished with elegant rococo devices. Three of the most important of these were executed by Turner (see No. 38); other elaborate examples (see Nos. 40, 41) were published by the tradesman Matthew Clarkson. In the 1760s, when resentment was mounting against the mother country's domination, the English-style cartouche began to show colonial modifications. Revere, in a view of

British troops landing at Boston in 1768, reduced the ornament of the title's cartouche to a palm tree, an image of an Indian, and one or two raffles.[75] In 1784, a similarly drastic transformation of rococo mantling, visible on Buell's engraving of the first map of the newly formed United States (No. 42), implies conscious rejection of a decorative style then seen as denoting fealty to England.

In the Germanic communities of Pennsylvania, rococo ornament was seldom employed, and then usually only on special commission. The drawings of the surveyor and builder Andreas Hoeger are an exception. Hoeger was born in Nuremberg in 1714, joined the Moravian Church (the United Brethren, or Unitas Fratrum) in Herrnhut in 1742, and came with a group of single brethren to Pennsylvania in 1754. Until he left there ten years later, Hoeger was busy with the physical needs of the expanding evangelical sect, especially at its three Pennsylvania settlements, Bethlehem, Nazareth, and Lititz.[76] Several highly finished plans and architectural drawings with ornamental title cartouches have been attributed to him.[77] The "Bethlehem Tract with all the adjacent Land. 1755" (**No. 37**) is the largest and, though its paper has darkened with time, the most decorative.[78] The layout of the drawing as well as the care with which it was rendered suggests that it was intended to be engraved.

Bethlehem, forty-five miles north of Philadelphia, on the banks of the Lehigh River (on the map inscribed "Lehey or the West Branch of Delaware"), was founded in 1740. Hoeger's plan contains three different representations: an overall plan of the Bethlehem tract (top middle), a plan of designated lands (bottom), and a bird's-eye view of the town center with each building depicted in perspective (top right). This last vignette is set apart by a wonderfully rococo frame whose top and bottom parts look to have been inspired by English pattern books. In a rococo variation on the cartographic convention of using trompe l'oeil scrolls to frame titles and other texts (see No. 38), Hoeger has represented the sides of his frame as having dissolved, leaving the unprotected edges of the paper to appear to curl up.

Delaware Bay, the water route to Philadelphia, is full of treacherous shoals and navigational hazards. Until the publication of Fisher's survey in 1756, there was no comprehensive, accurate chart of those busy waters. The chart, almost four feet wide (**No. 38**), was intended for use as a navigational aid. Joshua Fisher (1707–1783) began the survey while a hatter and fur trader in his native Delaware. In 1746, he moved to Philadelphia, where he developed a flourishing mercantile business. Ten years later, encouraged by Thomas Penn, son of the first proprietor, and his agent, Richard

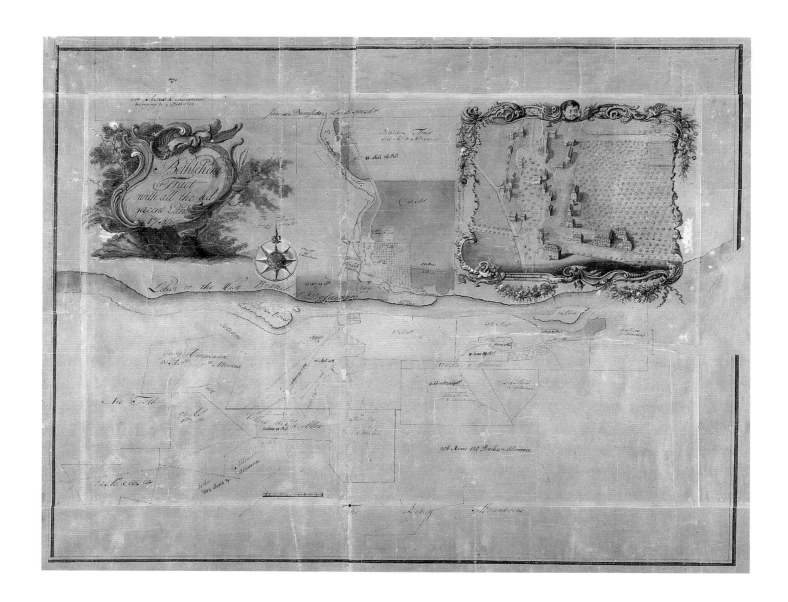

37

Plan of Bethlehem Tract
Attributed to Andreas Hoeger
Bethlehem, Pennsylvania, 1755
Ink and wash on paper, 24½ x 31¾ in.
Moravian Historical Society

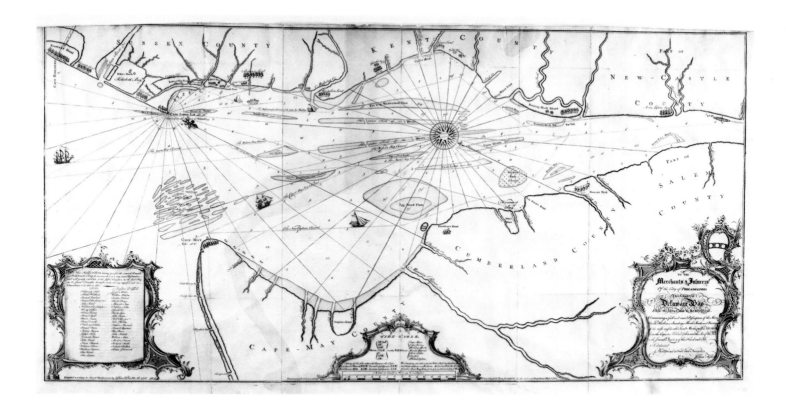

Peters, Fisher finally published his chart.[79] It was executed by James Turner, the most accomplished American engraver of the time, who may reasonably be credited with the actual design of the three splendid cartouches across the bottom of the chart. That at the right, under the Penn family arms, contains the title, the author's name, and the dedication "To the Merchants and Insurers of the City of Philadelphia"; that to the left, a list of subscribers (pilots and shipmasters) to the publication; that at the center, a tide table. The plan is dated 28 February 1756, an inauspicious timing, as it happened, for on 4 March, Provincial Governor Robert Hunter Morris ordered its publication postponed. As he wrote to Fisher, "We are in daily expectation of a French War . . . if your map of the Bay should be published, some Copys of it may fall into ye Enemys Hands."[80] Fisher had already delivered a few of the charts, but the stricture must have been generally effective: only this copy and one other are known.

38

Chart of Delaware Bay
James Turner, after Joshua Fisher
Philadelphia, 1756
Engraving on paper, 23⅝ x 45⅛ in.
The John Carter Brown Library, Brown University

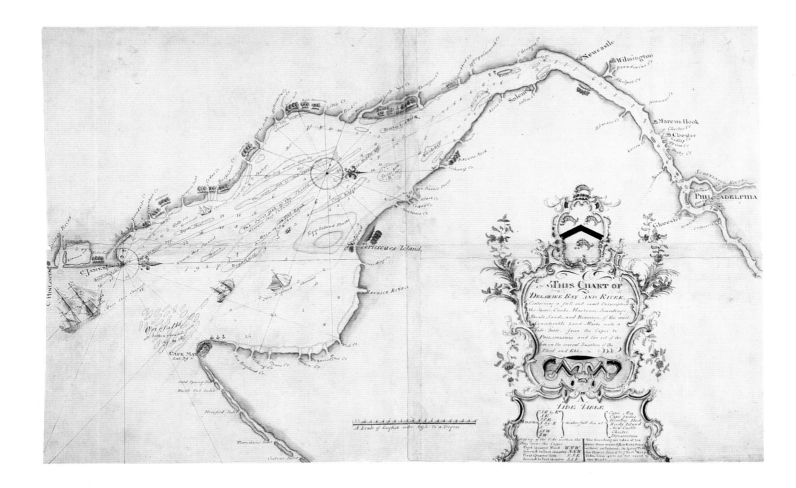

Fisher's monumental chart of 1756 was not reissued until the Revolution and then only in a reduced format and showing a larger area, all the way up the river to Philadelphia. While undated, it probably was engraved in 1775, in anticipation of armed conflict and in time to serve as the model for a spate of pirated London editions, all dated 1776 and all acknowledging that they were taken from the chart published by Fisher in Philadelphia. In this war, unlike that with the French, both sides were to have charts! A watercolor version of the second edition (**No. 39**) differs little from the engraving except that the three cartouches have been consolidated into one, and the dedication, the author's name, and the list of subscribers are omitted. In place of the Penn arms are a chevron and three fishes, perhaps a pun on the author's name, which has led to the speculation that this may have been Fisher's own copy.[81] The expertly drawn cartouche, in grisaille except for green spiky leaves and red flowers, is a tamer, more stately version of the rococo than that Turner had used two decades before.

39

Chart of Delaware Bay and River
Probably by Joshua Fisher
Philadelphia, ca. 1775
Ink and watercolor on paper, 17⅛ x 27¼ in.
The Historical Society of Pennsylvania

Nicholas Scull (1687–1761) was surveyor general of the Province of Pennsylvania from 1748 almost until his death. In that position, he was occupied in making the most important maps of Philadelphia: in 1752, one of the city and "Parts Adjacent"; in 1754, an "East Prospect"; in 1759, one of the whole province, engraved by Turner and having a rococo cartouche. Scull died in 1761, before completing a detailed map of Philadelphia based on his surveys of the city's streets and lots, but his daughter and executor, Mary Biddle, saw it to completion the following year. Dedicated to the elected officials and freemen of Philadelphia, "This Plan of the improved part of the City surveyed and laid down by the late Nicholas Scull Esqr." (**No. 40**) was published on 1 November 1762 and sold by "the Editors," Mary Biddle and Matthew Clarkson. Clarkson was first heard of in an advertisement of 1761, which proclaimed: "Copper-Plate Printing/By a workman from London,/Is performed, in all its Branches, for Matthew Clarkson."[82] While Clarkson, a tradesman, never divulged the name of the engraver, the skillful rendering of the title cartouche has the quality of London work. (With Turner dead, Dawkins is a likely candidate.) The map is the first that accurately recorded the placement of individual buildings in Philadelphia.

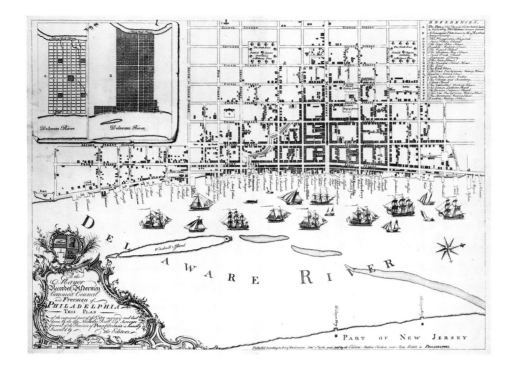

40

Plan of Philadelphia
Possibly by Henry Dawkins,
after Nicholas Scull, Philadelphia, 1762
Engraving on paper, 20⅛ x 26¾ in.
The New York Public Library

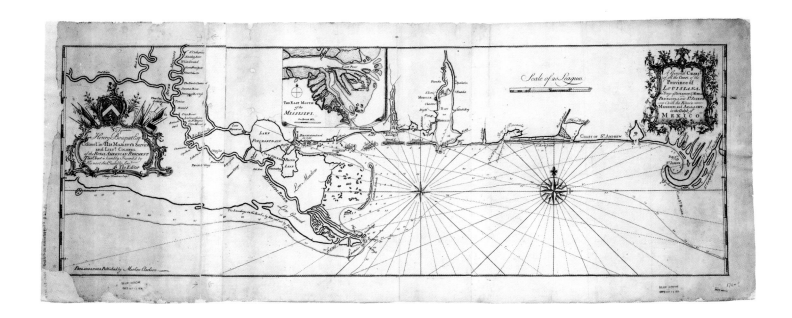

Clarkson was also editor and publisher of a "General Chart of all the Coast of the Province of Louisiana" (**No. 41**) — including what is now west Florida, Alabama, and Mississippi—for which he employed Henry Dawkins as engraver. A rococo cartouche is squeezed into the available space at either end of the long, narrow print. That at the right encloses the title; that at the left, executed in a more spirited style and with military standards and drums projecting from behind, contains a dedication to Henry Bouquet, "Colonel in His Majesty's Service and Lieut. Colonel of the Royal American Regiment." The Swiss-born Bouquet (1719-1765) received the latter rank in 1754, at the outbreak of the French and Indian War. In 1756, he sailed for America, where he distinguished himself militarily; in 1758, he was promoted to full colonel. In 1765, then a brigadier general, Bouquet was given command of the entire southern district of British North America, including the area of this chart, which was probably executed not long before Bouquet's last promotion. Stricken in a fever epidemic, he died at Pensacola that same year.

After the restoration of peace, in 1783, the first map of the new United States (**No. 42**) was the work not of a skilled London-trained engraver but of a native opportunist—Abel Buell, of New Haven. As he advertised in the *Connecticut Journal* of 31 March 1784: "Buel's Map Of the United States

41

Chart of the coast of Louisiana
Henry Dawkins, Philadelphia, 1760-65
Engraving on paper, 14½ x 40½ in.
The New York Public Library

of America, Laid down from the latest observations and best authorities, agreeable to the peace of 1783, is now published, and ready for subscribers. [This] Map is...the first ever compiled, engraved, and finished by one man, and an American."[83] Printed on four sheets and measuring not much under four feet square, it was intended as a wall map. While the cartographic features are all taken from other surveys, the title cartouche in the lower right corner is Buell's own creative effort. He has abandoned his precise engraving style and slavish imitation of English originals (see No. 36) in favor of an informal etched technique and American symbols: the American flag; a fringed oval containing the arms (three grapevines) of Connecticut; and the seated figure of Liberty holding a staff crowned with a liberty cap. The rococo title cartouche—a symbol of England—was done away with, except for two large raffles remaining at the bottom.

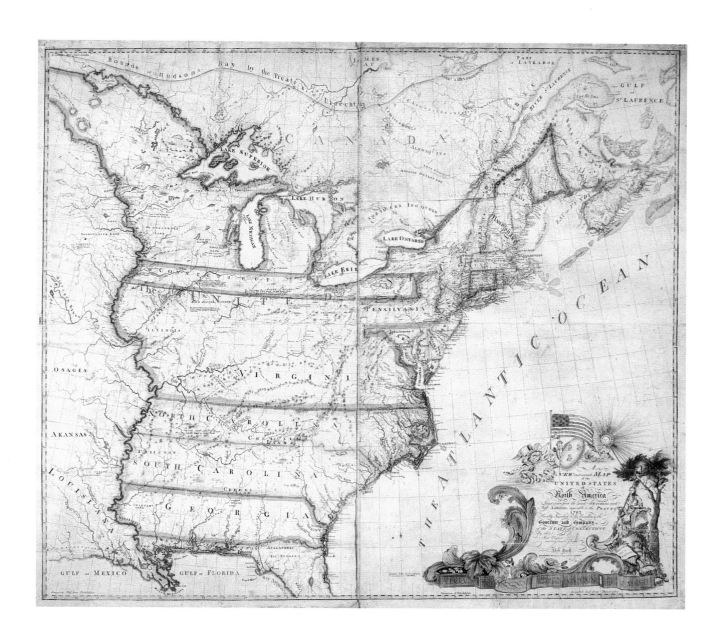

42

Map of the United States of America
Abel Buell, New Haven, 1784
Engraving on paper, 42¾ x 48 in.
The New Jersey Historical Society

Clock Dials

Clock dials made of sheet brass engraved with rococo ornament, while not intended for printing, nevertheless merit discussion as an adjunct to the more common types of engraving. In traditional eighteenth-century tall clocks, the dial, or face, fronted the clock movement, which was mounted in the bonnet of the wooden case. Made of brass, with applied chapter ring (a large circular band marked with the hours and minutes), seconds ring, and nameplate, all silvered to enhance legibility, it usually measured twelve inches to a side. It had spandrels filled with cast ornaments and, often, an arched top containing a moon phase. The dial, calibrated for telling time, had to proclaim the name of the clockmaker and the town where he worked. That type of dial was superseded in the mid-1780s by those made of sheet iron painted white and having black numerals and colored decoration. Many of the brass dials, and most of the painted, were imported, but a native alternative emerged about 1770: a dial consisting of a single flat brass sheet on which representations of applied chapter ring, nameplate, and other elements were engraved. When silvered, it was not unlike a painted dial in appearance—a domestic alternative to the "enamelled dial-plates" Philadelphia clockmaker John Wood had imported as early as 1773.[84]

The engraved face is not often found on fine urban clocks, though there are brilliant exceptions (see No. 43). The greatest flowering of this belated American rococo expression took place in Connecticut (see Nos. 44, 45), far from the major style centers, and, though with less originality, in Maryland and Virginia.[85]

The American engraved clock dial most closely approximating the style of the London rococo (**No. 43**)[86] is signed "Burrows Dowdney/Philadelphia," a maker about whom nothing is known except that during the years 1768–71 he advertised in the *Pennsylvania Chronicle* as a watch- and clockmaker in Front Street.[87] On the dial of his clock, which

43

Dial of clock by Burrows Dowdney
Philadelphia, ca. 1770
Brass, silvered, 16⅜ x 12 in.
The Dietrich American Foundation

has never been resilvered (in places, the brass shows through), the engraving, having the refined precision of the best English copper-plate work, is certainly the work of some master of the technique, perhaps Dawkins. It combines pictorial representation and rococo ornament: in the corners, raffles fill the spandrels; in the arched top, hissing serpents with twisting tails flank the moon phase; in the center, Father Time, holding his scythe in his left hand and resting his right hand on an hourglass, is seated on an asymmetrical rococo frame; at the left are another hourglass and scythe; an eagle tries to grasp the clock-hands' shank; raffles appear to grow organically out of the winding holes and from the bottom corners of the nameplate. The combination of ornament and the images of eagles, serpents, and Father Time suggests a familiarity with Thomas Johnson's *One Hundred and Fifty New Designs*.[88] In 1774, John Norman advertised that he supplied "Clock and Watch Graving,"[89] but the style he revealed in his illustrations (see No. 4) for the Philadelphia edition of Swan's *British Architect* (1775) is somewhat looser than that of Dowdney's clock dial.

Engraved clock dials ultimately achieved greater popularity in New England than in Pennsylvania. In 1773, the English clockmaker Thomas Harland settled in Norwich, Connecticut, and advertised "Clock faces engraved and finished for the trade."[90] Harland had a number of apprentices. The most illustrious of them was Daniel Burnap (1759–1838), who, after completing his indenture, continued to work for Harland as a journeyman until 1779. It was from Harland that Burnap learned to engrave clock faces and to make "chime" clocks—that is, clocks that played musical tunes.[91] In 1780, he established his own shop in East Windsor, a few miles north of Hartford, where he carried on what became the largest such business in the Connecticut Valley. Of the dozen known chime clocks that were his specialty, six are recorded in his surviving account books, five of them between the years 1790 and 1795. A dial (**No. 44**) with rococo raffles in the spandrels and intertwined vines looping around the inscriptions in the arched top and the center illustrates a late flowering of rococo ornament in rural America.[92] A hand in the arch can be pointed to select any of the six tunes that the movement is programmed to play four times a day. The sounds produced by these clocks, including such favorites as "Air by Handle," can be said to be the only authentic music that can be summoned from the eighteenth century.

44

Dial of musical clock
Daniel Burnap, maker and engraver
East Windsor, Connecticut, 1790–94
Brass, silvered, 16⅝ x 12 in.
Historic Deerfield, Inc.

Another outstanding engraved dial from Connecticut (**No. 45**) is that for a clock made by Reuben Ingraham of Plainfield, on the eastern border of the state, a few miles north of Norwich. In perhaps the only instance of an engraver's signing an American clock dial, John Avery's name appears in tiny letters within the seconds ring. Avery (1732–1794) was a silversmith and clockmaker in Preston, near Norwich. His arrangement of the names of the maker and the town in the arched top, the semicircular opening for the date ring, even the Four Seasons as motifs to fill the four spandrels, owe a debt to the design of Harland's dials.[93] The cartouche in the arched top, the spandrel motifs, and the various layered compartments into which the central area is broken up are all surrounded with borders of small-scale scrolled leafage, an engaging, if somewhat fussy, interpretation of the rococo at the end of the century.

LGB, MHH

45

Dial of clock by Reuben Ingraham
Engraved by John Avery
Plainfield, Connecticut, 1785–94
Brass, silvered, 16 x 12 in.
Collection of Mr. and Mrs. Frank A. Mauri

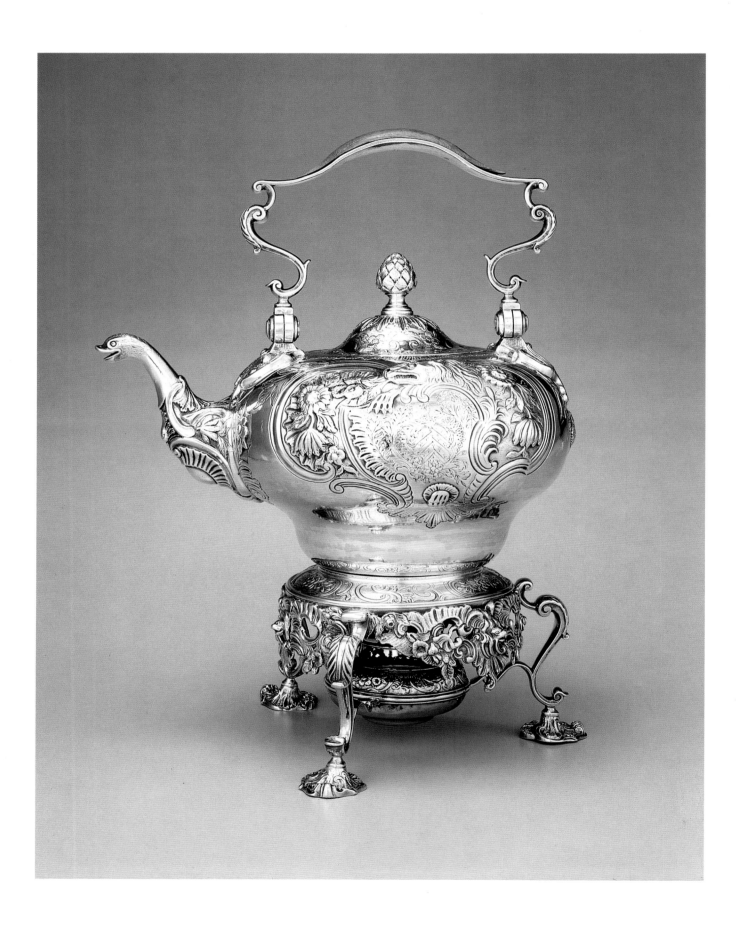

SILVER

American silver began to reflect the rococo style in the late 1740s, influenced by printed ephemera and silver imported from the mother country. Domestic silversmiths who had trained in the colonies could integrate aspects of the new taste into their repertoire, but most lacked the specialized schooling required to create the highly ornate surfaces of full-fledged rococo silver. Much of that decoration was contributed by immigrant journeymen, outworkers, or indentured servants,[1] who had benefited from training abroad (usually in London) and were already familiar with the new style.

Silver was an urban luxury, produced in America in the eighteenth century primarily in Boston, New York, Philadelphia, and Charleston. The finest domestic rococo silver traces to a few workshops in those cities, whose earliest examples postdate the introduction of the style in London by at least ten years, a phenomenon attributable to social and economic conditions. In England, rococo taste entered through aristocratic circles and gradually came within the reach of the upper-middle class; in America, it became available to prosperous merchants as it had to their London counterparts. The fashionable English imports appearing in the homes of colonial merchant princes naturally influenced local taste. Export and import records, period advertisements, and surviving examples of British silver with provenances in eighteenth-century America leave no doubt that imported silver was highly prized by wealthy colonials, who could have their orders to London filled and returned within ten months to a year.

A graphic demonstration of the influence of foreign silver is provided by an unusual London rococo coffee pot

owned in Salem in 1760 (**No. 46**). Uplifted on three C-scroll-and-shell feet, it is a departure from the standard English version elevated on a pedestal foot. The tripod design was a French innovation adopted only selectively by London silversmiths. The pot, crafted in London in the shop of Arthur Annesley and marked with the date letter for 1759–60, was given to Mary Vial (1737–1802) of Boston by her uncle Jonathan Simpson (1711/12–1795), probably in honor of her marriage in 1759 to Edward A. Holyoke (1728–1829), a Salem doctor. It can be no coincidence that the only two tripod coffee pots known in American rococo silver were both made for Salem patrons who had undoubtedly admired Mary Holyoke's fashionable London gift.[2] The two American versions spawned by the Annesley pot were created for separate members of the prominent Derby family of Salem (see p. 136). An unmarked example was made for Elizabeth Crowninshield when she married Elias Hasket Derby, in 1761; eleven years later, Paul Revere supplied Elias's father, Richard, with the most noteworthy American rendition of the design (**No. 47**).[3]

Not everyone in the colonies could afford to buy expensive imported silver,[4] and some of those who could undoubtedly preferred not to wait almost a year for the delivery of their goods. Those considerations, together with the nonimportation agreements that preceded the Revolution, encouraged the development of domestically produced rococo silver. American patrons—an elite and affluent class—were not remotely interested in encouraging local silversmiths to develop a uniquely American interpretation but continued to commission silver reflecting the latest London fashions.

Silver has always been associated with wealth. In the eighteenth century, objects fashioned of it were collectively known as plate and served as an owner's savings account, an asset that could be liquidated almost immediately for the value of the metal. Because there were several less expensive

---

Teakettle on stand, Joseph Richardson (No. 88)

mediums available, the use of silver was not a case of necessity but of choice. Silver had no utilitarian relation to any of the forms into which it was made; the merit of the forms rested in their intrinsic worth and the social status they proclaimed on an owner's table. Their value as currency did not include the cost of the work in fashioning them, therefore the amount of decoration applied to them was purely a matter of taste and affordability. Though the rococo did influence shapes in silver, the style was primarily an ornamental consideration that required costly additional labor for elaborate engraving, relief chasing, piercing, or castings.

The decoration on the majority of American rococo silver is limited to engraving and casting on forms that may not themselves exhibit rococo influence. Drinking and serving forms changed little throughout the period of the style's domination, but many tea and coffee vessels adopted the double-bellied shape that is a rococo signature. Engraved or cast decoration, the least laborious means of ornamentation, entailed minimal extra cost to patrons, most of whom were pragmatic merchants. Even if financial reverses did not demand the conversion of their plate to cash, changing styles might dictate its refashioning. Patrons ordering new silver often submitted their old, which was credited according to its weight, melted down, and used in the fabrication of new designs.

Engraving is the process of cutting fine lines into an object, thereby removing minute quantities of metal. The kind of rococo engraving found most frequently in American silver is an asymmetrical cartouche that often encloses the owner's arms or initials.[5] Engraving also served as a means of identification. If an object was stolen, its decoration of initials or family arms assisted immeasurably in its recovery, as is attested by eighteenth-century newspaper advertisements containing notifications of missing silver and descriptions of its engraving. This explains why silver was a safer means of storing surplus cash than the coinage itself. A thief wishing to profit from silver he had stolen had to sell it to a silversmith, who was likely to recognize it.

Casting—the pouring of molten silver into molds of sand into which a pattern had been impressed—was the usual process used to create spouts, handles, and finials. For most rococo designs, such as spouts decorated with shells and acanthus, carved wooden patterns were probably supplied by a local artisan[6] and could be used repeatedly, creating similar appendages for numerous vessels. Silversmiths were expected to have a supply of patterns from which their patrons could choose without additional cost.[7] Only when the patterns were particularly ornate (and the casting commensurately heavy) did a patron incur extra expense for the weight of the metal.

46

Coffee pot, 1759–60
Arthur Annesley, London
Silver, H.: 11½ in.
Essex Institute

Chasing and piercing, though more appropriate to rococo excesses, were also more extravagant ornamentations. On elaborate examples, the cost of such embellishment could approach the cost of the metal, an inconceivable expense except for the very rich. Chasing is the process of manipulating the metal into bolder, more sculptural designs by means of hammers and blunt tools, with no cutting devices employed. In modern parlance, the technique of decorating the metal from the exterior is still known as chasing, or flat chasing, but when the metal is also worked from within, resulting in a design both convex and concave, it is known as repoussé. Because of its sculptural relief quality, repoussé decoration characterized fully developed rococo silver in both Britain and America. In the period, however, it was known as chasing; the artisan who accomplished it, a chaser. The specialty was described in *The London Tradesman* (1747) as practiced by one of the "Dependants [of the] Goldsmith, or, as some call him, Silversmith," along with jewelers, refiners, burnishers, and gilders, among others.[8] Chased decoration appears on plate from the three major centers of American silver production—Boston, New York, and Philadelphia—as well as on work from Charleston, Baltimore, Annapolis, Rhode Island, Albany, and Lancaster. Piercing is just as exuberant as chasing but much rarer in American silver. The technique consists of laying out a pattern on the silver, then drilling holes in the areas to be removed, expanding the holes by means of a small fret saw, and, finally, filing the rough edges smooth.

The rococo, more than any preceding style, required specialized skills that exceeded the abilities of the average American silversmith. Recent research in London silver has dispelled the myth that the so-called maker's mark on a silver object could be interpreted as the artist's signature and has revealed the complex network of retailers, retailer-silversmiths, specialist-silversmiths, and silver artisans who were responsible for the production of any given shop.[9] *The London Tradesman*, "being a compendious view of all the trades" practiced in London, described the complement of a silversmith's shop:

The Goldsmith employs several distinct Workmen, almost as many as there are different Articles in his Shop; for in this great City there are Hands that excel in every Branch, and are constantly employed but in that one of which they are Masters. This gives us an Advantage over many Foreign Nations in this Article, as they are obliged to employ the same Hands in every Branch of the Trade, and it is impossible to expect that a Man employed in such an infinite Variety can finish his Work to any Perfection, at least, not so much as he who is constantly employed in one Thing.[10]

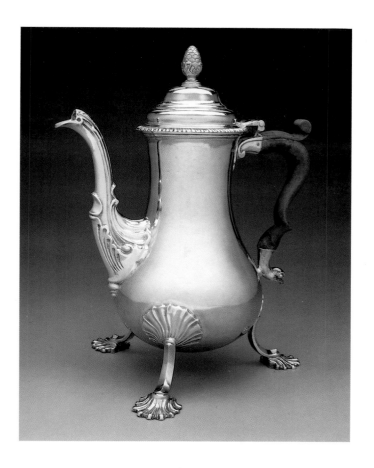

47

Coffee pot, 1772
Paul Revere, Boston
Silver, H.: 12 in.
Private collection

On a smaller, more provincial scale, American silversmiths operated in the same fashion, obtaining objects and services from one another. Paul Revere's ledgers reveal a network of such relationships with thirteen other silversmiths prior to the Revolution.[11] Fine armorial engraving was a talent beyond the rudimentary training of the average silversmith, and Revere, an accomplished engraver, supplied that service to a number of his colleagues.[12]

Chasing was a highly demanding skill, more challenging than engraving and one that American silversmiths were not likely to have practiced in the preceding Queen Anne period. In view of the paucity of hollowware commissions in most silversmiths' production (repairs and small work made up most of their trade) and the still smaller percentage of commissions calling for such expensive ornament, it is highly unlikely that domestic craftsmen could have developed chasing ability of a quality commensurate with the most accomplished essays in the American rococo.

Not only did American silversmiths contract among themselves for specialized services, they also employed fully trained silversmiths, some of whom were undoubtedly practiced in the techniques. One of the least understood areas of American silver is the identity and contribution of those men, most of whom were journeymen—silversmiths working for a master smith and under his mark. The term "master silversmith," designating the owner of a silver workshop, has led to the common misconception that he was always the most skilled and experienced craftsman. A master took on apprentices when they were thirteen or fourteen. They were then bound to him for a period of about seven years until, having served their term, they became wage-earning journeymen. The next transition, from journeyman to master, had less to do with exceptional ability than with access to capital and patronage and was by no means a foregone conclusion. The easiest way to become a master was to be born a master's son or to marry a master's daughter and so inherit tools, shop, and clientele. The journeyman wishing to embark on his own and lacking family connections had to accumulate substantial capital, not only to acquire the fundamentals of his trade but also to extend credit to his patrons. In addition, he had to earn the trust and respect of potential clients.

In the eighteenth century, American silversmiths functioned as brokers, transforming their clients' assets into a different kind of commodity. In England, patrons were protected by strict governmental regulations requiring that virtually every piece retailed be tested at an assay office. Those of satisfactory alloy were hallmarked and could then be offered for sale. Because no such official procedure developed in the North American colonies, a dishonest craftsman could cheat his clients by cheapening the alloy, using less silver than the standard expected.[13] Americans therefore tended to patronize silversmiths of proven reputation, a cautionary practice that further hindered journeymen struggling to establish their own shops, since they could not rely on a government hallmark to guarantee the integrity of their materials.

In the absence of governmental regulation, a system of trust developed between patrons and their suppliers that served to protect domestic silversmiths from their most threatening competition—foreign craftsmen who were thoroughly acquainted with current European fashion and often more technically proficient than the Americans. Though many British and European silversmiths migrated to the colonies, most of them worked for American masters as journeymen, outworkers, or indentured servants. Only a few succeeded in opening their own retail shops, thus permitting them to mark their wares and identify their contributions for posterity.

Without marks or documentation for most of those anonymous men, they constitute a large, overlooked group whose expertise undoubtedly made possible some of the finest American silver of the period. Fortunately, contemporary newspaper advertisements document the existence of some of them. Though certainly not comprehensive, period references do provide sufficient evidence to suggest that the adoption and development of the rococo style in the colonies were directly linked to immigrant artisans who had firsthand knowledge of the style as well as the specialized ability needed to create its attributes. Their contributions have been routinely assigned to shop masters.

In the study of American silver, the initial and name marks stamped on an object have traditionally been regarded as the means of identifying the maker. A given silversmith's ability was evaluated on the basis of objects stamped with his mark. Some American silversmiths may deserve the reputation they have garnered as a result of that misinterpretation, but others were almost certainly retailer-silversmiths who supervised thriving businesses. Until further research can untangle the web of the American silver trade or unless specific evidence suggests otherwise, the so-called maker's mark on high-style rococo silver should be regarded as a shop mark only—an indication of where the piece may have been assembled and where it was sold, but no proof at all of the authorship of the ornament.

Of the three silversmithing centers (Boston, New York, and Philadelphia), Boston was the most conservative in rococo interpretation. Although the city had as much access to the style as did New York and Philadelphia, a flagging economy and a shortage of foreign-trained specialists may explain her moderate response. English rococo silver can be documented in New England by the late 1740s,[14] but Bostonians seem to have ordered far fewer domestic interpretations of the new chased style. English records reveal that the total weight of silver articles shipped to New England exceeded that exported to Pennsylvania between 1746 and 1758, years of the adoption of the rococo in the colonies.[15] One of the first trades to be affected by Boston's decline in prosperity and population (maintaining at only fifteen thousand throughout the rococo period) was silversmithing. Though in its prime during the first decade of the 1700s, it had lost much of its promise by the 1730s and, consequently, attracted far fewer apprentices and immigrant craftsmen.[16]

Foreign silver workers bringing new styles into America were more likely to settle in New York or Philadelphia, where the chances of employment were greater. In contrast with New York, Philadelphia, and Charleston advertisements, those in New England newspapers are conspicuously lacking in mention of craftsmen lately from London or trained in Europe.[17] The majority of the city's silversmithing shops were run by American-born men, as might be expected. The lagging economy notwithstanding, Boston still had a number of affluent citizens, largely merchants. Some of them patronized the rococo, and chief among the local silversmiths who supplied them with objects in the fully developed mode were Benjamin Burt, Nathaniel Hurd, Samuel Edwards, Thomas Edwards, and Paul Revere. Stylistically, the rococo work from Revere's shop surpasses that of the others.

Paul Revere (1735–1818) was trained by his father, Apollos Rivoire (1702–1754), a French Huguenot brought to Boston at the age of fourteen and apprenticed to John Coney (1655/56–1722). Revere, though still a minor in 1754, when he assumed responsibility for his father's shop after Rivoire's death, had become a master goldsmith in Boston by 1757. Revere's career as a silversmith spans three style periods — Queen Anne, rococo, and neoclassical — but his most important works are from the last two. The fortuitous survival of his Day Books from 1761 to 1797 facilitates a more accurate assessment of the expense and incidence of rococo work. An accomplished engraver as well (see pp. 39, 40, 51 for more information on Revere and on that aspect of his work), Revere added such ornament to silver of his own and others' making.[18]

New York's commercial ties to England, so vital to her growth, produced a cosmopolitan city of wealthy merchants anxious and well able to afford to follow London fashions. English rococo silver can be documented in New York by

FIGURE 26. *Coffee pot*, 1762–63. Benjamin Brewood II, London. Silver, H.: 12 in. (30.5 cm.). The Metropolitan Museum of Art, Gift of James DeLancey Verplanck and John Bayard Rogers Verplanck, 1942 (42.88)

1757, when an advertisement for stolen silver describes a "chaced Salver," as well as a "chaced Coffee-Pot," among several other pieces, all of which were "Sterling Plate, have a Lion Stampt on the Bottom."[19] Judith Crommelin (1739–1803) and Samuel (1737–1820) Verplanck, who were married in 1761, owned some handsome rococo plate from London, including a lavishly chased teakettle on stand en suite with a coffee pot (FIG. 26), and a pair of tea caddies, all date-marked 1762–63.[20] The quantity of British silver exported to New York between 1747 and 1763 was generally high, averaging 1,068 ounces a year between 1747 and 1758 and reaching an average of 3,487 ounces a year between 1759 and 1762.[21] New York silversmiths seem to have been producing rococo silver by the late 1750s: the Myers silver made for Samuel and Susannah Cornell (see No. 82; FIG. 30, p. 123) most likely dates from their marriage in 1756; in 1758, one Joseph Pinto advertised chased silver milk pots.[22]

The city's newspapers document the existence of foreign silversmiths throughout the period. The earliest reference to one of them, in 1754, probably identifies the man responsible for bringing the style to New York. Daniel Christian Fueter (1720–1785) was born and trained in Switzerland and worked in Bern before fleeing to London as a political refugee. After at least two years in the English capital, he emigrated in 1754 to New York, remaining there until 1769, when he returned to Europe and, eventually, to Bern.[23] His European background probably accounts for his fluency in rococo interpretation. In 1754, he advertised his arrival in the *Snow Irene* from London, adding that he could make "all sorts of Gold and Silver work, after the newest and neatest Fashion."[24] Because Fueter succeeded in opening his own shop, his mark identifies some highly sophisticated rococo objects (see Nos. 74, 81, 85).[25] In the 1750s, the rococo was fully mature and flourishing in continental Europe, though it was still a relative newcomer to American shores. Fueter, who would have been well versed in the style when he came to the colonies, must have been instrumental in fostering its popularity in New York.

Other foreigners proficient in rococo decoration are documented in New York in the 1760s. In 1763, Otto Parisien advertised himself as from Berlin and proclaimed his prowess in "all Sorts of Plate Work, both plain and chas'd."[26] Fueter informed the public in 1769 that "Mr. John Anthony Beau, Chaiser, from Geneva, works with him."[27] Beau's presence in New York may well have predated Fueter's announcement. If so, Beau may have been working for other silversmiths, possibly for that Joseph Pinto, who, after advertising the milk pot in 1758, went on to offer in 1761 a tureen, candlesticks, coffee pots and teapots, sugar dishes, waste bowls, sauceboats, all chased, as well as "Chass'd and Plain" stands, mugs, salvers, milk pots, and whistles.[28] Regrettably, none of those works are known today. A connection among Pinto, Beau, and Fueter seems possible. Fueter, in his advertisement of 1769, also announced that he had moved into the house of Mrs. Pinto, which suggests that he had taken over her husband's silversmithing shop. If Beau had been working for Pinto, that may explain how Fueter came to hire him on.

The appeal of foreign-trained specialists is made apparent in an advertisement of 1771, in which Bennett and Dixon, a partnership producing jewelry and small silver and gold work, not only identified themselves as "from London" but also, following a list of their wares, added: "Likewise for the better carrying on the jewellery, [silversmith] and lapidary business, have engaged some of the best workmen in those branches, that could be had in any part of England."[29] Because New York was enjoying a period of prosperity in the 1750s and 1760s, it follows that the city was attracting a large number of foreign silversmiths (including at least one deserter from the British army),[30] who, in their own shops or working for others, substantially contributed to the local rococo style.

New York's finest rococo silver is marked not only by Fueter but also by Ephraim Brasher, Pieter de Riemer, John Heath, Myer Myers, Nicholas Roosevelt, and Richard Van Dyck. Of those, the shop of Myer Myers seems to have retailed the largest percentage of outstanding examples. Born in New York in 1723 to Dutch immigrant parents, Myers was probably educated at a school maintained by the family synagogue, the Congregation Shearith Israel. Though his apprenticeship is undocumented, he is known to have become a freeman of the city in 1746, at the age of twenty-three, and therefore entitled not only to open a shop but also to vote. His first marriage, to Elkalah Cohen (1735–1765), took place early in the 1750s; his second, after Elkalah's death, was to Joyce Mears, in 1767. Nine children survived from the two marriages. Myers prospered in his career and as a community leader, holding offices in the synagogue as well as in the local Masonic lodge. By 1755, he was trading with Jewish merchants in Philadelphia; in 1786, he was chairman of New York's Gold and Silver Smith's Society.[31] His shop enjoyed the patronage of some of New York's finest families, including the Livingstons, the Schuylers, the Cornells, and the Philipses. Except during the British occupation of the city, which he spent in Connecticut and in Philadelphia, Myers remained in New York until his death, in 1795.

An advertisement of 1761, in which Myers informed the public that his English indentured servant, Lewis Mears, "a jeweller by Trade, and can engrave," had run away, proves that Myers was using the skills of immigrant silversmiths.[32] It appears that Myers was supervising a jewelry business in addition to his silver firm, and possibly accepting engraving jobs as well. Some of the finest engraving of the period graces silver from his shop (see Nos. 66, 72, 87). The large amount of pierced work ascribed to him on the basis of his mark may also point to the services of a craftsman in his employ or available to him. Piercing was such a highly accomplished specialty that certain London silversmiths supplied the majority of English pierced wares in the rococo period. An immigrant journeyman from one of their shops may have worked for Myers, which would explain the piercing on some Myers silver and also the appearance of forms not commonly found in the colonies but routinely produced in London's specialized shops: coasters, a basket, a dish ring, and a fish slice.

FIGURE 27. *Teakettle on stand*, 1744–45.
Paul de Lamerie, London. Silver, H. (handle extended):
14¾ in. (37.5 cm.). The Metropolitan Museum of Art,
Gift of George D. Widener and Eleanor W. Dixon
(Mrs. Widener Dixon), 1958 (58.7.17)

a tea service (1744–45) marked by Paul de Lamerie (FIG. 27), probably a wedding gift from London relatives.[34] Among Philadelphia silversmiths importing plate were Richardson, John David, Philip Hulbeart, Richard Humphreys, John Leacock, and Edmund Milne. Statistics of the period reveal that the quantity of English silver exported to Philadelphia averaged 581 ounces a year between 1747 and 1758 and rose to an average of 2,832 ounces a year between 1759 and 1762, reaching a high of 5,221 ounces in 1760.[35] The same phenomenon already noted in New York points to the prosperity of the two cities, a result of the merchants' lucrative contracts to supply goods to the British army, then fighting the French and Indian War. Exports to both New York and Philadelphia declined after 1762 because of postwar recessions and increasing trade tensions.

Philadelphia's domestic production of rococo silver can be dated from the 1750s (see Nos. 62, 65, 75, 88). Notices of immigrant craftsmen appear in city newspaper advertisements throughout the 1760s and 1770s, but only two men are mentioned as chasers, and they do not appear until 1772 and 1774.[36] Though it is as yet impossible to identify specific foreign artisans who may have been responsible for such ornament on Philadelphia rococo silver in the 1750s and 1760s, that does not belie their existence. American master smiths, unless they were trying to recover an indentured servant, rarely published notices of immigrant silversmiths in their shops. The majority of references to foreign craftsmen were by the foreigners themselves, advertising either their services or the services of immigrant artisans working for them.

In addition to those mentioned above, Thomas Shields and Philip Syng, Jr., are among Philadelphia silversmiths traditionally acknowledged for their work in the rococo style; the two who can be regarded as the most prominent retailers of silver in the rococo taste are Richardson and Syng. Joseph Richardson (1711–1784) was a second-generation American and silversmith whose work spanned the Queen Anne and the rococo periods. Born in Philadelphia, he was trained by his father, Francis Richardson (1681–1729), whose tools and business he inherited at the age of eighteen. Richardson became a prominent Quaker silversmith and civic leader, as well as a prosperous landowner. In 1741, he married Hannah Worril, who died five years later, leaving him with a daughter. In 1748, Richardson married again. His second wife, Mary Allen, bore him three more daughters and two sons, Joseph junior and Nathaniel, who learned the trade from their father and assumed responsibility for his business when he retired in 1777. As a philanthropist, Richardson supported the Pennsylvania Hospital throughout his career. He was also a member and shareholder of the

Philadelphia was the foremost city in the colonies by the beginning of the rococo period. Not a few affluent Philadelphians maintained both city and country houses, and most of them made an effort to keep up with the current London tastes. Whereas Revere's production of teapots in Boston averaged one a year between 1761 and 1767, Joseph Richardson's orders to London between 1759 and 1767 averaged out to an annual six, in addition to those produced in his Philadelphia shop.[33]

English rococo silver was being exported to Philadelphia by the late 1740s, when David and Margaret Franks received

Library Company of Philadelphia and a respected leader in his Quaker congregation.[37] His letter book documents his considerable importing business with English silversmiths and merchants between 1758 and 1773, interrupted by periods of economic decline and by the colonial nonimportation agreements, which Richardson supported.[38] The substantial quantity of import orders recorded by Richardson suggests the possibility that he brought in unmarked English silver, to which he added his own stamp. That theory is easily refuted. English silver without hallmarks could not have been exported legally, and the small amount of fees saved by silversmiths evading the assay laws would not have justified the risk they ran.[39] Further, period advertisements in colonial newspapers leave no doubt that London silver identifiable by its hallmarks had great cachet.

Irish-born Philip Syng, Jr. (1703–1789), was also trained by his father, an English silversmith who worked in Bristol, brought his family to Annapolis in 1714, and moved to Philadelphia by the end of the year. When he went back to Annapolis, about 1724, young Syng assumed the Philadelphia business.[40] In 1725, he sailed for London and returned the next year, presumably with patterns and tools. In 1730, he married Elizabeth Warner. Like Richardson, Syng took an active role in the affairs of the city. He was a member of several respected organizations, including the Junto (Benjamin Franklin's intellectual circle) and the American Philosophical Society. He was also a director of the Library Company of Philadelphia and a trustee of the College of Philadelphia. Syng had acquired the services of a London engraver by 1748, the year Lawrence Hubert advertised as such.[41] In 1763, along with Richardson, he was appointed to settle the estate of fellow silversmith Philip Hulbeart. When he retired, in 1772, Syng rented his workshop to twenty-two-year-old Richard Humphreys and recommended his successor to his clients in a newspaper advertisement.[42]

Richardson was born in America and Syng immigrated at the age of eleven; both were trained in the colonies. Silver bearing their marks has some of the most accomplished chasing of any from the American rococo period. That either Richardson or Syng, who were schooled during the Queen Anne era in a style not known for chased decoration, could have acquired the skills to execute their own chasing is unlikely. Before the 1750s, when their finest works were created, their commissions for such expensive pieces would have been infrequent indeed. Richardson's coffee pot (No. 65) and a matching sugar dish for the Peningtons date from around 1754; his teakettle on stand for the Plumsteds (No. 88) was completed before 1755. Syng's coffee pot for the Galloways (No. 62) probably dates from their marriage, in 1753; his salver for the Peningtons (No. 75), from around

1754. That impressive group constitutes some of the earliest datable American rococo silver; that it is also among the most highly developed in style argues for the participation of foreign chasers. Nothing is known of journeyman chasers in either man's shop, but if neither possessed such ability among his employees, it seems certain that he would have contracted for it. Even if ghost chasers for Philadelphia's finest rococo silver cannot yet be identified, the likelihood of their existence is undeniable. Philadelphia's size and prosperity would have attracted immigrant craftsmen and dictated that her silver industry follow closely the London model.

The fourth major colonial city was Charleston, but too little silver survives from there to document it as an eighteenth-century silversmithing center. Wealthy southerners were not merchants with cash but planters with credit in England; as a consequence, they imported a substantial amount of their silver directly from London. Between 1750 and 1769, exports of British silver into the Carolinas exceeded the combined total exported into New England, New York, and Pennsylvania for the same period.[43] Charleston's strong economic ties with London would have lessened the demand for locally produced silver. Nonetheless, London-trained John Paul Grimke advertised in 1760 that he had acquired the services of a journeyman chaser and, a year later, John Winckler proclaimed himself a "Silver-smith and Chaser from London."[44] Moreover, period advertisements reveal several foreign silversmiths working in Charleston and five local silversmith-retailers selling imported silver between 1761 and 1772.[45] The sole surviving example of mature rococo silver from Charleston (No. 64) must represent a larger group of high-style domestic silver that was converted to cash or destroyed in the Civil War.

The rococo style was never the last word in fashion for all American patrons. Even in imported silver, orders for objects in the rococo mode were accompanied by orders for plain, unchased pieces. The rococo was, after all, a stylistic choice, almost always more expensive than the plainer forms of the Queen Anne period. The style flourished during the 1750s and 1760s, one of the most prosperous periods in colonial history, but its progress was interrupted by one of the most turbulent. Recessions in the wake of the French and Indian War, followed by conflicts with England over taxes levied on imported goods, culminating in the Revolution, certainly limited and disrupted the natural course of the rococo style. By the resolution of the War of Independence, in 1783, the neoclassical was the new style of choice for fashionable silver patrons.

Tea and Coffee Forms

The majority of American rococo silver is represented by the forms crafted in the colonies beginning in the late 1740s for a domestic ritual then recently imported from England: the serving of tea and coffee. Those exotic beverages, the first introduced to Europe from the Orient; the second, from the Mideast (with a third, chocolate, imported from the Americas), exercised a social influence that was palpable in London by the last quarter of the seventeenth century. In 1660, Samuel Pepys recorded his first tea-tasting. In 1652, London's first coffeehouse opened, followed in 1670 by the first in Boston.[46] Specialized forms made for the service of each beverage are well documented by 1700. Tea was believed to have medicinal properties, while coffee was extolled in a London advertisement of 1660 as "wholesome, preserving health until extreme old age, good for clearing the sight [and able to] make the body active and lusty."[47] Both contained caffeine, a stimulus to the nervous system, as did the less popular chocolate. Prior to their introduction, the gentry had achieved the same effect by consuming large amounts of sugar at meals, a practice they abandoned in favor of the new drinks.[48]

By 1700, the more privileged Americans were enjoying tea, coffee, and chocolate. The partaking of tea, associated with a ceremonial custom originating in Japan, was adopted in the colonies, as it had been in England, as a highly important social ritual frequently administered by women.[49] The most popular of the three beverages, it was becoming increasingly affordable by the middle of the eighteenth century; in the year 1759, more than sixteen thousand pounds of tea were consumed in Boston alone.[50] In England, when Pepys first tasted it, a pound of fine tea cost three pounds ten shillings; by 1700, it cost only a pound; by 1760, its price had dropped to ten shillings. Though that was still not inexpensive when compared with the price of meat (threepence a pound), it was a more affordable luxury.[51]

In eighteenth-century America, "the tea ceremony, sometimes simple, sometimes elaborate, was the very core of family life."[52] The beverage was served by a lady of the household seated at a tea table, around which guests mingled, sitting or standing. A fully equipped table held a teapot, waste bowl, cream pot, tea canister, sugar dish, sugar tongs, cups and saucers, and teaspoons. High society preferred cups—without handles for tea, with handles for chocolate or coffee—and saucers to be of porcelain, but the remainder of the equipage was most desirable in silver.

The repast might have consisted of cakes, pastries, nuts, sweetmeats, fruit—depending on the host's means. Teatime was the most social time of the day; besides family members, participants included friends who called, visitors in town, and gentlemen courting marriageable young ladies. The courting aspect could extend the event well into the evening, when a variety of entertainments were offered. Two such occasions were recorded by Nancy Shippen of Philadelphia in a journal she kept from 1783 to 1786:

> Mrs Allen & the Miss Chews drank Tea with me & spent the even'g. There was half a dozen agreable & sensible men that was of the party. The conversation was carried on in the most sprightly, agreable manner . . . till nine when cards was proposed, & about ten, refreshments were introduced which concluded the Evening. . . .
>
> Saturday night at 11 o'clock. I had a very large company at Tea this Evening. . . . I don't know when I spent a more merry Eveng. We had music, Cards, &c &c.

Not all tea parties were so jocular. As a European visitor complained: "The only thing you hear . . . is the whistling sound made by the lips on edges of the cups. This music is varied by the request made to you to have another cup." Foreigners were distressed when they found themselves ignorant of the proper way to prevent their hostess from refilling their cups. A French nobleman described his dilemma as a guest at tea in the Philadelphia home of the Signer Robert Morris:

> I partook of most excellent tea and I should be even now still drinking it, I believe, if the [French] Ambassador had not charitably notified me at the twelfth cup, that I must put my spoon across it when I wished to finish with this sort of warm water. . . . It is almost as ill-bred to refuse a cup of tea when it is offered to you, as it would [be] indiscreet for the mistress of the house to propose a fresh one, when the ceremony of the spoon has notified her that we no longer wish to partake of it.

Sometime later, another French visitor admired a clever but uninitiated foreigner, who, having consumed repeated cups of tea, "decided after emptying it to put it into his pocket until the replenishments had been concluded."

Tea sets—consisting variously of a teapot, coffee pot, sugar dish, cream pot, and additional accoutrements, all made en suite—were new in the rococo period. Two existing English sets are documented in Philadelphia. One, marked by the London firm of Whipham and Wright, dating from 1763 and engraved with the Lloyd coat of arms, was part of the dowry of Elizabeth Lloyd, who married John (later General) Cadwalader (see p. 185) in 1768; the other is known in surviving pieces from the Franks family silver (see FIG. 27, p. 77), which show that they were part of a set marked by Paul de Lamerie in 1744–45.[53]

American examples dating before the 1790s are rare. Joseph Richardson's accounts record that he supplied a set to Samuel Blunston in 1737.[54] As early as 1759, Richardson ordered from England a list of objects that included "3 Double Bellied Silver tea Potts with Stands or weighters Neatly Chast" and "3 Double Bellied Shugar Dishes with Covers Neatly Chast to Suit the tea Potts." A year later, his book contains the same sort of order, but that one requested two teapots with accompanying sugar dishes engraved instead of chased and with the addition of "2 Cream Potts or Ewers to Suit the Above."[55] How literally the London recipients of those orders interpreted "to suit" cannot be determined. Did they supply sets with identical decoration or pieces with similar decoration? In view of Richardson's repeated hope that his orders would be "Shipt Per first Oppertunity,"[56] it is not illogical to assume that many of the "sets" were assembled from stock on hand to satisfy Richardson's continual pleas for haste. The earliest set recorded in Paul Revere's ledgers was made in 1764 for Captain Joseph Goodwin and consisted of a teapot, sugar dish, and cream pot.[57]

What is traditionally considered one of the earliest existing American rococo tea sets[58] is marked by Pieter de Riemer (**No. 48**). Its individual elements, not identical in decoration but similar in style, may have been entirely consistent with English prototypes of the kind imported by Richardson. The set's pieces, if not made en suite, were certainly commissioned within a short period of time, possibly for a patron whose abraded, partly illegible initials, engraved in Roman capitals, are visible on the foot rim of each. If they are correctly interpreted as *L/PC*, the initials may be those of Philip Schuyler Van Rensselaer's grandparents Philip (1716–1778) and Christina (Ten Broeck) Livingston (1718–1801).[59] (Each piece has later engraving of the initials *PSVR* and crest of the grandson, born in 1766.) If so, the set would most likely date between about 1763, when Riemer became active, and 1778, the year Livingston died.

48

Tea set, ca. 1765–75
Pieter de Riemer, New York
Silver, H.: teapot, 6¾ in.,
sugar bowl, 4¾ in., cream pot, 5½ in.
Museum of the City of New York

Pieter de Riemer (1738–1814), an American of Dutch descent, was born to Catharine and Steenwyck de Riemer and was baptized in the Reformed Dutch Church in New York in 1739. Apprenticed to New York silversmith Nicholas Roosevelt, whose expertise in the rococo style is discussed elsewhere (see No. 77), he married in Albany in 1763, the year he became an active silversmith in New York City.[60]

The sole documented American tea set to survive from the rococo period was part of a service ordered from Paul Revere by Dr. William Paine for his bride, Lois Orne (a distant cousin of Revere's first wife), in 1773 (**No. 49**). Paine (1750–1833) graduated from Harvard in 1768 and established a medical practice in Worcester shortly thereafter. A Loyalist, he was forced to leave Worcester in 1774 after signing a protest against a resolution passed by the town meeting. He went to Boston and joined the British army, and the following year went to Scotland to continue medical studies. In 1778, he returned to America as an apothecary to the British forces in Rhode Island and New York.[61]

Paine's commission of forty-five pieces was recorded in Revere's ledgers on 2 September 1773. Not a set but a service, it consisted of a teapot, a coffee pot, a cream pot, a tankard, a pair of canns, a pair of butter boats, a pair of porringers, a pair of tea tongs, twelve large spoons, eighteen teaspoons, four salt spoons, and a wooden case to contain the service. Every piece was engraved with the Orne arms, crest, or initials, some with all three. Revere charged Paine £74 for the silver and £34 for his labor. The service is largely intact but for twelve spoons (including the four salt spoons), the porringers, the cream pot, and the wooden case.[62]

Except for the spoons, nearly all the forms in the service are in the rococo mode. Least rococo are the tankard and the canns: on the tankard, only the finial and engraved arms bespeak the style; on the canns, the arms are the signature element, though the addition to the foot of a spiral fluted band suggests a rococo consciousness. As discussed below, the teapot (see p. 85) is a superb interpretation of the style. It is appropriate that the coffee pot (see p. 97) ranks as the finest rococo example from Boston, since it was clearly intended as the centerpiece of the service. The sauceboats, or butter boats, display the scrolling handles and feet, scalloped rims, and shell knees typical of both English and American examples, augmented by the engraved arms. The tea tongs have shell grips, pierced fretwork derived from chinoiserie designs, and peaked raffles engraved at the top of the arms. On the arms, the pierced fretwork relates to designs published in Chippendale's *Director* and also found on rococo furniture (see No. 121). Similar tea tongs are referred to in Joseph Richardson's letter book as "Peirced Spring tea tongs."[63]

It has been noted that the teapot made for Dr. Paine in 1773 was one of only two recorded in Revere's books between 1769 and 1775, a paucity reflecting the political climate.[64] Revere customarily recorded from one to two teapots a year, but escalating tensions over the Townshend duties imposed in 1767 and the Tea Act of 1773 would seem to have influenced not only the amount of tea consumed in Boston but also the production of the vessels for serving it. As a Loyalist, Paine would not have hesitated to order a teapot, but his order should not be considered an extravagant proclamation of his political sympathies, a "monumental tea service," as has been suggested.[65] The commission as a whole was a general silver service, consisting of eating, drinking, and serving forms, as well as the actual tea and coffee vessels. Its components suggest not a political statement but a bridegroom's desire to delight his wife with an impressive gift. It was the largest single order recorded in Revere's ledgers, and it would have been only natural for the silversmith to treat it as the masterpiece of his career.

49

Selections from a wedding service, 1773
Paul Revere, Boston
Silver, H.: coffee pot, 13½ in.,
teapot, 6⅝ in., cann, 5 in.,
butter boat, 4⅜ in., L.: dessert spoon, 8¾ in.,
teaspoon, 5⅜ in., tea tongs, 5⅜ in.
Worcester Art Museum

FIGURE 28. *Teapot*, 1745. Jacob Hurd, Boston. Silver, H.: 5¼ in. (13.3 cm.). Hood Museum of Art, Dartmouth College; Gift of Louise C. and Frank L. Harrington, Class of 1924 (M.967.42)

50

Teapot, ca. 1753
John Coburn, Boston
Silver, H.: 6½ in.
Historic Deerfield, Inc.

TEAPOTS

Whether produced in sets or individually, hollowware forms for the serving of tea and coffee were transformed into some of the most representative and most lavish demonstrations of the style in American silver. Not only were they ornamented with rococo engraving, chasing, and casting, but their shapes became rococo as well. The focal point of the tea service, the teapot, began as a small, squat form of globular or pear shape but, as the rococo period progressed, evolved into an apple shape rising from a stepped foot. By the full maturity of the style, rococo teapots had become more dramatic in design: tall and top-heavy, with swollen shoulders above smaller, rounded bellies and with domed lids that provided a visual counterpart to those fulsome elements. The mere reversing of the simple pear shape resulted in a surprisingly elegant form, which silversmiths described as "double bellied." When correctly interpreted, the mass of the pot was elevated well above the surface of the table, giving the impression of a vessel in graceful defiance of gravity, an implied instability that was characteristic of the rococo style's penchant for flouting convention. Such a shape conceded practicality to aesthetics, since the best-tasting tea required a pot expansive enough at the bottom to permit a maximum quantity of boiling water to suffuse the tea leaves.

Engraving was the avenue of entry for rococo design in the colonies. By 1745, English printed ephemera, including bill heads, trade cards, and bookplates, had begun to make popular the asymmetrical cartouche that was a signature motif of the new style. It is therefore to be expected that the earliest instance of the rococo in silver would be the engraved application of a readily available printed design.

The first documented rococo decoration to appear in American silver occurs on a Boston teapot (FIG. 28) dated 1745 and marked by Jacob Hurd (1703–1758).[66] Queen Anne in style, the conventional pot, globular and with a flat lid, is nevertheless enlightened with engraving of asymmetrical cartouches composed of raffles, *C*-scrolls, and foliage that appear on either side of the vessel, on one side framing the arms of the Fayerweather family of Boston, on the other enclosing the inscription "The Gift/OF/Edwd Tyng Esqr/to/H. Fayerweather/Decr 9/1745." (Hannah Fayerweather was married on 10 December 1745 to Farr Tolman, a Boston bookbinder.)[67] Despite that rococo decoration, the engraving around the lid of the pot remains baroque, a dichotomy that suggests that the engraver, possibly James Turner (see p. 39),[68] copied the armorial cartouches from an English bookplate or other rococo engraving but was less assured in adapting the new style to the lid decoration.

A teapot (**No. 50**) marked by John Coburn was commissioned by Thomas Welles (1692–1767) of Glastonbury, Connecticut, for his daughter Mary (1735–1814), along with a silver cream pot and a sugar caster, probably on the occasion of her marriage, in 1753.[69] The pot, more than an inch in height over the one marked by Hurd, has an apple-shaped body elevated on a stepped, circular foot. Its taller profile, though not double bellied, is still indebted to the influence of rococo design, as are the spout with its cast scrolled designs, the domed lid, and the flame finial. The most mature stylistic aspect of the pot is the engraving: rococo C-scrolls and diapered panels encircle the lid, and the Welles family arms appear on the body in an asymmetrical cartouche of raffles, scrolls, and foliage. The pot is typical of numerous New England counterparts, fledgling in form and limited to subtle engraved decoration for their fullest expression of the style.

John Coburn (1703–1758), a Boston silversmith born in York, Maine, who probably apprenticed with Thomas Edwards of Boston, is best known for his tea and church silver. Coburn occasionally ordered silver objects from Paul Revere and also contracted for his services as an engraver.[70] Thus, the Welles teapot may have been engraved by Revere.

The best example of a New England rococo teapot with engraved decoration is the one supplied by Revere as part of the Paine service (No. 49). The pot (see detail) is double bellied in shape; the circular foot is elevated and adorned with a fluted band; the finial is in the form of a large, crisply detailed pineapple. The asymmetry of the engraved cartouche, which is more florid and expansive than that of the Welles pot, is accentuated by a trailing ribbon, or motto scroll, here left blank. Revere, who is known to have copied English engravings line for line (see Nos. 12, 13), may have borrowed the cartouche from an English armorial device with motto intact. In addition, rococo flourishes, diapering, and C-scrolls are engraved on the lid and around the handle and spout junctures, while the spout is cast with rococo C-scrolls and acanthus leaves.

The finest surviving rococo teapot from Boston is also marked by Revere (**No. 51**). Like the Paine set counterpart, it is fully rococo in form and has the same cast spout design. Instead of the engraving that appears on the majority of Boston rococo teapots, chasing mantles the shoulders and forms the cartouche on this example. The iconography of the pot's decoration is the most exotic of any observed on Boston teapots. As well as the usual flowers, raffles, and C-scrolls, it features a bird and a chinoiserie pavilion (see detail). The Ross family arms engraved on the cartouche are probably for the patriot John Ross (1726–1800), a shipping merchant who emigrated from Perth, Scotland, to Philadelphia in 1763 and later served as purchasing agent for the Continental Congress. His recent arrival in America would have ensured his familiarity with more ornate

British rococo teapots; his means would have enabled him to order a pot similar to them and more elaborate than most American examples of the time.[71]

The Ross teapot illustrates the fully developed rococo interpretation of the form, a double-bellied shape with chased decoration. The formula, derived from imported British examples, was common in England but relatively rare in American silver. Since the combination was the most expensive of available designs, that was probably as much a matter of cost as of taste.

No. 49 (detail)

51

Teapot, ca. 1765–70
Paul Revere, Boston
Silver, H.: 5⅞ in.
Museum of Fine Arts, Boston

As with Boston work, most New York rococo teapots are engraved, but examples with chased decoration survive in numbers comparable to those known from New England. The finest of these is the one marked by Pieter de Riemer (No. 48), with its accompanying cream pot and sugar dish. Like the Ross family pot supplied by Revere, it has a stepped foot, domed lid, and pineapple finial; while it lacks the other's central cartouche, it has a more elaborate acanthus-and-shell-cast spout. The shoulders are ornately decorated with a fluid, sinuous design of flowers and raffle-draped C-scrolls carefully proportioned to the curve of the pot.

With few exceptions, Philadelphia's exemplary rococo teapots fall short of the double-bellied and chased formula observed in Boston and New York. One of the finest chased Philadelphia teapots (**No. 52**) is apple-shaped, akin in form to the one Coburn supplied for the Welles family. Crafted in the shop of Joseph Richardson, its shape, stepped foot, and domed lid are considered traits of early rococo teapots. Fully mature, however, is its exuberant decoration of chased flowers, raffles, and C-scrolls, which extends nearly halfway down the pot's profile and adorns the spout, handle juncture, and lid. Equally rococo is the cast pineapple finial embellished with C-scrolls beneath furling leaves. En suite with the teapot is a sugar dish having an identical finial and similar chased decoration.[72]

Most of the surviving double-bellied teapots from Philadelphia are not chased but engraved. Among the finest is one (**No. 53**) marked by Philip Syng, Jr., which is engraved with the arms of the Bayard family, possibly for Maryland-born but later Philadelphian John Bubenheim Bayard (1738–1807), merchant, statesman, and member of the Continental Congress from Pennsylvania. The slightly exaggerated form of the pot results from the expansive swelling-out of the shoulders over a proportionately small belly. Lacking the vertical balance of the usual domed lid (this lid is low and gently curved), the pot, poised on its small, tucked-in base, has a horizontal emphasis that accentuates its rococo defiance of rules.

The quintessential American rococo teapot was produced in Baltimore (a satellite of Philadelphia prior to nationhood) and so must be considered a relative of Philadelphia examples. The teapot (**No. 54**), marked by Gabriel Lewyn, is a superb composition of form, proportion, and decoration. The sumptuous, integral chased design, its folded tendrils trailing onto the lower body in imitation of nature, carefully conforms to the double-bellied shape of the vessel. As a result of its spool-shaped pedestal, the foot is higher than

52

Teapot, ca. 1755–60
Joseph Richardson, Philadelphia
Silver, H.: 6 in.
The Historical Society of Pennsylvania

53

Teapot, 1760–70
Philip Syng, Jr., Philadelphia
Silver, H.: 5½ in.
Department of State

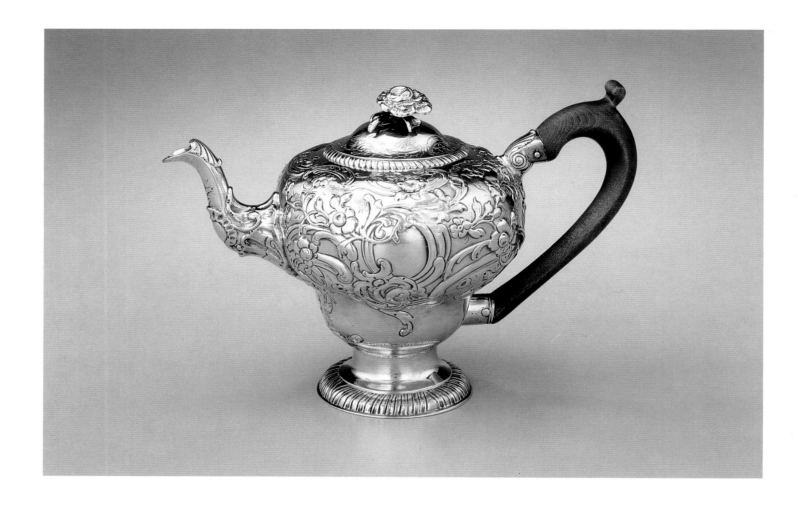

those of its contemporaries. Fluting on the foot rim is repeated around the lid, which is crowned by a cast three-dimensional flower—a sculptural element rare in American rococo silver. Among the handful of related finials known are a flower on the Richardson coffee pot (No. 65) and accompanying sugar dish, and bird finials found on Albany sugar dishes, including one attributed to Jacob Gerritse Lansing (No. 57). Also richly cast are the shells, scrolls, and foliage of the spout, which is among the most ornate of its kind.

Little is known about the silversmith Lewyn. His whereabouts are a mystery before 1770, when he appeared in Annapolis and in the same year moved to Baltimore. The masterly design and execution of his teapot suggest that he was either trained abroad or had access to the services of a superb chaser. English rococo silver owned in Baltimore could have influenced the design.[73] Barrister Charles Carroll (1723–1817) of that city had some very fine London examples: a set of tea canisters dated 1763–64 and a double-bellied chased coffee pot dated 1765.[74]

54

Teapot, 1760–70
Gabriel Lewyn, Baltimore
Silver, H.: 6 in.
Phillips Collection, Yale University

A discussion of tea forms in American rococo silver necessarily includes the ancillary vessels for sugar and cream. Perhaps because they constituted less of an investment, sugar dishes and cream pots (as they were called in period accounts) occurred as sets that survive in greater numbers than those that include a teapot, possibly because they were ordered to accompany a china teapot with matching cups and saucers. Most often, however, they were made as individual forms, as is attested by Paul Revere's ledgers.[75] The designation "cream pot" or "cream ewer" is used apart from "milk Potts or Ewers" in Joseph Richardson's orders to London, but the terms were probably interchangeable: Richardson's specification for the milk vessels, "to weigh from 3 to 4 oz.," matches exactly the range of weight he specifies for cream pots. (In his ledgers, Revere recorded the same range of weight for the same forms.) Doubtless because cream pots were smaller and less expensive than sugar dishes and the sugar itself more costly than the more easily obtained cream, orders for single cream pots greatly outnumber orders for individual sugar dishes in Revere's ledgers. Richardson routinely ordered dozens of cream pots but ordered sugar dishes only to accompany tea or coffee pots.[76] His orders for both frequently specified double- or single-bellied shapes, plain, engraved, or chased; as with teapots, the most rococo and most costly of them were double bellied and chased.

The superlative Philadelphia cream pot is one marked by Philip Hulbeart (**No. 55**) sometime before 1763, the year of his death. Despite its traditional single-bellied form, the pot is distinctly rococo, as seen in the chased decoration added all over the body and in the modification of certain elements of the vessel: the rim more deeply scalloped, the spout more elongated than on earlier examples, and, in place of the typical cast scrolling handle, one created by the use of a special mold of more intricate design. Further scrolls and leafage adorn the lower return of the handle, and, at its upper juncture with the rim, atop the usual C-scroll, there are raffles and scrolls that support a vestigial caryatid related to those found on the handles of late-seventeenth-century cups in England and America.[77] Hulbeart also redesigned the feet of the pot; in place of the usual cabriole or scroll feet, he substituted cast Indian figures, an allegory for the American continent common in period iconography (see FIG. 4, p. 14; No. 34) and found in broadsides and European works in several mediums.[78] Such human figural references were part of the standard vocabulary in European rococo silver but are seldom found in American work. They characterize the

55

Cream pot, ca. 1760
Philip Hulbeart, Philadelphia
Silver, H.: 4¼ in.
Philadelphia Museum of Art

56

Sugar dish and cream pot, 1760–75
Myer Myers, New York
Silver, H.: sugar dish, 6¾ in.,
cream pot, 6¾ in.
Collection of the Brinckerhoff family

most ebullient English rococo forms: for example, on a ewer of 1742 from the shop of Paul de Lamerie, a female figure forms the handle.[79] On the body of the Hulbeart pot, the chasing is loose and all-encompassing—a floral design that relates to patterns on the palampores made of cotton chintz that were then being imported from India,[80] but with added raffles and scrolls.

Philip Hulbeart (d. 1763), son of William Hulbeart, of Bristol, England, was briefly a resident of Philadelphia. The earliest reference to him in that city is in the year 1761, when he advertised in the *Pennsylvania Gazette*.[81] Nothing is known of his apprenticeship or immigration to America, but he likely came to join an uncle who already resided in Philadelphia. Like Joseph Richardson, Hulbeart evidently imported English silver, for he advertised it along with the work of his own shop. When he died, in 1763, Richardson and fellow Philadelphia silversmith Philip Syng, Jr., were appointed to settle his estate. Among the objects sold, primarily to other Philadelphia silversmiths, were shoe buckles, "a neat gilt silver whistle and corel with eight bells," "a neat chased Slop Bowl," "a Sugar Dish," "a Caster," and thirteen cream pots.[82]

Two surviving New York silver sugar-and-cream sets, marked by two different silversmiths, display variations in treatment and in design. Both sets illustrate the double-bellied and chased interpretation of the forms. The first is part of the tea set made by Pieter de Riemer (No. 48), which also includes a teapot.[83] Centered on both cream pot and sugar dish is an asymmetrical cartouche enveloped by flowers and C-scrolls. Each of the vessels has typical New York characteristics: the sugar dish has the reel lid retained from the earlier Queen Anne fashion and the cream pot has the pedestal foot and twisted-scroll handle associated with New York rococo milk pots. It is interesting to note that the cream pot is endowed with one of the rare incidences of animal decoration in American rococo silver, a large chased bird perched to the left of the cartouche.

The second sugar-and-cream set (**No. 56**) survives with an English coffee pot assayed in 1761–62 by the London partnership of William and Robert Peaston. The sugar dish is marked by Myer Myers; the cream pot, though unmarked, is attributed to his shop on the basis of its similarity to the sugar dish. Assembled as a set sometime in the eighteenth century, all three pieces are highly rococo, are engraved with

57

Sugar dish, Albany, 1760–75
Attributed to Jacob Gerritse Lansing
Silver, H.: 4⅝ in.
Albany Institute of History and Art

the initials *DR* for their original owner, Dorothea Remsen, and descended in her family. The Myers pieces are unusual in their display of imbricated scales arranged in vertical panels, an English rococo motif associated with the shop of Paul de Lamerie in the 1730s[84] and virtually absent from the American rococo vocabulary. (The Peaston coffee pot, lacking such ornament, does not appear to have been the model for the American vessels.) Logic points to an English-trained chaser, familiar with the style in London. The cream pot is of typical rococo shape and decoration; its handle has the characteristic New York twist seen on the Riemer version. The sugar dish, however, is atypical; its slimmer and more attenuated proportions suggest the influence of an English double-bellied tea caddy, an elegant, elongated form often made in pairs en suite with a sugar dish of conventional globular form. No such sets are known in American silver, but at least one from London was owned in Maryland by Margaretta (Tilghman) Carroll (1742–1783), the gift of her bridegroom, Barrister Charles Carroll, to whom she was married in June 1763.[85] Similar sets were possibly owned in New York.

Dorothea Remsen (1750–1834) was married to Abraham Brinckerhoff (1745–1823) in 1772. The couple resided in New York City, in a fashionable house on Broadway, and had their portraits painted—hers by John Trumbull; his by Gilbert Stuart.[86] Abraham was the son of the merchant George Brinckerhoff and his second wife, the former Maria Van Deusen. Dorothea's father was Peter Remsen, also of New York City.

While the design of the Peaston coffee pot has little in common with any element of the Myers sugar-and-cream ensemble, its bird finial is similar to that found on a double-bellied sugar dish (**No. 57**) attributed to the shop of Jacob Gerritse Lansing, of Albany. At least three other bird finials appear on surviving sugar dishes—also double bellied, two of them chased—from Albany.[87] Bird finials are sufficiently uncommon in American rococo silver that one can assume that the Albany group was influenced by an imported example or by an immigrant craftsman. The Van Rensselaer collections at their family estate, Cherry Hill (then outside Albany), included a double-bellied and chased London teapot of 1762 having a cast bird finial.[88] New York City sugar dishes often have the reel top of the type seen on the sugar dish of the Riemer set (No. 48). This Albany sugar dish is adorned with relief chasing of *C*-scrolls, flowers, and leafage. Although unmarked, it has long been attributed to Lansing on the basis of its provenance. It has the engraved initials *F/I L* for the silversmith's second wife and cousin, Femmetje Lansing, and for himself, as well as the initials *M/I L* for her parents and Lansing's aunt and uncle, Marytje and Colonel Jacob J. Lansing. The similarity of the bowl's chasing to that of two examples having marks associated with Abraham Schuyler has suggested reattribution of the piece to that Albany silversmith. An alternate explanation would be the existence in Albany of a chaser who decorated all three dishes, as well as other examples of chased rococo silver from Albany.

Jacob Gerritse Lansing (1736–1803) was born in Albany, son of Gerritse Lansing and grandson of silversmith Jacob Gerritse Lansing (1681–1767), possibly the boy's master. Lansing married his first wife, Neeltje Roseboom, in 1767; his second, Femmetje, in 1774. Lansing was evidently highly regarded by Albany town officials, for in 1784 they commissioned him to craft a gold box for presentation to General Washington.

The most notable cream-and-sugar ensemble surviving from Boston (**No. 58**), marked by Paul Revere, was commissioned by silversmith Benjamin Greene (1747–1807) for his sister-in-law Lucretia Chandler (1728–1768) in honor of her marriage, in 1761, to John Murray (d. 1794). Lucretia kept house for Greene after the death of his wife, Mary, Lucretia's eldest sister. The sugar dish, recorded in Revere's ledgers on 11 March 1762, is invoiced at £4-17-8 for the silver content of nearly fourteen ounces. Revere charged £1-12-0 to make it, bringing the total cost of the dish to £6-9-8.[89] (Curiously, there is no mention of the cream pot in Revere's ledgers.) The cream pot illustrates the double-bellied shape elevated on three feet in place of the pedestal foot common in New York. On the sugar dish, the pineapple finial is of the same casting found on several of Revere's rococo forms.[90] Both double-bellied pieces are ornately chased with rocaille-edged C-scrolls, raffles, acanthus, and flowers. Revere, an engraver himself, probably had a skilled chaser in his employ: his ledgers record his supplying other silversmiths with chased silver.[91]

58

Sugar dish and cream pot, 1761–62
Paul Revere, Boston
Silver, H.: sugar dish, 6½ in.,
cream pot, 4⅜ in.
Museum of Fine Arts, Boston

Newport, Rhode Island, though not one of the three colonial silversmithing centers, was a thriving urban seaport in the eighteenth century, with a prosperous merchant class. Silversmith Samuel Casey (ca. 1724-ca. 1780) must have drawn some of his clients from Newport, though he lived in nearby South Kingstown. A cream pot with Casey's mark (**No. 59**) has become a favorite among historians of the American decorative arts because of its cast claw-and-ball feet and their similarity to those found on contemporary Rhode Island furniture. Claw-and-ball feet also occur on rococo salvers of the period (see Nos. 61, 73), but they are uncommon on vessel forms.[92]

The elongated talons and oval ball do indeed correspond to the regional characteristics of feet on Newport furniture, and with good reason. Silversmiths frequently acquired their casting positives (original models from which they made their molds) from carvers; the same craftsman who supplied these to Casey was probably also carving full-sized feet for chairs, tables, and case pieces. (The rendering of the talons is in the manner of the great Newport cabinetmaker John Goddard.) The single-bellied shape of the Casey cream pot is not unlike the form of the Hulbeart example (No. 55), but the height and nature of the feet give it an altogether different aspect—less elegant but more lively. The chaser used punches to create the effect of ruffled edges that contain a broad band of foliate scrolls flanking, under the spout, a central cipher (*IC*) of a design derived from a book of ciphers published by Samuel Sympson (London, 1726).[93]

Casey, presumedly born in Newport, apprenticed in Boston with Jacob Hurd (see FIG. 28, p. 84). In 1745, he was made a freeman in Exeter, Rhode Island, where he first established a silversmithing business. He moved to South Kingstown by 1750 and within a few years married Martha Martin. Despite the skill and quality manifested in the cream pot, Casey was a sad contrast to the many colonial silversmiths who prospered and became civic leaders. A series of misfortunes led to his declaration of insolvency in 1770 and his subsequent imprisonment for counterfeiting. In 1779, his wife successfully petitioned the General Assembly for his pardon, describing him as "forlorn and forsaken and destitute of every means of support to make his life even desirable, separated from his wife and offspring."[94]

59

Cream pot, 1755-70
Samuel Casey, Rhode Island
Silver, H.: 4 in.
Museum of Fine Arts, Boston

COFFEE POTS

Opposition to the Townshend Acts, which had imposed duties on several imported commodities in 1767, resulted in boycotts of the taxed items. (Three years later, the tax was repealed on all but tea.) The controversy intensified with the passage of the Tea Act of 1773, which gave the East India Company a virtual monopoly on exportation of the commodity to the colonies. The famous Boston Tea Party followed, and the abstention from tea drew more support in America.

A humorous renunciation, titled "A Lady's Adieu to her Tea-Table," appeared in several colonial newspapers on the eve of the Revolution:

> FAREWELL the Tea-board with your gaudy attire,
> Ye cups and ye saucers that I did admire;
> To my cream pot and tongs I now bid adieu;
> That pleasure's all fled that I once found in you.
>
> Farewell pretty chest that so lately did shine,
> With hyson and congo and best double fine;
> Many a sweet moment by you I have sat,
> Hearing girls and old maids to tattle and chat;
> And the spruce coxcomb laugh at nothing at all,
> Only some silly word that might happen to fall.
>
> No more shall my teapot so generous be
> In filling the cups with this pernicious tea,
> For I'll fill it with water and drink out the same,
> Before I'll lose LIBERTY that dearest name,
> Because I am taught (and believe it is fact)
> That our ruin is aimed at in the late act,
> Of imposing a duty on all foreign Teas,
> Which detestable stuff we can quit when we please.
>
> LIBERTY's the Goddess that I do adore,
> And I'll maintain her right until my last hour,
> Before she shall part I will die in the cause,
> For I'll never be govern'd by tyranny's laws.[95]

There seems no doubt that the imbroglio served to elevate the social status of coffee as an acceptable alternative to the traditional beverage in many afternoon social gatherings. A visitor to Nomini Hall, the Virginia plantation of Colonel Robert Carter, noted in his journal on a Sunday in May 1774: "After dinner we had a Grand & agreeable Walk in & through the Gardens—There is great plenty of Strawberries, some Cherries, Goose berries &c.—Drank Coffee at four, they are now too patriotic to use tea."[96]

Before the crisis, coffee pots were rare entries in Paul Revere's ledgers: only two were recorded between 1761 and 1767. In 1769, however, when the British military's attempt to enforce the duties enraged Boston citizens, six more were entered, and an additional four appeared in 1772 and 1773. That total of ten ordered between 1769 and 1775 is in sharp contrast with the listing of only two teapots in the same six-year period, though they had formerly been produced at the rate of one to two a year.[97]

In early-eighteenth-century America, if observations of foreigners are to be trusted, only the privileged few had the time to indulge in the leisurely ritual of afternoon tea, with its porcelain cups and saucers and its silver serving vessels. By mid-century, however, tea, coffee, and chocolate were common staples in most colonial larders. Naturalist Peter Kalm, visiting Pennsylvania in 1748, observed that all three beverages "at present constitute even the country people's daily breakfast," a remark borne out by that of the historian and author Israel Acrelius a few years later: "Tea, coffee, and chocolate are so general as to be found in the most remote cabins, if not for daily use, yet for visitors, mixed with Muscovado, or raw sugar."[98]

Coffee, while consumed in the home, was also associated with the male domain of public coffeehouses, those "centers of political, social and literary influence as well as of commercial life,"[99] where the beverage was dispensed in serviceable tin pots, as it was in most colonial homes; only the most affluent could afford silver. Available at breakfast along with tea, coffee could also be taken in the late afternoon with its oriental cousin. Dinner was customarily served at two o'clock. As Claude Blanchard, a visitor from France, noted, "[Americans] do not take coffee immediately after dinner, but it is served three or four hours afterwards with tea; this coffee is weak and four or five cups are not equal to one of ours; so that they take many of them. The tea, on the contrary, is very strong. This use of tea and coffee is universal in America."[100]

Coffee pots, evolving from a cylindrical, lighthouse shape into a curving baluster, matured in the rococo period into a double-bellied form with a stepped domed lid balancing the curving lower profile. Rococo decoration, like that of teapots, was achieved through cast elements, with the addition of chasing or engraving or both. On the coffee pot, a form more statuesque than the teapot, the double-bellied shape was even more arresting; a fully rococo coffee pot was an imposing and expensive object. A perfect comparison between the teapot and the coffee pot is documented in Paul Revere's ledger entry for the Paine service, which includes both. The two pots have similar decoration, as befits a set, yet in labor alone the cost for "making and engraving" the coffee pot was £7-9-4; for the teapot, it was only £4-12-0. The real disparity, however, was in the silver content: the weight of the coffee pot was recorded as just over forty-five

ounces; the teapot, at eighteen ounces eleven pennyweight, was less than half that.[101]

The Paine example (No. 49, see detail), made in 1773, is the finest surviving double-bellied rococo coffee pot from Boston, distinguished from its local counterparts (including others marked by Revere) by the broad band of spiral fluting on its foot, the shell casting at its upper handle juncture, its size, and its weight. (The latter exceeds that of most of Revere's coffee pots, which are not more than forty ounces.) Eight years later, on a pot (**No. 60**) he supplied to Paul Dudley Sargent (1745–1828), an officer in the Revolution and later a prominent Maine jurist, Revere repeated the same design with only slight modifications. He used a different mold for the pineapple finial, dispensed with the cast shell at the upper handle juncture, and, on the foot, substituted a gadrooned rim for the spiral fluted band.

A new neoclassical taste, traces of which are visible in 1774 in Philadelphia silver,[102] had begun to influence design in the decorative arts by 1781. Though Revere started to alter his style in hollowware as early as 1782,[103] harbingers of the new mode can be seen in the cartouche on the Sargent pot of the previous year. The Sargent arms are gloriously engraved in rococo fashion, but a closer examination reveals that neoclassical motifs are intermingled with the raffles, C-scrolls, and foliage. The lower half of the cartouche is adorned with asymmetrically placed pendent swags of drapery and a bellflower garland. The cartouche itself, when compared with one Revere devised in 1764 to surround the family arms on a Sargent bookplate (No. 16), shows a simplified and tightened composition. While still rococo in style, the later interpretation has less froth and foliage, the leaves are treated as two distinct branches, and the right one is contained in the suggestion of a classical urn.

Similar to the Paine and Sargent pots is a patrician example that probably dates from the 1770s. Made in Philadelphia and marked by Richard Humphreys, the pot (**No. 61**) differs from the two Revere models chiefly in the shape and placement of the spout, here mounted low on the belly and rising almost vertically before curving out at the lip. All three pots have rococo armorial engraving, but the arms on the Humphreys pot, contained in a cartouche, are unidentified. They may have been the work of James Smither (see Nos. 32, 33), who engraved a similar cartouche on a tea urn supplied by Humphreys in 1774 for Charles Thomson, first secretary of the Continental Congress.[104]

Because the double-bellied coffee pot with engraved decoration was common in English silver and was probably imported into all the colonial urban centers, the similarity of

No. 49 (detail)

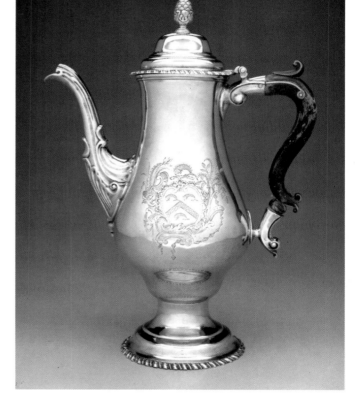

60

Coffee pot, 1781
Paul Revere, Boston
Silver, H.: 12⅞ in.
Museum of Fine Arts, Boston

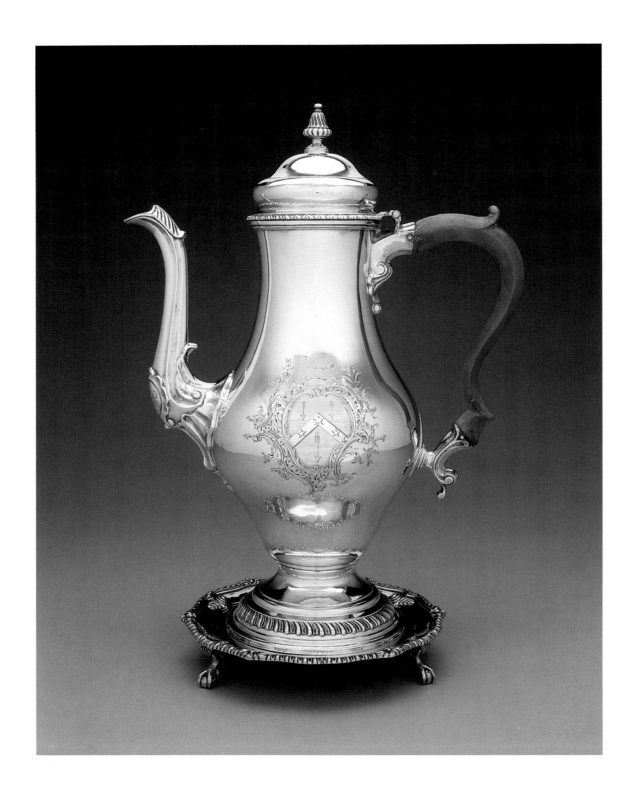

61

Coffee pot on stand, 1770–80
Richard Humphreys, Philadelphia
Silver, H., pot: 13⅝ in.; Diam., stand: 6¾ in.
Museum of Fine Arts, Boston

the Revere and Humphreys coffee pots, as well as of certain New York examples revealing the same formula, supports the conclusion that the form's design had its source in imported British models.[105] The elongated shape of all three pots imitates the increasingly attenuated British interpretation of the form, which evolved in London in the 1760s (see FIG. 26, p. 75). A demonstration of the influence of foreign silver is provided by the trio of tripod coffee pots from Salem (see p. 71). An English model imported into that city (see No. 46) was an unusual design that spawned two American copies for another Salem family (see No. 47), but the tripod form occurs nowhere else in the colonies.

The Humphreys pot is particularly unusual in that it survives with its original matching stand (see detail), of a scalloped rococo shape with shell and leaf castings punctuating the gadrooned border and with central armorial engraving that is nearly identical to that on the pot. Joseph Richardson's import records leave no doubt that he routinely ordered teapots and coffee pots with stands. (Perhaps that was a practice centered in Philadelphia, for it is not one reflected in Revere's ledgers.) Between 1758 and 1773, Richardson ordered thirty teapots, twenty-four of them with stands, and twenty-four coffee pots, twenty-one of them similarly accompanied.[106] An inventory taken in 1771 of John Cadwalader's silver closet listed a chocolate pot, a coffee pot, and a teapot, each with a stand.[107]

Richard Humphreys (1750–1832) was one of the leading silversmiths of Philadelphia. Born into a distinguished Quaker family in Tortola, in the West Indies, Humphreys was orphaned as a boy and placed with relatives in Wilmington, Delaware. He was apprenticed to Quaker silversmith Bancroft Woodcock (1732–1817), as noted in part in the minutes of the Wilmington Monthly Meeting from 1765: "This meeting received some lines from a few Friends in Tortola dated 19th 5th Month 1765 signifying that Richard Humphreys an apprentice to Bancroft Woodcock, is a Friends son."[108] Humphreys evidently completed his apprenticeship by 1769, returned to Tortola for a year, and came back to Wilmington in 1770. In 1771, he married Hannah Elliott of Philadelphia, and the following year the couple moved to Philadelphia, where Humphreys rented a house and workshop from retiring silversmith Philip Syng, Jr. Syng recommended Humphreys to his clients as a "person qualified to serve them on the best terms, and whose fidelity in the above business will engage their future confidence and regard."[109] Hannah Humphreys died in 1773 and the next year the silversmith married Ann Morris, who bore him five children. In 1774, when he was twenty-four, Humphrey's career and reputation as a fine silversmith were undoubtedly aided by his important commission from the Continental

62

Coffee pot, ca. 1753
Philip Syng, Jr., Philadelphia
Silver, H.: 11⅞ in.
Philadelphia Museum of Art

Congress for the Charles Thomson tea urn, an interpretation in the latest London taste. It was an extraordinary opportunity for the young silversmith, not just because of the patron but because of the gift itself, for the tea urn is the largest and rarest hollowware form in American silver. In 1776, despite his Quaker religion, Humphreys joined the military, whereupon his Meeting disowned him. (He was reinstated in 1783.) Whether his prosperity derived from his success as a silversmith or from the Tortola estates he inherited from his family, he died a wealthy man, with a fortune valued at $108,998.50.[110]

Rococo chasing is far rarer than engraving on both coffee pots and teapots. Chasing on coffee pots was practiced almost exclusively in Philadelphia and its environs, mostly on pots of an earlier, single-bellied baluster shape. No coffee pot having such relief ornament survives from New York or New England, with one exception.[111]

As early as 1760, Richardson's London import orders specified "2 Chast Silver Coffe Potts to hold 3 wine Pints," accompanied by "2 Chast Stands or weighters for Do. with Chast Shells on the Border." Four months later, he ordered four more such coffee pots and stands.[112] Since he was careful to specify "double bellied" when ordering teapots, it is likely that the coffee pots he requested were single bellied and had curving baluster profiles. The finest known Philadelphia essay of this type is a pot, marked by Philip Syng, Jr., made for Joseph and Grace (Growden) Galloway.

The Galloway pot (**No. 62**), virtually identical to British examples,[113] is probably of the kind that Richardson was importing. Though its single-bellied form predates the rococo period, the pot is unarguably rococo by virtue of its lavish ornament: chased C-scrolls, foliage, and flowers that encircle the upper and lower parts of the pot, the two steps of the domed lid, and the spout. Further, the spout is distinguished by cast decoration—shell, cartouche, and acanthus leaves—as is the upper junction of the handle, where there is a sculptural shell. Similar decoration adorns a salver (No. 75) Syng supplied in 1754 to Edward Penington and Sarah Shoemaker as part of their wedding silver. The coffee pot is traditionally dated 1753, the year of Joseph Galloway's marriage to Grace Growden, a supposition supported by the pot's affinity to the Penington salver of 1754. Since the Galloway pot and the Penington salver are the only surviving examples of such chased work in Syng's oeuvre (and their chasing is among the most refined of the period), it is likely that the ornament was added by a London-trained artisan.

Grace Growden (ca. 1732–1782) was the daughter of Laurence Growden, of Philadelphia, owner of Trevose, a five-thousand-acre estate in Bucks County, and one of only

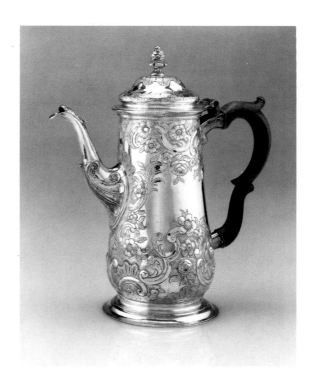

FIGURE 29. *Coffee pot*, 1755–60. John Inch, Annapolis. Silver, H.: 11¼ in. (28.6 cm.). Virginia Museum of Fine Arts, Museum Purchase: The Adolph D. and Wilkins C. Williams Fund (52.20.1)

eight Philadelphians to possess a four-wheeled coach in 1760.[114] The politically prominent Joseph Galloway (1730–1803), son of Peter Galloway, of White's Hall plantation, Anne Arundel County, Maryland, was a wealthy Quaker lawyer. A longtime member of the Provincial Assembly, he was among the more controversial figures of the American Revolution. A friend of Isaac Norris's and Benjamin Franklin's, he served on the Whig delegation to the Continental Congress. He resigned in 1775 and joined the Royal Army in New York in the following year, whereupon Franklin and his other Whig friends denounced him. In 1777, he was sent to Philadelphia under the command of General Sir William Howe. When the British evacuated the city in 1778, Galloway fled to England with his daughter, leaving Grace behind to try vainly to recover their estate, much of it her dowry.

Three other coffee pots similar in shape and decoration to the Galloway pot survive from Annapolis and Lancaster (both within Philadelphia's sphere of influence) and from Charleston. Nothing is known of the provenance of the Annapolis vessel (FIG. 29) and little is known of John Inch, who marked it, but it seems likely that he was familiar with

63

Coffee pot, 1760–75
Charles Hall, Lancaster
Silver, H.: 10¾ in.
Henry Ford Museum & Greenfield Village

64

Coffee pot, 1755–65
Alexander Petrie, Charleston
Silver, H.: 10⅜ in.
Museum of Early Southern Decorative Arts

English examples or possibly with the pot Syng supplied to Galloway; the Galloways were, after all, a Maryland family. The Inch pot is heavily chased with rococo motifs that nearly cover the surface. Like the Syng example, it has a cast shell-decorated spout mounted high on the body and a stepped dome lid with additional chasing surmounted by a pineapple finial.

No information survives on the Lancaster pot (**No. 63**) marked by Charles Hall. The Inch pot appears to copy the Syng model, but the Hall version exhibits a subtle variation in shape, as illustrated by an examination of the profiles of all three. That of the Inch pot is the most conservative, conforming to those of earlier traditional examples of nearly cylindrical form and with a rounded base; that of the Syng pot more closely approximates a baluster, with the belly proportionately broader than the diameter of the neck. (Both pots flare outward from rim to belly and both have roots in known English prototypes.) The profile of the Hall pot, even more curvaceous, is the only one of the three to sport a waist, visible where the body narrows between the flaring rim and the expansive belly.[115]

Charles Hall (1742–1783) is well documented as a Lancaster silversmith.[116] His older brother David was a silversmith in Philadelphia and in Burlington, New Jersey. Charles worked with him for several years but was recorded in Lancaster by 1763. He took an active role in the Revolution,

serving as a lieutenant in the local militia, an agent for confiscating British property, and, in 1778 and 1779, a Burgess. His familiarity with high-style rococo may have resulted from the time he spent in Philadelphia at his brother's shop, and the chasing on his pot could be the work of a Philadelphia artisan. Conversely, chasing skills may have been available locally, as implied by the existence of another chased rococo silver form—a tureen—from the workshop of a fellow Lancaster silversmith.[117]

A Charleston coffee pot (**No. 64**) is the sole surviving example of mature rococo domestic silver from that city, a paucity resulting partly from the Charlestonian preference for English silver and partly from the destruction of property during the Civil War. The pot, marked by Alexander Petrie (act. 1744 to 1765–d. 1768), is conservative in shape and in profile closely resembles the Inch example, though it lacks the higher, stepped-lid design found on all three related examples from the Philadelphia area (FIG. 29, p. 101; Nos. 62, 63). Thus, it is entirely Queen Anne in shape, as are three other Petrie coffee pots,[118] all four having spouts, foot rims, and handle sockets cast from the same molds. This example is the only survival of chased silver from Petrie's shop, but the smith's probate inventory included chased teapots and coffee pots, with stands, and "1 large Chased Coffee pott 32½ ozs.," as well as imported silver.[119]

At least one and possibly two chasers are recorded in Charleston newspapers of the period. John Winckler, from London, who made such mention in a notice of 1761, may have been the journeyman chaser advertised by John Paul Grimke in 1760.[120] Petrie himself may have been qualified in the skill if he emigrated from Britain, as is believed. First recorded in Charleston in 1744, he married Elizabeth Holland in 1748 and offered imported plate in 1756 and 1761.[121] His probate inventory also included a slave silversmith named Abraham, valued at £400, who was subsequently sold to another Charleston silversmith.[122]

Double-bellied coffee pots having chased decoration are even rarer than teapots. Joseph Richardson's letter book records several orders of "chast" London coffee pots, but none with double bellies. Philadelphia silversmith Edmund Milne, however, advertised in 1763 that he had "just imported in the last vessels from London, an elegant Assortment of Goldsmiths and Jewellry ware, consisting of Chased and plain double and single belly'd coffee-pots."[123] At least one double-bellied and chased English example survives from Philadelphia, part of a set made for the Lloyd family by Whipham and Wright in 1763 and owned after 1768 by the Cadwaladers (see p. 80). Barrister Charles Carroll of Maryland had a similar London-made pot, marked by the date letter for 1765–66, as did Judith and Samuel Verplanck of New York, theirs dated 1762–63 (see FIG. 26, p. 75).[124] The single American example of this common English design is a coffee pot (**No. 65**) supplied by Joseph Richardson as wedding silver for Edward Penington and Sarah Shoemaker, who were married in 1754 (see also No. 75). The pot's profile is similar to that of the earlier double-bellied British coffee pot of the late 1740s and 1750s, which is lower and less statuesque than the version of the 1760s. Its unusual floral finial and shell-and-C-scroll foot rim relate to the same models.[125] A similar finial occurs on a richly chased sugar bowl marked by Richardson that is also part of the Penington silver.[126] The relief decoration of the Penington pot, ringing the lid, neck, and spout but conspicuously absent from the lower body, is more limited in application than that found on the Syng, Inch, Hall, and Petrie pots (No. 62; FIG. 29, p. 101; Nos. 63, 64), as well as on the English examples.

Edward Penington (1726–1797) was the son of Isaac and Ann Penington of Philadelphia. A Quaker merchant, he married Sarah Shoemaker (1729–1797) of nearby Germantown in 1754. Penington was a member of the Colonial Assembly in 1761, a justice in the county court, and a member of the Provincial Council in 1774. A pacifist, he was among twenty Philadelphia Quakers exiled to Virginia in 1778 for suspected collaboration with the British.[127]

65

Coffee pot, ca. 1754
Joseph Richardson, Philadelphia
Silver, H.: 11 in.
The Historical Society of Pennsylvania

Drinking and Serving Forms

TANKARDS

The tankard, a large, circular drinking vessel having a hinged lid and a cast handle, is a venerable form in the history of Anglo-American silver. Recorded in fourteenth-century accounts in England, where actual examples date from as far back as 1556,[128] tankards are also among the earliest hollow-wares made in American silver, known from the last quarter of the seventeenth century. In the colonial period, alcoholic beverages were routinely consumed in much greater quantities than they are today. Potable water was far less easily procurable and spirituous drinks were associated with social gatherings, hospitality, and conviviality. Tankards and canns—the latter a mug identical to the tankard but without the hinged lid—were used for the consumption of ale, beer, and cider.

In both England and America, vessels for alcoholic beverages were less influenced by the rococo style than other forms. In contrast with the enormous effect the style had on the more status-laden tea and coffee equipage, it made virtually no impression on the outlines of tankards or canns. Rather, the traditional cylindrical shape remained popular for tankards in New York, as it did in Boston. The advent of the style may have encouraged the adoption of the curving baluster shape seen on some tankards and more canns from the rococo era. That shape, however, was not a rococo innovation but one introduced in the earlier Queen Anne period. Though the baluster had the strongest influence in Philadelphia and can also be found in New York, in Boston it was rarely employed for tankards but reserved primarily for canns. ("Cann," the period term for the drinking vessel whether of baluster or cylindrical shape, is used today for those of baluster shape; "mug," for those cylindrical, or straight-sided.)

The only concession to the new taste in these drinking vessels is in their applied engraving and the modification of

66

Tankard, ca. 1770
Myer Myers, New York
Silver, H.: 6¾ in.
Wadsworth Atheneum

their cast handles from a single scroll to a double, with the chasing seen on tea and coffee forms noticeably absent.[129] Mugs and canns outnumber tankards, but all survive in large numbers. (The Paine service cann [see No. 49], with the Orne arms engraved in a cartouche, represents the fullest rococo expression of the form.) The three tankards chosen for inclusion in this discussion illustrate some of the finest examples of rococo engraving on these objects.

The production of flat-topped tankards continued in New York long after it was discontinued in Boston and Philadelphia. An example marked by Myer Myers (**No. 66**) has masterly engraving consisting of a large cartouche that encloses the arms of its owner, Robert Livingston. Though not identical in composition, the design of the cartouche is similar to that found on a Myers ale jug (No. 87). Myers, probably not himself the author of the decoration, may have employed the same engraver for both pieces, possibly Lewis Mears, the indentured servant with engraving skill for whom Myers advertised in 1761 (see p. 76). Whoever the engraver, he either copied a prototype faithfully or was himself familiar with English heraldry, for, using standard methods, he correctly indicated color, here the vertical and horizontal lines denoting sable, or black, in the background of the lower left, or third, quarter.[130] Such specificity is rare in American armorial engraving. The Livingston arms are unusual among American armorial devices because of the motto scroll and the legend appearing on it. When Robert Livingston (1654–1728), the first Livingston to emigrate to America, survived a shipwreck in 1694, the family was inspired to alter their crest to a ship.[131]

The tankard may date from Livingston's marriage to Mary Stevens, in 1770, as it bears the couple's initials in triangular format on the base. Robert Livingston (1746–1813) was a native of New York City, son of Judge Robert R. Livingston and his wife, Margaret Beekman. He practiced law, as did his father and grandfather, and from 1773 to 1775 served the Crown as recorder of the City of New York. Dismissed because of his patriot sympathies, he was subsequently elected to the Continental Congress, where he served from 1775 to 1776, from 1779 to 1781, and from 1784 to 1785. (In 1790, as chancellor of the State of New York, a position he held from 1777 to 1801, he administered the oath of office to President Washington.) When Jefferson, who described him as "one of the ablest of American lawyers," became president of the Republic in 1801, he appointed Livingston minister to France, in which post he was instrumental in negotiations for the Louisiana Purchase in 1803. He left public service in 1804 and returned to New York.

67

Tankard, New York, 1750–58
Attributed to William Bradford, Jr.
Pewter, H.: 7⅛ in.
Winterthur Museum

Similar in shape to the Myers tankard is an example (**No. 67**) attributed to New York pewterer William Bradford, Jr., because of its mark, *WB* with a fleur-de-lis.[132] Pewter, much less expensive than silver, was not usually used to interpret the costly rococo style. The lavish engraved cartouche on this tankard therefore makes the vessel a rare, possibly unique, survival of American rococo pewter. Since the pewterer's trade did not call for an engraver's skill, Bradford may have subcontracted the cartouche, but it is more probable that the patron commissioned it himself later in the rococo period. Engraving on pewter was easily come by: many artisans or masters working on silver also worked on pewter. (For example, Joseph Richardson recorded engraving on the metal in 1738 and Philip Syng, Jr.'s engraver-assistant, Lawrence Hubert, advertised "Engraving on Gold, Silver, or Pewter" in 1748.)[133] The unknown engraver of this cartouche, which is larger and more complex than most examples known on silver, was a highly competent man. Unfortunately, the identity of the patron, whose initials, *CS*, form a central ornamental cipher in the engraving, is also unknown.

William Bradford, Jr. (1688–1759), was born in Philadelphia, the son of a printer. The family moved to New York, where in 1725 the senior Bradford published New York's first newspaper. Young Bradford learned the printing trade and then tried the sailor's life. He settled into matrimony with Sytie Santvoort in 1716 in New York. In 1719, he was made a freeman of the city and was recorded as a pewterer. His son Cornelius continued in the trade, sharing his father's shop in Hanover Square before locating in Philadelphia by 1753.

A Philadelphia tankard marked by John Bayly (**No. 68**) demonstrates the baluster form with glorious engraving of a composition well suited to its curving profile. Though the elaborate arms elude identification, they are notable for the architectural plinth on which the bird crest is perched, as well as for the suggestion of water dripping from the lower *C*-scrolls and rocaille of the cartouche.

John Bayly advertised intermittently in Philadelphia newspapers between 1754 and 1783. The son of a Philadelphia cordwainer (shoemaker), Bayly is first recorded in 1750, when he married Jane Watkin. His earliest known advertisement, in the *Pennsylvania Gazette* of 5 September 1754, announced his goldsmithing business at the sign of the teapot in Cherry Alley. Like many of his colleagues, Bayly had other business interests; in his case, a hotel in the environs of the city, in what is now Chester Springs, that he owned from 1752 until at least 1773.[134]

68

Tankard, 1760–75
John Bayly, Philadelphia
Silver, H.: 8 in.
Wadsworth Atheneum

BOWLS

As with tankards, there is no discernible change in the shape of bowls in the rococo period.[135] Rococo decoration is all that distinguishes them from earlier counterparts. That decoration is usually engraved, as seen on a bowl with the arms of the Lardner family (**No. 69**) marked by Philip Syng, Jr. The elaborate armorial cartouche might have been done by Syng or, possibly, by one of Philadelphia's expert engravers. The arms—those of the Lardner family impaling those of the Bransons—are for the original owners, Lynford and Elizabeth (Branson) Lardner, of Philadelphia.

Lynford Lardner (1715–1774), an English wool merchant, emigrated to Philadelphia in 1740. His business partner and brother-in-law Richard Penn, proprietor of Pennsylvania, made him receiver general of the colony and a member of the Governor's Provincial Council. His estate, Somerset, was on the Delaware River near present-day Tacony, a suburb of Philadelphia. Lardner was well acquainted with Philip Syng, Jr., as both men were directors of the Library Com-

69

Bowl, 1750–70
Philip Syng, Jr., Philadelphia
Silver, Diam.: 9 in.
Philadelphia Museum of Art

pany of Philadelphia, members of the American Philosophical Society, and trustees of the College of Philadelphia. In 1749, Lardner married Elizabeth Branson (1732–1761), daughter of the Philadelphia Quaker merchant William Branson. A pair of canns, also marked by Syng, has armorial engraving similar to that of the bowl, suggesting that all three pieces were made for the couple's marriage.[136]

Unique on American bowls from the rococo period is the chasing found on a New York example marked by Richard Van Dyck (**No. 70**). The bowl is virtually covered by a flat chased design consisting of flowers and rocaille enhanced by fine engraving and two cartouches, one centered on each side, the whole contained within a shaped lower border of *C*-scrolls and curves. The initials *GP* engraved in one of the cartouches for the original owner are unidentified. The decoration has been compared to delicate chasing found on an Irish silver bowl.[137] The prototype for the bowl, however, might have been made in England, since the same design occurs in English rococo silver.[138] In 1768, James Beekman

(see p. 155) recorded purchasing a "Silver chaisd Bowl" from Simon Coolley,[139] probably the silversmith Simeon Cooley, who, spelling his name "Coley," advertised himself "from London" in 1767.[140] Whatever the design source, Van Dyck was, or had access to, a chaser accomplished in this style; the same type of decoration occurs on two of Van Dyck's tankards,[141] though such decoration is common on neither bowls nor tankards from the period.

Very little silver survives by the maker Richard Van Dyck (1717–1770), son of the more famous silversmith Peter Van Dyck. Richard, also known as an engraver and importer, had a shop in Hanover Square. In 1746, he was commissioned to engrave the bills of credit used to help finance an expedition into Canada during King George's War (1744–48). Van Dyck advertised imports in 1753, including wrought plate, looking glasses, sconces, pictures, and best "French oyl."[142] He married Elizabeth Strang, of Rye; their son Henry was a graduate of King's College and one of the first Episcopal ministers ordained after the Revolution.[143]

70

Bowl, 1755–70
Richard Van Dyck, New York
Silver, Diam.: 7⅜ in.
Garvan Collection, Yale University

71

Salver, ca. 1761
Paul Revere, Boston
Silver, Diam.: 13⅛ in.
Museum of Fine Arts, Boston

SALVERS

Engraving also embellishes the finest rococo salvers. "Salver" is the period term for a flat serving form, distinguished from a tray because it is elevated either on a base or on multiple feet. A salver (**No. 71**) made in the shop of Paul Revere for Lucretia Chandler is of typical English border pattern and shape and is enhanced by the Chandler coat of arms engraved within a rococo cartouche. The salver, along with a sugar dish and a cream pot marked by Revere (No. 58), was made for Lucretia in honor of her wedding, in 1761, to John Murray. Although Revere also engraved the Chandler arms for the bookplate (see No. 17) of Gardiner Chandler, brother to Lucretia, it is worth noting that there he altered slightly the design of the cartouche.

Three salvers from New York, among the most outstanding examples of the form, illustrate three variations in border design. The most typical is that on one marked by Myer Myers (**No. 72**)—a shaped hexagonal design with gadrooned rim, common prior to the advent of rococo design. What sets the salver apart is its extraordinary engraving. A departure from the usual cartouche enclosing arms, it covers almost the entire surface in an illustration of an allegorical scene within a shaped surround over a commemorative inscription, the design bordered above and below by Latin phrases.[144] The scene consists of an angel crowning an allegorical female figure symbolizing justice (righteousness), while another angel showers her with gold from a cornucopia, the whole illuminated by the radiance of the sun (representing the presence of God), on which is engraved "Ps:34:15,Ve," a reference to the Psalm depicted: "The eyes of the Lord are upon the righteous, and his ears are open unto their cry." The size, quality, and rococo design of the engraving make it the most arresting of any on American silver of this period. Might the engraver have been Myers's runaway indentured servant of 1761, Lewis Mears (see p. 76)?

The salver was especially commissioned as a gift to Theodorus Van Wyck (1718–1776), as confirmed by its English inscription: "In testimony of exemplary justice and as a small acknowledgment for kindness received, this plate is humbly presented to [Theodorus] Van Wyck by his friends [Samuel] Schuyler, [William] Lupton and [Cornelius] Swits." The donors recorded were all related to Van Wyck, the last two by marriage to his nieces Johanna and Catherine Schuyler. In 1752, on the death of Brandt Schuyler, father of Samuel, Johanna, and Catherine, Theodorus assisted his sister, Magretta Van Wyck Schuyler, in rearing her children. The salver was an expression of the children's gratitude.

72

Salver, ca. 1768
Myer Myers, New York
Silver, Diam.: 12 in.
Collection of Philip Van Rensselaer Van Wyck

73

Salver, 1765–70
John Heath, New York
Silver, Diam.: 15⅛ in.
Winterthur Museum

74

Salver, 1754–69
Daniel Christian Fueter, New York
Silver, Diam.: 15⅝ in.
The Metropolitan Museum of Art

A second New York salver, this one marked by John Heath (**No. 73**), is directly related to an English model. The border design, not commonly found in American silver, is identical to that of a London salver from the 1760s, made for the De Peyster family of New York. It consists of standard lobed gadrooning but is embellished by an inner border of shell-like ruffles punctuated by rosettes alternating with acanthus leaves. Two other New York salvers also have this unusual border design.[145]

Completing the salver's rococo presentation are the Schuyler family arms, engraved in the center within a cartouche of C-scrolls, foliage, and rocaille. The salver, like the English model, rests on four claw-and-ball feet. The Schuyler family, founded in the colonies in 1651, is closely associated with Albany. Among its most famous eighteenth-century members was Major General Philip Schuyler (1733-1804), veteran of the revolutionary war, member of the Continental Congress, and later a United States senator.

John Heath married Edith Pell in 1760 and became a freeman of New York in 1761. In 1763, Heath advertised a house for sale at "Van Gelder's alley in the Broadway," noting that his shop was in Wall Street.[146] In addition to this salver, a punch bowl survives from his hand, also beautifully engraved with a rococo armorial for Pierre Van Cortlandt. Heath's bill for the punch bowl charged Van Cortlandt one pound sterling for engraving "A Cot Armes & a Crist."[147]

The third salver in this impressive New York group was marked by Daniel Christian Fueter (**No. 74**) and made for a member of the prominent Provost family of French Huguenot extraction. Of the three salvers, this has the most vigorous border, defined by bold peaks and curves and rimmed with gadrooning. The Provost family arms grace the elaborate central cartouche.

Chased decoration is extremely rare on American salvers. Not surprisingly, the only instances known occur on two examples from Philadelphia.[148] The finer of the two (**No. 75**), dating to 1754 and marked by Philip Syng, Jr., was, like the Richardson coffee pot (No. 65), part of the wedding silver of Edward and Sarah Penington (see p. 104). The salver, set on three cast scroll feet, is rimmed with a highly intricate cast border of asymmetrical raffles, scrolls, and foliage. The interior surface is exquisitely chased with raffles, flowers, leafage, C-scrolls, and diapered panels in a broad band encircling a central engraved cipher. So similar is the chased decoration to that of the Syng coffee pot made for the Galloway family (No. 62) that one may presume they were decorated by the same unidentified chaser.

75

Salver, ca. 1754
Philip Syng, Jr., Philadelphia
Silver, Diam.: 8½ in.
The Historical Society of Pennsylvania

SAUCEBOATS

Most of the period's sauceboats resemble the pair made by Revere for the Paine service (see No. 49), a form established by English examples in the prerococo period and accommodated to the new style by the addition of shell and scroll castings at handle and feet. The outstanding American sauceboats are a pair (**No. 76**) supplied by Richard Humphreys to George Emlen (1741–1812), a wealthy Quaker merchant who married Sarah Fishbourne (1756–1823) in 1775.

Instead of the typical three-footed base, each of the Humphreys pair is elegantly uplifted on a pedestal foot having fluted, curving borders. The shaped design of the foot is repeated in the rim of the vessel, where it is edged with gadrooning to correspond to the fluting below. The rim resolves into a graceful, sculptural scrolled terminal at the handle juncture, and a cast scrolled handle completes the composition and balances the mass of the pouring spout. Superbly proportioned and gracefully designed, the two sauceboats are further enlivened by the addition of engraved cartouches enclosing the script initials *GE*, for the original owner.

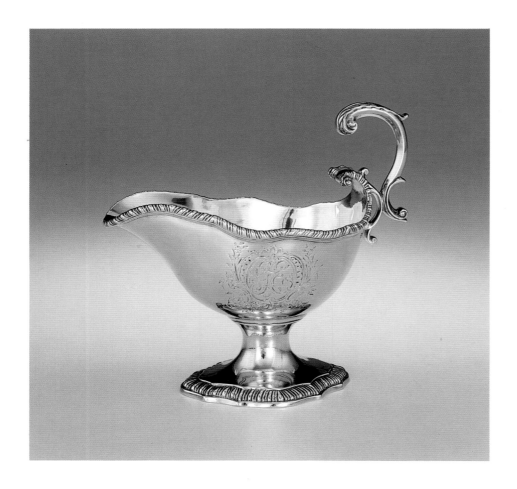

76

One of a pair of sauceboats, 1770–80
Richard Humphreys, Philadelphia
Silver, H.: 6¾ in.
Private collection

Rare Forms

Some of the finest achievements in American rococo silver are extremely rare forms. Though a number of them are related to the ritual of tea and the serving of meals, they are still so scarce as to warrant inclusion here. Silver dish rings, cake baskets, and teakettles, and gold shoe buckles and snuff boxes were luxuries, even among those who might regard a silver teapot as a social necessity. The very selection of such forms was an act of conspicuous consumption on the part of the owners; that the rococo style was chosen for their interpretation followed in natural progression. It is therefore not surprising that engraving, the most modest kind of rococo ornament, is, when present, overshadowed by more pretentious, and more expensive, chased, pierced, or cast decoration.

Moreover, it is among these precious, singular forms that the rare incidence of gold is found. In the eighteenth century, the terms "goldsmith" and "silversmith," referring to an artisan who worked in precious metals, were interchangeable. Even in England, where the title of the silversmiths' guild was the "Worshipful Company of Goldsmiths," members seldom had the opportunity to work in solid gold, more frequently using it only in measured quantities for gilding objects of silver (a technique practiced infrequently in the colonies). Without exception, eighteenth-century American gold objects are small, personal accessories, such as buttons, shoe buckles, or snuff boxes, attributes reserved for the very wealthy.

One of the most engaging forms in American gold is the whistle and bells, an ornament popular in Europe in the seventeenth and eighteenth centuries. Made for a child's amusement and complete with a branch of coral (considered as having protective powers) for teething, it is depicted in paintings hanging from the small owner's waist.[149] Gold and silver examples imported from London are documented in colonial newspaper advertisements.[150] Joseph Richardson

77

Whistle and bells, 1755–68
Nicholas Roosevelt, New York
Gold; coral, H.: 6⅛ in.
The Metropolitan Museum of Art

ordered both plain and chased "Correll & Bells," usually with the specification "8 Bells to Each." Between 1758 and 1773, he sent for seventy-six plain and fifty-four "chast"; on 27 June 1759, he ordered "2 Chast Correls with 8 Bells Gilt with Gold," the only two so specified. Occasionally, he also requested "Correll Pieces for Whisels & Bells," evidently for toys made in his own shop.[151] Paul Revere recorded a "Silver childs Wisel" in 1762 (though the form is otherwise virtually absent from his ledgers), and, on 18 August 1770, Philip Syng, Jr., received forty shillings ninepence from John Cadwalader for a whistle and bells.[152]

Only four examples in gold by American artisans are known.[153] A gold whistle marked by Nicholas Roosevelt has survived without provenance, but the lucky recipient got an extravagant plaything (**No. 77**). Such trinkets, whether in gold or silver, were usually the gift of a doting relative,[154] often at the child's christening. The form lends itself to a style that seeks to charm and amuse. The Roosevelt example, which retains six of its original eight bells, is meticulously decorated with rococo flowers, leafage, rocaille, and a fountain, on a stippled ground, all framed in panels and reserves of shells and *C*-scrolls. A child's pleasure in these precious toys is reflected in *The Rambler*, where Samuel Johnson remarked: "Of all the toys with which children are delighted, I valued only my coral."[155]

Nicholas Roosevelt (1715–1769) was born in New York and probably apprenticed to Cornelius Wynkoop (b. 1701). He was married twice; first to Catherine Confoort, in 1737, then to Elizabeth Thurman, in 1754. He was active as a silversmith from 1737 through 1768. In January 1769, he advertised for let property on the wharf that included a "roomy and convenient house, with seven fire-places," as well as a silversmith's shop, tools of the trade, and "a parcel of ready made silver . . . which he will sell very reasonable, as he intends declining business, and to move in the Country in the spring."[156] Nicholas, the grandson of the first Roosevelt to settle in New Amsterdam, was related to the presidential Roosevelts, who descended from his brother.

A gold shoe buckle marked by Myer Myers (**No. 78**) further illustrates the rococo style's suitability for accentuating the importance of small, valuable objects. Its cast and chased decoration, formed variously of interwoven leafage, flowers, and scrolls, would have glittered in the light, drawing attention to this ornate, ground-level accessory.

While American gold examples are extremely rare, large quantities of silver buckles were made on both sides of the Atlantic for American buyers. A single London order placed in 1759 by Joseph Richardson included 110 pairs, but the production of his own shop would appear to have been far

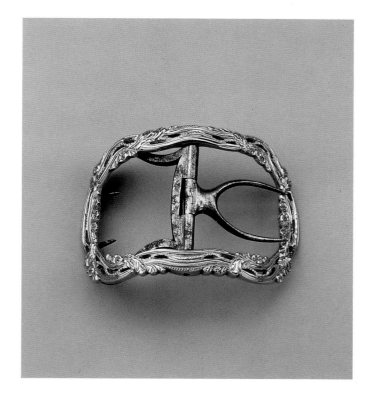

78

Shoe buckle, 1755–75
Myer Myers, New York
Gold; steel, L.: 2⅜ in.
Garvan Collection, Yale University

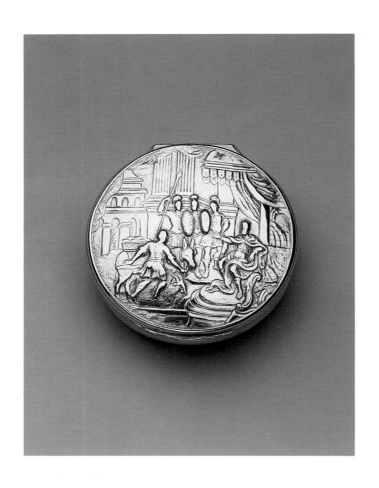

79

Snuff box, 1755–75
Myer Myers, New York
Gold, Diam.: 2⅜ in.
The Metropolitan Museum of Art

in excess of that figure. In 1761, he ordered seventeen gross (2,448) of steel chapes and tongues in varying sizes for making both shoe and knee buckles.[157] The personal quality of the buckle form made it particularly suitable as a gift. The Myers example, its steel chape and tongue probably imported from London, is engraved "The Gift of Robt. Arcdeckne Esqr. to Danl. McCormick." McCormick (1742–1834) was an illustrious New York banker who later became an alderman of the East Ward.[158]

Another luxury was the snuff box, a rare form employed in the aristocratic practice of inhaling the costly tobacco-derived substance. American snuff boxes of gold are extremely scarce, since their size required more of the precious metal than smaller forms such as buttons or buckles. The elaborately chased example marked by Myer Myers (**No. 79**) was probably created as a special gift; its biblical iconography and Myers's Jewish heritage suggest that it may have been commissioned for use in a synagogue with snuff or perhaps with spice, as on the Day of Atonement.[159] Its primary decoration, a depiction of David before Saul, recounted in I Samuel 16: 17–22, fills the box's cover, unimpeded by traditional panels or decorative devices.[160] The scene itself is narrative, but its high-relief chasing and a rococo diapered panel contained within an *S*-scroll at the edge of the box (about four o'clock) signals its stylistic debt. On the bottom is an unusual rococo cartouche, in design vigorous and anarchic in comparison with typical English examples and, like the unfettered cover scene, evocative of Continental interpretations.

More English in stylistic derivation is a silver snuff box (**No. 80**) with the mark of Joseph Richardson. The precious vessel features the asymmetrical arrangement characteristic of the mature rococo style, as illustrated by a cartouche composed of *C*-scrolls enclosing a basket of fruit and surrounded by more *C*-scrolls, ragged shells, and festoons, all contained within the box's serpentine-shaped lid. Here demonstrated in microcosm are the same assured handling, fluid composition, and sophisticated vocabulary used more extensively on a tour de force from the Richardson shop, the Plumsted teakettle on stand (No. 88). In shape and decoration, the box is similar to one documented from 1757, which also bears Richardson's mark. In 1759, the silversmith ordered from London three "Chast Silver Snuf Boxes Gilt inside with Gold."[161]

Though chasing characterizes the fullest expression of the style, piercing was an equally suitable form of rococo decoration on appropriate forms. More functional than decorative on earlier eighteenth-century American silver—caster

80

Snuff box, 1755–70
Joseph Richardson, Philadelphia
Silver, L.: 3 in.
Private collection

81

Basket, 1754–69
Daniel Christian Fueter, New York
Silver, L.: 14⅞ in.
Museum of Fine Arts, Boston

lids, braziers, and strainer (slotted) spoons—it came into its own with the advent of the rococo. The group of highly accomplished luxury forms that ensued have elaborate piercing that far exceeds any utilitarian concern. Baskets, dish rings, and fish slices, in addition to coasters and salts, manifest not only the confluence of style and social convention but also the increasing prosperity in the colonies, which enabled patrons to commission such indulgences. The taste for lacy hand-piercing, admirably suited to the intricacies of the rococo mode, was adopted first in England, thence in America.

That most American pierced silver was made in New York suggests the existence of a specialist in such work there: all the piercing represented in these pages comes from that city. Though the majority is from one shop—that of Myer Myers—the most sophisticated piece is a basket (**No. 81**) marked by Daniel Christian Fueter and made for Richard Harison, a delegate to the Constitutional Convention in 1788 and a prominent New York attorney whom Washington appointed the first United States district attorney for New York in 1789. Both in design and quality of execution, the basket—its heavy cast border and light openwork body serving as foils for each other; the movement expressed in its shaped rim repeated in the feet and handles—could easily be mistaken as London made. Every element from its curving feet to its contoured handle expresses a theme of the rococo repertoire. The body is pierced with a delicate foliate-and-*C*-scroll design, and cutwork on the rim, handle, and leg junctures is complemented with intricate castings. The inner surface of the bottom is engraved with an elaborate rococo cartouche containing the Harison arms (see detail). The cast border decoration of rocaille, *C*-scrolls, and fruit-and-flower festoons, perhaps the best example of its kind in American rococo silver, is rivaled in achievement only by the raffle-framed female masks that adorn the basket's handle. This incidence of figural relief decoration is common in European rococo silver but rare in American interpretations. Of the more than fifty examples of American silver illustrated in these pages, only two display human allusions: this basket and the cream pot marked by Philip Hulbeart (No. 55). Among these and other known depictions, including a cherub on a whistle and bells also marked by Fueter, the two Fueter pieces illustrate the most masterly command of integral human references in American rococo silver.[162]

   Though baskets appeared in English silver late in the 1500s, they did not become a well-known table accessory until the rococo period, when their combination of piercing and casting made them an ideal exponent of the frothy style. The Fueter example is not dissimilar to those marked by the

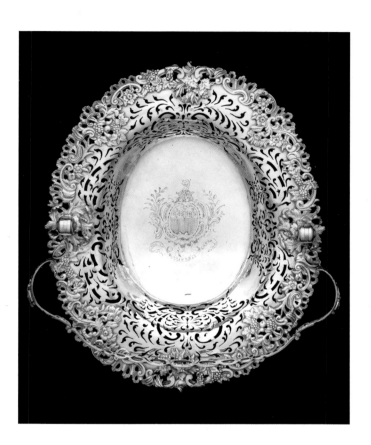

London silversmith Paul de Lamerie, the French Huguenot whose shop is renowned for works that characterize the finest English rococo. At least one Lamerie basket was owned in the colonies. It was ordered in 1743, along with other wedding silver, for the Philadelphia merchant David Franks and his bride.[163] Other London-made baskets were owned in the colonies by the Hancock family of Boston, the Byrd family of Virginia, and the Lloyd family of Maryland.[164]

   Fueter, European trained and arriving from London at an auspicious moment, probably introduced rococo-style silver to New York. He may also have been responsible for setting the fashion for pierced decoration in the city's silver.

82

Basket, ca. 1756
Myer Myers, New York
Silver, L.: 14½ in.
The Metropolitan Museum of Art

The only other American rococo basket known (**No. 82**) was supplied by Myer Myers to Susannah and Samuel Cornell of New York, whose initials, *SSC*, are engraved on its interior. Myers's commission for the Cornells included a pierced dish ring, a coffee pot, a cann, and a pair of pierced wine coasters.[165] Though members of New York's aristocracy were more likely to have imported silver such as the basket and the dish ring, the variety of forms from the same maker suggests that, like the Paine service (No. 49) from the shop of Paul Revere, they were ordered by a bridegroom as a gift to his bride.[166] The theory is supported by later engraving on the coffee pot, which indicates that Cornell gave it to Susannah in the year of their marriage. The knowledge that a third of the American pierced work surviving from the rococo period belonged to the Cornells is a cogent illustration of just how vital the patronage of a very few affluent families was to the development of American rococo silver.[167]

Samuel Cornell (1731–1781) married Susannah Mabson (1731/32–1778) in 1756. Cornell, a wealthy New York merchant of Loyalist sympathies, moved his family to New Bern, North Carolina, early in the 1770s. He was a member of His Majesty's Council of that state in 1775, when he strongly advised the governor to outlaw Whig meetings. Cornell was in England during the outbreak of the Revolution, but he returned to New York and set sail for New Bern under a flag of truce. On his arrival, he was denied reentry and reunion with his family unless he took an oath of allegiance to the state, then under Whig rule. He refused and, while still in the harbor, made an effort to save his property by deeding it to his children. He then obtained permission to remove his family to New York. His conveyances of property were not honored, and his holdings were confiscated by the state and sold.[168]

Unlike the Fueter basket, where the maker has used every means of rococo decoration at his command, the

Myers basket relies solely on piercing for ornamental drama. Its elaborate filigree body is contained visually between a simple arching handle and a circular foot that are rococo in decoration but not in shape, and the castings at the rim, foot, and handle junctures are composed of routine gadrooning. The basket was created at a time when such expanses of openwork were virtually unknown; Fueter, perhaps more accustomed to the technique, treated piercing as one element in a dialogue. Whereas the Myers example is an exemplification of piercing in American silver, the Fueter basket is a triumph of rococo design that utilizes piercing.

In its cutout decoration, the Myers basket includes the three stylistic variations of English rococo explained in Chippendale's *Director*—French, or Modern, Chinese, and Gothic. Reserves of French scrollwork alternate with diapered panels of Chinese latticework, and the baseband is pierced with a design of Gothic quatrefoils and diamonds. (The piercing on the Fueter basket, less intricate, is limited to the French taste.)

Dish rings, used under hot serving dishes, require piercing to ventilate the heat away from the table. The only example known in American silver is one Myers supplied to the Cornells (FIG. 30), though wicker and pewter examples are recorded.[169] The form, which occurred in England early in the eighteenth century but was replaced by the dish cross[170] in the 1740s, remained especially popular in Ireland. On Irish rococo examples, the design is usually naturalistic, with chasing to articulate leaves and flowers and with the occasional application of cast decoration. Imported Dublin examples may have come to the attention of either Myers or the Cornells, but it is more likely that Myers contracted with a foreign piercer who may also have suggested the form. A dish ring was more adaptable to the sizes of serving dishes when it was composed of two silver circles of varying diameters, as is the Myers example. Complementing its shape is a medial band of scrollwork framed within Gothic diamond-and-lozenge decoration. The initials *SSC* for the Cornells are engraved on an applied heart-shaped shield; both rim and foot are undecorated. As does the Myers basket, the dish ring relies solely on piercing for its aesthetic effect.

Though the Myers basket and dish ring, both exceedingly ornate in the context of American silver, are conservative in comparison with British models, the fish slice with Myers's mark (**No. 83**) is virtually identical to examples popular in England in the 1760s. Its pierced design, composed of diapering and foliate scrolls enhanced with engraving, is similar to that found on English prototypes, as is the splayed shell

FIGURE 30. *Dish ring*, ca. 1756. Myer Myers, New York. Silver, Diam.: 8⅞ in. (22.5 cm.); H.: 4⅜ in. (11.1 cm.). Yale University Art Gallery, The Mabel Brady Garvan Collection (1936.136)

with openwork ribs that adorns the handle juncture. In its vigor and flare, the shell represents a marked progression from the tight, restrained shell castings at the junctures of the Myers basket. His shop produced at least one other similar slice,[171] but no other American examples are known from the rococo period. The form itself, however, is documented in the colonies: the records of William Byrd, of Westover, Virginia, mention a fish slice in 1769, with no indication of its origin, and the Tayloes of Virginia had one made in London in 1767 that was engraved with the family arms.[172]

American silversmiths rarely followed the English practice of applying weighty, expensive castings purely for decoration, but instead used the process where necessary for appendages such as handles, handle junctures and terminals, rims, and feet, which required solidity and reinforcement. A ladle (**No. 84**) marked by Pieter de Riemer demonstrates that usage while at the same time exploiting the capacity for ornamentation inherent in the technique.

The Riemer ladle, unique in American silver and elaborate even by English standards, was probably inspired by a Continental example exhibiting the more florid character of the French or northern European rococo. The fluted chasing of the bowl is conventional, but the handle terminal, cast as a large, imposing cartouche, is extraordinary. Though cartouches decorate the handles of most English flatware forms, here the maker has employed the device as a separate sculptural element by composing it of flower-strewn raffles framing a central reserve that terminates in a strikingly asymmetrical scroll. Pendent flowers and rocaille adorn the back of the cartouche (see detail), where the initials *R* over *RS* are engraved for the original owners, Richard (1717/18–1763) and Sarah (Bogart) Ray (1728–1781). The script monogram *CR* on the front, inside the cartouche, was added for Cornelius Ray (1755–1827), who inherited the ladle from his parents. Its subsequent descent in the family is recorded on the back of the bowl in engraving added about 1912.[173] The Ray family, prominent in New York business and society, was founded in America in the seventeenth century by John Ray, of Exeter, England.

A more complex use of casting is to be found on rococo cruet stands, as exemplified by one, made for the Van Voorhis family in the shop of Daniel Christian Fueter, that is decorated with cast scrolls, shells, and cartouches (**No. 85**). Several American rococo cruet stands, made by both Philadelphia and New York makers, are known.[174] All have the same general design, patterned after English prototypes well documented in the colonies—primary decoration consisting of a cast central cartouche, a scrolled handle and legs,

83

Fish slice, 1755–75
Myer Myers, New York
Silver, L.: 14⅛ in.
Wadsworth Atheneum

84

Ladle, ca. 1763
Pieter de Riemer, New York
Silver, L.: 13⅝ in.
Private collection

and cast shell feet. In 1757, George Washington acquired an example made by Jabez Daniel of London; other London-made stands were owned by Benjamin Faneuil and by the Apthorps in Boston, by the Brownes in Salem, and by the Chases in Maryland.[175] The standard design (known as the Warwick type, possibly because one made for the earl of Warwick in 1715–16 was once thought to be the earliest)[176] called for two glass cruets, for vinegar and oil, and three silver casters, for sugar, mustard, and pepper. The stand therefore consisted of a framework with five adjoining rings to contain those vessels and two smaller rings at either end to hold the cruet covers when the cruets were in use. Although several American examples of the form survive, none are known with domestic fittings; those that remain intact, including this one, have English casters and cruets ordered from London. As requested by the Philadelphia silversmith Joseph Richardson, these were sometimes "plain" and sometimes "Double Bellyed"; in a letter of 1760, Richardson even ordered a "Silver Caster frame with a Sett of Double Bellyed Casters Neatly Chast with Ground Glass Cruits tipt with Silver."[177] The earliest reference to stands in Revere's ledgers was in 1781, when he recorded a "Silver Frame for Casters"[178] but made no mention of accompanying casters. The double-bellied and chased casters on the Fueter stand are marked by Samuel Wood of London and are date-marked 1752–53. The cartouches on both casters and stand are engraved with the Van Voorhis family crest.

Only two American snuffer stands are known, one of which was marked by Philip Syng, Jr. (**No. 86**); the other, by Myer Myers. The complete form consisted of a stand, or tray, holding a pair of snuffers, a scissorslike device used for trimming the burnt wicks on candles.[179] A specialized form of this nature was not necessarily of silver; most American snuffers and stands were made of a base metal. Paul Revere recorded making a "Pr. of Snuffers & Snuff Dish" in 1762; John Cadwalader of Philadelphia, according to an inventory of the contents of his silver closet taken in 1771, owned at least two snuffers and stands, one with "snuffers part silver part steel," the other "all silver."[180]

Syng's example, now without its snuffers, has a particularly capricious air, the result of the plenitude of cast decoration applied around its hand-wrought surface: the shaped profile is rimmed by *C*-scrolls and leafage embellished with four ragged, asymmetrical shells, one centered on each side. Uplifted on four scrolled pad feet, the stand is memorable for the unusual raffled *C*-scroll that surmounts its scrolling handle. The cast border decoration is similar to that found on the most famous work from Syng's shop, an inkstand commissioned by the Pennsylvania Assembly in 1752 and

85

Cruet stand, 1754–69
Daniel Christian Fueter, New York
Silver, H.: 10 in.
Historic Deerfield, Inc.

later used by the signers of the Declaration of Independence and of the Constitution.[181] Though it is engraved in the center with the crest of the Hamilton family, and may have been owned by Andrew Hamilton, its provenance is not recorded.

Most of the rare forms discussed in these pages have fallen into groupings by ornament. With the possible exception of the Fueter basket (No. 81), each example has expressed the rococo style primarily through one of three techniques: chasing, piercing, or casting. Hollowware forms allowed rococo silversmiths greater latitude to integrate various types of decoration. As demonstrated by the basket, where cast and pierced decoration are combined to stunning effect, the results can be even greater expressions of mature rococo design.

An ale jug marked by Myer Myers (**No. 87**) is a splendid example of rococo hollowware, though the form itself is not a rococo innovation. Here, the commanding eleven-inch height enhances the effect of the superb engraving and castings. Though jugs, tankards, and canns did not echo the double-bellied profiles found on tea and coffee forms, the baluster shape introduced in the previous period lent itself gracefully to the addition of rococo ornament. This jug is engraved with the arms of David Clarkson (1726-1782) of New York, probably the "jug with cover" referred to in his will as the "Share" of his daughter Ann Margaret Clarkson.[182] The arms are contained within a luxuriant asymmetrical cartouche surmounted by a winged-griffin crest. The sweeping curve of the body is balanced by a vigorous double C-scroll handle marked by rococo castings at the upper and lower junctures. A three-dimensional raffle cocked on the lid's hinge serves as a thumbpiece and adds to the visual success of the vessel. Both the thumbpiece and the upper handle juncture are elaborate rococo castings that complement the expansive engraving. Another jug from the Myers shop, of similar size and shape and with identical handle and upper juncture, is at the Henry Ford Museum. In its lack of rococo thumbpiece and armorial engraving, however, it falls short of the Clarkson example.[183]

The most monumental form produced in American rococo silver was the teakettle, or tea urn, two variations on the same theme. It is suitable that the only rococo examples known are from New York and Philadelphia, the two centers of high-style colonial silver in the rococo taste.[184] The kettle, designed to hold hot water for replenishing teapots, was introduced into the tea equipage in England late in the seventeenth century. More common in base metals, the form traditionally included a stand furnished with a spirit lamp for

86

Snuffer stand, 1750–70
Philip Syng, Jr., Philadelphia
Silver, L.: 7⅜ in.
The Metropolitan Museum of Art

87

Ale jug, 1755–75
Myer Myers, New York
Silver, H.: 11¾ in.
Private collection

heating the water. Intended to be lifted for pouring, the vessel was provided with a spout and a swinging handle either made of wood or wrapped with wicker for insulation. In the mid-eighteenth century, the teakettle began to be replaced by the tea urn in England, though the transition occurred somewhat later in the colonies. (James Beekman of New York recorded purchasing a "New Kettle & Stand" in April 1766; in May 1773, he acquired a "Tea Urn.")[185] Both versions fulfilled the same function, but the urn differed from the kettle in that it was designed to remain stationary on the table, the hot water dispensed through one or more spigots, thus relieving the host or hostess from lifting a heavy vessel and directing its contents into small teapots.

A tea urn marked by Ephraim Brasher (FIG. 31) is the earliest example of its kind in American silver and the only rococo one known. Though such three-legged vessels are French in origin, they were copied in contemporary English silver (see No. 46). The Brasher urn was probably patterned after an English coffee pot, undoubtedly as a commission for an unidentified patron whose initials, *JDW*, are framed in a grand cartouche engraved on the side. The design suggests that the maker was neither well versed in the production of such urns nor in possession of casting molds exactly suited to them.[186] He evidently borrowed molds from more common forms to create this unique piece, its feet composed of shells and scrolls that were part of the period's casting vocabulary, its handles of the type occurring on jugs, ewers, and two-handled cups, and its finial typical of that found on coffee pots, including one with Brasher's mark.[187]

The urn is technically competent, but because it was not designed and created as an integral piece, it betrays an inconsistency of scale and decoration, particularly at the feet and the handles. When plotted correctly, the large upper curve of such *S*-curved handles swung out well beyond the smaller lower reverse curve, the scroll tip of the lower juncture kept well inside a vertical line dropped from the outermost point of the upper curve. Here, however, the scrolling terminals abut such a line. The feet are equally disproportionate to such a massive vessel. The maker's probable unfamiliarity with the form may explain the placing of the handles and the engraving without regard for the tripartite arrangement of the feet and the spigots below.[188] The urn's naiveté notwithstanding, the castings and the engraving are above reproach. The urn itself is imbued with rococo spirit, movement, and sprightliness, and remains one of the most ambitious efforts in American silver.

Ephraim Brasher (1744–1810), a silversmith of Dutch descent, was born in New York and worked in the city throughout his career. He married Anne Gilbert, sister of New York silversmith William Gilbert, in 1766, and was

FIGURE 31. *Tea urn*, 1765–75. Ephraim Brasher, New York. Silver, H.: 17¼ in. (43.8 cm.). The Art Institute of Chicago, Gift of the Antiquarian Society (1959.58)

88

Teakettle on stand, 1745–55
Joseph Richardson, Philadelphia
Silver, H.: 14¾ in.
Garvan Collection, Yale University

recorded as a member of the Gold and Silver Smith's Society in 1786; his name appeared in the city directories from 1786 to 1807. In 1792, he was an assayer for the United States Mint.

More accomplished than the Brasher essay in the form is the unparalleled teakettle on stand marked by Joseph Richardson (**No. 88**; see also ill. opp. p. 71). Unique in the oeuvre from Richardson's shop, it ranks as the greatest accomplishment in American rococo silver. Every bit the equal of outstanding London examples, Richardson's teakettle on stand is a unified composition of form and ornament, in every detail fully expressive of the highly elaborate style.

The Richardson masterpiece (which is absent from his accounts and his orders from London) was made for Clement Plumsted (1680–1745), former mayor of Philadelphia, or for his third wife and widow, Mary (Curry) Plumsted (d. 1755), who bequeathed it in her will to her husband's granddaughter Elizabeth Plumsted. Richardson had long had business relations with Plumsted, from whom he acquired property and for whom in 1737 he witnessed a business transaction.[189]

The probable inspiration for the fluent handling of such a rare design is the Franks family teakettle on stand (FIG. 27, p. 77), marked in 1744–45 by that master of English rococo silver, Paul de Lamerie, for David and Margaret (Evans) Franks of Philadelphia. The kettle was part of a tea service, from which also survive a basket and a waste bowl, all displaying the same arms—those of Franks impaling those of Evans. David Franks had two brothers who lived in London, one or both of whom probably commissioned Lamerie to supply the service in honor of the couple's marriage, in 1743.[190]

The Richardson kettle is identical in form and composition to the Lamerie example. The two, differing in height by less than half an inch, are beautifully proportioned double-bellied vessels uplifted on scroll-footed stands, display chasing, casting, and engraving in the same places, and vary only in ornamentation. The iconography on the Lamerie kettle, true to the silversmith's style, is more animalistic and fantastic—lion's masks and paws, demicherubs and cherub masks, human masks, snails, and eagles with outstretched wings. The less exotic vocabulary on the Richardson kettle is composed primarily of C-scrolls, shells, flowers, leafage, and rocaille. It does, however, possess a few exceptional elements, perhaps the chaser's response to the Lamerie animal references: a bird's head forming the spout, winged masks on the stand, and a demilion draped over the cartouche. Tucked among the foliage, peering out from behind C-scrolls, they contribute a feral drama of surprise and move-

ment that is unique in American rococo silver, where the incidence of chased fauna, while more common than that of human references, remains a rarity in comparison with its frequency in English work. Other occurrences represented in this book are birds on the Riemer cream pot, on a Revere teapot, and on the Lansing sugar dish (Nos. 48, 51, 57). The maker may have obtained molds for his kettle-on-stand castings from a carver who also exercised his ornamental talents on Philadelphia rococo furniture. It is unlikely that Richardson would have had occasion to use most of those molds for another client, which would have further increased the kettle's expense.

A commission of that kind was a once-in-a-career opportunity for an American silversmith. The quality of design and chasing on the Plumsted kettle makes it the supreme example of American rococo silver. Though Richardson may have wrought the form, the chasing, which bespeaks European training and experience, was probably the accomplishment of an immigrant silversmith working in Philadelphia.

LGB

FURNITURE

Furnituremaking was one of the most universal of colonial enterprises. Not an industry susceptible to supervision from England, it was carried on domestically in small shops by no more than a handful of craftsmen at any one time. Endless supplies of suitable woods were readily at hand, a factor that, when combined with the cost of shipping, meant that imports were seldom competitive with local products. In urban centers, cabinetmakers labored year round at their craft, employing journeymen and apprentices and subcontracting such specialist activities as carving. In rural areas, cabinetmaking tended to be a winter occupation undertaken by farmers having little opportunity to develop specialized skills.

Furniture is made of primary and secondary woods: the primary, that which is visible and finished; the secondary, that which is used for the unseen inner parts. Mahogany, shipped in huge logs from Honduras and the islands of the Caribbean, was the preferred primary wood in both England and America during the second half of the eighteenth century. As well as for its beauty and the ease with which it could be worked, it was chosen for its strength and imperviousness to rot and insect infestation. Most of the other woods, both primary and secondary, used in the colonies were native to North America; it is their presence that helps to identify the place of origin of individual pieces. In Pennsylvania and Virginia, the local primary wood was walnut, which was not so very different from mahogany; in New England, it was maple or cherry, both almost too hard to carve. In America, furniture was mostly fabricated out of solid pieces of primary wood rather than out of veneers over a secondary-wood carcass, as in England. That manner of construction saved on labor and also withstood the dramatic shifts in temperature and humidity of the native climate. In New England, the favorite secondary wood was northeastern white pine; in the middle colonies, tulip poplar and yellow pine; in the South, cypress. Wherever wood was to be carved and gilded or painted (as with frames for pictures and looking glasses), the universal American preference was for northeastern white pine because of its lightness, strength, and carvability.

Most furniture was assembled using two basic joinery techniques, the mortise and tenon and the dovetail. Structural elements such as stiles and rails were united by cutting away part of the end of one member to form a tongue, or tenon, which was then inserted into a slot, or mortise, cut into the other member. Boards were joined at right angles by fashioning their ends into interlocking wedge-shaped keys, called dovetails.

In American furniture, the rococo is manifested in the art of the carver. The signature of the style is the realistic portrayal of elements from nature: leafage and raffles, flowers and fruit, shells and rocaille work. All those motifs were combined with C- and S-shaped scrolls, occasionally forming a trefoil or quatrefoil shape suggesting the Gothic. To that repertoire must be added the use of pierced work or blind fretwork, which distinguished the Chinese mode made popular in Chippendale's *Director*. Rococo slab tables and looking-glass and picture frames were exclusively the work of carvers. Carving, which could either be cut from the solid or applied, defined the shape, or outline, of forms it embellished (see No. 131). Chairs with rectangular backs were given projecting corners and pierced splats; ornament was added to other established forms to bring them up to date. A Philadelphia furnituremaker's *Price Book* printed in 1772, at the height of the rococo (see p. 184), describes the full range of available furniture. It lists many forms introduced first in

Cadwalader furniture now in the Powel house ballroom at the Philadelphia Museum of Art (Nos. 124, 125, 154, 155)

the 1740s and 1750s and spells out just how much more a piece of mahogany furniture with rococo carving cost than a piece of walnut left plain. The book clearly demonstrates that the style was a luxurious option, the purview of the well-to-do.

The carvers of the most stylish and accomplished American rococo furniture were mostly immigrants from England, Scotland, and Ireland who had served their full apprenticeships, usually in London, before coming to the New World. There were sporadic arrivals in New York, Philadelphia, Williamsburg, and Charleston in the 1750s, but the great craftsman migration began in the mid-1760s and crested with the incidence of the nonimportation agreements, around the end of the decade. Those dates coincide precisely with the introduction and height of the rococo style. It is no happenstance that Boston, of the great colonial ports the least welcoming to immigrant craftsmen, has so few pieces of identifiable rococo furniture and that Philadelphia, the most hospitable, has so many.

In the major cities of colonial America, the cabinetmakers nurtured local furniture styles so distinctive, so different from one another, that they form the natural units by which American furniture can be examined. The regional styles are the result of a combination of factors unique to each place: the taste of the local gentry; the mix of native-born and immigrant craftsmen; and the availability of imported English pattern books and furniture as design sources. In the pages that follow, the furniture of Boston, New York, Williamsburg, Charleston, and Philadelphia is treated separately and in that order. Philadelphia, with more furniture in the rococo style than all the other cities put together, is taken out of geographic order to become the grand finale, showing how close Americans could get to the London rococo.

Boston

Boston was the dominant colonial city in the seventeenth and early eighteenth centuries, but the economic recessions she suffered after Queen Anne's War (1702–13) and King George's War (1744–48), along with the increasing prominence of New York and Philadelphia, impeded her ability to expand and to continue her development as a center of urban creativity. By the 1750s, her heyday was over. The city's gallant, incendiary role prior to the Revolution and her occupation by the British, which began in 1768 and did not end until 1776, only contributed to her woes. Her stand against import duties[1] began a decade of wartime sacrifices from which she never fully recovered. Nonetheless, Boston rococo furniture, while limited in quantity, compares favorably in quality with that of other colonial urban centers.

In the great majority of furniture made in the city between 1760 and 1790, the old styles were maintained with only slight, and usually belated, accommodation to the emerging rococo sensibility for lighter forms and ornamental carving. The few pieces of wonderful rococo furniture fashioned by Boston woodworkers are the exception rather than the rule. The reason is simple. The arrival of the rococo style in Boston coincided with the period of decline in the city's population and economy, and there were not many newly rich merchant princes prepared to flaunt the fresh modes. Moreover, Boston cabinetmakers were understandably conservative. Some had participated in the creation of a uniquely New England style in the vibrant years of the 1730s; others were their descendants. In either case, the native-born artisans were unwilling to admit outsiders, even if (or, perhaps, especially if) they were London trained and schooled in the new rococo fashion.

The manufacture of furniture was a widespread enterprise in colonial Boston. As the English traveler James Birket observed of the city in 1751: "The Artificers in this Place Exceed Any upon ye Continent And are here also Most Numerous as Cabinet Makers."[2] Of some 562 furnituremakers known to have been working in the city before 1800,[3] about 160 were practicing their trade between the years 1750 and 1790. To be sure, much of their labor was focused on shipbuilding. The wood-carvers, only about fifteen of them active between 1750 and 1800, were situated mostly around the wharves and must have been employed primarily in carving ships' figureheads and other fittings, such as ornamental scrolls and brackets.

Furnituremaking was also an important industry in the other major cities of coastal New England. To the north, Newburyport, Marblehead, and Salem all produced furniture in the Boston manner, but each added a touch of local color. There are houses in Newburyport and Marblehead with rococo architectural ornament that is clearly the work of Boston artisans, but the locally made furniture is uncarved, and no one then active as a carver has been recorded in those areas.[4] The inference to be drawn is that when a grandee such as Jeremiah Lee of Marblehead wanted the latest fashion (the rococo), he sent to Boston for carvers to embellish his house and for carved furniture to add to examples he had doubtless imported.

In Salem, there is a recognizable variation in uncarved block-front and bombé Boston forms; there are also a number of ornate rococo-style case pieces thought to be of Salem manufacture but with carving that looks to be Boston. Their authorship has yet to be sorted out. Further north, in Portsmouth (in what is now New Hampshire), ties with Boston were much weaker. Though Ebenezer Dearing of nearby Kittery did architectural carving, Portsmouth-made furniture in the rococo style is unknown, except for a famous group of china tables (see No. 102) that have no apparent stylistic debt to the city.

South of Boston, in Newport, Rhode Island, members of the Townsend and Goddard families made some of the finest of all American furniture. Those locally trained artisans, whose primary stylistic inspiration came from Boston (where it predated the rococo and remained in fashion until the mid-1790s), combined the traditional Boston block-front with magnificent lobed shells of their own devising. What resulted was a compact, self-contained, block-and-shell design that was essentially baroque. Even on cabriole-leg tables, the carving, not the work of specialized craftsmen but of the cabinetmakers themselves, is so stylized and controlled as to defy any suggestion of rococo.

Contemporary information about Boston cabinetmakers is spotty at best. Local newspapers frequently carried advertisements for sales of furniture and household effects, usually by auction, but furnituremakers almost never advertised their wares or their skills. Well known in the community, often the third or fourth generation in the profession, they saw no need for such promotion.

The shop accounts that survive are only marginally helpful in the quest for the Boston rococo. Nathaniel Holmes was probably the most financially successful of the Boston cabinetmakers at mid-century. His miscellaneous bills and receipts, dating from 1728 to 1759, are of greatest use for their implicit recording of the introduction of the Queen Anne style in the 1730s and for their description of shop practices, which included workmen employed in such outlying towns as Marblehead.[5] There are also the account books of the prominent upholsterer Samuel Grant (1705–1784) for the years from 1728 to his death.[6] Upholstery methods were not much affected by the introduction of the rococo style, but Grant's petty ledgers establish that two of Boston's leading carvers, John Welch (1711–1789) and Simeon Skillin (1716–1778), were in his employ. He paid Welch £11-19-0 in 1756 and 1758 and Skillin £35 in 1762 and 1763 for, among other things, carving cornices, headboards, and branches for bedsteads. The "Carvg a Set open cornishes" for which Skillin received £3 on 1 October 1763 is a sure description of pierced work in the rococo style.[7]

The wording of Skillin's receipt is one of the earliest pieces of evidence that manufacturing in the rococo taste was being practiced in colonial Boston. The receipt, following on the heels of the innovative architectural carving for the Vassall (1759) and Apthorp (1760–61) houses in Cambridge (see p. 18), is contemporaneous with the appearance of the first Boston-made carved-and-gilded picture frames, probably by Welch, on portraits painted by John Singleton Copley. Chairmakers may have been a little slower to adopt the "modern" style. Advertisements in the *Boston Gazette* for auctions of "Carv'd Frame Mehogany Chairs" (20 November 1753) and "an exceeding good Sett of Mehogany carv'd Chairs, new Fashion" (17 November 1755)[8] describe pierced and carved splat patterns, a total break from traditional New England seating furniture. Although they suggest the new mode, they most probably refer to imported pieces. Domestic rococo production (see No. 96) seems to have been triggered by a particular design (FIG. 36, p. 148) in Robert Manwaring's *Cabinet and Chair-Maker's Real Friend and Companion* (London, 1765), a book available in Boston by 1767. A set of chairs ordered in 1769 by Josiah Quincy, Jr., shows its influence, as does one made for Jonathan Bowman the following year by George Bright, "esteemed the neatest workman in town."[9]

Cabinetwork did not show such a drastic change. High chests and dressing tables in the traditional Queen Anne style were still being made. The block-front treatment of chests and desks introduced in the late 1730s and the bombé-front treatment introduced in the early 1750s continued unabated in the 1770s and 1780s. The scroll pediments, moldings, and feet of those heavy baroque pieces (see No. 93) were embellished with rococo leafage by carvers employed to satisfy the demands of a handful of wealthy, fashion-conscious clients.

The form of some Boston case furniture, however, was ultimately altered to accommodate the new style. A graceful, continuously curved front—called "serpentine" if the center projects and the sides are recessed and "oxbow" if the center is recessed and the sides project—supplanted the block and the bombé. It might be assumed that the new shapes were introduced in the early 1770s, but the earliest documented instance of the oxbow is a chest-on-chest made in 1780 by Nathan Bowen and Ebenezer Martin of Marblehead; just three years later, a magnificently carved serpentine chest was made by Thomas Needham of Salem (FIG. 35, p. 144). On rare occasions, testing the cabinetmaker's skill to the limit, the bombé and the serpentine were united in Boston's most rococo form (see No. 95).

The names of Welch and Skillin, who worked on bedsteads for the upholsterer Samuel Grant, are most frequently associated with carving on Boston furniture.[10] Welch, son of a Boston carver, rented a shop on the town wharf from 1733 until 1758, when he sold many of his possessions preparatory to going to London. He returned to Boston about 1760. He had dealings with Copley in the 1770s and undoubtedly made many of the painter's picture frames. Skillin, whose earliest recorded commission was carving for the ship *King George* in 1758, was a friend of Bright's.[11] Both men had sons who were also carvers. In 1791, two of Skillin's heirs, John and Simeon junior, carved an extraordinary chest-on-chest, part rococo, part neoclassical in style, made by Stephen Badlam of Dorchester Lower Mills, now a part of Boston, for the most famous member of the Derby family of Salem.[12]

Elias Hasket Derby (1739–1799), son of Richard Derby, a successful Salem merchant, made a fortune in shipping during the Revolution and is renowned as the first and greatest of the China traders and a munificent patron of the Salem neoclassical architect Samuel McIntire.[13] The name of Derby, who was apparently an avid buyer of Boston rococo furniture, has been associated with ownership of several of the major monuments of the style: John Cogswell's chest-on-chest, 1782 (No. 93), Thomas Needham's serpentine chest, 1783, and a fine set of chairs (see No. 100). Presumably, the furnishings were all intended for his Derby Street residence, by the wharf, the first of four great houses he was to acquire in Salem. Begun by McIntire in 1780, it was left uncompleted sometime after 1782, when Derby bought the even grander house of Benjamin Pickman, on Washington Street. The rococo must have represented the nouveau-riche style until at least 1790, for it was not until the following

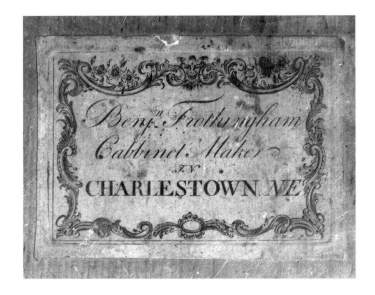

FIGURE 32. *Label of Benjamin Frothingham*, 1760–70, Nathaniel Hurd, Boston. Engraving on paper, 2⅞ x 4 in. (7.3 x 10.2 cm.), on desk. Historic Deerfield, Inc. (62.181)

year that Badlam made the great double chest, the first of Derby's commissions in a predominantly neoclassical mode.

Other illustrious New England patrons of the rococo included Jeremiah Lee, whose mansion remains wonderfully intact architecturally (see p. 20), and Nicholas Boylston, of whose house John Adams said in 1766, "[The furniture] cost a thousand Pounds sterling. A Seat it is for a noble Man, a Prince."[14] The contents of those and of all other high-style interiors have been dispersed.[15]

The only Boston-area cabinetmaker habitually to identify his own work was Benjamin Frothingham (1734–1809), son of a Boston joiner of the same name, who set up shop across the river in Charlestown in the early 1750s and, except for a hiatus during the war years, carried on the furniture business until his death.[16] His printed paper label with its rococo-style border (FIG. 32), the work of the local engraver Nathaniel Hurd (see Nos. 14, 26), is preserved on about fifteen of his pieces. The ornate label notwithstanding, Frothingham's cabinetwork is notable for its lack of ornamental carving.[17] Fortunately, three of the greatest carved case pieces from the region are signed by their makers or have marks that identify them: Cogswell's chest-on-chest of 1782; Needham's serpentine chest of 1783; and a desk and bookcase made by George Bright about 1775–85.[18]

A few furniture pattern books containing engraved rococo illustrations were available in New England, but all promoted a style for which there was little market, a lack of interest once again attributable to the conservative predilection of most Yankee makers and their clients. Though Chippendale's *Director*, the largest and most famous of the pattern books, is documented in eighteenth-century New England four times (a copy inscribed "Boston 1768"; the title's presence in the 1772 catalogue of the booksellers Cox and Berry; a copy in the 1782 inventory of the Salem gentleman-cabinetmaker Nathaniel Gould; and a copy owned by the Newport maker John Goddard),[19] not one identifiable motif was culled for use by a New England craftsman.[20] The only other furniture books recorded are a handful of modest volumes by Crunden, Baretti, and Manwaring, which had been brought to Boston and advertised for sale by Cox and Berry on the first day of 1767, shortly after the partners' arrival from London.[21] Among the books, only Manwaring's, a copy of which was owned by the Boston mason and architect Thomas Dawes (1731–1809),[22] exercised any real influence. As related above, most Boston chair splat patterns were modeled to one degree or another after one of its designs (FIG. 36, p. 148).

FRAMES

John Singleton Copley was the towering figure among pre-Revolutionary New England painters. It was to complement his prolific outpouring of portraits that a distinctive Boston type of carved-and-gilded rococo-style picture frame was developed. It is among the masterpieces of the New England rococo. An inventory of the frames of Copley's oeuvre has not been completed, but some two dozen locally made rococo examples, which survive with the pictures for which they were originally intended, are already known.[23] Conversely, no single native rococo frame on any other New England painter's work has yet been identified, not even on that of Joseph Blackburn, an artist who came to Boston from London in 1755 and who exerted a marked influence on Copley's style.[24]

Copley was born in Boston in 1738. Shortly after his father's death, in 1748, his mother married Peter Pelham, a London-trained engraver and portrait painter who during the three years prior to his death in 1751 introduced young Copley to the world of art and artists. By 1753, Copley's career was under way; by 1760, his style was set and his supremacy among American painters apparent.[25]

In 1763, at a charge of £2-13-4, engraver and jack-of-all-trades Thomas Johnston (see Nos. 15, 25) made "a handsome Half length Picture Frame inside edge Carvd & Gilt" for his friend Samuel P. Savage, presumably for Copley's painting of Mrs. Savage.[26] Such relatively inexpensive frames—plain molded and black painted except for the inside edge—were then standard for colonial portraits. Copley may not have concerned himself with the enclosures for his likenesses until about that year, when he first chose a Boston-made rococo frame with a gilded surface.[27] The ensuing examples are virtually all of one basic model. The design has three parts: next to the painting a narrow molding, either leaf carved or gadrooned; then a large, deep cove pierced in places, its bed embellished with leaf streamers and rosettes; finally, the outer edge, a curved or scalloped applied piece that extends over the cove's cutaway spaces.

Differences in the fashioning of the known Copley frames suggest that at least two artisans were employed in their manufacture, but the only one who can be documented is John Welch, probably Boston's preeminent carver. In 1771, while Copley was briefly in New York to paint the local gentry, he wrote to his half brother, Henry Pelham, "I have parted with the two small frames, but cannot yet give orders for more . . . you must let me know the price of the small ones . . . let me know what you paid Welch for Carving and Whiting for Gilding."[28] Stephen Whiting (1728–1789), a japanner, advertised in 1757 "Pictures and Maps framed and

89

Picture frame, Boston, ca. 1765
White pine, gilded, 29½ x 24½ in.
With portrait of Mrs. Edward Green
by John Singleton Copley
The Metropolitan Museum of Art

varnish'd" and, ten years later, "Any sort of Frames that will suit the Buyer."[29] (No American frame has been found on any of Copley's New York portraits.) In 1773, Harvard College paid Copley £56 for a full-length replica of his portrait of Nicholas Boylston (1767); subsequent entries in the Harvard accounts refer to payment for the frame and for carving by Welch.[30]

Several of Copley's paintings of the mid-1760s have a readily distinguishable kind of frame, the work of a single carver. That of the pastel portrait (1765) of Mrs. Edward Green (**No. 89**) is characteristic: a leaf-carved inner edge, an outer edge formed into a gentle central point. Similar frames surround the huge, full-length portraits of Harvard College benefactors Thomas Hancock, painted in 1764–66, and Thomas Hollis, painted in 1766 (FIG. 33), for the library of Harvard Hall, a building that replaced one destroyed by fire in 1764.[31] Their white pine frames, each surmounted by the sitter's coat of arms, were unquestionably locally made.

On 9 July 1766, Edward Holyoke, president of Harvard College, wrote Hollis's nephew, then in England: "The Carver who hath made a frame for yr excellent Uncle's Picture (which we have got drawn at Large By a Painter who takes a fine Likeness) hath constructed it so, as to have an Eschucheon for his Arms on the Top of it wherefore if you will please to send us the Blazonry They shall be added."[32]

Among Copley's most perceptive portraits are those of members of the Boylston family of Boston. Their exceptionally well preserved frames are of two types. The first, exemplified by that on the likeness of Mrs. Thomas Boylston (1696–1774), painted in 1766 (FIG. 34), is marked by the shallowness of its cove and by the molded and finished treatment of its sides.[33] Fashioned of the red pine preferred by English makers, it must be of English manufacture and was probably copied for the frames of the second type (a locally made version having a deep cove and unfinished sides), represented by the one that surrounds the original portrait (1767) of Nicholas Boylston (**No. 90**).[34]

Of the same model and probably by the same carver are the frames on the pair of fifty-by-forty-inch seated portraits of Ezekiel Goldthwait (1710–1782) and Mrs. Goldthwait (1714–1794). In a bill of 1771, Copley charged Goldthwait £19-12-0 for each portrait and listed "two carved Gold Frames" for £9 each,[35] leaving little question that the painter chose the design and the carver to execute it. (The bill also documents the eighteenth-century carvers' frequent practice of doing their own gilding.) The Goldthwait frames compare with the one carved by Welch for Harvard's replica (1773) of the Nicholas Boylston portrait. On that basis, the entire group may be assignable to Welch.

FIGURE 33. *Picture frame*, Boston, 1766. White pine, gilded, 108 x 70 in. (274.3 x 177.8 cm.). With portrait of Thomas Hollis by John Singleton Copley. The Harvard University Portrait Collection, Commissioned by the President and Fellows of Harvard College, 1765 (H25)

FIGURE 34. *Picture frame*, England, ca. 1766. Red pine, gilded, 57⅜ x 47¼ in. (145.7 x 120 cm.). With portrait of Mrs. Thomas Boylston by John Singleton Copley. The Harvard University Portrait Collection, Bequest of Ward Nicholas Boylston, 1828 (H16)

90

Picture frame, Boston, ca. 1767
White pine, gilded, 66¾ x 47⅜ in.
With portrait of Nicholas Boylston
by John Singleton Copley
The Harvard University Portrait Collection

91

Picture frame, Boston, ca. 1770
White pine, gilded, 65¾ x 60½ in.
With portrait of Richard Dana
by John Singleton Copley
Collection of the Richard Henry Dana family

92

Frame, Boston, ca. 1767
White pine, gilded, 24 x 24 in.
With the Williams family arms
Collection of Mr. and Mrs. George M. Kaufman

About 1770, Copley painted a half-length portrait in the fifty-by-forty-inch format of Richard Dana (1700–1772), lawyer and Justice of the Commonwealth of Massachusetts (**No. 91**). The overpowering figure of the jurist and Copley's subdued palette—black for the coat, dark blue for the curtain, and only sporadic touches of light—are offset by a carved-and-gilded rococo frame that represents the structurally most daring of the Copley types. Its corners are cut away so dramatically that wrought-iron brackets were needed from the start to hold the joints together. The iron extends into the voids, where it has been painted ocher to make its transgression less obvious. Almost identical frames surround the pair of half-length portraits of Isaac Smith and his wife (a daughter of the Ebenezer Storers), painted in 1769 at a cost of £20-10 each, plus £9 per enclosure.[36] Copley's larger frames often have removable central ornaments at the top. Those of the Smiths are surmounted by pierced-shell central finials, but Dana's has his family coat of arms: three stags separated by a chevron, with a fox for its crest and *Cavendo tutus* ("By caution secure") for its motto. For sitters with armigeral pretensions, that was the perfect personalization for a picture frame.

Copley, never known to have neglected the financial side of his profession, was routinely involved with ordering and selling frames for his pictures, but that was surely as much for artistic reasons as a matter of business. The somber palette of his maturing style was effectively set off by his carved-and-gilded frames. For Copley to have allowed his

exceptional paintings to be encased in anything less than the finest and most fashionable frames would be unimaginable.

A frame probably executed by the same hand as those of the Dana and Smith portraits but the sole instance known of a carved-and-gilded Boston rococo frame *not* on a Copley portrait encloses a Williams family coat of arms (**No. 92**).[37] Lozenge-shaped panels displaying coats of arms and crests, inspired by funerary hatchments, were popular in New England by the 1750s. Their function was primarily decorative. Of the well over fifty embroidered examples (usually in satin stitch on a black satin ground) now known, the great majority are from the Boston area, where between 1755 and 1769 a number of Bostonians advertised drawing coats of arms for embroidery.[38] While the arms and crests vary, the rich and leafy mantles, inspired by painted examples from the early eighteenth century, are all of one or two stock patterns.

The right to a coat of arms was not granted many American colonists, but when John Williams (1727–1782) of Boston was in London in 1767 for his induction as Inspector General of the American Board of Custom Commissioners, he received just such a grant. The Letters Patent describe his arms as having a lion rampant and two doves. These are visible in the needlework quartered by three bells, a reference to the alliance by marriage of the Williams and Bell families. The needlework probably dates shortly after 1767, when Williams ordered London silver engraved with his new arms.[39]

CASE FURNITURE

Perhaps the best known of the few bombé- or serpentine-shaped Boston case pieces on which rococo carving appears is the chest-on-chest John Cogswell made at his Middle Street shop and signed with his name and address and the date of manufacture (**No. 93**).[40] The combination of forms in a double chest—the lower unit with a shaped front, the upper unit flat with flanking pilasters—was a Boston favorite from mid-century. Cogswell's masterpiece represents a very traditional and conservative form onto which rococo ornament was applied but not always fully integrated.

The profile of the bombé-shaped lower section, which, with its two straight top drawers and its two bulging bottom drawers, lacks the continuous curve of the rococo, is of a type generally acknowledged to have been inspired in Boston by a double chest believed to have been imported by Charles Apthorp prior to his death, in 1758.[41] Bands of blind fretwork, a standard feature in *Director* designs but rare in New England, accent the junctures of the pediment and the upper case and the upper case and the lower. The visual focus of the piece is the luxuriant high-relief carving concentrated in the scroll pediment and superimposed on the typically plain scallop-edged Boston brackets of the claw feet. In the pediment, the applied rocaille scrolls that conform to the squashed openings are the closest the carver comes to capturing the spirit of the style.

Cogswell was born in Ipswich in 1738, married in Boston in 1762, and died in early 1818. He was selling furniture to Boston's merchant aristocracy by 1769, and his cabinet-making activities continued for at least two decades.[42] His chest-on-chest, which descended in the Derby family of Salem, was apparently ordered by Elias Hasket Derby for his Derby Street house, on which work was begun in 1780.[43] Can any significance be attached to its central finial, an eagle on a sphere? Is it perhaps emblematic of the global ventures of the insatiably ambitious Derby?

The serpentine front became fashionable on New England chests and desks shortly after its introduction about 1780. Its graceful curves endow it with a certain rococo feeling, but the form was rarely highlighted with carving. Two chests of drawers are not only exceptions to the rule but extraordinary statements in the New England rococo style. The first (FIG. 35) is unusual for its commanding scale (its forty-four-inch width greatly exceeds the norm), for its carefully chosen woods—its four drawer fronts veneered from a single board whose surface is covered with graphlike patterns—and for its fine carving lavished on the canted corners, the skirt pendant, and the claw feet.[44] The oversize brackets of the feet,

93

Chest-on-chest, 1782
John Cogswell, Boston
Mahogany; white pine, H.: 89½ in.
Museum of Fine Arts, Boston

FIGURE 35. *Chest of drawers*, 1783. Probably by Thomas Needham, Jr., Salem. Mahogany; white pine, cedar, 36½ x 44¼ x 24½ in. (92.7 x 112.4 x 62.2 cm.). Private collection

unlike the brackets on the Cogswell chest, are of a shape that conforms to the *C*-scrolls and rocaille mantles with which they are carved. Except for the skirt pendant, all the carved areas are in low relief and have a star-punch background that unifies them and causes them to sparkle with light, an attribute also conferred by the figure of the veneered drawer fronts. The chest, though massive in form and endowed with huge, heavy brass drawer pulls, has an air of elegance that demonstrates a remarkable advance in the rococo style over the Cogswell chest it succeeds by a year.

Inscribed on the bottom of the chest are the initials *TN* (probably those of Thomas Needham, Jr.) and the date 1783. Needham, son of a Boston cabinetmaker who moved to Salem in 1776 and whose family members carried on the business until they returned to Boston in 1796, is recorded as making furniture for Elias Hasket Derby of Salem in the year 1783.[45] Did the master merchant of Salem order this chest, too? In the evolution of the form, it is the link between Cogswell's double chest of 1782 and the one made by Stephen Badlam in 1791.

The second chest of drawers (**No. 94**), with its delicate air, exhibits an altogether different aesthetic, particularly in the scale and the handling of the carved ornament and the

brasses. Nowhere is there to be found a piece of New England rococo furniture that looks more London. The plasticity of the skirt scrolls, the manner in which the carving integrates the skirt and the bracket feet, the freedom with which the foliage rests on the flat surfaces of the canted corners, the nut-brown patina, even the veneered top, the slide with its hinged mirror frame, and the once-fitted upper drawer—all speak with an English accent. Yet there can be no doubt that the chest has been locally produced, for the interior is made entirely of native woods (white pine and cedar) worked in the New England manner and the carving is flat and sketchy in comparison with that of English prototypes.

It is tempting to imagine the chest to be the work of a British craftsman right off the boat, but it is so clearly New England made that it must be the creation of a local man emulating an imported example. He employed the design only once more, on the lower half of a double chest now associated with Samuel McIntire.[46]

Though lacking the ministrations of a wood-carver, another chest of drawers, this one exhibiting extraordinary gilt

94
Chest of drawers, Salem, ca. 1780
Mahogany; white pine, L.: 45¼ in.
Collection of Erving and Joyce Wolf

bronze mounts (**No. 95**), may also be adjudged rococo. The chest, which is inscribed inside with the name Green, has been traced back to its original owner, Gardiner Greene (1753-1832), of Boston. Presumably, it was made around the time of Greene's first marriage, in 1785, or his second, in 1788, as part of the furnishings of his Tremont Street town house, once known as "the most splendid private residence in the city."[47] The bombé-and-serpentine profiles of the drawer fronts—the ultimate in complexity of Boston cabinetwork—cause the grain of the wood to appear in undulating curves and reinforce its innate sense of movement. The top and sides, formed respectively of figured and crotch mahogany, display an almost elemental, and very American, sense of the rococo. The mounts, elaborately cast and chased with chinoiserie motifs of trellis and pagoda roof as well as with the more standard rococo scrolls and foliage, take the place of carved woodwork. The cabinetmaker may well have considered that his primary role in creating this diminutive chest was to provide a backdrop for the magnificent mounts, one of only two such sets ever seen in Boston.[48] The drawer pulls, of a size probably intended for a much larger piece of furniture, were certainly imported from England, and at great expense.

95
Chest of drawers, Boston, 1775–85
Mahogany; white pine, L.: 35¾ in.
The Dietrich American Foundation

Like New England case furniture, elaborately carved rococo chairs and tables from the region are rare. The few that are known are associated with Boston or, tangentially, Salem.[49] All have tall cabriole legs ending in claw-and-ball feet with raked-back side talons or, more exceptionally, talons delineated with tufts of hair. On the basis of their knee treatment, the chairs and tables can be separated into two groups, presumably the work of two carvers.

On the first group, the knees have a square corner edge overlaid with the central stem of an acanthus leaf whose flatly carved leafage emerges on either side from the seat rails. This tight, schematic ornament has no known English prototype, nor, oddly, is similar carving to be found on any Boston case piece. Chairs of the group have backs that seem to have been heavily influenced by Manwaring's *Cabinet and Chair-Maker's Friend* of 1765. For example, Plate 9 (FIG. 36) was copied exactly for the back of one of a set of chairs (**No. 96**) made for Clark Gayton Pickman (1746–1781) of Salem, who married in 1770. A number of other sets are based on the same engraving, though they usually have less carving on the splat. A felicitous variation on the basic outline is employed on a chair (**No. 97**) from the De Wolf family of Bristol, Rhode Island. Though these examples represent two of the most ornamental of Massachusetts rococo chairs, their design relates to a modest pattern in a very modest book. The engraving shows a straight-legged (read inexpensive) chair, but, as frequently happened, the colonial interpretation has been upgraded with carved cabriole supports.

On the second group, the legs have altogether different, and much more rococo, carving: the knee is wrapped round with mantling composed of a single large C-scroll and an acanthus leaf. The asymmetry and movement in the knee design as well as the much greater three-dimensionality in the carving place this group with the best of the New England rococo. A card table (**No. 98**) that is also exceptional for being constructed with hinged side rails (the so-called accordion action) rather than the standard hinged-back leg is the only table known from the group. First owned by Captain Thomas Frazar (1735–1782) of Duxbury,[50] who married in 1760, it was certainly made to special order, with no expense spared. The same C-scrolled legs appear on a settee (**No. 99**) that is one of a pair. With its pleasing combination of the conical arm supports typical of New England easy chairs and an indented serpentine crest in place of the so-called camel back that was the familiar colonial shape, the settee is a high point in American rococo-style upholstered furniture.[51]

96

Side chair, Boston, 1765–85
Mahogany; maple, H.: 38¾ in.
The Metropolitan Museum of Art

FIGURE 36. Design for a "Parlour" chair, Robert Manwaring,
The Cabinet and Chair-Maker's Real Friend and Companion
(London, 1765), Plate 9 (detail). Engraving on paper,
5½ x 8⅛ in. (14 x 20.6 cm.). The Metropolitan Museum of Art,
Harris Brisbane Dick Fund, 1932 (32.9.6)

97

Side chair, Boston, 1765–85
Mahogany; maple, H.: 38 in.
The Metropolitan Museum of Art

98

Card table, Boston, 1765–85
Mahogany; maple, L.: 35½ in.
Collection of Erving and Joyce Wolf

99
Settee, Boston, 1765–85
Mahogany; maple, L.: 57½ in.
The Metropolitan Museum of Art

The same knee carving is sported on Massachusetts chairs of various patterns, including two sets having a splat design of interlaced figure eights, one of which (**No. 100**) is said to have been owned by—who else?—Elias Hasket Derby.[52] The entire design, including splat and knee, is copied from an English chair (**No. 101**) owned in eighteenth-century Boston by one William Phillips.[53]

100

Side chair, Boston, 1765–85
Mahogany; maple, H.: 37½ in.
The Chipstone Foundation

101

Side chair, England, ca. 1750
Mahogany; beech, H.: 37¼ in.
Museum of Fine Arts, Boston

102

China table, Portsmouth, 1762–80
Mahogany; white pine, L.: 36½ in.
The Carnegie Museum of Art

Apart from those pieces made in Boston and in Salem, about the only New England furniture that can be said to have serious rococo aspirations is a group of china tables from Portsmouth. Of the four of the group that have histories of descent in that city, one can be identified with the "raild Tea Table" valued at forty-eight shillings in merchant William Whipple's inventory of 1788.[54] The frame of another (**No. 102**), which once belonged to the merchant Stephen Chase (d. 1805), is by far the most elaborate: the table is covered with blind fretwork in a Chinese pattern of interlaced diamonds on the skirts, a Gothic pattern of repeated arches on the legs. The fundamental design—a rimmed rectangular top and four legs joined by crossed arched stretchers—has a family resemblance to a *Director* pattern for a china table (Plate LI), but the ornament on the skirt is taken directly from a dressing table (Plate XL) in Ince and Mayhew's *Universal System*, a book not recorded as having been in colonial Boston.[55]

New York

New York City developed its own interpretation of the rococo in furniture design during the third quarter of the eighteenth century. Major examples of the local rococo style, long overshadowed by the glorious Philadelphia Chippendale of nearby Pennsylvania, long overlooked because they were not always distinguishable from English prototypes and because some of the best pieces must have been taken abroad by their Loyalist owners at the time of the Revolution, are only now being identified.

Furnituremaking was a big business in colonial New York. Some hundred and forty-eight craftsmen, their shops spread throughout the city, are recorded as having been engaged in the trade prior to 1775. Of that number, sixty-three cabinetmakers, thirty-four chairmakers and turners, fourteen upholsterers, and six carvers began work after 1750.[56] What little is known about those men, many of them English trained, comes in good part from the advertisements with which they began to pepper the New York press in the mid-1750s.[57]

Few of the era's household inventories or other forms of documentation exist. The only New York cabinetmaker's accounts surviving from the period are those of Joshua Delaplaine, a Quaker. Typical among them is his daybook for the years 1753 to 1755, which records the manufacture of large numbers of beds and tables.[58] Unfortunately, little furniture can be ascribed to an individual artisan, but many pieces can be identified as of local origin by their histories in prominent eighteenth-century families. The large body of work represented must have been what Governor William Tryon was referring to when he reported to the British Board of Trade in 1774 that most household goods were of English manufacture "except Cabinet and Joiner's Work, which is Generally made here."[59]

The 1750s, a prosperous time for New Yorkers, forged the unusually close ties with the mother country that would affect all aspects of social life and style for the remainder of the century. A Royal Colony, centrally located, with about twenty-two hundred houses and a population of thirteen thousand and forty souls, the city was chosen in 1755 as the western terminus for the newly instituted British mail packet service and as the seat of Britain's admittedly modest general administrative authority in America. Local merchants developed thriving businesses through the provisioning of the British forces engaged in the French and Indian War (1754–63). As historian and New York jurist William Smith observed in 1759:

> In the city of New-York, through our intercourse with the Europeans, we follow the London fashions; though by the time we adopt them, they become disused in England. Our affluence during the late war introduced a degree of luxury in tables, dress, and furniture with which we were before unacquainted. But still we are not so gay a people, as our neighbors in Boston and several of the Southern colonies.[60]

With the peace, London instituted such revenue-producing taxes as a sugar act in 1764 and the Stamp Act of 1765, which New Yorkers were quick to denounce. The city's merchants formed a society to encourage local manufacturers and instituted the first nonimportation agreement, which held until the repeal of the Stamp Act in 1766. By 1770, the port of New York was fourth in order of tonnage shipped in and out of America, coming after Philadelphia, Boston, and Charleston.

Exactly when the rococo style of ornament in woodwork was introduced into New York cannot be pinned down, but it could not have been before the late 1750s. There is no mention of ornament in any of Delaplaine's accounts. The prize for a lottery advertised in the *New-York Gazette or the Weekly Post-Boy* for 31 December 1753 was "a good Mahogany Chest of Drawers, with Eagle's Claw Feet, a Shell on each knee, and fluted Corners, with good Brass Work and Locks." The unusually complete description of the stylistic features of the chest makes it patently clear that none of them could yet be considered rococo. Not until the late 1750s can the first traceable glimmer of the rococo style be seen in New York work, visible in the leaf-carved ornament on the knees of a settee that bears the label of Joseph Cox, upholsterer, at the Dock Street address he maintained from 1757 to 1760.[61]

The first of the six known carvers active before 1775 was Henry Hardcastle, who was listed in 1751 as a freeman carver in New York, where he remained active until about 1755, when he moved to Charleston.[62] He has been associated with what are certainly the earliest surviving instances of the rococo in New York architecture, the southeast parlor and

FIGURE 37. *Label of Samuel Prince*, New York, 1760–75.
Engraving on paper, 4½ x 5½ in. (11.4 x 14 cm.),
on chest of drawers. Museum of the City of New York,
Gift of Mr. and Mrs. Eric M. Wunsch (70.4)

chamber in the manor house built in Yonkers by Frederick Philipse (see p. 22, where see also FIG. 9). The carving, indisputably New York in origin if of uncertain date, is the Rosetta stone for deciphering the first phase of the New York rococo style. In 1755, Stephen Dwight, "late an apprentice to Henry Hardcastle, carver," announced that he had set up as a carver of "all sorts of ship and house work...and all kinds of work for cabinet makers."[63] The American-born Dwight was soon engulfed in competition from abroad; the 1760s and early 1770s saw a virtual invasion of New York by British craftsmen.

Cabinetmakers came from Ireland, from the west of England, and especially from London. In 1762, "John Brinner, Cabinet and Chair-Maker," advertised that he had "brought over from London six Artificers, well skill'd in the above Branches."[64] He was followed by James Strachan in 1765 and a Mr. Minshull in 1769, both of them carvers and gilders from London. All three men are known today primarily from the notices they put in the New York newspapers to promote their trade. Another carver, John Gibbons, is known only from a newspaper mention in 1771, which describes him as a twenty-seven-year-old deserter from the British army.[65] The last of the six men who could have executed rococo ornament in prewar New York was Richard Davis, in partnership with Stephen Dwight in the early 1770s.[66]

While the names of many of the craftsmen are known, little of what they made can be identified, for only two New York cabinetmakers consistently labeled their work. The first

was Samuel Prince (d. 1785), who was active by about 1760 and who after his death was praised by a former apprentice as "a conspicuous character in his way, and esteemed one of the first workmen in this city."[67] Prince's ornate rococo label (FIG. 37), which has been found on several pieces, must have been engraved before 1775, when the name of the street of his shop address was changed from Horse and Cart to William. The second was Thomas Burling, who had been apprenticed to Prince, was made a freeman in 1769, and advertised as an independent cabinetmaker between 1773 and 1796.[68] Burling's engraved label, though neoclassical in style and probably dating from the late 1780s, is adorned with a rococo chest, chair, and table. The pieces of furniture labeled by Prince and Burling, while of fine quality, are generally plain. Carving plays very little part on them, and they cannot be seen as rococo.

English furniture pattern books containing engraved rococo illustrations became available in New York for the first time in the 1760s. The most easily procurable was *Genteel Houshold Furniture in the Present Taste*.[69] Issued in four parts between 1760 and 1762 and republished about 1765 with a variant title, it received timely mention in 1760 in the first advertisement of James Rivington, a bookseller newly arrived from London.[70] Two years later, it was listed in the catalogues of the city's leading booksellers, Rivington & Brown, and Garett Noel.[71] The handy little book was an inexpensive version of Chippendale's *Director*, no copy of which is known to have existed in New York. Not surprisingly, the chair and the chest illustrated on Samuel Prince's engraved trade card were copied directly from the widely disseminated *Houshold Furniture*. In 1771, the catalogue of booksellers Noel and Hazard listed the pattern book again and at the same time offered one of the earliest pamphlets of rococo carving designs, Copland's *New Book of Ornaments*, which had been first published in London in 1746.[72] Copland, with coauthor Matthias Lock, had produced another volume in 1752, that one titled *A New Book of Ornaments with Twelve Leaves*. It was reissued by Robert Sayer in London on 1 January 1768, just in time for its Plate 10 to be used as the precise pattern for the carved spandrels (FIG. 10, p. 24) in the archway of Stephen Van Rensselaer's manor house, then being finished in Albany.[73]

Such direct copying, however, was not the rule but the exception in New York. Only one design in all *The Director* (Pl. 12, 1762 ed., a splat pattern for a chair) was widely adopted in New York work, but that use was probably inspired not by the engraving but by an English export. Though in 1774 Thomas Burling advertised his cabinet shop with a woodcut illustration of a ribbon-back chair derived from Plate xv in *The Director*,[74] no New York-made example of any such chair is known.

Imported furniture probably exercised more influence on local design than did pattern books. In 1772, London-made furniture destined for New York was valued at £2,415, far more than for any other colony.[75] In one case, an English easy chair that descended from Peter Townsend, of Albany (he who forged the iron chain that was stretched across the Hudson to stop British ships during the Revolution), has eagle's-claw feet and leaf-carved knees that are nearly indistinguishable from New York work.[76] When newlywed Lady Susan O'Brien (née Strangways) arrived in the city in 1764 as the bride of an aspiring thespian, she brought to her new life household furnishings made for her in London in Chippendale's shop at a cost of £247.[77] Oh, to know what they looked like!

James Beekman (1732–1807) is probably representative of the generation of New York merchants who came to prominence in the 1760s and 1770s and furnished their houses in the fashionable rococo style. A member of a Dutch family established in New York in the seventeenth century, Beekman went into the dry-goods business in 1750, married in 1752, and by 1760 was able to buy a substantial house on Queen (now Pearl) Street, to which he made major alterations and additions during the succeeding four years. At the same time, in 1763 and 1764, he built Mount Pleasant, his country house overlooking the East River at what is now Fifty-first Street. Perhaps the most telling statements of his prominent position in New York society are the carriages he bought for going about the city: in 1765, a chaise; in 1767, a chariot and

a phaeton; and in 1771, an imported coach. (He lost no time in having his arms emblazoned on the doors of the coach.) From that luxurious domestic habitude there remain at The New-York Historical Society, along with the coach, a chimney breast (No. 11), the frames on two sets of family portraits (see Nos. 103, 105), and a pair of card tables, which in all constitute the largest body of rococo-carved work that can be documented to a single New York family.

Beekman's household furniture accounts record his purchases between 1761 and 1796.[78] In 1761 and 1762, busy doing up his green drawing room, he was patronizing New York's best craftsmen. From Samuel Prince he got eight mahogany chairs, a sofa, a settee chair, and a fire-screen stand; from upholsterer George Richey he bought thirty yards of green damask and thirty-six yards of green binding; and from carver Stephen Dwight he got the gilded frames for the portraits of his wife, Jane, and himself that had been painted by James Kilburn, a Danish artist who had come to New York in 1754. Only the pictures and their frames have been identified, and they represent but a tentative essay in rococo ornament. Between 1766 and 1768, Beekman seems to have engaged in outfitting another room. In 1767, the carver James Strachan, who in the previous year had made Beekman two pairs of looking-glass frames, provided carved and gilded enclosures for portraits of the Beekman children, then numbering six (Mrs. Beekman was to bear four more). Her husband paid cabinetmaker Marinus Willett £15 for two armchairs and ten side chairs, as well as £3-12-0 for what were described in the account book as six "open window cornishes." The "open" refers to pierced work like that on Strachan's rococo picture frames, a demonstration that by then Beekman had acquired a taste for the fully matured rococo style. Beekman's furniture accounts also illustrate the popularity in New York of "vendue," or auction, sales conducted by merchants seeking to promote commerce. There, in every year from 1761 until 1771, he bought a quantity of furniture and silver, new or used. Between 1773 and 1783—a period that included the years of the British occupation, when Beekman moved his family to Kingston, New York— he made no purchases. Thereafter, the taste for things rococo having run its course, his buying consisted only of Windsor chairs and other painted furniture.

Beekman's acquisition of a town house and his construction of a country estate coincided with his best years as an importer and seller of dry goods. Beginning in 1765, with the mother country's imposition of various restrictive mercantile policies, trade became unsettled, and Beekman appears to have reacted by subsequently acquiring his domestic luxuries at a prudent, more measured pace.[79]

FRAMES

There is no question that frames for pictures and looking glasses were made in New York City; most of the carvers' advertisements in newspapers of the 1760s and 1770s mention them specifically. Though no looking-glass frame has yet been attributed to a local source, picture frames that still protect and enhance images of members of the James Beekman family have been identified as the work of the New York carvers Stephen Dwight and James Strachan.[80]

Dwight, the first New Yorker to advertise the making of frames, probably produced the city's first carved examples. On 21 July 1755, he announced that he had "set up his business, between the Ferry Stairs and Burlington Slip, where he carves all sorts of ship and house work: also tables, chairs, picture and looking glass frames, and all kinds of work for cabinet makers."[81] On 11 March 1762, the day James Beekman paid Kilburn £20 for his and his wife's portraits, he also paid Dwight "for carving 4 flowers for my New Roome" in the Queen Street house and "for the two Frames for [myne & my Wife Pictures]...@ £5.15 [a total of] £11.10."[82] That Dwight received payment for architectural ornament and picture frames at exactly the same time strongly suggests that both forms of carving were considered an integral part of the decoration of a room.

The basic design of Dwight's carved-and-gilded frames (**No. 103**), conservative in the early 1760s, has all the elements of English counterparts from the 1740s and 1750s: next to the picture a narrow carved ogee molding; then a flat, sand-finished fascia, or band; finally, a broad, stippled ovolo molding whose carving of rosettes and C- and S-scroll leafage is the only concession to the playful new rococo style.

The origin of Dwight's frames is not hard to trace. He borrowed both the decorative motifs and their arrangement from the imported English frame on a portrait Kilburn had painted of Abraham Beekman, James's older brother (**No. 104**). Abraham's picture, while undated, can be adjudged to precede that of James on the basis of the sitter's approximate age. The frame, more elaborate than Dwight's and of heavier stock, is made of European red pine, and its mitered corners are reinforced with tapered dovetail splines, both characteristics of English manufacture. In making his versions of native white pine, Dwight probably lacked the means to duplicate the British model: a circular punch by which to produce the textured background on the ovolo molding, fine-grained sand for the granulated surface of the fascia, and the technical skill to articulate precisely the scrolled leafage. For this last, he compensated with flourishes of his own, notably by piercing the scrolls that project at the corners and at the middle on all four sides. A simplification consonant with his colonial limitations, and not bad for a native talent. Much more fully rococo examples had been carved a decade earlier for the portraits of New York worthies painted by John Wollaston, an Englishman who practiced in New York from 1749 until 1752. The typical Wollaston frame, made of European red pine and so surely imported, is exemplified by those on Philipse family portraits: a carved ogee inner molding, a single large cavetto molding with rococo mantling, and a pierced-and-scrolled outer edge.[83]

In 1767, when it came time to commission portraits of his children, Beekman chose a different artist and a different framemaker. On 12 November 1767, he paid John Durand £19 for "drawing my Six Childrens Pictures," and on 31 December, he paid James Strachan "for 6 Gilt Frames @ £3.14 [for a total of] £22.4."[84] Durand, possibly of French extraction, was a painter who made a specialty of studies of children; his oil-on-canvas "drawings" (almost without modeling) of the Beekmans' three sons and three daughters have a certain naive freshness and directness. Strachan's frames provide the perfect visual foil (**No. 105**). They consist of a gadrooned inner edge surrounded by a broadly conceived, boldly pierced leaf-and-scroll-carved mantle. The carving, though symmetrical, is fully rococo in style. Wrought of native white pine and gilded, they represent one of the two choices of finish Strachan advertised in 1765: "Carved and gilt in Oil or burnish'd gold."[85]

Strachan, who died in New York in 1769, had but a four-year career in America. In 1765, he advertised himself as "Carver and Gilder, from London, in the Broadway near the old English Church, in New York; Makes and sells all Sorts of Picture and Glass Frames."[86] Sometime afterward, he must have carved the frames (virtually identical to those he made for Beekman) that enclose Durand's portraits of members of the Richard Ray family.[87] Their design can now be seen as a characteristic New York pattern.

Other than Wollaston, Kilburn, and Durand, the few painters then at work in New York include Thomas McIlworth, active in the environs between 1757 and 1767, and John Singleton Copley, of Boston, who painted dozens of exceptional portraits during a hectic visit to the city in the second half of 1771. None of their known New York works are enclosed by a locally made frame.

103

Picture frame, 1761–62
Stephen Dwight, New York
White pine, gilded, 52¾ x 40 in.
With portrait of James Beekman
by Lawrence Kilburn
The New-York Historical Society

104

Picture frame, England, ca. 1760
Red pine, gilded, 54¼ x 45¾ in.
With portrait of Abraham Beekman
attributed to Lawrence Kilburn
The New-York Historical Society

105

Picture frame, 1767
James Strachan, New York
White pine, gilded, 43½ x 35½ in.
With portrait of James Beekman, Jr.,
by John Durand
The New-York Historical Society

TABLES

In pre-Revolutionary New York, the consumption of tea was so great, the ritual surrounding the taking of afternoon tea so fixed, that as early as 1731 excessive tea drinking was seen as a public health problem.[88]

Tea tables were the altars on which the afternoon tea ceremony was celebrated. Though both round and rectangular models were made in New York, examples of the former —what was called a "round Mahogany Pillar and Claw Table" in an advertisement of 1763—survive in greater numbers and probably represent the more popular of the two types. They were a staple product in the Delaplaine shop in the mid-1750s, and a number of them existing today are labeled by Thomas Burling, active from 1769 to 1800. The Burling tables are largely plain, but do illustrate distinctive regional features: rimless round tops; central pillars in the shape of a cup-and-flared-shaft or a baluster; colonettes repeating those shapes in the box, or so-called bird cage; and claw feet with pinched-in side talons.

Of round tea tables identifiable as New York, only a handful having the piecrust tops and the carved pillars and knees more commonly associated with Philadelphia work are worthy of the name rococo. In 1751, in one of the earliest references to these New York tables, a cabinetmaker named John Tremain advertised that he made "Dining and Tea-Tables, plain or scollopt," the "scollopt" obviously a reference to the piecrust top.[89] Of the two here illustrated, one is unusually small, the other unusually large. Since both have the same serving height, the proportions of their pedestals differ dramatically. The first (**No. 106**) stands tall, trim, and proud. Its top, which is but twenty-nine inches in diameter, has a raised rim consisting of an outer bead and a gadroon-like ruffle divided into six repeats, or divisions, each cut out in a pair of serpentine curves. Equally typical of New York design are the colonettes of the box, with their cup-and-flared-shaft profile. The acanthus-leaf decoration on the baluster-shaped pillar closely resembles that on a New York bedstead (FIG. 38, p. 165), while the cabochons carved in high relief on the knees and the paw feet parallel features found on the legs of an easy chair from Charleston (No. 122). The similar motifs embellishing furniture from both New York and Charleston may perhaps be associated with the carver Henry Hardcastle.

The second table (**No. 107**), said to have descended from the Van Vechten family of New Jersey,[90] is massive and squat. Its immense top is about a foot larger than a tea table of regular size. Was it bespoke for a place of public assembly or for a grand domestic establishment? To keep it at serving

106

Tea table, New York, 1760–75
Mahogany, Diam.: 29 in.
The Chipstone Foundation

107

Tea table, New York, 1760–75
Mahogany, Diam.: 45⅜ in.
Van Cortlandt House, Bronx, New York

108

Card table, New York, 1765–75
Mahogany; tulip poplar, L.: 34⅛ in.
Collection of Mrs. Murray Braunfeld

Card table, New York, 1765–70
Mahogany; tulip poplar, L.: 35 in.
The Metropolitan Museum of Art

height, the legs are perforce almost awkwardly low slung, the ankles hugging the floor. The rim is divided into ten repeats, the pattern of each identical to those of the first example. The New York features of the table are the cup-and-shaft pattern of the pillar, the baluster-shaped colonettes of the box, and the pinched-in claw feet. The carving, characteristic of a sizable number of New York rococo pieces, includes a quatrefoil rosette centered in the shell on the knees and, on the knees and the pillar, leafage articulated in simple, incised lines, all carved elements set off against a textured background.

New York–made tables having hinged tops that enable them to be put against the wall when not in use were designed especially for card playing and survive in large numbers from the colonial period. Their ubiquity is not unexpected, since gaming—card playing in particular—was a fashionable, often passionate, pastime in colonial New York.[91] Though the card tables were certainly in use earlier, one of the first specific references to them appeared in a newspaper advertisement of 1766.[92] It was not until the early 1770s, however, that New York's leading craftsmen—Joseph Cox, Samuel Prince, and Marinus Willett—promoted the sale of mahogany card tables of the best quality.[93] They were undoubtedly referring to the serpentine type, often made in pairs and known today in a large number of fine examples. The distinguishing features of this kind of table are: a boldly serpentine front, semiserpentine side rails, and large, square front corners supported on cabriole legs that end in claw-and-ball feet. The bottom edge of the rails has gadrooning, the knees have *C*-scroll and leaf carving, and the baize-covered playing surface has recessed corners for candlesticks

and dished-out areas for gaming counters. Most of the tables have a fifth, swing leg that provides a more stable and symmetrical form than that of the four-legged type favored in New England and Pennsylvania.

On the basis of consistent differences in proportion and decoration as well as of methods of construction, many of the best of these surviving five-legged serpentine tables fall into two distinct groups, demonstrably the work of two separate, unidentified shops.[94] The first group includes a pair of tables from the Beekman family, one of them marked on the underside with the chalk initials *IWB*, for James William Beekman (1815–1877). Though they are not mentioned in the household furniture accounts of James William's grandfather, they may well have been made for him in the late 1760s. The tables, remarkable for the shallowness of their skirts, the delicacy of their gadrooned edges, the sense of movement conveyed by the pairs of inward-facing *C*-scrolls on their knees, and the attenuated elegance of their legs, have a lightness, an airiness of stance, that captures the essence of the rococo. Identical in design and clearly from the same shop is a table, its provenance unknown (**No. 108**), that differs from the Beekman example only in certain aspects of the carving.

The tables of the second group are represented by one (**No. 109**) that descended in the Van Rensselaer family. It was quite likely made for Stephen II for use in the manor house he built on the Hudson River, near Albany, between 1765 and 1768. The table's deep skirts, bold gadrooning, and heavy legs and feet result in an effect of massive solidity. That static quality is reinforced by stark, stylized knee carving, which consists of symmetrical, outward-facing pairs of *C*-scrolls surrounded by mantles articulated with vigorous parallel furrows and displaying a minimum of modeling.

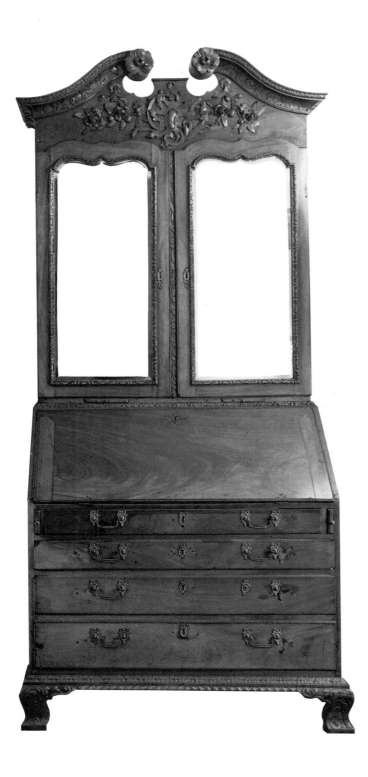

CASE FURNITURE

The most common case-furniture forms in New York were chests, chests-on-chests, linen presses (chests of drawers surmounted by a cabinet having drawers or trays), desks, and, more rarely, desks and bookcases. Missing from the list are the high chest (highboy) and the dressing table (lowboy) so popular in New England and Pennsylvania. Since those uniquely American forms, with their scroll tops and cabriole legs, were the most susceptible of all case furniture to rococo ornament, their absence is perhaps the most cogent evidence that by the third quarter of the century fashionable New Yorkers wanted proper "English" furniture and rejected all colonial variations. It was surely no accident that Samuel Prince, undisputed leader among New York cabinetmakers, decided to call his shop At the Sign of the Chest of Drawers and that he chose to picture on his engraved label a chest-on-chest (FIG. 37, p. 154). Though chests and linen presses labeled by Prince or Burling are known, they are all solid and four-square and do not merit the accolade rococo.

Only on the occasional chest or desk and bookcase is rich carving in a local interpretation of the style to be found. A desk and bookcase (**No. 110**) featuring a scroll pediment and mirrored doors with scalloped top rails is the most elaborate of those known from the 1750s. All the major moldings are carved, and the pediment board, or tympanum, has applied scrolls and leafage and a central asymmetrical cabochon. The decoration looks to be the work of the carver of the first-floor chimneypiece at Philipse Manor (FIG. 9, p. 22): grape leaves with similar veining and fruit with similar modeling, even similar trilobate rosettes in the scroll pediment.

The flat-carved moldings and feet on the desk and bookcase compare closely with those on the most elaborate of all New York chests of drawers (**No. 111**). The name Van Ranslaer inscribed on the reverse of the writing slide documents its provenance in that family. Characteristically diminutive, squat and solid, it nonetheless commands respect for its combination of serpentine facade, projecting canted corners, carved ornament, and pierced brasses.

110

Desk and bookcase, New York, 1755–60
Mahogany; tulip poplar, H.: 99½ in.
The Chipstone Foundation

III

Chest of drawers, New York, 1755–65
Mahogany; tulip poplar, L.: 35½ in.
Winterthur Museum

112

Side chair, New York, 1765–75
Mahogany; sweet gum, H.: 38⅞ in.
The Metropolitan Museum of Art

113

Armchair, New York, ca. 1775
Mahogany; red oak, H.: 39½ in.
The Metropolitan Museum of Art

SEATING FURNITURE

A well-known type of New York chair—its splat of the tassel-and-ruffle design and so known as the tassel-back—seems to have been one particularly favored by the Van Rensselaers; at least four different sets of tassel-back chairs have associations with branches of that family. The tassel-back has a better claim than most New York chairs to be called rococo, as is demonstrated by one of the Van Rensselaer examples (**No. 112**). Here, a C-scroll with rocaille mantle on the crest rail and a tassel over a ruffled band on the splat are both flanked by pairs of carved leaf fronds. The mantle, embellished with carved peanuts and pinwheels, is similar to that found on the knees of some New York card tables (see No. 108). In other respects, the Van Rensselaer chair exhibits a purely New York sensibility: broad, unrelieved flat surfaces on stile and seat rail, shaped rear legs, and four-square claw feet.

The most fully rococo of New York seating furniture, illustrated here in the armchair (**No. 113**) from a set made about 1775 for Samuel Verplanck (1737–1820), has what appears on first glance to be a Gothic-style splat, the result of paired lancet openings within a pointed arch in the lower section. The splat, while a variation on a Manwaring pattern (FIG. 36, p. 148) especially popular in Massachusetts, was a standard design on examples imported from England. The chair itself has carved motifs characteristic of New York: a ruffled mantle below a central C-scroll on the crest, ruffled bands forming the outer edges and the bottom edges of the two circular openings on the splat's upper section, rosettes in the lancet-like openings on the splat's lower section, eagle's-head arm terminals, and ruffled bands forming the legs' top edges.

A mahogany bedstead with elaborately carved footposts and rails (FIG. 38), long thought to be English, can be plausibly attributed to New York because of affinities between its carving and that of chimneypieces in Philipse Manor. For example, the bedstead's oversize capitals in the form of baskets of fruit and grain reveal the same combination of grapes, grape leaves, and plums as the garlands on the side scrolls of the Philipse second-floor overmantel; both elements, having a verisimilitude unusual in New York carving, are probably the work of the same hand. The bedstead's knees have paired C-scrolls and dependent grapevines, a combination of motifs that also appears on a Charleston ceremonial chair (FIG. 40, p. 169). Perhaps the carver Henry Hardcastle, active in New York from 1751 to 1755 and in Charleston in 1755 to 1756, can be credited with all this work.[95]

FIGURE 38. *Bedstead*, probably New York, ca. 1755. Mahogany, H.: 89⅛ in. (226.4 cm.). Society for the Preservation of New England Antiquities, a bequest of Janet M. Agnew (1975.152)

Williamsburg and Charleston

Until recently, the South has been disproportionately neglected in the history of eighteenth-century American furniture. The region's plantation economy was thought to have precluded development of the urban centers necessary to the cabinetmaking business, and distinctive regional styles were not recognized, in the belief that most furniture, especially any of stylistic consequence, must have been imported.

There is some truth to those old assertions. A comprehensive study of the furniture trade in coastal North Carolina has revealed but one modest instance of the rococo, a pair of chairs, based on a design in Chippendale's *Director*, that have been attributed to New Bern, the capital city in the colonial era.[96] The uniqueness of their discovery is consistent with the absence of any mention of a carver in North Carolina records prior to 1790. The study did, however, reveal a widespread production of furniture in the rural areas—often the part-time work of farmers, often of recognizable local style. That pattern probably typifies much of the South, with important exceptions, principally Williamsburg, Virginia, and Charleston, South Carolina,[97] two cities sufficiently established at mid-century to rise to the challenge of the emerging rococo style.

Williamsburg, situated in the Tidewater on the peninsula between the James and the York rivers, was the capital of the Virginia colony from 1699 until it was supplanted by Richmond in 1779. With a population of about three thousand permanent residents throughout the quarter-century prior to the Revolution, it was also the largest city. To its citizenry must be added the seasonal influx of delegates from Virginia's fifty-nine counties for the meetings of the House of Burgesses and for sessions of the General Court. The proprietors of innumerable Virginia plantations, many from families grown rich in the tobacco trade, were also frequent visitors. With their splendid plantation houses, they constituted a pool of clients ready for the latest fashions—

that is, on those occasions when they did not order their goods directly from England.[98]

The city was clearly the center of furniture manufacture in colonial Virginia.[99] Though no comprehensive list of the region's furniture craftsmen has been published, fully thirty-three of fifty-seven furnituremakers' advertisements appearing in the *Virginia Gazette* were those of Williamsburg men; second-place Fredericksburg was represented by only four. Because the newspaper notices were mostly appeals by shop masters for journeyman cabinetmakers rather than of cabinetwork for sale, it is apparent that during the boom years before independence Williamsburg had only a handful of established cabinet shops and that the skilled woodworkers needed to man them were in short supply.

None of the furniture attributed to the city's shops is labeled, but a Masonic master's chair (No. 123) is signed by its maker, Benjamin Bucktrout (d. 1813), who in 1766 advertised as a "Cabinet Maker, from London, [who] makes all sorts of cabinetwork, either plain or ornamental, in the neatest and newest fashions."[100] Bucktrout's extraordinary chair, surely his masterpiece, ranks among Williamsburg's greatest contributions to the American rococo. The chair's front legs are directly copied from Plate XXI of *The Director*, a book that Bucktrout may well have brought with him from England and possibly the one recorded as being a fixture in a shop where he was employed.

Robert Carter, of Nomini Hall, one of Virginia's leading planters, lived in Williamsburg from 1761 to 1772 and kept accounts that are the most detailed evidence of Virginians' buying of Williamsburg-made furniture.[101] During his sojourn in the city, Carter bought almost all his furniture from local makers, mainly from the two leading shops. The first was the establishment of Peter Scott (1694–1775), who had come to Williamsburg by 1722 and set up in business by 1733.[102] A half-dozen newspaper notices are about the only record we have of Scott, but he is known to have been a man of local prominence. He was a member of the Common Council for forty years, and the site where he toiled even longer was a well-known landmark. (One of his patrons was Thomas Jefferson, who purchased much of his furniture in Williamsburg before the Revolution.) Scott remained active until his death, in 1775. A considerable body of locally made furniture has now been attributed to his shop, a few of the pieces, mostly chairs, decorated with passages of carving that may be read as rococo.

The Nicholson Street concern of Anthony Hay, begun about 1751 and carried on by Hay's successors for more than a quarter-century, blossomed into the second of Williamsburg's leading workshops.[103] Employing London-trained cabinetmakers and carvers, and even possessing a copy of

The Director, it was surely the paramount source of rococo-style furniture in the city. With nearly a dozen men identified with its operation during the 1760s[104] (and probably twice that number associated with it during its existence), one can reasonably assume that in time a certain continuity—a house style—developed in its work. Hay, who first advertised for journeyman help in 1751, had within a few years engaged the services of James Wilson, a carver from London, to assist in the new fashion for ornament. In 1755, Wilson himself advertised that he worked in plaster and wood "and is to be spoke with at Mr. Anthony Hay's, Cabinet-Maker."[105] Wilson has been credited with an official armchair (FIG. 39) whose elaborately carved *C*-scrolls and acanthus leaves are not unlike motifs found on the knees of certain Massachusetts and New York work (see Nos. 98, 108). The chair, made for use in the capitol sometime after it was rebuilt following a fire in 1747,[106] therefore exhibits what is possibly the earliest instance of the rococo in Williamsburg. It is probable that Wilson's arrival coincided with the city's introduction to the new style, and it may be his hand that is seen in the nascent rococo carving of tables and chairs associated with Hay's shop.

In 1765, Bucktrout was working for Hay. Two years later, probably because of failing health, Hay announced his retirement, confident that "the Gentlemen who have bespoke Work of the subscriber may depend upon having it made in the best manner by Mr. Benjamin Bucktrout."[107] Though Hay continued to own the property, Bucktrout served as master in the shop until December 1770, when Hay died and Bucktrout was replaced by Edmund Dickinson (d. 1778), who had also worked briefly for Hay in the mid-1760s. Bucktrout then set up shop on Francis Street and flourished during the 1770s.

Dickinson, like Hay, formed an association with an English-trained carver. George Hamilton, a "Carver and Gilder, just from Britain," advertised his services at Dickinson's shop on 28 July 1774.[108] Hamilton must have worked on the furnishings for the Governor's Palace, for which Dickinson was paid £92 in 1776. Dickinson prospered in his new position until 1778, when, as a major in the 1st Virginia Regiment, he was killed in battle. The inventory of his library listed "Chippendales Designs" (i.e., *The Director*),[109] the only reference to a furniture pattern book in eighteenth-century Williamsburg and likely the copy Bucktrout presumably brought to the Hay shop.

Among Virginians, even the wealthiest, there seems to have been a preference in locally made pieces not for the richly ornamented but for what was called the "neat and plain." Except for some modest tables and chairs associated with the Scott shop and a few elaborate china tables and a

FIGURE 39. *Capitol chair*, Williamsburg, 1750–55. Mahogany; beech, H.: 49 in. (124.5 cm.). The Colonial Williamsburg Foundation (30-215)

series of grand Masonic chairs associated with the Hay shop, examples of Williamsburg rococo carving are as yet too rare to establish a distinctive Williamsburg style.[110]

Charleston, founded in 1680 and incorporated in 1783, was the capital of South Carolina until 1790, when the government removed to Columbia. The oldest city in the colony, as well as the largest and most prosperous, Charleston is situated at the tip of a long, narrow peninsula flanked by the Ashley and Cooper rivers. Where the rivers meet, they form the large and well-protected harbor, the finest in the southeast, that enabled the city to become the region's leading seaport and the economic center of the Carolina Low Country.

In 1770, Lieutenant Governor William Bull counted 1,292 houses in the colony, from which he extrapolated a population of 10,900.[111] In the decade before the Revolution, Charleston's exports to Great Britain—primarily rice and indigo—were worth almost three times as much as exports shipped from second-place New England.[112] The city's resulting wealth was acknowledged to be equal to or greater than that of anywhere else in the American colonies. In *London Magazine* of June 1762, the city was described as "the politest, as it is one of the richest in America."[113] Josiah Quincy, Jr., visiting the capital in 1773, wrote home to Boston that "in grandeur, splendour of buildings, decorations... and indeed in almost everything, it far surpasses all I ever saw, or expected to see, in America."[114]

Even in the colonial period, Charleston had a considerable furniture industry and employed great numbers of artisans, several hundred of whom are known by name.[115] Among the more prominent are those who advertised in the local press between 1750 and 1785: some twenty-six cabinetmakers, ten carvers and gilders, fourteen upholsterers, and three looking-glass makers,[116] whose shops were interspersed among the houses of their wealthy merchant clientele on the principal thoroughfares of the city—Tradd, Meeting, Broad, King, and Queen streets. Their notices, unlike those for journeyman help published by their Williamsburg peers, sought to sell cabinetwork in a highly competitive buyer's market. The tenor of their entreaties was expressed by John Fisher, a cabinetmaker from London, in the *South Carolina Gazette & Country Journal* of 5 May 1767: "Those Gentlemen and Ladies who please to favour him with their commands, may depend on having their orders well executed, and on the shortest notice." The advertisements also illustrate that Charleston was the center for the manufacture of fashionable furniture throughout South Carolina. As one artisan proclaimed in 1754: "All Letters and Orders for the Country shall be punctually answered; and the Goods put up in a safe Manner for Carriage, and sent by whatever Conveyance

directed."[117] Abraham Pearce, a carver recently arrived from London, boasted an even wider influence in 1768: "Orders from the country, or any of the northern provinces, will be punctually complied with."

Though no signed or labeled or otherwise documented Charleston furniture in the rococo taste has been discovered, the name of one maker, Thomas Elfe (ca. 1719-1795), has long been synonymous with eighteenth-century Charleston cabinetwork.[118] His celebrity stems from the chance survival of his account book for the years 1768-75, the apogee of the fashion for the rococo. The book records that during that time, with the assistance of handicraft slaves (sawyers, joiners, cabinetmakers) and specialist contract employees, such as carvers, his shop made some fifteen hundred pieces of furniture both plain and ornamented and was patronized by most of the city's leading families. The book further shows that over those years Elfe ran a successful business, invested in real estate, and achieved a measure of local prominence. Though most Charleston case furniture is routinely attributed to Elfe's shop, particularly those pieces having figure-eight-patterned frets, we can only guess what his work from the 1760s and 1770s looked like.

Elfe, whose origins are obscure, was probably English born and London trained, as were so many of Charleston's craftsmen. By 1747, he had an established shop; in 1751, he advertised having "a very good upholsterer from London" to do work in "the best and newest manner."[119] In 1756, he went into partnership with another cabinetmaker, Thomas Hutchinson, and together they were employed on the lavish new State House (built 1753-56; burned 1788). On 13 March 1756, the Commons House of Assembly resolved to order furniture for the New Council Chamber, and on 14 March 1758, Elfe and Hutchinson submitted a bill for £728-2-6 for furniture for the room. What appears to be one piece from that group survives (though now missing its ornamental crest)—the South Carolina royal governor's chair (FIG. 40).[120] Its eagle's-head armrests, knees with C-scrolls and dependent grapevines, and hairy-paw feet qualify the chair to be the earliest documented carving in Charleston in any way suggesting the rococo style. Though most of the ornament is executed in a less advanced manner than that of the contemporaneous capitol chair at Williamsburg (FIG. 39, p. 167), the treatment of the knees and arms is markedly similar to New York work of the same decade. Again, is there a connection with the carver Henry Hardcastle, who moved from New York to Charleston sometime between 1755 and 1756?

At the beginning of the next decade, Charlestonians exhibited a predilection for the Chinese taste (an aspect of the rococo generously represented in Chippendale's *Director*). In 1761, Peter Hall, cabinetmaker from London, offered to

FIGURE 40. *Royal governor's chair*, Charleston, 1756–58.
Mahogany; sweet gum, H.: 53⅜ in. (135.6 cm.).
McKissick Museum, The University of South Carolina

supply "Chinese tables of all sorts, shelves trays, chimney pieces, brackets, etc, being at present the most elegant and admired fashion in London." A "Chinese Tea Table" is mentioned at the beginning (1768) of Elfe's surviving accounts. During the years from 1771 to 1774, Elfe was an enthusiastic proponent of the fashion for chinoiserie, crafting many such tea tables having applied rims and tops and desks and bookcases having glazed "Chineas dores." Elfe's ledger shows that in the 1770s he also specialized in a variety of forms embellished with other rococo ornament. They included double chests with fretwork and pierced scroll tops, bedsteads with eagle's-claw feet, chairs with carved or scroll backs, and mahogany picture frames.[121]

The height of the vogue for the rococo style must have coincided with the increased immigration to Charleston in the late 1760s of highly skilled British cabinetmakers, carvers, and other craftsmen. Several of them were associated with Elfe: London cabinetmaker John Fisher (arrived 1767) was in partnership with him between about 1768 and 1771,[122] carvers Thomas Woodin (arrived by 1764), to whom he owed money in 1768,[123] and Abraham Pearce (arrived 1768), who worked steadily in his shop from 1769 until 1774. John Lord (arrived 1766) advertised in 1767 that he provided "gilding and all branches of house and furniture carving, in the Chinese, French, and Gothic tastes."[124] Lord, who appears in Elfe's accounts just once, in 1774, trained a number of apprentices, including Henry Hainsdorff and Joseph Parkinson (probably Charleston's first native carvers), before returning to England in 1775.[125]

London fashion, the standard by which Charlestonians measured their furnishings, was available in the work of immigrant craftsmen and in the imported furniture that served as models for locally made counterparts. Richard Magrath, for example, offered in 1772 "carved Chairs of the newest fashion, splat Backs, with hollow slats and commode fronts, of the same Pattern as those imported by Peter Manigault, Esq."[126] In addition, the craftsmen of Charleston had access to pattern books showing engraved rococo ornament, principally Chippendale's *Director.*[127] The local bookseller Robert Wells advertised it in 1766 and again in 1772, along with the other deluxe folio pattern book of the period, Ince and Mayhew's *Universal System.* Copies of Chippendale's book were recorded in the inventories of the builder and carver Ezra Waite (d. 1771) and of Walter Russell (d. 1776), an upholsterer from London who had rooms in Elfe's house in 1773.[128] Whole designs or individual motifs from the book, however, were rarely copied. The exception is a well-known library bookcase (FIG. 43, p. 179) only slightly amended from Plate XCIII in *The Director.*

The Swiss-born painter Jeremiah Theus (1716–1774) arrived in South Carolina in 1735 and settled in Charleston by 1740, where he dominated the portrait-painting business during the third quarter of the century. At his death, he was succeeded by Henry Benbridge (1743–1812), of Philadelphia. Certain other artists visited the city for brief periods, including John Wollaston in 1766–67. A fair number of the resulting portraits of Charlestonians have their original rococo frames. Which of them are of local manufacture is just now being determined. From Elfe's accounts, for example, it is known that Theus purchased stretching frames for his canvases and, after late 1772, mahogany picture frames.[129] On 18 November 1774, the brothers John and Hamilton Stevenson, painters who had recently started a drawing and painting academy, advertised: "The better to accommodate their Employers, and to lesson the great expence of Framing, they have contracted with, and brought out a Carver & Gilder, and Frame Pictures, Prints &c, at the London Prices."[130]

Possibly Theus's earliest dated picture having an American frame is that of Mrs. Algernon Wilson, painted in 1756 (FIG. 41). Of white pine, carved and gilded, the frame tends to overpower the small (some 16½-by-14-inch) picture. Though the frame's immediate prototype is unknown, its pierced rocaille mantling within a large cavetto molding is a pattern frequently found on imported frames, such as those of Wollaston's large-format New York portraits of a few years earlier (see p. 156).

About 1750, Theus painted seven small-format portraits of the planter Barnard Elliott, his wife, and his children, all having simple mahogany frames. About 1766, he painted full, fifty-by-forty-inch images of the patriot Colonel Barnard Elliott, Jr. (1740–1778) (**No. 114**), and his bride, Mary Elizabeth (Bellinger). They are among the artist's most splendid efforts: the decorative stylishness of the subjects' attire more than compensates for the figures' lack of anatomical accuracy. The frames, of New England pine, are spectacular examples of the full rococo taste. Composed of a broad, flat, black-painted area between an inner molding and scrolled outer edges that are both carved and gilded, they have an expansive grandeur reminiscent of the pierced frames of the same date carved by James Strachan of New York (see p. 156).

Wollaston's Charleston portraits, all realized in a palette of delicate rococo pastels, present an assurance and a softness of modeling not found in his earlier work.[131] Prime examples of the seventeen known paintings of this phase of the artist's oeuvre are the portraits of John Beale and Mrs. Beale (**No. 115**). The frame may lack the coherence of design and

FIGURE 41. *Picture frame*, Charleston, ca. 1756.
White pine, gilded, 22½ x 20⅛ in. (57.2 x 51.1 cm.).
With portrait of Mrs. Algernon Wilson by Jeremiah Theus.
Museum of Early Southern Decorative Arts (2024.52)

114

Picture frame, Charleston, ca. 1766
White pine, gilded and painted,
61⅜ x 51⅝ in.
With portrait of Barnard Elliott, Jr.,
by Jeremiah Theus
Gibbes Museum of Art

the conviction of execution possessed by that of Theus's *Colonel Elliott*, but though it is heavy in scale and the pierced rocaille mantles attached to the outer scrolls look like afterthoughts, it nonetheless has an endearing rococo charm. The Beales were Tories who fled to England in 1775, doubtless taking with them the portraits, which were found there some years ago. The frame of Mrs. Beale's picture is of native Carolina cypress, but that of her husband's is of European red pine, from which one may conclude that the original frame was lost and a replacement made abroad.

The monument to Lady Anne Murray (**No. 116**), now in First Scots Presbyterian Church, erected in 1814 at 57 Meeting Street, but originally part of an earlier building on the same site, is carved of New England white pine and marbleized rather than chiseled from marble itself in the English manner. A rare and magnificent example of pre-Revolutionary church furnishing, it is unusual for its size and use of rococo ornament[132] and remarkable for being, apparently, the only example of early Charleston architectural carving that has never been repainted.

The material of which the memorial is made is known to have been shipped to Charleston from New England. In 1768, the local Assembly authorized payment "for New England Pine plank for the Carver £55:17:19."[133] The carver, Thomas Woodin, had in the previous year fulfilled a commission for the State House. One of two prominent English artisans then in the city,[134] he is a likely candidate for the authorship of the memorial to Lady Anne.

The monument, which was completed by 1772, consists of a heavy crossetted and marbleized frame with rococo scrolls and leafage carved in high relief at the sides and on the top, where they form an oversize cartouche framing a coat of arms, those of Lady Anne's husband's family quartering those of hers. The stone-colored moldings and the carving are highlighted against a dark ground. The inscription, painted in gold on a rectangular black field, reads in part: "In this Cemetery lie the Remains / of / The Right Honourable / Lady Anne Murray, / Third Daughter / of George Earl of Cromarty / A young Noblewoman as / conspicuous for Piety & Virtue / as she was for / High Birth & illustrious descent / She died the 17th of January 1768 / much lamented."

Lady Anne's first marriage was to the Honorable Edmond Atkins, president of the Council of South Carolina; her second was to John Murray, a Scots physician who had come to the Carolinas during the 1740s. Her inscription does not fill the tablet, but the space reserved for that of her husband, who died in 1774, was preempted to commemorate one of his relatives, "Geo Murray Esqr. deputy Secretary of So. Carolina," who died 24 September 1772.

115

Picture frame, Charleston, ca. 1767
Cypress, gilded, 37 x 32 in.
With portrait of Mrs. John Beale
by John Wollaston
Museum of Early Southern Decorative Arts

116

Memorial to Lady Anne Murray, Charleston, 1768–72
White pine, marbleized, H.: 73½ in.
First Scots Presbyterian Church, Charleston

TABLES

To identify the origin of round tea tables—a standard form having no secondary woods—is not always easy, but the source of some southern examples has been postulated. One such table (**No. 117**) has recently been established as of Virginia manufacture. It descended in the Lee family of Stratford and remains part of the furnishings of Stratford Hall, the ancestral Lee mansion, on which building was begun about 1738. On the basis of the carving, in particular the characteristic three-part bellflower on the knees, the table has been attributed to the Williamsburg shop of Peter Scott.[135]

The pattern of carving on the table's piecrust edge may be the most elaborate of any on an American example; its combination of shells and *C*- and *S*-scrolls repeats almost exactly the applied cast border decoration of mid-century silver salvers—circular trays that were part of the tea equipage. Though a few American salvers are known with the same border design, such as one made in the shop of Paul Revere about 1761 for the Chandler family (No. 71), they were produced in far greater numbers in London. (Peyton Randolph, speaker of the House of Burgesses in Williamsburg in 1766-67, owned a pair of such salvers, his made by the London silversmith William Peaston between 1753 and 1755.)[136] It must be to one of those English models that the tabletop design is indebted. The elaborate carving extends to the pillar and legs, with the leafage on the vasiform part of the pillar—asymmetrical, flamelike, and lapping at the base of the column—the table's most rococo aspect.

Another round tea table (**No. 118**) descended in the Gibbes and Holmes families of Charleston, where it is thought to have been made. The piecrust top edge has an unexceptional scallop pattern but the outer molding is gadroon-carved in a manner again suggesting work in silver (see No. 74). The pedestal is very like that of the Lee family table. Though the carving of the Virginia example is more lively, the two share the same program of ornament, even to the acanthus leafage on the knees with the pendent three-part bellflower that has been associated with the Scott shop.[137]

In Virginia furniture, mature rococo ornament is most evident in a handful of rectangular tables having straight legs and pierced galleries and believed to have been made in Williamsburg between about 1765 and 1775 in the shop of Anthony Hay. Like their counterparts from Portsmouth, New Hampshire (see No. 102), they are sometimes called "China Tables," after the two illustrated in *The Director* (Plate LI). According to Chippendale, they were intended "for holding each a Set of China, and may be used as Tea-

117

Tea table, Williamsburg, 1755-70
Mahogany, Diam.: 32⅞ in.
Robert E. Lee Memorial Association

Tables." The ornament of the Virginia examples is either pierced (sawed out) or a combination of pierced and carved. Thus a rococo effect could be achieved without the participation of a professional carver.

One of the pierced-work tables (**No. 119**), especially distinguished for its design and condition, has a tradition of ownership in the Lewis and Byrd families of Virginia. There has long been speculation that the profile of a bird centered within its pierced side rails is an allusion to the name of the latter family. An engaging hypothesis is that the table was commissioned around 1762–63, when the interiors of Westover, the James River plantation of William Byrd III (1728–1777), were being updated with stucco ceilings in the rococo style.

The table is made entirely of mahogany, now having developed a lustrous deep red patina.[138] The legs and the gallery are cut from the solid, a practice unusual in English work but not in American. Except for the top, all elements of the table are extensively pierced: the gallery sawed out in a guilloche pattern formed by pairs of undulating curves; the legs, with a repeated pattern of figure eights, diamonds, and rosettes. The effect of the openwork, even within a rigidly four-square form, is unmistakably rococo. It is also, literally, Chinese Chippendale. *The Director* contains a number of illustrations of "Chinese Chairs," "Chinese Cabinets," and "china Cases" of noticeably similar treatment. In another design, Chippendale says, "The Feet and Rails ... are cut through; which gives it an airy Look."[139] Elsewhere (Plate CXXIII), he notes, "The Frame is pierced through, but may be solid, and the Fret glued on," the latter an option employed on the next table.

The most fully developed of the carved southern china tables (**No. 120**) has serpentine rails and tapered legs carved with undulating vines and ending in guttae feet (so called after a triangular element of the Doric order).[140] A closely related counterpart, but with straight sides, has a history of Washington ownership at Mount Vernon. Since on this serpentine-railed example the delicate tapering of the legs heralds the emerging neoclassical style, the table would date from the mid-1770s, when the Scots carver George Hamilton joined the shop of Anthony Hay,[141] or later. On that basis, and because of similarities with Hay shop construction and carving, it has now been credited to Williamsburg.[142]

A case can be made for associating tables of this sort with Charleston. Elfe's accounts demonstrate that china, or Chinese, tea tables were a favored local furniture form. Here, the blind fretwork of interlaced hexagons with scrolled central tablet that is carved into the table rails almost matches the fret above the cupboards of a library

bookcase (FIG. 43, p. 179) securely ascribed to Charleston. The table would also seem to conform nicely to the "commode fret China table" for which Elfe charged £45 in February 1774. What *is* the connection between these Williamsburg and Charleston tables? Was there a carver who moved between the two cities?

118

Tea table, Charleston, 1755–70
Mahogany, Diam.: 31¼ in.
Museum of Early Southern Decorative Arts

119

China table, Williamsburg, 1760–75
Mahogany, L.: 36⅜ in.
The Colonial Williamsburg Foundation

120

China table, Williamsburg, ca. 1775
Mahogany, L.: 36 in.
Collection of Mr. and Mrs. George M. Kaufman

Among the most distinctive forms in southern rococo furniture is the Charleston version of the pembroke, or breakfast, table: a serpentine top, straight legs, end rails carved with elaborate scrollwork framing pierced Chinese latticework, and flat stretchers with exaggeratedly broad baluster profiles. The two known examples are almost identical. One (**No. 121**) was found in Charleston in 1954; the other descended in the Middleton family and is still at Middleton Place, outside Charleston. The second table was most likely made for Arthur Middleton (1742–1787), a signer of the Declaration of Independence, after he and his wife, Mary (Izard), returned in 1771 from three years abroad and settled permanently at their plantation. To attribute these tables to Thomas Elfe is not farfetched, for in January 1772 he described just such a piece: "Breakfast table the Ends Carved—£28."

121

Pembroke table, Charleston, 1770–75
Mahogany; ash, L.: 42 in.
The Charleston Museum

CASE FURNITURE

Though no rococo-style case furniture has been identified from Williamsburg cabinet shops, it has long been considered a staple in Charleston work. A chest-on-chest (FIG. 42) that descended in the Deas family of Charleston, presumably made for John Deas (1735-1790), has secondary woods—native cypress and yellow pine—that reinforce a local attribution. The drawer fronts have the figured veneers, beaded edges, and hardware with simple, circular escutcheons suggesting the impending neoclassical taste and a date in the 1770s or later. The only rococo features on the piece are a fretwork of a figure-eight pattern surmounted by a scroll pediment and its pierced tympanum. Centered in the tympanum—here a thin and lacy screen of scrollwork—is a platform meant for a ceramic bust or other ornament. Pieces of this general design are often associated with the name of Thomas Elfe, whose accounts for the years 1771-74 include references to double chests with frets and pierced pediment heads. His descriptions of a "Double Chest of Draw's wth. a pediment head, cut through—£82" and "a Large Close press with a pediment head Culopin [cut open]" admirably suit this double chest.

A library bookcase (FIG. 43) straight out of Chippendale is one of Charleston's most famous pieces of furniture. Cypress secondary woods and a figure-eight fret just under the pediment associate it with the city and possibly even with Elfe's shop. In November 1772, Elfe billed one John Dart £100 for a "Library Book Case wth Chineas doors & Draws under them" (here there are only doors). The design is altered only slightly from Plate XCIII in *The Director*. Faithful to the engraving are the glazed, mullioned doors, including the carved fronds in the arched tops of the end units, but the chest's proportions are vertically oriented in keeping with the high ceilings of southern interiors and a fret has been added above the cupboards.[143]

FIGURE 42. *Chest-on-chest*, Charleston, ca. 1775. Mahogany; cypress, yellow pine, H.: 87 in. (221 cm.). The Colonial Williamsburg Foundation (1974-166)

FIGURE 43. *Library bookcase*, Charleston, 1765–75. Mahogany;
cypress, H.: 106 in. (269.2 cm.). Museum of Early Southern
Decorative Arts (949)

An easy chair (**No. 122**) is one of the few examples of upholstered rococo furniture from the South. The lively, small-scale leg carving—a naturalistically rendered cabochon and leafage on the knees and hairy paws for feet—is so much in the Philadelphia idiom (see No. 149) that the chair was long thought to be from that city. Nevertheless, it is one of a handful with conical arm supports and shaped rear legs of a design that can now be ascribed to Charleston. All have frames with southern woods (all with cypress, some also with red bay), as well as either yellow pine or poplar; two have Charleston histories of ownership.[144] Elfe's accounts list only two easy chairs: in November 1772, "1 Easie chair Eagle claws" for £30; in November 1773, "an Easy chair & Casters Carved feet" for £32, the latter a description that could apply to this chair.

The most magnificent piece of eighteenth-century Virginia furniture is a great ceremonial chair (**No. 123**),[145] its back stamped with the signature of Benjamin Bucktrout, who arrived in Williamsburg about 1765 and was initiated into the Williamsburg Masonic order in February 1774.[146] The high back consists of a compendium of Masonic emblems, its arch-and-keystone crest attesting that the chair was made as a master's chair. Each of the Masonic motifs is of symbolic import; the trowel at upper left, for example, represents the

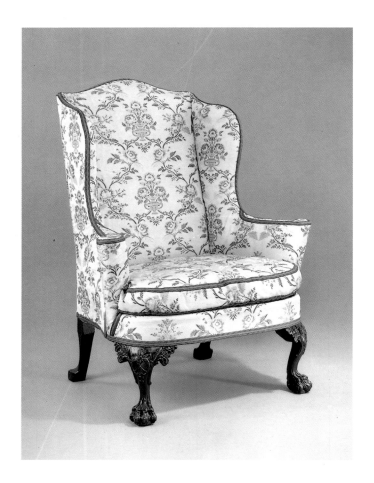

122

Easy chair, Charleston, 1765–75
Mahogany; cypress, H.: 48½ in.
Winterthur Museum

spreading of fraternal love. The significance of the bust of Matthew Prior (1664–1721), after his statue in the Poet's Corner in Westminster Abbey, is now lost. Which Virginia lodge originally commissioned the chair is no longer known, but in 1778 it was taken to Edenton, North Carolina, to preserve it from wartime destruction.

Apart from its Masonic iconography and except for the height of the seat, Bucktrout's masterpiece is readily recognizable as an oversize rococo armchair fashioned from the densest mahogany. The dolphin legs—twisted tail on the knee, fish scales on the ankle, and open-mouthed head forming the foot—are taken from Plate XXI of *The Director*, the only direct cribbing from Chippendale in Williamsburg furniture. Bucktrout, despite his obvious familiarity with the design of English ceremonial chairs, may have been better at execution than at design, for it must be admitted that his great effort lacks total coherence. The front skirt is not without grace, but the carving on the side skirts fails to accommodate the arm supports; the arch and the pilasters from which it springs are unduly heavy; and the medley of artisans' tools cling to the sides of the openwork back as if tossed into a magnetized box. Despite any aesthetic shortcomings this chair and at least two other richly ornamented Williamsburg-made Masonic examples may possess,[147] they all bear witness to the importance in Virginia of a fraternal order to which such luminaries as Washington and Jefferson belonged.

123

Masonic master's chair, 1767–75
Benjamin Bucktrout, Williamsburg
Mahogany; walnut, H.: 65½ in.
The Colonial Williamsburg Foundation

Philadelphia

The most fertile ground for the cultivation of the rococo taste in American furniture was Philadelphia, from which more rococo-style pieces survive than from all the other American cabinetmaking centers combined. Some show rococo ornament grafted onto local forms and some are full expressions of the fashionable London idiom, but nearly all are readily recognizable as what has come to be known as Philadelphia Chippendale. The rococo mode that evolved in that city, enthusiastically adopted by client and craftsman alike, had a powerful influence throughout eastern Pennsylvania and western New Jersey and, to the south, in Delaware and Maryland.

Philadelphia was established by William Penn in 1682 and incorporated in 1701. From 1701 until 1751, during the tenure of James Logan as proprietary agent, the city grew and prospered. Her golden age came in the second half of the century, when she reigned supreme among the American colonies: the nation's first capital, from 1789 to 1800, as well as the state capital, until 1799. During the 1750s, while the population of Boston remained static at about 15,000, that of Philadelphia first exceeded New York's and then continued to grow, reaching some 19,000 in 1760 and 28,500 in 1774.[148] Situated some hundred miles from the sea on the Delaware River (see No. 39) and stretching west to the Schuylkill, the city had unparalleled access to the vast hinterlands of the middle colonies. Commerce and trade in the region's abundant natural produce made Philadelphia rich at precisely the time that the fashion for the rococo in England was at its height.

The city had a large contingent of woodworkers. The names of 172 active between about 1730 and 1760 are known,[149] as are documented pieces by more than 30 working between 1750 and 1785; at least 37 others advertised in the local press between 1731 and 1785,[150] and over 100 are recorded in the tax list of 1783.[151] Many of the craftsmen were native born, but there were also numerous immigrants.

Newspaper advertisements were mostly announcements of the opening or closing of shops or changes of address; few were detailed descriptions of objects for sale. Of about twenty carvers active between 1750 and 1793, nine are known to have been immigrants and those nine constituted the source of almost all the currently known or attributed Philadelphia carving of their era. A survey of all the makers of documented pieces demonstrates that as a rule native-born craftsmen produced plain, uncarved furniture and the immigrants turned out pieces enriched with carved ornament.[152] That finding is hardly surprising: carving was a highly specialized craft for which scant training would have existed in the city.

Intimations of the rococo style began to appear in Philadelphia furniture in the early 1750s. A scroll-top high chest (FIG. 47, p. 199), signed by the cabinetmaker Henry Clifton and dated 1753, is the earliest documented use of naturalistic carving. The knees of the cabriole legs have leafy ornament, the large central drawers have recessed and frilly-edged rocaille shells flanked by streamers of foliage, and a pierced and asymmetrical shield, or cartouche, forms the central finial. All that stylish embellishment is applied to the somewhat old-fashioned and uniquely American high chest with scroll pediment, which had developed in New England during the 1730s and was to remain popular there for four decades. Philadelphia, with her close commercial ties to Boston, took up the form and added up-to-date ornament. Similar shells and leafage were used on seating furniture. Presumably, that was the style of decoration on the eight walnut chairs with "Carved Claw and Knee open back" and the easy-chair frame with "Carved Claw and Knee" sold to Judge Edward Shippen by John Elliott in 1754.[153]

The English-born Elliott (1713–1791) arrived in Philadelphia in 1753 and immediately set about making furniture for fellow Quakers, Shippen among them. He still called himself a cabinetmaker in 1756, but the following year spoke of his looking-glass store. His printed labels, found on many looking glasses, the great majority of them imported, are evidence that the pieces were in Philadelphia in the eighteenth century. Other types of furniture were also imported into the city at that time but lack labels or other documentation that would locate them there. In 1772, furniture valued at £1,085 was shipped to Philadelphia (£860 worth from London alone). That the total represented only about a third the value of furniture imported into the neighboring colonies of New York or Maryland and Virginia gives some indication of the relative importance of the city's own furniture businesses.[154]

The publication in 1762 of the third, enlarged edition of Chippendale's *Director* can now be seen as having heralded the era of the Philadelphia Chippendale, the most thoroughly rococo of all American interpretations of high-style London cabinetwork. In the decade that followed, in a political climate that discouraged the buying of English goods, the city witnessed a confluence of talented young London-trained artisans and worldly and wealthy young Philadelphians eager to assert their standing in colonial society. The time was ripe for Chippendale-style furniture to be produced locally.

The Director was readily available in the colony.[155] Sometime between 1764 and 1769, a copy of the third edition was acquired by the Library Company of Philadelphia (the first subscription library in America), which in 1769 counted nine furnituremakers among its readers. Two of them, Thomas Affleck and Benjamin Randolph, are known to have owned copies.[156] In addition, Robert Bell, a Philadelphia bookseller, advertised the book in 1776, and bookbinder James Muir charged a client for covering a copy a decade later.

In 1775, Bell published the first book on architecture to be printed in America, a Philadelphia edition of Swan's *British Architect* (see p. 6). The illustrations were by John Norman, an English engraver newly arrived in America. Bound into some copies, opposite the title page, was a broadside proposal for printing by subscription a book of furniture designs to be titled *The Gentleman and Cabinet-Maker's Assistant* (No. 5). In typography and phraseology, the broadside apes the title page of the first edition of *The Director* (No. 6). If plans for the book had not been canceled because of the outbreak of war, the illustrations would almost certainly have been modeled after the same source. There could be no more telling evidence of Chippendale's appeal to Philadelphians. The furniture designs were to have been the work of John Folwell, a cabinetmaker best known for the massive mahogany case for David Rittenhouse's orrery (1771) at the University of Pennsylvania and for the Speaker's Chair (1779) in the House of Representatives, both pieces having straight, fret-carved front legs of a type much favored by Chippendale.[157]

The actual use of designs or motifs from *The Director*, while practiced to a greater degree in Philadelphia than anywhere else in the colonies, was limited to a handful of plates illustrating a few chairs and a couple of writing tables and desks and bookcases. Only once is a design copied in toto (see No. 147). Usually, elements from one or more designs are combined in new ways (see No. 138); occasionally, Chippendale's designs are so assimilated as to be almost undetectable (see No. 130).[158]

The only other furniture pattern book recorded in colonial Philadelphia was *Houshold Furniture* (1760–62), advertised in 1762 by Rivington and Brown, booksellers in New York

(see p. 154) and Philadelphia. No fewer than seven of its designs were illustrated on cabinetmaker Benjamin Randolph's trade card, in company with one from *The Director* and one from carver Thomas Johnson's *One Hundred and Fifty New Designs* (London, 1758; 1761).[159]

Randolph (1721–1791), born in Monmouth County, New Jersey, and settled in Philadelphia by 1762, became probably the most prominent of all the native furnituremakers. His surviving ledgers refer to a variety of business ventures.[160] By 1766, he was employing skilled carvers; the following year, he purchased property on Chestnut Street, between Third and Fourth streets, where in 1769 he built a substantial house and a shop, The Golden Eagle. To celebrate, he had James Smither engrave his grand, London-style advertisement (No. 32), which offered "all Sorts of Cabinet & Chairwork Likewise Carving Gilding &c Perform'd in the Chinese and Modern Tastes." In 1769 and 1770, Randolph was extensively occupied in providing architectural carving and furniture for John Cadwalader's incomparable house on Second Street.[161] In early 1770, he advertised that he made wooden buttons, a pointed reminder to Philadelphians not to buy the imported ones made of brass or silver. An outspoken patriot, Randolph joined the First City Troop in 1774. His pocket almanac for 1775 records his association with both Washington and Jefferson, who were in the city for the Second Continental Congress.

More than anything else, the influx into Philadelphia in the 1760s of trained woodworkers, most notably carvers from London, must be the explanation for the extraordinary quality of the Philadelphia rococo. The men came individually, though some of them might have been enticed with specific promises of employment. One of the first and most successful of those artisans was the Aberdeen-born cabinetmaker Thomas Affleck (1740–1795), who had apprenticed in Scotland before moving to London in 1760.[162] Doubtless with high hopes, he sailed for Philadelphia in 1763, a copy of *The Director* under his arm. Though John Penn (1729–1795), grandson of the founder and the colony's new lieutenant governor, arrived at the same time, apparently on the same ship, the claim that he was Affleck's principal patron has not been confirmed.[163] In 1768, Affleck moved from his first shop, on Union Street, to his permanent habitation on Second Street, announcing in the *Pennsylvania Chronicle* of 12 December that he carried on "the cabinet-making business in all its various branches." Thereafter, he was engulfed in the building boom, from which he emerged the wealthiest of Philadelphia craftsmen.[164]

On 25 November 1762, an announcement appeared in the *Pennsylvania Gazette*: "Just imported...from London, and to be Sold by Bernard and Jugiez Carvers and Gilders, at their Looking-Glass Store, in Walnut-Street... A Compleat assortment of Looking-Glasses," the proprietors also offering "All Sort of Carving in Wood or Stone and Gilding done in the neatest Manner."[165] That notice by two men presumably recently arrived from London is the first evidence of a partnership that was to loom large in the Philadelphia rococo. Nicholas Bernard promoted the business by setting up shop briefly in other colonial cities—in Charleston during the fall and winter of 1765/66; in New York in the summer of 1769.[166] He and Martin Jugiez specialized in carving coats of arms, such as that of King George III, for the Council Chamber of Charleston's new State House, and, for Thomas, Lord Fairfax, proprietor of five million acres in the Northern Neck of Virginia, that of his family, featured in a pattern to be cast into chimneybacks.[167] In 1766, Benjamin Chew paid the men for architectural carving at Cliveden, his country house (see p. 26). After their advertisements in Philadelphia papers in 1767 and 1769, their business took off.

When Bernard and Jugiez signed the first Philadelphia nonimportation agreement, on 25 October 1765, they were joined by another recently arrived carver,[168] one Hercules Courtenay, a man who had been trained in the hotbed of the London rococo. On 13 May 1756, he had begun a seven-year apprenticeship with "Tho: Johnson of St Giles in the fields Carver"; duty or tax of £30 on the indenture was not paid until 14 February 1760.[169] In the years immediately following the first edition of *The Director* (1754), Thomas Johnson (b. 1714) was the most active promoter of carving in the rococo style. The fifty-three engraved plates he issued in 1756 and 1757, while Courtenay was in his shop, and reissued in book form in 1758 and 1761, had great influence.[170]

Courtenay entered the employ of Benjamin Randolph by late 1766. Between 1766 and 1769, there are numerous references to him in Randolph's accounts, the most instructive of which is a tailor's charge for "making your Carver Courteney a...Coat."[171] He finally went out on his own in 1769. On 14 August, he advertised in the *Pennsylvania Chronicle* as "Carver and Gilder, from London," who "undertakes all Manner of Carving and Gilding, in the newest Taste, at his House in Front-Street, between Chestnut and Walnut Streets." By the summer of 1770, he was busy with the finest commissions in town.

The last of the immigrant carvers about whom anything much is known is James Reynolds (d. 1794).[172] His arrival with his wife was announced in the *Pennsylvania Gazette* of 21 August 1766. An advertisement appeared in the same newspaper within two weeks: "James Reynolds, carver and gilder, Just arrived from London... at his House in Dock-Street... undertakes to execute all the various Branches of Carving and Gilding in the newest, neatest, and genteelest

Taste."[173] The next year, Reynolds moved to Front Street, between Chestnut and Walnut (just where Courtenay was to settle in 1769). He advertised heavily in the fall of 1767 and in 1768, offering imported looking glasses as well as "All the several Branches of Carving and Gilding." By 1770, he too was involved in many of the city's major projects.

While those men were to be the key players in the Philadelphia rococo up to the Revolution, there were others active in the style, though generally at a less brilliant level. Native-born James Gillingham (1736–1781), a partner of Henry Clifton's between 1761 and 1768, labeled chairs based on Plate X in *The Director* and at least once employed Bernard and Jugiez to embellish his work. Thomas Tufft (d. 1788), whose label (FIG. 44) is affixed to some competently carved pieces, took over Gillingham's shop in 1773.

By the end of the 1760s, there had been a sea change in Philadelphia high fashion. Whereas at the beginning of the decade carving had been limited in scope and heavy in execution, now, in the hands of the London-trained talent, it was exhibiting a spirit of dazzling excess, just what the rococo did best. What happened next vividly demonstrates the factors that nourished the style in Philadelphia: John Cadwalader and Samuel Powel, two rich and influential young men, both recently married, bought fine, nearly new town houses and set about having the interiors totally remodeled in the most elaborate rococo manner. The work on the houses and their furnishings, proceeding concurrently, required the combined efforts of the best woodworkers in the city. Affleck and Randolph (the two leading cabinetmakers) and Bernard and Jugiez, Courtenay, and Reynolds (the four leading carvers) were all engaged. The result was architecture and furniture in the fullest rococo style America was to achieve. Thereafter, until war broke out, anyone aspiring to the height of fashion—including Benjamin Chew, who purchased John Penn's town house in 1771; Penn himself, who built Lansdowne, the most magnificent of the region's country seats, in 1773; and Cadwalader's cousin John Dickinson, who redid the great house of John Ross (see p. 85) in 1774 (all buildings now gone without a trace)—would have looked to the Cadwalader and the Powel houses as the stylistic benchmark.

A book of *Prices of Cabinet & Chair Work*, published in Philadelphia in 1772,[174] is a unique document of rococo furniture; there is nothing comparable in the other colonies or in England. Compiled in an effort to regulate what cabinetmakers should pay journeymen for specific tasks and what they should charge their clients for completed pieces, the book gives a remarkably detailed picture of the furniture obtainable in Philadelphia during the height of the rococo. (Traditional forms from the Queen Anne period, which had

FIGURE 44. *Label of Thomas Tufft*, Philadelphia, ca. 1770. Engraving on paper, 1⅜ x 2⅝ in. (3.5 x 6.7 cm.). Private collection

been the fashion in the 1750s, were also included.) Listed in the *Price Book* were the various optional embellishments for every type of chair, table, and chest, and the going rate for each, according to the patron's choice of wood, which could be either Pennsylvania walnut or the more costly Caribbean mahogany. Thus, a Philadelphia high chest, made of walnut, having a flat top and no carving, was priced at £13 (including the journeyman's pay of £3-10-0); another chest, of mahogany, having a scroll pediment and carved work, cost £21 (the journeyman receiving £5-10-0). The full rococo style—implicit in the listed chairs and tables with crooked (cabriole) legs and leaves on the knees or Marlborough feet (straight legs) with bases, brackets, and frets; and chests with scroll or pitch pediments with dentils, frets, and shields—was by far the most expensive.

Philadelphia chairs or tables with straight, square legs, usually either molded or plain and ending in applied cuffs, are described by the sobriquet Marlborough. On exceptional pieces, the sides of the legs are cut away to form ornamental panels of naturalistic foliage and blind fretwork in Gothic and Chinese patterns, and are linked to the chair or the table skirt by pierced brackets. These are the rococo features of the Marlborough style. The Marlborough leg and the alternate cabriole type were probably both offered simultaneously from the 1750s, though the earliest known use of the eponymous term is in 1766, on Philadelphia cabinetmaker Samuel Mickle's drawing of a straight-leg chair.[175] The *Price Book*, in devoting separate sections to "Chairs Marlbrough

feet," "Soffas Marlborough feet," and "Card tables with Marlbrough feet," shows how important the straight leg had become. The same option appears in all editions of *The Director*, but the term "Marlborough" seems not to have been used in England. Its origin and any connection with the ducal house have yet to be determined.

John Cadwalader may be considered the exemplar of the great Philadelphia patrons of the rococo.[176] Born to the wife of an eminent physician, Cadwalader attended the College of Philadelphia before completing his education in England and doing the grand tour in France and Italy. His marriage in 1768 to Maryland heiress Elizabeth Lloyd provided him with tremendous resources. Between 1769 and 1772, he spent some £3,500 on remodeling his house and another £1,500 on its furnishings (Nos. 124, 125; 153–156)—an altogether princely sum. He alone shared with Governor Penn the distinction of owning "all sorts" of carriages.[177] On 3 June 1774, Silas Deane, a member of the Continental Congress from Connecticut, wrote: "I dined yesterday with Mr. Cadwallader, whose furniture and house exceeds anything I have seen in this city or elsewhere."[178] Washington, whose admiration of his "military genius" led to Cadwalader's appointment to the rank of brigadier general in 1776, was a not infrequent visitor.

Though Cadwalader's house was torn down about 1820, the voluminous surviving records of its remodeling and furnishing give a detailed portrait of the creation of a colonial rococo setting. Moreover, much of the furniture, all of which Cadwalader had made locally (most of it by craftsmen fresh from London), can now be identified. The upstairs pieces, of walnut and uncarved, were made by the native-born joiner William Savery (1722–1787). The parlor suites were the work of Affleck, with Bernard and Jugiez and Reynolds. Of the seating furniture, three sofas were upholstered by the native craftsman Plunket Fleeson, but the blue and yellow silk damask covers were fitted by John Webster, upholsterer from London, who in the *Pennsylvania Journal* of 20 August 1767 advertised that he had "had the honour of working with applause, for several of the nobility and gentry in England and Scotland."[179] Cadwalader limited the orders he made through his London agent, Matthias Gale, to what could not be made in Philadelphia: the silk damasks and Wilton carpets for his parlors; damask tablecloths and napkins, knife cases, and flatware for his dining table; and a four-in-hand carriage for his peregrinations about town. Andirons, including "one Pare of the Best Rote [wrought] fier Dogs with Crinthen [Corinthian] Coloms," were made by Daniel King, brass founder, at a cost of £25; and a dozen leather fire buckets were provided and painted by the artist James Claypoole.[180]

FRAMES

The only known Philadelphia-made rococo picture frames are a matching group of five enclosing the portraits of members of John Cadwalader's family, which he commissioned of Charles Willson Peale (1747–1827) and intended as part of the furniture in the parlors of his house. The frames for the likenesses of his parents, Dr. and Mrs. Thomas Cadwalader, and of his brother, Lambert (**No. 124**), all painted during the summer of 1770, were made by James Reynolds. On 15 March 1771, the carver billed Cadwalader "To 3 [half-length] Picture frames in Burnish'd Gold @ £18," for a total of £54.[181] Since Peale had charged £12-12-0 per canvas, the frames cost a third again as much as the pictures. The other portraits followed: that of John's sister, Martha, is dated 1771, as is a family group (**No. 125**)—John, his wife, Elizabeth, and their daughter, Anne—begun at that time but completed the following summer at a cost of £25-4-0. Though the carver's bills for the frames of the last two pictures are lost, the frames are identical to those of the first three portraits and are presumably by the same hand.[182]

Unfortunately, the scrolled projections at each corner and at the middle of each side of all the frames were sawed off some years ago, which destroyed much of the open quality of the work. The Boston-made frames used by John Singleton Copley (see Nos. 89-91), however, are of the same general model—narrow carved molding next to the picture, deep cove with leaf-and-flower fronds, and projecting pierced C-scrolls flanking central shells—and suggest how the Philadelphia counterparts were intended to look.

Peale, who moved to the city in 1775, was the first artist of real stature in Philadelphia.[183] Born in Maryland, he was sent to London in 1766 to study painting and returned three years later, settling in Annapolis. In 1770, he was commissioned to paint the lawyer John Dickinson, recently made famous by his *Letters from a Farmer in Pennsylvania* (1768), who in turn introduced Peale to his cousin John Cadwalader. The original black and gold molded neoclassical frame of the Dickinson picture (Historical Society of Pennsylvania) is of a type described exactly by carver Gabriel Valois in an advertisement in the *Pennsylvania Journal* of 30 March 1774: "Family Pictures, Neatly framed in the newest taste, varnished in black, with three members carved and gilt in burnished gold."[184] Consistent with Peale's neoclassical-style portraiture, it was to be his favorite type of frame, which helps to explain the dearth of Philadelphia-made rococo enclosures. The Cadwalader frames, in the full rococo taste, must have been the choice not of the artist but of the client, part of the ornamental program for a particularly luxurious room.

124

Picture frame, 1770–71
James Reynolds, Philadelphia
White pine, gilded, 60 x 50 in.
With portrait of Lambert Cadwalader
by Charles Willson Peale
Philadelphia Museum of Art

The manufacture and sale of looking glasses was a special branch of the furniture trade. Mirror glass, which required techniques of grinding and polishing unavailable in colonial America, was always imported, but the supporting frames could be locally made. Some Philadelphia artisans went into the business of importing framed looking glasses: in 1757, cabinetmaker John Elliott was the first to advertise a looking-glass store in Philadelphia. He was followed into the trade by the carvers Bernard and Jugiez in 1762 and James Reynolds in 1768. No looking glasses made or sold by Bernard and Jugiez have been identified (though in March 1773 Jugiez offered "frames of any kind, to come as nearly as cheap as can be imported"),[185] but we have a number of important documented examples from Reynolds.

Elliott, best known from the numbers of looking glasses he labeled, first announced in the *Pennsylvania Gazette* of 30 December 1756 that he imported and had for sale "A Neat assortment of looking glasses"; also "Looking glasses new quick silver'd, or framed, in the neatest manner." The next September, he mentioned "his Looking-glass store in Chestnut-street,"[186] and, by April 1758, at "the Sign of the Bell and Looking-glass."[187] Four years later, he moved the business to Walnut Street, where it was to remain until after the war. More than a hundred looking glasses are known with Elliott's printed paper label affixed to the backboard.[188] Those with the Chestnut Street address can be dated between 1758 and 1762; those with the Walnut Street address, from 1762 or later. A few, having a variation on the Walnut Street label,[189] may date from the late 1760s or the early 1770s.

Only in the examples of the later period, such as that of the looking glass he supplied to Richard Edwards (**No. 126**), is Elliott found selling frames made in Philadelphia of northeastern white pine.[190] Edwards (1744–1799), a merchant in nearby Burlington County, New Jersey, commissioned in 1775 several stylish rococo pieces of furniture from Thomas Tufft, including a diminutive, pierced-skirted pier table, above which his looking glass long hung.[191] The account book that recorded those pieces also contained a transaction with Elliott.[192] The Tufft commission came at the end of the interval from 1769 to 1775 when Elliott did not advertise— nonimportation or the spirit of nonimportation cramping his normal trade.

Edwards's looking glass, the only fully carved rococo-style example having an Elliott label, retains its original white-painted surface, a treatment then popular for looking-glass frames intended to be set against a colored wall.[193] Elliott either retailed it or repaired it, but he did not make it. The frame consists of parallel-gouged shellwork with an

125

Picture frame, 1772
Probably by James Reynolds, Philadelphia
White pine, gilded, 60 x 50 in.
With portrait of the John Cadwalader family
by Charles Willson Peale
Philadelphia Museum of Art

126

Looking-glass frame
Philadelphia, ca. 1775
White pine, painted;
cedar, 48 x 26 in.
The Metropolitan Museum of Art

outer mantle of pierced scrollwork. At the top is a vibrantly asymmetrical acanthus leaf, at the sides are pendent leaves and flowers, and at the bottom is a serenely floating swan. The work, very much in the manner of Reynolds, bespeaks the hand of an artisan dedicated to carving.

In the *Pennsylvania Chronicle* of 14 November 1768, Reynolds offered imported looking glasses "in carved and white, or carved and gilt frames."[194] During the early 1770s, he made elaborate frames for a number of leading families, including the Cadwaladers, the Chews, the Pembertons, and the Penns. He billed Cadwalader for four large carved looking glasses on 5 December 1770 and for another large one the next October. They must have captured the imagination of Philadelphians.[195]

Two pairs of Chew family looking glasses at Cliveden are likely the work for which Reynolds received £51-10 on 20 April 1772.[196] One pair, among the grandest and largest of all American examples, have mirrors composed of two pieces of glass with an overall size of five feet by two (**No. 127**). Here, Reynolds used remnants of tall and narrow Queen Anne looking glasses, honoring his advertisement in the *Pennsylvania Chronicle* of 14 November 1768: "Old Glasses new framed and quicksilvered."[197] The frames, on the lower panes flanked by colonettes; on the upper, by rocaille work, are not a perfectly unified design, but they give the effect of an extraordinary confection of rococo motifs.[198] The other Chew pair, of the girandole type (FIG. 45), have the most irregularly shaped of all American mirrors, a central glass area of rococo vasiform shape.

127

Looking-glass frame, 1772
Probably by James Reynolds, Philadelphia
White pine, painted, 78 x 42 in.
Cliveden of the National Trust

FIGURE 45. *Looking-glass frame*. Probably by James Reynolds, Philadelphia, 1772. White pine, painted, 38½ x 23¼ in. (97.8 x 59.1 cm.). Cliveden, a co-stewardship property of the National Trust for Historic Preservation (NT 73.55.24 [2])

Together with looking-glass and picture brackets are a kind of furniture that was the exclusive domain of the wood-carver. The book of *Prices of Cabinet & Chair Work* published in Philadelphia in 1772 therefore contains no mention of those forms. The only known carved rococo wall bracket of local origin is an example (**No. 128**) whose design—a bird in a nest of *C*-scrolls, its outstretched wings supporting the shelf—was inspired by an engraving (FIG. 46) in Johnson's book of designs. In this instance, however, the carver deleted the spiky grasses and simplified the scheme to suit his standard repertoire of scrolls, leafage, and feathers. The bracket is carved from a single piece of white pine, plus a top board whose elegantly scalloped bottom edge is visible when the bracket is mounted high on the wall. The translucent golden brown surface is the result of a thin pigmented coating over layers of white ground.[199] The masterly work has been ascribed to James Reynolds,[200] an attribution strengthened by the resemblance of the bird's stance and feathers to those of a bird finial (No. 143) to which there are documentary links with Reynolds.

128

Wall bracket, Philadelphia, 1765–75
White pine, painted, H.: 16¼ in.
Winterthur Museum

FIGURE 46. Design for a wall bracket, Thomas Johnson, *One Hundred and Fifty New Designs* (London, 1758; reissue, 1761), Plate 42. Engraving on paper, 9⅞ x 7 in. (25.1 x 17.8 cm.). The Metropolitan Museum of Art, Harris Brisbane Dick Fund, 1932 (32.61)

TABLES

The largest and some of the most rococo of Philadelphia tables were made to have marble tops. The *Price Book* classified them as "frames for Marble Stands" or "frames for Marble Slab," four or five feet in length and having either Marlborough or claw feet. They were usually found in parlors, but they could be positioned against a wall wherever a large serving table was needed. Their marble tops made an indestructible surface on which hot foods and beverages could be placed. An advertisement in the *Pennsylvania Gazette* of 1 December 1768 offered "To be sold twelve marble slabs, well pollished, four feet six inches long and two feet six inches wide."[201]

Those advertised pieces of marble would have been just the right length for a masterpiece of the type (**No. 129**), which, sadly, has no known history. The legs, however, are so similar to those on a high chest from the Van Pelt family (No. 137) that the two pieces may have been made en suite. Massive in scale and with a serpentine-shaped skirt and conforming top of great movement, the table is one of the most imposing examples of Philadelphia rococo furniture. Though it has been suggested that the abrupt termination of carving at the junction of leg and skirt resulted from the separate workings of a cabinetmaker and a carver,[202] this rhythmic division of plain and ornamented surfaces is characteristic of much English and American rococo furniture. The table displays such a unity of design that it must have been the inspired creation of a single artisan. The totality of its swirling, figured marble (in shades of purple, gray, white, and yellow), its shimmering pattern of mahogany skirt veneers, and its nervous knee carving makes it an unparalleled example of American rococo.

The Cadwalader slab table (**No. 130**), so called because it descended in that family and was presumably part of the furnishings of the general's magnificent Second Street house, does not match the parlor furniture supplied to Cadwalader by Affleck in 1770–72. It may have been one of "2 marble Slabs etc [Cadwalader] had of C. Coxe," his neighbor, in 1769.[203] Whatever its source, the table is the supreme example in American furniture of the fully developed French rococo. Though it proclaims its American origin in its secondary woods (yellow pine backboard and walnut corner braces), there is no separation between leg and skirt; in direct opposition to standard American design (see No. 129), the curving planes and the carving of one are continued unbroken into the other. Unique among identified Philadelphia tables, it is entirely a carver's work, rather than a cabinetmaker's work embellished by a carver. Examples of the

French taste so fully realized were rare, even in England. Chippendale illustrated a few such designs (see Plate CLXXV), but he did not make them. That he left in the realm of the carver.

The table seems to incorporate elements of pattern-book designs completely integrated into a new whole. The configuration of scrolls that make up the legs compares with that shown in Plate CLXX of *The Director*, but even more with that in Plate LXXIII of Ince and Mayhew's *Universal System*. There is no printed inspiration for the plump-cheeked young girl, indefinably oriental in character, who reclines in the middle of the skirt, a bird in her upraised left hand and a faithful hound between her feet.

Originally, the table was a deep red mahogany surmounted by a black, gold-veined marble top. Now the wood has a dark, matte finish. Only where the carved parts have been rubbed—as on the girl's belly—does the luminous dark red of the wood shine through. Most of the pierced scrollwork depending from the bottom of the skirts is gone, but the stumps of eight extensions remain. Despite the loss, the carving is of such broadness of concept, such grandeur of scale, that it was surely the result of meticulous London training; it is found nowhere else in colonial furniture.

129

Slab table, Philadelphia, 1765–75
Mahogany, marble; pine, L.: 54 in.
Museum of Art, Rhode Island School of Design

130

Slab table, Philadelphia, ca. 1770
Mahogany, marble; yellow pine, L.: 48¼ in.
The Metropolitan Museum of Art

131
Card table, Philadelphia, 1765–75
Mahogany; northern white cedar, L.: 34 in.
Winterthur Museum

Card tables were made in Philadelphia in large numbers. The *Price Book* listed three categories: with Marlborough (straight) feet, with crooked (cabriole) legs, and with round corners. The crooked-legged ones usually have only modest amounts of ornament. The price of such a table as one (**No. 131**) having claw feet and carved knees and moldings was £5. The skirt decoration may have made this example a bit more costly, but the result is an understated, particularly lovely vision of rococo beauty. Light and airy leafage defines the scalloped outline of the front skirt, an integration of form and ornament achieved by cutting away the surface of the skirt board to the basic scrollwork pattern and then piecing it out as needed with additional carved wood. The carving is crisp and the wood has the burnished quality of the best London work. The scalloped, foliate bottom edge of the skirt blends harmoniously with the graceful carved legs, and the straight skirt somehow presents the perfect foil for the serpentine-shaped top. The original color of the dense reddish mahogany is still apparent on the skirt rails, but the top has faded to a mellow nut brown.

Though its skirts and legs are also unified in design, another card table (**No. 132**) is an altogether different aesthetic experience. Card tables with round corners were a Philadelphia favorite. When the tables were open, the projecting cylindrical corners provided places for the candlesticks that illuminated the playing surface. Plain, such card tables cost £5; with leaves on the knees and carved moldings, £8; with carved rails, as here, £10. Add the carving on the legs, which continues up the round corners in a diapered shield, and the table constitutes one of the most lavish of all Philadelphia rococo statements. There is but a handful of these tables, all apparently made in pairs, and all with more or less similar carved designs.[204] On this example, which has descended in the family of Cornelius Stevenson, of Philadelphia, the carving has a particularly strong sense of fluidity.[205]

132

Card table, Philadelphia, 1765–75
Mahogany; yellow poplar, L.: 34½ in.
Collection of George G. Meade Easby

133

Tea table, Philadelphia, 1765–75
Mahogany, Diam.: 35⅜ in.
The Dietrich American Foundation

With very few exceptions, Philadelphia tea tables had a round top on a tripod stand. In the *Price Book*, a tea table was round unless otherwise specified. In 1769, James Gillingham charged £5 for making a rococo-carved example: "To 1 Mahogy. Tea Table Top scolloped Claw feet & leavs on Knees."[206] The *Price Book* offered an additional embellishment—a carved pillar—for a total charge of £5-15-0. Writing in 1828, historian J. F. Watson recalled Philadelphians' having had "mahogany tea boards and round tea tables, which being turned on an axle underneath the centre, stood upright, like an expanded fan or palm leaf in the corner."[207] Great numbers of Philadelphia rococo-carved tea tables exist, differing principally in the design of the pillar and in the carving. The two discussed next represent the two basic carved pillar designs and are the work of two separate hands.

An example of the vase-and-column-pillar-type tea table (**No. 133**) is notable for its perfect sense of balance and repose. The legs have an upright stance, the layout of the carving is symmetrical and tightly controlled, and the top, of straight and even-grained wood, has ten scalloped units. The attribution of the table's carving to Bernard and

134
Tea table, Philadelphia, 1765–75
Mahogany, Diam.: 33⅜ in.
The Metropolitan Museum of Art

Jugiez[208] is based on the pillar's leaf-carved urn, closely similar in treatment to that of the Cadwalader fire screens the partners embellished in 1771 at the behest of Thomas Affleck (see No. 156). The table is one of a matching pair that descended in the same family as the previous card table.[209]

In contrast, a table of the second type (**No. 134**) — of the flat ball-and-column pattern — exhibits movement and tension. The compressed ball, or ring, on the pillar is a configuration unique to Philadelphia craftsmen. The legs cant down at their junction with the pillar and splay out at the feet, attributes that convey the effect of elements squashed by a weight from above. The top, a board with a lively allover figure, has an edge formed of eight boldly scalloped units. The carving — assured, asymmetrical, and naturalistic, the foliage playfully lapping over the knees and forming a garland around the ball — suggests the London rococo of Thomas Johnson and has been attributed to his erstwhile apprentice Hercules Courtenay. The top has been polished, showing the wood's figure to advantage, but the pedestal has an attractive buildup of old finishes.

135

Tea table, Philadelphia, ca. 1775
Mahogany, painted iron;
tulip poplar, L.: 30¼ in.
Private collection

A Philadelphia tea table (**No. 135**) is rare for being rectangular (the "square tea tables" of the *Price Book*) and unique in
having a sheet-iron top, its raised rim and edges folding
down over the skirts and ending in scalloped edges.[210]
Retaining as it does much of its original white paint (now
with a golden patina) and gilded border, the top must have
been colored to match the white or gold frames of Philadelphia-made looking glasses. It would have glistened in the
dark of an eighteenth-century interior, its undulating edges
giving an impression of lightness that belied the weight of
the iron. The legs are attenuated and delicate, almost colt-
like. The carving is crisp and, just below the top, sketchy. In
overall handling (for example, the knee brackets' forming a
continuous curve with the legs), the woodwork is in the
manner of Thomas Tufft, who took over the shop of James
Gillingham in 1773. One of the few references to sheet iron
in the period appeared in an advertisement in the *Pennsylvania Evening Post* of 23 April 1776 by Thomas Mayberry,
ironmaster of Mount Holly, New Jersey, for "Sheet and
Rod Iron of different sizes."[211]

CASE FURNITURE

That particularly American form, the high chest of drawers, has long been the symbol of the rococo style in Philadelphia. Of all case pieces, it is the most susceptible to rococo ornament. Like the chest-on-chest, the desk and bookcase, and the tall clock, it has a pedimented top that can be richly ornamented, but it is alone among large, two-part case pieces in having high legs and scalloped skirts that cry out for elaborate carving.

Within the general category of high chests of drawers, the Philadelphia *Price Book* includes the chest-on-frame (today's highboy) and the chest-on-chest. Both were listed, along with an optional matching "Table to Suit Ditto" (today's lowboy, or dressing table). The *Price Book*, in describing the decorative choices open to a Philadelphian shopping for one of these monumental storage chests, demonstrates that by the early 1770s the chest-on-frame was available in what can be called three successive models.

Carved Philadelphia high chests are still numerous today, but none of the best examples in the fully developed rococo style is documented to maker or original client. The sole instance of a high chest inscribed and dated by the cabinetmaker is the one made by Henry Clifton in 1753 (FIG. 47), which also exemplifies the first model in the evolution of the Philadelphia type. The top extends upward in an exaggerated scroll pediment, which houses a large, central shell drawer in the scroll board, or tympanum; a similar shell drawer is centered above the scalloped front skirt. Carving is limited to the leafage on the knees, the shell drawers, and the finials. In the terminology of the *Price Book*, Clifton had made a chest on a frame, with claw feet, leaves on the knees, shell drawers in the frame, scroll pediment head, shield, roses, and blases. (The "shield" is the central cartouche; the "roses" are the rosettes terminating the pediment scrolls; and the "blases" [blazes] are the flame finials at either side. The carved work was not to exceed £3-10-0.) With the addition of quarter-columns, this description fits all the high chests discussed below.

Sometime during the mid-1760s, the form evolved into a second stage, lighter and more graceful. There is perhaps no more beautifully proportioned or more satisfying example than a high chest (**No. 136**) and its matching dressing table.[212] The scroll pediment, no longer housing a boxy central drawer, has a serpentine-curved profile and is open in back. The scroll board, now an uninterrupted surface, is suited to all sorts of carved rococo ornament: here, a floating shell and its flanking streamers fill the entire tympanum. The wood is walnut with a mellow nut-brown patina. The

FIGURE 47. *High chest*. Signed and dated by Henry Clifton, Philadelphia, 1753. Mahogany; tulip poplar, white cedar, 95½ x 44¼ x 22½ in. (242.6 x 112.4 x 57.2 cm.). The Colonial Williamsburg Foundation (1975-154)

136

High chest, Philadelphia, 1765–75
Walnut; yellow poplar, H.: 96¾ in.
Garvan Collection, Yale University

137

High chest, Philadelphia, 1765–75
Mahogany; tulip poplar, H.: 90¼ in.
Winterthur Museum

quarter columns at the front edges and elements of the moldings and carvings are highlighted with the original glossy black paint and, on a fillet of the scroll cornice, gilding. While a rare survival today, that sort of picking out of decorative elements, giving added emphasis to the ornament, was once commonplace.

The carving has a distinctive and particularly rococo character. The shells in the pediment and skirt areas have frilly outlines within which taut, membranous surfaces have been manipulated as if to simulate the irregular surface of shells. On all the carving, delicate incised lines with tapered ends provide texture and a sense of shading. The unidentified artisan has been dubbed the "Garvan Carver" after this high chest and its matching dressing table, among the best-known pieces in the Mabel Brady Garvan Collection at Yale University.[213]

A high chest particularly noteworthy among Philadelphia examples for the carving on its scroll board (**No. 137**) is a rare instance where the local preference for a central shell and streamers was abandoned in favor of colonettes and scrolls dripping with what resembles stalactites—a gentle essay into the whimsical world of engraved designs by Chippendale and Thomas Johnson. The carving has decisive and angular chisel marks that break up and reflect the light, just as the wood of the drawer fronts has a figure that suggests rippling water. The combination of the carving, the figured wood, and the pierced brasses gives a light and ever-changing look—the essential rococo quality—to what would otherwise be a bulky mass. The same aesthetic is found on a slab table (No. 129) with carving by the same hand. According to family tradition, the chest was originally owned by William Turner and his wife, Mary King Turner, and descended by marriage in the Van Pelt family.[214]

An example of the third and final model is a famous high chest (**No. 138**), popularly called the "Pompadour highboy" because of the supposed French character of the portrait bust in its pediment. Not only is it among the best known of American furniture but it also provides a graphic illustration of the creative manner in which pattern books influenced that style. The Pompadour embodies more passages, borrowed from more different engravings, than any other American piece.[215] The pictorial tableau (a spouting serpent and two swans) on the large bottom drawer is a faithful rendition of a 1762 chimneypiece tablet design by Thomas Johnson (FIG. 48). The precise configuration of cornice moldings and dentils comes from a desk and bookcase in *The Director* (Plate CVII), and the draped urns are from the central finial of that piece. The general arrangement—a con-

tinuous horizontal cornice surmounted by a portrait bust within a pediment from whose tympanum leafage springs—copies another of Chippendale's designs for a desk and bookcase, though there is no Chippendale prototype for the pierced scroll board of the pediment.

The Director's influence resulted in a new approach to the design of Philadelphia pedimented case furniture. The horizontal cornice, which effectively separates the carved scroll pediment from the flat, unadorned facade of drawer fronts, resolved the awkwardness inherent in a field of ornamental carving on the same plane as the drawer fronts. The resulting design may legitimately be called Philadelphia Chippendale. That such pediment treatment was probably employed first on the Pompadour high chest is implied in the manner of its construction.[216] Though this, the sole instance of a bust on a high chest, probably set the precedent, male portrait busts on desks and bookcases soon became the standard.

For all its importance, nothing is known about the Pompadour's early history. The carving, of an exceptional realism and immediacy, must be the work of a London-trained master. Pictorial narrative carving like that on the center drawer is found only rarely on Philadelphia chimneypieces and furniture.[217] The choice of a tablet design by London carver Johnson encourages the speculation that his apprentice Hercules Courtenay (who arrived in Philadelphia by 1765) was the artisan.

FIGURE 48.   Design for a chimneypiece tablet, Thomas Johnson, *A New Book of Ornaments* (London, 1762), Plate 5. Engraving on paper, 8 x 13¾ in. (20.3 x 34.9 cm.). The Metropolitan Museum of Art, Gift of Harvey Smith (1985.1099)

138

High chest, Philadelphia, 1762–75
Mahogany; tulip poplar, H.: 91¾ in.
The Metropolitan Museum of Art

139

Shield finial, Philadelphia, 1760–65
Mahogany, H.: 11⅜ in.
From a high chest
Philadelphia Museum of Art

140

Scroll finial, Philadelphia, 1760–70
Mahogany, H.: 14¾ in.
From a desk and bookcase
Philadelphia Museum of Art

FINIALS

The scroll or pitch pediment that capped most tall Philadelphia case furniture offered expansive opportunities for the carver. The tympanum board was often enriched with carving or piercing or a combination of both. Rising out of it, through the center of the pediment, was a carved finial. A number of designs were used for the finials: shield-shaped or rococo-scrolled cartouches, baskets or vases of flowers, or birds. Even independent of the structures they were intended to grace they are among the most engaging manifestations of the American rococo.

The earliest type of Philadelphia finial is an asymmetrical kidney-shaped shield—called by early collectors the "Philadelphia peanut"—with a surrounding mantle of scrollwork. The design was current in the early 1750s, witness the example on the Henry Clifton high chest of 1753 (see FIG. 47, p. 199), where it is the most rococo part of the entire piece. The immediate source is unknown, but the ultimate inspiration for these motifs must be something like Matthias Lock's *Book of Shields* (London, 1746). Among the largest and best-preserved shield finials is one (**No. 139**) that comes from a high chest of the Garvan type (see No. 136) probably dating from 1760-65.[218] The shield is larger than usual, more symmetrical than most, and not in the least upstaged by its mantle. The curling-over of the top frond and the incised work so like engraving are characteristics of the Garvan carver.

The shield cartouche waned in importance as the rococo style advanced. An alternative design (**No. 140**), consisting of a delicate asymmetrical framework of *C*-scrolls enclosing a central rosette, is found on high chests and, occasionally, on desks and bookcases. This example of a quintessential rococo motif comes from a large and stately secretary probably made soon after the marriage of Caspar Wistar and Mary Franklin, in 1765.[219]

The use of baskets or vases of leafage and flowers, common on English furniture, offered the carver an opportunity for finial treatment of a more pictorial type. One of the most luxuriant versions of the basket model (**No. 141**) has a high background screen of branches and berries and a low foreground of open flowers and blossoms. An identical finial appears on a high chest, one of a pair for which Richard Edwards paid Thomas Tufft £22 in 1775.[220] A finial in the form of an urn (**No. 142**), from a Philadelphia desk and bookcase, is a version of the vase model.

Birds, another popular finial pattern, usually appear on double chests and tall clocks. An outstanding example (**No. 143**), usually described as a phoenix, is one on the double chest thought to have been ordered by William Logan at the time of his daughter Sarah's marriage to Thomas Fisher, in 1772.[221] It may have been included in the work for which Logan paid Thomas Affleck £72-15-0 that year, £50 of it owed to the carver James Reynolds. An eagle or another bird was a standard ornament on looking glasses (Reynolds's specialty). The asymmetrical treatment of this one, poised for flight, one leg lower than the other, recalls the handling of birds in elaborate rococo designs from Johnson's book.

An altogether different form of ornamental finial was the carved portrait bust,[222] among the few instances of figural sculpture made in colonial America. With the exception of the female portrait on the Pompadour high chest (No. 138), the busts are found only on desks and bookcases having continuous cornices beneath their pediments. The most frequently used subject was John Locke, followed by John Milton. Such images of renowned literary figures come out of a tradition for library busts with roots in antiquity, which saw a revival in mid-eighteenth-century England. In great English houses, busts were placed on large breakfront bookcases.[223] Perhaps the closest the colonists came to that conceit was the massive cabinet surmounted by some of "the best enrichments of sculpture," four busts (now gone) made by John Folwell for David Rittenhouse's orrery for the College of Philadelphia.[224] The standard place for busts in Philadelphia furniture (one recommended in Plate CVIII of *The Director*) was in the pediment of the desk-and-bookcase form that served the city's cognoscenti as a movable library.

Portrait busts were readily available in Philadelphia by 1765, when the carvers Bernard and Jugiez advertised "a great variety of figures, large and small busts in plaister of Paris, and brackets for ditto."[225] Four years later, Edmund Physick, attorney to John Penn, bought from a local shopkeeper "three Carved Mahogany Brackets, two Busts & a Figure of Milton."[226] The largest was some fifteen inches high; the smallest, some seven. From about 1750, the principal manufacturer of such plaster statuary was John Cheere (1709–1787), of London.[227] As yet unlocated examples of his small versions were likely the models for the mahogany busts made by Philadelphia carvers. Cheere's busts all follow the same basic composition and all stand upon paneled plinths. Though those mass-produced plasters, colored to look like ancient bronze, were of satisfactory appearance when viewed from a distance, they were softly modeled and lacking in detail. The market demanded something better. Between 1765 and 1775, the Philadelphia wood-carver breathed new life into those visages. Only in the mid-1770s, too late to influence American artisans, did Josiah Wedgwood, the Staffordshire potter and genius of industrial mass-production, begin to manufacture beautifully worked

141

Basket finial, Philadelphia, 1765–75
Mahogany, H.: 13¾ in.
From a chest-on-chest
Philadelphia Museum of Art

142

Urn finial, Philadelphia, 1765–75
Mahogany, H.: 9¼ in.
From a desk and bookcase
Winterthur Museum

143

Bird finial, 1770–75
Probably by James Reynolds, Philadelphia
Mahogany, H.: 12½ in.
From a chest-on-chest
The Metropolitan Museum of Art

144

Finial bust of John Locke
Philadelphia, 1765–75
Mahogany, H.: 10½ in.
From a desk and bookcase
Bernard and S. Dean Levy, Inc.

145

Finial bust of John Milton
Philadelphia, 1765–75
Mahogany, H.: 12¼ in.
From a desk and bookcase
Private collection

busts in what he called black "basalte."[228] Though sometimes more refined, they were never more lively and compelling than the best of the Philadelphia versions in wood.

Of all the carved busts of the philosopher John Locke, one (**No. 144**) that comes from a desk and bookcase having a pitch pediment and a pierced and leaf-carved tympanum board[229] is noteworthy for the anatomically convincing articulation of the face and for its reflective modeling. On the eve of the Revolution, Locke (1632–1704) was a particular favorite of the colonists; his two *Treatises on Government* provided the intellectual underpinnings of their claim to the right to rebel. In the Library Company of Philadelphia's catalogue of 1741, Locke's *Essay Concerning Human Understanding* was held to be the best book of logic in the world.[230] Understandably, he was the most popular subject for these busts. Though demonstrably executed by three different carvers, all five known examples are based on the same model, dressed informally in an open-neck shirt.[231] The plaster busts that inspired the American carvers rest on plinths having tapered sides and a paneled front inscribed with the subject's name. The wood versions copy that favored type, but without the inscription.

The bust of John Milton (1608–1674) crowned at least two Philadelphia desks and bookcases.[232] The poet may have been chosen because of his polemic writings in tireless defense of religious, civil, and domestic liberties. This example (**No. 145**) demonstrates the heights to which Philadelphia artisans could rise. The features of the head—narrow face, receding forehead, pointed jaw—appear to be an almost generic prescription for an intellectual (note the resemblance to Locke); only the blank eyes (a convention in classical sculpture and appropriate here because of Milton's blindness) and the scholar's collar tabs identify the sitter.[233] But how beautifully realized! The carver has chiseled the faceted surfaces of the face and the collar tabs more in the manner of a sculptor in marble than in wood, creating a tautness and a play of light that is the heart of the rococo.

Another bust finial from Philadelphia, that of a young man (**No. 146**), is of a thoroughly rococo sensibility.[234] With his long neck, upright and aristocratic bearing, and classical drapery pulled aside to display elegantly embroidered finery, he is far more stylish than our literary figures. He cries out for identification.

146

Finial bust of a young man
Philadelphia, 1765–75
Mahogany, H.: 8½ in.
From a desk and bookcase
Private collection

SEATING FURNITURE

A superbly carved chair (**No. 147**), of a commanding presence, is the only piece of Philadelphia furniture that attempts to execute a design from *The Director* in its entirety. The splat pattern and the ornament of the back and legs faithfully follow Plate XII (No. 1) and were clearly a client's special order. Otherwise, the chairmaker chose to follow standard Philadelphia practice, employing a slip (removable) seat and simple, rounded back legs. The bold and assertive front legs, with scroll feet and high-relief carving that has been attributed to Bernard and Jugiez,[235] may have caused the maker to add the gadrooning to the seat rail, a creative touch that completes the integrity of the design.

A considerable variety of splat patterns were popular in Philadelphia, a number of them based on Chippendale designs, a number of others having pointed arches or various arrangements of interlaced strapwork. None combine coherent design and fine carving better than does this example (**No. 148**). The figure-eight strapwork in the splat merges effortlessly into the crest rail, an even more flowing interpretation than that of the previous chair.

147

Side chair, Philadelphia, 1760–70
Mahogany; cedar, H.: 39¾ in.
The Dietrich American Foundation

148

Side chair, Philadelphia, 1765–75
Mahogany; cedar, H.: 38 in.
The Metropolitan Museum of Art

Only very occasionally were easy chairs in Philadelphia made with carved seat rails and arm supports, true essays in the rococo style. The ultimate inspiration for the design of those elements appears to be the cabriole-leg version of the "French Chairs" in *The Director* (Plates xx–xxiii). A chair of that type (**No. 149**) has carving that is the work of an altogether superior and exceptional talent. All four legs end in naturalistic hairy-paw feet, and the skirts are carved with sprightly foliage against a diapered pattern and with a human mask (a great rarity in American furniture, as in American silver) at the center front. Tips of the leafage extend artfully over the upper-edge molding of the skirts. Here is one of the greater moments in Philadelphia carving. It can be attributed, with reasonable assurance, to Hercules Courtenay,[236] who between 1766 and 1769 worked for Benjamin Randolph. The chair is said to have descended from Mary W. (Fennimore) Randolph, Benjamin's second wife.[237]

149

Easy chair, Philadelphia, 1765–70
Mahogany; white oak, H.: 45¼ in.
Philadelphia Museum of Art

A sofa (**No. 150**), a fixture at Benjamin Chew's Cliveden (see p. 26) since the late eighteenth century, is the most elaborate of Philadelphia Marlborough examples, the only one to conform to the *Price Book*'s description of "Soffas Marlborough Feet" with all the extras: "a fret on feet & rails and carved mouldings...£10-10-0." Its scalloped serpentine back—the so-called camel back with points—is a classic Philadelphia design, as are the three front legs, square and with cuffs, and the straight stretchers. The armrests, which form nearly horizontal rolls extending far forward, however, are more in the English manner. On the skirt, above the applied gadroon, is a blind fret of overlapping ogival arches; on the front legs is fretwork in the form of arches and lattices.

The sofa is the most stately piece of colonial American upholstered furniture. The present covering, a bright yellow silk damask, reproduces the color the Chew family traditionally had on their drawing-room furniture. It is the deep mahogany skirt that gives this piece its air of monumental architectural majesty. The longstanding association of the sofa with Governor John Penn is circumstantial. Chew, in purchasing Penn's Third Street house, paid £5,000 for a building that in 1770 had been valued at £2,000, which could imply that he bought it fully furnished. That idea is reinforced by the lack of bills for furniture at the time in the multitudinous Chew papers.

150

Sofa, Philadelphia, 1763–71
Mahogany; tulip poplar, L.: 90⅜ in.
Cliveden of the National Trust

151

Armchair, Philadelphia, 1765–75
Mahogany; white oak, H.: 40¾ in.
Promised gift to Los Angeles County Museum of Art

More closely associated with the Penn family are two sets of elaborate chairs, made in two variations of the "French Chairs" in *The Director* (Plate XIX). The type is listed in the *Price Book* as "Chair frame for Stuffing over back and Feet with Marlborough Feet," in mahogany for £1-5-0, and with arms, brackets, bases, and carved moldings available as extras. A standard form in England, the great open-armed, upholstered-back chair was exceptional in Philadelphia.

The chairs of the first set (see **No. 151**) have acanthus leafage on the arm supports, gadrooned molding under the seat rails, and, on the legs, carved fretwork that matches that of the Chew sofa. Nine chairs from the set are known. Two, listed as "2 Large Armchairs formerly ownd by Governor Penn," were given to the Friends Hospital of Philadelphia in 1817.[238] The set may have been en suite with the sofa made for the Third Street house John Penn acquired shortly after his marriage to Ann Allen, in 1768.[239] The famous Speaker's Chair with the Masonic emblem of the rising sun in its crest rail, commissioned on 17 December 1779 from John Folwell and now on view in Independence Hall,[240] has arms and legs identical in design to those of the Penn chairs. Though the inspiration for the carving is evident, its execution is flat and unconvincing in comparison.

The chairs of the second set have plain arm supports, bead-and-reel molding under the seat rails, and carved bellflowers above hollow-cornered inset panels on the legs.[241] This example (**No. 152**) was long called the "William Penn" chair, certainly a mistaken reference to John.

152

Armchair, Philadelphia, 1765–75
Mahogany; white oak, H.: 43 in.
The Metropolitan Museum of Art

153

Easy chair, 1770
Thomas Affleck, Philadelphia
Mahogany; yellow pine, H.: 45 in.
Collection of H. Richard Dietrich, Jr.

CADWALADER PARLOR SUITE

By sheer good fortune, the most aggressively rococo of all groups of Philadelphia furniture is also the best documented. It is the furniture (see ill. opp. p. 133) made for the front and back parlors of John Cadwalader's house on Second Street. During the autumn of 1770, Randolph, Courtenay, and Bernard and Jugiez submitted bills for the architectural carving they had completed. The rooms were designed and executed as an ensemble, though the front parlor was larger and more lavishly ornamented. Invoices for the furniture arrived shortly afterward. The principal document is Affleck's bill, for the sum of £119-8-0, meticulously rendered in a copperplate hand, for work completed between 13 October 1770 and 14 January 1771.[242] (At the bottom, Affleck added separate charges for his carvers, Reynolds and Bernard and Jugiez, totaling £61-4-0.) Among the furniture listed are some pieces clearly intended for the front room:

2 Mahogany Commode Sophias for the Recesses @ £8	£16-00
one Large ditto	10-00
an Easy Chair to Sute ditto	4-10
2 Commode Card Tables @ £5	10-00

Because all are described as "commode" (having a serpentine front), they must have been more or less en suite. Though the three sofas are now lost, surviving are the easy chair (**No. 153**) and the card tables (see **No. 154**), of an identical pattern. Their skirts are serpentine and have a small asymmetrical shield in the middle; their legs end in paw feet. Of the same distinctive group is a large set of side chairs (see **No. 155**)[243] that can be identified with upholsterer Plunket Fleeson's charge, "To covering over Rail finish'd in Canvis 32 Chairs." Since the entry on the bill was dated 18 October 1770, the chair frames would have been listed on the Affleck invoice (now missing) that predated the one quoted above. The following January, Fleeson upholstered the easy chair, finishing it in canvas,[244] and billed for cases, or slipcovers, of "fine Saxon blue Fr.Chk. [French check]" for the three sofas and for seventy-six chairs.[245] That August, "Rich Blue Silk Damask," together with deep and narrow blue silk fringes and large and small blue silk tassels, was ordered from London.[246] Upholsterer John Webster, late of that city, made the curtains and covered the three sofas and twenty of the chairs for the front parlor.[247]

The only other furniture on Affleck's invoice that is now identifiable with that room is the "4 Mahogany fire screens @ 2-10 [a total of] £10-0" (see **No. 156**).[248] Their paw feet help to identify them as a part of the suite. Of equal importance to the mahogany chairs and tables of the front

154

One of a pair of card tables, 1771
Thomas Affleck, Philadelphia
Mahogany; yellow pine, L.: 39¾ in.
The Dietrich American Foundation

155

Side chair, ca. 1770
Thomas Affleck, Philadelphia
Mahogany; white cedar, H.: 37 in.
The Metropolitan Museum of Art

parlor were the carved-and-gilded frames on the walls—enclosing a looking glass and five family portraits (Nos. 124, 125)—all by Reynolds and contained in an inventory of the room taken in 1778, after the British occupation of Philadelphia had ended. Also listed were fifteen chairs and four tables—two of mahogany and two marble slabs, one of which may have been No. 130. The inventory taken at the time of the general's death, in 1786, included one large and one small settee and two (fire) screens.[249]

The back parlor had its own matching set of furniture, which, in keeping with its subsidiary role, is of somewhat simpler design. The legs of the card tables and the chairs end in paw feet, almost a signature for Cadwalader furniture, but their skirts are straight and uncarved.[250]

Cadwalader's large front parlor was a splendid and exceptionally pure instance of the rococo taste in America. It was rushed to completion by the concerted effort of many of the leading artisans in the city. While some of their names are known and some of their work can be identified, differences in the commode card tables—even differences between the carving of the backs and legs of the chairs[251]—signify that the commission was the work of myriad hands, all of them skilled in the rococo mode.

MHH

156

Fire screen, 1771
Thomas Affleck, Philadelphia
Carving probably by Bernard and Jugiez
Mahogany, H.: 62⅞ in.
The Metropolitan Museum of Art

CAST IRON, GLASS
AND
PORCELAIN

Unlike the production of engravings, silver, and furniture, which was accomplished in workshops by small numbers of artisans, the manufacture of cast iron, glass, and porcelain had different requirements: large numbers of workers, massive masonry structures to house the furnaces or kilns, and thousands of acres of woodland to provide fuel for them. The launching of those industries therefore represented an extensive capital investment. England countenanced domestic manufacture of some iron, as well as utilitarian glass and pottery, but discouraged the development of table glass and porcelain. Because the mother country considered the colonies not only a source of raw material but also a market for her own exports, the more stylish domestic goods represented direct rivalry with English counterparts. In the 1760s, the growing American sentiment for boycotting imports fostered domestic production of such luxuries, though ultimately the young factories could not compete with England's established industries. When the brief trade embargo was over, fashionable colonists reverted to purchasing the less expensive wares from abroad. A few objects that survive from the period attest to the efforts of local entrepreneurs to break into that lucrative market. In view of the need for both substantial capital and prosperous consumers, it is not surprising that the three fledgling American industries—iron, table glass, and porcelain—were concentrated around Philadelphia.

Pickle stand (No. 172)

Cast Iron

Colonial America, abundantly supplied with the requisite iron ore, wood, limestone, and water power, was well suited to the successful manufacture of cast iron: wood, for the charcoal with which to fuel the blast furnace; limestone, to provide the necessary flux for the heated ore; and water, to power the bellows that fanned the furnace's fire. Wealthy urban investors were essential. Though there were foundries in New England and New York, by far the greatest concentration of iron manufactories was around Philadelphia: to the east in New Jersey; to the west in the Schuylkill Valley of Pennsylvania; and to the south in the Shenandoah Valley of Virginia.

England generally encouraged the colonial manufacture of cast iron, but only in the form of "pigs" (ingots), which could be shipped across the Atlantic for fabricating into finished products. Nevertheless, a local market for American-made iron goods, having mostly to do with cooking and heating, had emerged by the beginning of the eighteenth century. The British Board of Trade apparently left the stove industry pretty well alone, since what it produced was not suited to the home country's needs. Whereas in England most people heated their houses by burning coal in fireplace grates,[1] in America wood was to remain the primary fuel for heating and cooking until the nineteenth century.

The carbon-rich iron turned out by American foundries was admirably suited to objects required to withstand heat.

These included, notably, chimneybacks (today called "fire-backs")—iron plates attached to the backs of fireplaces—and stoves, freestanding fireboxes made up of several iron plates. The plates themselves were sand cast: made of molten metal poured into a mold of damp sand that had been impressed with a pattern. The patterns were made of solid pieces of mahogany mortised and tenoned together, that wood chosen for its durability and "because it warps least."[2] If there was to be decoration on the plate, the pattern was carved correspondingly.

In the late 1760s, precisely coincident with heavy investment in the iron industry by a number of wealthy Philadelphians, rococo ornament, cast from patterns created by accomplished artisans, suddenly began to appear on the chimneybacks and stove plates of the area.[3] In January 1768, a New York newspaper carried an advertisement on behalf of Charles Read's Etna Furnace, in southwest New Jersey, for "any Workman who well understands the making of such Moulds as are made of Wood...and can produce good Characters, may meet with extraordinary Encouragement. It is expected that the Mould should be finished with great Skill and Accuracy."[4] In December 1770, the carvers Bernard and Jugiez were paid £8 "for the carving the Arms of Earl of Fairfax for a Pattern for the Back of Chimney,"[5] later cast at Marlboro Furnace, Virginia; in November 1774, the multi-talented John Folwell was paid £5 for carving stove molds for Atsion Ironworks, another of Read's New Jersey ventures.[6] That those three men were among the leading proponents of the rococo in Philadelphia does much to explain why some of the local triumphs in the style are cast in iron.

CHIMNEYBACKS

The only evidence of the rococo style in New England cast ironwork is found in the prancing-stag chimneybacks retailed by Joseph Webb and others. They are a modest effort stylistically and the furnace that manufactured them is not known. Webb (1734–1787) was a Boston merchant whose advertisement, engraved by Revere in 1765 (see No. 27), offered "All sorts of Cast Iron work, done in ye best Manner, on short Notice," including "Chimney Backs of all sizes." Four prancing-stag chimneybacks remain in place in the Jeremiah Lee house, completed in 1768 in Marblehead (see p. 20), all four with an arched top containing an image of the sun—a round human face encircled by sixteen rays.[7] On three of them, a ribbon at the base is emblazoned with the legend "SOLD BY JOSEPH WEBB BOSTON,"[8] each is let into its fireplace brickwork, and each is cracked. The fourth, an unbroken chimneyback (**No. 157**) loose in the fireplace of the state drawing room,[9] is slightly narrower than the others (the arched top encompassing the image of the sun appears cramped) and the modeling of its stag and scrolled edges is less finely worked. Its trailing ribbon is marked "SOLD BY JAMES RUSELES," an as yet unidentified retailer, but the casting appears to be from a mold made from a Webb original. Did Webb, perhaps with not enough castings in stock to supply all Lee's fireplaces, have to go to Ruseles for his knockoff of the same design?

The device of the sun is copied precisely from that cast on the front plate of the "Pennsylvanian Fire-place" (the Franklin stove), invented by Benjamin Franklin in Philadelphia in 1742 and publicized in his pamphlet of 1744, which stated that the stoves were available in Boston from the inventor's brother James. Since Lee had built what may have been the most stylish of all rococo New England houses, his choice of the prancing-stag chimneybacks suggests that they were the most fashionable ones available.

Another chimneyback with the same motif, this one marked AETNA (**No. 158**), is clearly the inspiration for the version retailed in Boston by Webb and must rank among the most irrepressibly rococo of all American ironwork. The casting, large in scale and with robust high-relief carving and a well-modeled stag's body, is unpitted by rust. Though it is cracked at one side and worn by fire at the bottom, it is otherwise wonderfully preserved.[10] In both composition and carving, the ornamental design bears a strong resemblance to the tympanum boards of some Philadelphia case furniture (see No. 136). One other rococo-style chimneyback on which the name Aetna looms large in its arch is surrounded

157

Fireback, Massachusetts, ca. 1768
James Ruseles, retailer
Cast iron, 29 x 26 in.
Marblehead Historical Society

158

Fireback, ca. 1774
Aetna Furnace, New Jersey
Cast iron, 31½ x 30 in.
Winterthur Museum

with scrollwork and has an image of a crowing cock perched on a central water-dripping ledge.[11]

Aetna (initially spelled Etna) was one of four furnaces Charles Read established in the mid-1760s in Burlington County, New Jersey, just east of Philadelphia. Read (ca. 1713–1774), who came from a prominent Philadelphia merchant family, was one of the most influential men in the colony. He was also widely traveled, having visited London before settling in Burlington in 1739. He built the foundry on a tributary of Rancocas Creek in 1766–67 and began operations the next year.[12] On 23 January 1769 (his second year of production), a notice in a New York newspaper declared: "At Etna Furnace, *Burlington* County, which will begin to be in Blast the Middle of April, are wanted, a good Keeper, two Master-Colliers, Moulders and Stock-takers."[13] Late in 1770, Read offered his holdings for sale, noting that they included "a variety of nice patterns and flasks for casting ware."[14] He found no buyers, however, and in 1773, in financial and physical ill health, he conveyed his interest in the furnace to his son and namesake. The junior Read (1739–1783) had been its manager since at least 1769; it was he who changed the spelling of the name to "Aetna." Thus, the pattern for this chimneyback was probably carved between 1773 and 1774.

In 1766, Charles Read, Sr., obtained permission to dam up the Batsto River near its junction with the Atsion and Mullica rivers, some miles south and east of Aetna Furnace. Shortly afterward, on that site, he and his fellow investors established Batsto Furnace. When Read had to step aside, in 1773, he was bought out by John Cox (1731–1793), a Philadelphia merchant.

In common with the Aetna example, a chimneyback from the Batsto Furnace (**No. 159**) has a cavetto-molded edge and the name of the furnace prominent in the arch, but the use of a bead-and-reel molding to create a border for flanking pendent leaves and flowers makes for a more formal, ordered design. The large and handsome vase that holds a stylized bouquet is not unlike finials on Philadelphia case furniture (see No. 142); the pattern for the mold must have been carved by a Philadelphia artisan. While the casting is now pockmarked by rust, much of the detail, including the projecting pegs securing the mortise-and-tenoned boards of the wooden pattern, is still visible. Two Batsto furnace stove plates in the rococo taste are known, one of which is signed and dated 1770 on the ribbon scroll. The lettering of the factory name matches that of the present example and suggests for it a similar date.[15]

159

Fireback, ca. 1770
Batsto Furnace, New Jersey
Cast iron, 26¾ x 22¼ in.
New Jersey State Museum

For most of the colonial period, the standard American heating device other than the fireplace was the jamb stove, made up of five plates: a front, two sides, a top, and a bottom. Its open back was let into an interior wall, with the fire fed from the adjacent room. Its stove plates, the specialty of Pennsylvania-German iron founders, were decorated with biblical scenes and stylized ornament. Only in the 1760s, after the introduction of new and more efficient types of heating appliances, was the rococo style employed on ornamented stove plates. The six-plate model (a front, a back, two sides, a top, and a bottom), introduced about 1760 and based on Continental prototypes,[16] remained current for little more than a decade. It was then superseded by a ten-plate model, the four additional plates creating an internal baking oven accessible through a large door cut in each side plate. Both types were supported on an iron trestle base.

The new version, which originated about 1765 and now combined cooking with the heating function, was to remain the standard type until well into the nineteenth century.[17] Of the innumerable iron manufactories located in the Schuylkill Valley, which runs north and west of Philadelphia, one of the largest and best preserved is Hopewell Furnace, some forty miles from the city in the French Creek area of Berks County, Pennsylvania. It was established by Mark Bird, Jr., about 1770–71.[18] The following year, Bird commissioned the carving of the wooden patterns for two of the finest of all rococo-decorated American stoves, one of the six-plate type, one of the Franklin type.

The six-plate stove (**No. 160**), while missing its original trestle base, is more completely embellished with rococo decoration than any other American stove. (For an example having its original base, see No. 163.) The stove box is held together with a rod that runs in front of each of the decorated side plates and fits through holes in tabs extending from the top and bottom. Centered in each side plate is a magnificent footed vase with asymmetrical handles; from the vase flow branches with flowers and berries, filling the middle ground; at the bottom corners are lively raffles. At the top, on a ribbon scroll, is the motto "MARK BIRD HOPEWELL EURNACE [sic]" and the date 1772. The front panel has intertwined, fruit-laden grapevines flanked by engaged half columns decorated with running vines; on the back plate is depicted a man, arms akimbo and wearing a high-domed hat (an ironworker?), surrounded by rococo scrollwork. Despite the ravages of rust, the carving has a clarity of design and an assured execution that proclaims the hand of one of Philadelphia's master carvers.

160

Six-plate stove, 1772
Mark Bird, Hopewell Furnace, Pennsylvania
Cast iron, 35 x 41 x 18 in.
Birdsboro Community Memorial Center

The other great rococo design from Hopewell Furnace was a Franklin stove, from which survives only the arched front plate (**No. 161**),[19] ornamented with a pastoral vignette—two goats flanked by leafy branches. Above, in a ribbon, is the legend "MARK, BIRD HOPEWELL: FURNACE." Flanking the legend are numerals of the date, 1772. There is an exceptional realism in the carved ornament. Apart from the right side, which is pitted with rust, the casting is crisp and fresh, obviously derived from a carved pattern in excellent condition. Benjamin Franklin was interested in such matters. Writing from abroad to a Philadelphia merchant in 1765, he said: "A Friend in Paris has requested me to procure him two of our Pensilvania Fire Places. I wish you could get me a Couple of those that were cast by our Friend Grace, when the Moulds were good."[20]

A number of stove plates with rococo decoration have been found in Virginia and are now attributed to Marlboro Furnace, situated in the upper Shenandoah Valley a few miles south of Winchester.[21] In 1767, Isaac Zane (1743–1795), a well-born Philadelphian recently returned from London and the grand tour, purchased shares in the furnace and soon afterward bought out the other investors. It was he who in 1770 commissioned Bernard and Jugiez to carve the pattern for the massive Fairfax chimneyback (see p. 184). In view of his Philadelphia and London connections, it is not unreasonable to associate Zane with the production of a series of stove plates found locally, all with finely carved rococo ornament derived from the engraved designs of Thomas Johnson or Lock and Copland.[22] On one of them (**No. 162**), the Buddha-like figure is taken from the design for a chimneypiece in Lock and Copland's *New Book of Ornaments* (No. 2), which had been reissued in London in 1768.

It is only fitting that Henry William Stiegel, one of the most flamboyant of eighteenth-century American industrial entrepreneurs, should have produced the masterpiece of American rococo stoves at his Lancaster County furnace.[23] In 1750, Stiegel (1729–1785), who was born in Cologne, emigrated to Pennsylvania, where he was soon employed by the ironmaker John Jacob Huber at Elizabeth Furnace, near Brickerville. In 1752, Stiegel married his employer's daughter, Elizabeth, and by 1757, in partnership with Philadelphia merchants Charles and Alexander Stedman, he assumed control of the ironworks.

At first, Stiegel used Huber's stove-plate patterns, decorated with static arrangements of hearts and tulips. He altered only the inscriptions, which were biblical quotations in German, inserting in their place his name and the name of

161

Front plate from a Franklin stove, 1772
Mark Bird, Hopewell Furnace, Pennsylvania
Cast iron, 15 x 31¼ in.
The Historical Society of Pennsylvania

162

Side plate from a six-plate stove, ca. 1770
Attributed to Marlboro Furnace, Virginia
Cast iron, 22 x 27¼ in.
Private collection

163

Ten-plate stove, 1769
Henry William Stiegel
Elizabeth Furnace, Pennsylvania
Cast iron, 63¼ x 44¼ x 15 in.
Hershey Museum

his furnace. Stove plates bearing dates between 1758 and 1766 testify to that initial practice.[24] In 1769, Stiegel made a dramatic switch to the most florid rococo style. Clearly, he did so in an effort to attract the Philadelphia gentry (whose purchases abroad had been cut off by that year's nonimportation agreement) to a type of stove previously intended for Pennsylvanians of German origin. He commissioned carved wooden patterns for three different stoves. One, with his name and the date, is known only by individual side plates having a central vase surrounded by scrolls and leafage, none of it particularly well executed.[25] The other two exist in complete stoves—a six-plate and a ten-plate model—and have decoration of outstanding quality. The ornament is cast from patterns carved by the best of Philadelphia artisans; that of the six-plate stove has mostly to do with Masonic emblems.[26]

Stiegel's ten-plate stove (**No. 163**) was his attempt to produce a version so stylish that it would fit into the finest Philadelphia interiors.[27] For the decoration at either end of the side plates, which had to fit around the oven door, Stiegel chose splendid rococo raffles, mirror images of each other, and then proudly identified the manufacturer in ribbon scrolls: at the top, "H. W. STIEGEL"; at the bottom, "ELIZABETH FURNACE." The numerals of the date, 1769, are fitted into available space under the door. The back plate has a not particularly rococo hunting trophy; the front plate has within a rococo-scrolled and asymmetrical surround a vignette of a building in the background and, in the foreground, the dog of Aesop's fable contemplating his reflection in the water. The waterwheel next to the building signifies that it is part of an industrial complex, doubtless Elizabeth Furnace. The same image was employed for the tablet of the chimneypiece of the ballroom in Samuel Powel's town house, probably carved by Hercules Courtenay about 1770.[28] In 1769, the year the stove plate was carved, Powel had purchased the house from Charles Stedman, one of Stiegel's partners in the iron business. Was that a mere coincidence? Or does it support the theory that Courtenay was the carver of Stiegel's stove-plate patterns?

Reading (also spelled Redding) Furnace was in the French Creek region of the Schuylkill Valley, in the same area as Mark Bird's Hopewell Furnace.[29] Established in the 1730s, it was taken over in 1772 by James Old, who operated it for six years. Surviving rococo ironwork from Reading Furnace is limited to three stove plates, all with scrollwork and the inscriptions "IAMES.OLD" and "READING.FURNACE" in upper and lower ribbons. One, with a central basket of flowers reminiscent of finials on Philadelphia case furniture, is dated

164

Side plate for a ten-plate stove, ca. 1772
James Old, Reading Furnace, Pennsylvania
Cast iron, 23 x 30 in.
Pennsylvania Historical and Museum Commission

1772, the year of Old's succession.[30] The side panel to a ten-plate stove (**No. 164**) was his most ambitious effort in the rococo. The design, copied almost exactly from that of the preceding stove, is one step removed from its precision and vitality. In this casting, the oven aperture was filled in for use as a six-plate stove without the oven. The insert appears to have been makeshift; disparate carved motifs—a sheaf of wheat, the scales of justice, a sailing ship—have been combined with a fragment of a larger scrollwork pattern.

The type of wooden pattern from which the side of a ten-plate stove was cast is exhibited by a finely preserved example signed in its upper ribbon "BATSTO FURNACE," for the New Jersey ironworks (**No. 165**). Though as early as any of the known stove patterns, it is ornamented in a late rendition of the rococo. Vigorous, large-scale motifs have been replaced by refined low-relief carving. The triangular colonettes and scrollwork of the style have now been tamed to coexist with elegant neoclassical urns and vases. The pattern was probably made during the tenure of William Richard, who owned Batsto from 1786 to 1807.[31] Of solid mahogany, it is mortised and tenoned and pegged together to form a frame around the oven-door opening. The separate board that fills the opening is held in place with removable cleats.

MHH

165

Side-plate pattern for a ten-plate stove, 1785–95
Batsto Furnace, New Jersey
Mahogany, 26 x 33 in.
Burlington County Historical Society

Glass

During the period of rococo influence, the manufacture of domestic glass was limited to a very few factories whose output consisted almost entirely of bottles and windowpanes.[32] The making of fine table glass was attempted by only two manufacturers—first, Henry William Stiegel, subsequently, John Frederick Amelung—both of whom ultimately failed to compete with fashionable British goods. However, rococo influence is certainly perceptible among the few surviving tablewares from their two efforts, chiefly in the engraved ornament.

Henry William Stiegel, mentioned earlier in this chapter as proprietor of Elizabeth Furnace, Lancaster County, expanded his commercial interests in 1764 when he founded a glassworks at Manheim, also in Lancaster County. Stiegel hired German-trained glassblowers to produce bottles, windowpanes, and small amounts of tableware in the German style for the local Pennsylvania-German community. His production, realized late in the year, was advertised the following February: "Notice, that the Glasshouse, which he has erected in the Town of Manheim, is now compleatly finished, and the Business of Glassmaking in it carried on; where all Persons may be suited in the best Manner, with any Sort of Glass, according to their Order."[33]

The small amount of German-style table glass he made for domestic markets consisted primarily of tumblers, mugs, salts, cream pots, sugar dishes, and plates, of thick, unrefined green glass. When London trade commissioners asked Governor John Penn about American industries under his jurisdiction that might threaten the English exports, he called Stiegel's glassware "of very ordinary Quality, but to supply the small demands of the Villages and Farmers in the adjacent inland Country"; Benjamin Franklin described it as "coarse wear [sic] for the country neighbors."[34] Though Penn and Franklin undoubtedly downplayed Stiegel's production, his glass was certainly not comparable to that imported from the mother country.

Contemporary English table glass was finely blown of a sparkling, colorless lead-oxide composition. Colorless glass, called "white glass" in the period, was the most difficult to produce, requiring refining to rid it of the chemical impurities that would otherwise have shaded it green, amber, or brown. Coloring glass intentionally was easier than removing offending impurities; the addition of such chemical oxides as cobalt or manganese produced more pleasing tones of blue or purple, respectively. The introduction of lead into colorless glass, a discovery made in England late in the seventeenth century, enhanced its clarity and brilliance. This lead glass, called "flint glass" in the period, was commonly employed for fine English tablewares throughout the eighteenth century. Affluent colonials could purchase flint glass in all manner of drinking and dessert vessels, punch bowls, and serving forms, the most lavish of which had cut or engraved decoration. English glass responded to the rococo style not only with naturalistic foliate and armorial engraving but also with lighter shapes. The heavy, Germanic, knop-stemmed baluster of early-eighteenth-century English goblets was supplanted by a more delicate, attenuated, knopless stemmed form. Often, a spiral twist, achieved with a clear air bubble or with an opaque white cane of glass, was embedded in the stem, catching the light and investing the form with rococo delicacy and movement.

Stiegel made dramatic changes in his German-style production in 1769, when Philadelphia merchants voted to uphold the local nonimportation agreement. Hoping to take over urban markets previously supplied by imported tablewares, he hired English glassblowers, named his factory the American Flint Glass Manufactory, and became the first American manufacturer to produce fine lead-glass tablewares in the English style. The secret of the technology, brought to America that year by John Allman, was first put to use at Stiegel's glassworks.[35] Stiegel continued to produce bottles, windowpanes, and vernacular tablewares, but added to that repertoire a range of luxury items in flint glass as well as in colored glass: scent bottles, sugar dishes, cream pots, tumblers, mugs, salts, cruets, decanters, and glasses for wine, beer, water, and dessert. After 1769, cream pots were sometimes described in the records as "three-feeted,"[36] indicating an English form well known in silver (see Nos. 55, 58, 59). Stiegel advertised his new line actively, engaged the support of important glass merchants, and sought independent endorsements. One of these last, signed by an anonymous "Pennsylvania Planter," appeared in the *Pennsylvania Gazette* of 1 August 1771:

Every Person seems pleased with the late Success of Mr. *Stiegel*, who has erected the first House in *America* for making white Flint Glass. We have already seen that Work brought to Perfection; Decanters, Wine Glasses, etc. etc. now manufactured in this Province, equal in Whiteness, Transparency and Figure, to those which are imported from *Europe*; that many Thousands of Pounds must be saved to Pennsylvania by this Manufacture alone, will readily be granted.[37]

By 1773, Stiegel was able to embellish his wares with engraved decoration. In that year, he hired the earliest known glass engraver active in America, Lazarus Isaac, an English immigrant who had been working in Philadelphia. Earlier in the year, Isaac had announced in an independent advertisement that he undertook "to cut and engrave on glass of every kind, in any figure whatsoever, either coats of arms, flowers, names, or figures."[38] Stiegel signed a one-year contract with Isaac in June of 1773, paying him £5-10-0 a month (the same wages he paid his master blowers) and providing him with a house and land for a garden.

In glassmaking, engraving is considered a form of cold decoration—that is, adornment added to a fully fashioned article after it has been removed from the annealing oven and cooled—in contrast with that accomplished while the material is still hot and malleable. Thus, as in silver, engraving can be added by an independent artisan. The glass-engraving process, however, differs considerably from that employed on silver. By means of a lapidary-like procedure, the engraver manipulates copper wheels lined with an abrasive to cut away glass in specific areas, leaving them frosty in appearance. The rotating technique lends itself to flowing, curvaceous rococo designs.

The earliest example of American table glass with rococo decoration is a goblet (**No. 166**) that descended in the Stiegel family and is therefore attributed to Stiegel's factory.[39] The only known example of his English-style production, it is of lead glass and has an opaque white-twist stem. Its bowl is engraved in the rococo style: on one side, with a naturalistic, asymmetrical rose; on the other, with a foliate cartouche enclosing the engraved inscription "W & E OLD," for Elizabeth and William Old, Stiegel's daughter and son-in-law. Old was probably a son of iron manufacturer James Old, of Reading Furnace (see p. 227). The couple were married in 1773, shortly before Isaac was officially employed at Manheim; Stiegel undoubtedly had him engrave the goblet to commemorate their wedding. In composition and decoration, the goblet for the Olds is similar to contemporary English prototypes also having naturalistic engraving and stems that encase twists of opaque glass canes—a type that corresponds to Stiegel's advertisements for "enameled" glass.[40]

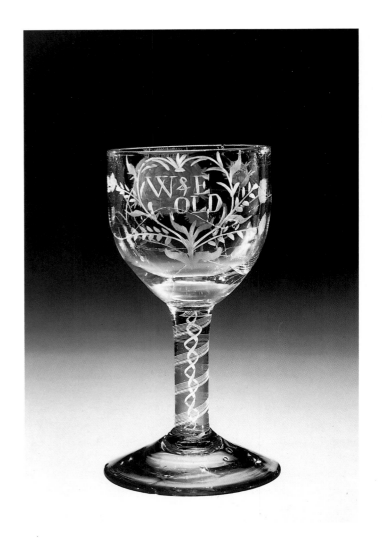

166

Goblet, 1773–74
Attributed to Henry William Stiegel
American Flint Glass Manufactory
Manheim, Pennsylvania
Engraving attributed to Lazarus Isaac
Glass, H.: 6¾ in.
The Corning Museum of Glass

From 1769 until the factory's closing in 1774, Stiegel produced both German- and English-style glass, but his foray into new markets was frustrated in 1770 by the repeal of Philadelphia's nonimportation agreement. That setback, combined with the large expense entailed in converting his factory to the production of lead glass, bankrupted Stiegel (who was already overextended in other business ventures), and his glass production ceased in 1774.

The finest rococo engraving on American glass dates from the twilight of the style, around 1790, and was produced at John Frederick Amelung's New Bremen Glassmanufactory, in Frederick County, Maryland. The German-born Johann Friedrich Amelung (1741–1798) began his work as technical director at his brother's mirror factory at Grünenplan, south of Hanover, in 1773. In 1784, after convincing a group of Bremen merchants to invest in a glass factory he planned to establish in America, Amelung bought equipment, hired German workers, and arrived in Maryland. He acquired an existing glassworks in Frederick County, about forty miles west of Baltimore, and set up production. Within a few months, he advertised window glass and hollowware (the latter, presumably, only bottles). In the following year, he published his intention to build a complete glass factory, to "consist in making all kinds of glass-Wares, viz. Window-Glass, from the lowest to the finest sorts, white and green Bottles, Wines and other Drinking-Glasses, as also Optical Glasses, and Looking-Glasses, finished compleat."[41]

There is no evidence to prove that Amelung ever succeeded with optical or mirror glass; the majority of his production was composed of utilitarian glass for bottles and windowpanes. Like Stiegel before him, Amelung attempted to break into the luxury market with colorless, engraved table glass of high quality. As an advertisement of 1789 reported: "He makes...all Kinds of Flint-Glass, such as Decanters, and Wine Glasses, Tumblers of all Sizes, and any other Sort of Table Glass. —He also cuts Devices, Cyphers, Coats of Arms, or any other Fancy Figures on Glass."[42] The "Flint-Glass" must have been colorless glass; there is nothing to document that Amelung ever produced lead glass. If surviving examples are any indication, his table glass differed from Stiegel's wares mainly in their forms: while Stiegel adopted his from the English, Amelung continued to produce the heavy, baroque kind of vessels he had known in his native country: knop-stemmed goblets, or Pokals, fitted with covers crowned by fat, robust finials; elaborately tooled sugar dishes with pincered handles and animal finials; and large tumblers, often fitted with finialed covers.

Engraving superior to that displayed on Stiegel's goblet for the Olds appears on Amelung's finest products. A consistently delicate, sophisticated style argues for a single hand, probably a German-trained engraver who executed the rococo flowers, birds, scrolls, and armorials, as well as lettering in a style analogous to that on German rococo glass but nonetheless retardataire by 1790, as were the baroque shapes of the glasses. An Amelung advertisement of 1791 suggests the availability of custom engraving and mentions the flowers typical of the rococo style: "Glass may be had, cut with *letters, cyphers, crests, flowers,* or *devices,* agreeable to the fancy of the purchasers, from 4d....to 40s. a piece, besides the price of the glass."[43]

To promote his wares, Amelung, like Stiegel, advertised and enlisted the retailing services of key glass merchants in neighboring Baltimore and Fredericktown, as well as in New York and Philadelphia. Amelung also produced a series of outstanding presentation glasses for prominent politicians and merchants in the hope of attracting political and mercantile support for his embryonic American endeavor. All the glasses had elaborate engraving that prominently featured the name of Amelung's factory; all seem to date between 1788 and 1792. Although goblets Amelung gave to George Washington do not survive, a published account of their presentation reveals much about the patriotic attitude toward the young country's fledgling domestic industry:

> I am just returned from Mount-Vernon, where I was present at a scene which made every patriotic pulse vibrate with the most pleasurable sensation. This, Sir, was a tribute of a new citizen of the United States, to their illustrious President.
>
> Mr. John F. Amelung, a native of Germany and an artist of considerable eminence...through his vast exertions he is now enabled to supply the United States, with every species of GLASS, the quality of which is equal if not superior to that imported....
>
> To the testimony of the ablest connoisseurs and characters of trade and respectability, it only remained for Mr. Amelung, to court the patronage of the great Patriot, and I had the good fortune to have been present at an offering to his Excellency of two capacious goblets of double flint glass, exhibiting the General's coat of arms, &c.[44]

The political ramifications of the gift were palpable; Washington approved a duty on imported glass four months later.

A covered tumbler and a goblet represent Amelung's splendid presentation pieces, collectively the most elaborate decorated glass made in eighteenth-century America. The tumbler (**No. 167**), Amelung's gift to his wife, Carolina Lucia (Magdalena Carolina Lucia von Leseburg), is dated 1788. The inscription, "Happy is he who is blessed with Virtuous Children Carolina Lucia Amelung 1788," is engraved as an arch over a central scene framed in rococo scrolls and foliage. The vignette depicts an angel leading Tobias, son of Tobit, on his journey to cure his father's blindness. (Tucked under Tobias's arm is a fish he will use in the cure.) The lid of the tumbler is also engraved with a rococo design of *C*-scrolls and foliage.

The finest rococo composition on Amelung's known glass occurs on the goblet (**No. 168**) made for the glassmaker himself around 1792. The bowl is engraved with his name and a German inscription (said to be the family's motto) that reads in translation: "Seek Virtue and when you find Her leave everything else to Providence."[45] The rococo cartouche surrounding the "J Amelung" consists of *C*-scrolls, flowers, foliage, drooping ears of wheat, a diapered panel, and a ribbed shell directly beneath Amelung's name; the small, bursting rose emerging from the scrolling *J* of his initial is a virtuoso touch (see detail). Throughout the design, the engraver has controlled the cuts of the wheel so as to shade certain areas lightly, creating an impressive sense of three-dimensionality.

By 1790, Amelung was the head of a thriving factory with a dependent village of forty-five hundred persons. During that decade, however, a disastrous fire at the glassworks and ensuing financial difficulties reversed his fortunes. In 1795, Amelung, in ill health, deeded the factory to his son; in 1798, it was subdivided and sold for debts.

LGB

167

Covered tumbler, 1788
John Frederick Amelung
New Bremen Glassmanufactory
Frederick County, Maryland
Glass, H.: 11⅞ in.
The Corning Museum of Glass

168

Goblet, ca. 1792
John Frederick Amelung
New Bremen Glassmanufactory
Frederick County, Maryland
Glass, H.: 6¾ in.
Collection of Mrs. Graham John Barbey
Courtesy of the Maryland Historical Society

Porcelain

Porcelain, the finest of the ceramic bodies and, because of its high firing temperature, the most difficult to produce,[46] was a highly prized oriental commodity until the secret of its manufacture was discovered in Germany early in the 1700s. Once revealed, the formula spread throughout Europe; by the mid-eighteenth century, Chinese imports were being rivaled by porcelain tablewares and figures of both oriental and Western design from a number of European and English factories. Yet porcelain, whether Chinese or European, remained a cherished possession, affordable only to the wealthy. American merchants, limited to trade with Britain, imported English ceramics almost exclusively, though Chinese porcelains were also obtainable from London suppliers. Most American tables were furnished with increasingly fine English pottery that served as less expensive alternatives to porcelain—delftwares, salt-glazed stonewares, and cream-colored earthenwares—while the most affluent colonials could indulge in English porcelain produced at Bow, Derby, Liverpool, Plymouth, and Worcester. The only American porcelain made during the rococo period imitated wares from those English centers and reflected their version of rococo taste.

The first documented attempt at American-made porcelain was made by Andrew Duché, a Philadelphia stoneware potter who found the kaolin essential to its production in Savannah, Georgia. In 1738, several years before porcelain was first produced in England, he recorded a successful kiln firing. The veracity of his claim has yet to be proved, and little is known of his subsequent career,[47] but he undoubtedly did find kaolin in Georgia (it was also available in South Carolina and Delaware). Though scattered reports of further American porcelain manufacture in the 1760s cannot be substantiated, the desire for domestic production is made particularly evident in the writings of Benjamin Franklin, who, on his travels in England and France, sent his wife examples of porcelain from Bow and Worcester. He also concerned

himself with the identification of domestic clays suitable for porcelain production and sought American-made enamels with which to decorate it. Writing from Paris to a correspondent in Pennsylvania, he recounted a French chemist's favorable assessment of white clays sent from America and added, "If we encourage necessary Manufactures among ourselves, and refrain buying the Superfluities of other Countries, a few Years will make a surprizing Change in our favour."[48] Franklin's hopes were shared by the noted physician Benjamin Rush, who in a letter from Edinburgh in 1768 spoke of his desire to see a china manufactory founded in Philadelphia.[49]

In such an optimistic climate, it is not surprising that experiments in the manufacture of American porcelain should begin in Philadelphia. In January of 1770, Gousse Bonnin (1741?–1780?) and George Morris (1742/5–1773), partners in a new Philadelphia china-producing venture, announced their success in a local newspaper:

> New China Ware. Notwithstanding the various difficulties and disadvantages, which usually attend the introduction of any important manufacture into a new country, the proprietors of the China Works, now erecting in Southwark [Philadelphia], have the pleasure to acquaint the public, they have proved to a certainty, that the clays of America are productive of as good Porcelain as any heretofore manufactured at the famous factory in Bow, near London.[50]

Bonnin was a wealthy Englishman who had brought his wife and children to Penn's colony in 1768; Morris was the son of a prominent Philadelphia family. The first indication of their partnership was a land agreement in late 1769 (it can be no coincidence that Philadelphia merchants had enacted a nonimportation agreement the previous April). Despite their announcement of January 1770, the "proprietors" did not actually produce porcelain until late in the year, after nine master workers they had hired from England arrived in Philadelphia that October.[51]

The partners, who called their business the American China Manufactory, made soft-paste porcelain[52] in style and shapes analogous to English wares. In their advertisements they offered "compleat sets for the dining and tea table together, or dining singly," including pickle stands, fruit baskets, sauceboats, bowls, and plates. Later, they added cups, teapots, sugar dishes, cream pots, and toilet sets to their line.[53] Technically, the surviving Bonnin and Morris interpretations are surprisingly proficient, undoubtedly due to the skilled English immigrants in their employ. The workers' various backgrounds probably explain the distilled English style of the manufactory's wares, copying not one factory's production but displaying motifs and characteristics related to many. For example, a given piece might have

169

Sauceboat, 1770–72
Gousse Bonnin and George Morris
American China Manufactory, Philadelphia
Porcelain, H.: 4 in.
The Brooklyn Museum

170

Sauceboat, ca. 1770
Probably Plymouth Factory, England
Porcelain, H.: 4¼ in.
High Museum of Art

border decoration common to one factory, a shape derived from another, a handle from a third.

Like their English counterparts, Bonnin and Morris decorated their wares primarily in underglaze blue,[54] a tradition originating with the blue-and-white oriental porcelains imported to Europe in the sixteenth and seventeenth centuries. Those imports had led to imitations in low-fired English stonewares and in English and Dutch delftwares, as well as in English porcelains, to the extent that blue and white was a widely favored color scheme in tablewares. Surviving examples from the Bonnin and Morris factory (fewer than two dozen) are stylistically consistent with contemporary English blue-and-white porcelains decorated in the rococo style with naturalistic flowers and insects or with chinoiserie scenes.

A comparison of a Bonnin and Morris sauceboat (**No. 169**) with an English example of the same period is illustrative not only of the factory's implicit mission to copy and to compete with English wares but also of its ability to produce alternatives of high quality. The sauceboat has been likened to Liverpool examples,[55] a resemblance that warrants mention, for the chinoiserie vignette that decorates it is certainly similar in composition to that of scenes on Liverpool prototypes.[56] Nevertheless, it also closely relates to one assigned to Plymouth (**No. 170**): both are molded in the rococo style with scrolls and shells on the body, shaped rims, double-scrolled handles, and lobed-and-ruffled pedestal feet. That signature rococo shape in ceramic sauceboats merits comparison with the premier example of the form in American rococo silver, a pair marked by Richard Humphreys (see No. 76). Like the Plymouth sauceboat, the Bonnin and Morris example is decorated with a landscape scene and with intermittent rococo floral sprigs in underglaze blue. The American interpretation differs from the Plymouth version in its oriental latticework border, the composition of the landscape scene in its cartouche, and the placement of floral sprigs on its inner border, handle, and foot rim.

The fashion for pierced serving dishes in the rococo period, already explored in silver (see pp. 119–24), can also be documented in porcelain. Because the ceramic medium is less malleable than silver, the results are more staid, but rococo nonetheless. A Bonnin and Morris basket (**No. 171**), fashioned after English prototypes from Worcester, Lowestoft, and Bow, has openwork sides of interlaced circles joined by horizontal crossbars, punctuated on the exterior with applied flowers picked out in blue, and surmounted by a serpentine rim. Like its English models, the basket has underglaze blue painting on the interior of a rococo still life,

171

Basket, 1770–72
Gousse Bonnin and George Morris
American China Manufactory, Philadelphia
Porcelain, Diam.: 5⅞ in.
Collection of Eric Noah

172

Pickle stand, 1770–72
Gousse Bonnin and George Morris
American China Manufactory, Philadelphia
Porcelain, H.: 5⅝ in.
The Metropolitan Museum of Art

173

Pickle stand, 1770–72
Gousse Bonnin and George Morris
American China Manufactory, Philadelphia
Porcelain, H.: 5⅛ in.
Collection of Mr. and Mrs. George M. Kaufman

typically consisting of a lush, asymmetrical, naturalistic bouquet of different varieties of flowers, usually with insects (here, a butterfly) hovering nearby. The technical difficulties of producing porcelain are graphically demonstrated by the border decoration on the American basket, originally a concise design of shells, flowers, and foliage, but reduced to a blur in the high-temperature firing.[57] The form undoubtedly corresponds to the "fruit baskets" billed to John Cadwalader at ten shillings apiece in 1771.[58] The Bonnin and Morris firm evidently offered at least two sizes of fruit baskets, in diameters of approximately six inches, seen here, and eight inches.[59]

The most elaborate shape produced at the Philadelphia porcelain factory was the double-tiered sweetmeat dish, referred to as "pickle stands" in period accounts and the most expensive form documented.[60] Four of these splendidly rococo serving dishes are known to survive, three with substantial blue decoration; the fourth, a less expensive version, embellished only with feathered blue borders.[61] All four are composed of three shell-shaped dishes clustered around a pillar of simulated coral encrusted with smaller shells on which is elevated a central shell-like bowl. The model, produced in England at both Bow and Plymouth, is related to various rococo forms in silver and ceramics that draw upon naturalistic renderings of shells and sea creatures.[62] The decorated example shown here (**No. 172**; see also ill. opp. p. 219) has rich rococo floral painting akin to that found on the preceding basket, with a butterfly fluttering in the uppermost bowl; all four dishes are painted in underglaze blue with delicately rendered flowers. Characteristically, the encrusting shells are picked out in blue, as are the feathered rims of the dish. Without the additional flower decoration (**No. 173**), the stand has the trompe l'oeil effect of being actually encrusted with sea life — a rococo whimsy unusual in American interpretation and more typical of English and French expressions.

At least two prominent Philadelphians may have used dishes like these at dessert. John Cadwalader and Thomas Wharton each ordered pickle stands from Bonnin and Morris for which they were charged fifteen shillings — five shillings more than the price of a fruit basket.[63] Both men made their purchases in 1771 from Archibald McElroy, Bonnin and Morris's Philadelphia retailer. Cadwalader ordered two; Wharton, only one. Also included on Wharton's bill, under the heading "American China," were a dozen "handled Cups," a total of three sugar dishes, two cream ewers, three teapots, four bowls, one fruit basket, thirteen plates, a set of "quitted" (quilted) cups, as well as a set of plain cups, a pair of sauceboats in addition to a smaller sauceboat, and six pint bowls.[64] Cadwalader, one of the richest and most influential tastemakers in Philadelphia, ordered his porcelain late in 1770, at the same time he was paying for architectural carving in the front and back parlors of his rococo showplace (see pp. 214–17). He had presumably received it by January 1771, when he paid McElroy's bill, the same month his lavish furniture suite had been completed by Affleck (see Nos. 153–156).

The disproportionately large numbers of surviving luxury forms, particularly baskets and pickle stands, leads to speculation that Bonnin and Morris emphasized top-of-the-line luxuries in the same way that Amelung produced his special presentation glasses. Despite the numerous forms documented, the only examples known to survive from the Bonnin and Morris factory are sauceboats, pickle stands, sweetmeat dishes (of single-shell shape), baskets, and covered openwork dishes.[65] Less lavish forms, possibly unmarked, may have been mistaken for English goods.

The patronage of such prominent Philadelphians as the Cadwaladers, the Penns, the Franklins, the Shippens, and the Whartons[66] notwithstanding, the American China Manufactory encountered many difficulties. In the face of setbacks inevitable to the launching of an ambitious new industry, and hampered further by America's resumption of trade with England in 1770, Bonnin and Morris closed their factory in November of 1772. Porcelain was not successfully produced again in the United States until well into the nineteenth century.

L G B

Notes

THE AMERICAN ROCOCO
pp. 1-15.

1. Kimball 1943, 4; for a summary treatment of the Continental origins of the rococo, see Snodin 1984, 27-31.

2. For Meissonnier, see *Oeuvres de Juste-Aurèle Meissonnier* (Paris, ca. 1750), reprint, with an introduction by Dorothea Nyberg (New York: Benjamin Blom, 1969).

3. Illustrated in ibid., folios 6-8.

4. As quoted in ibid., 19.

5. Snodin 1990, 16.

6. For the complete engraved works of Lock and Copland, see Heckscher 1979.

7. See ibid., 8, for a reference to *Chippendale's Ornaments and Interior Decoration* (London: John Weale, ca. 1840), which contains one design by Lock and none by Chippendale.

8. As quoted in MFA 1975, 13.

9. Prime 1929, 20.

10. William B. Willcox, ed., *The Papers of Benjamin Franklin*, vols. 15-26 (New Haven: Yale University Press, 1972-87), 19: 336-37.

11. Ibid., 12: 250, letter of August 1765 from Franklin, in London, to Deborah, in Philadelphia.

12. Ibid., 62, letter of 14 February 1765, from Franklin, in London, to Deborah, in Philadelphia.

13. Wainwright 1964, 65.

14. The standard book on the subject is Arthur Meier Schlesinger, *The Colonial Merchants and the American Revolution, 1763-1776* (New York: Facsimile Library, 1939).

15. Ibid., 107, quoting *The Boston Post-Boy*, 26 October 1767.

16. Prime 1929, 176.

17. Quoted in Hornor 1935, 168.

18. For a general treatment of the Kentucky rifle, see M. L. Brown, *Firearms in Colonial America* (Washington, D.C.: Smithsonian Institution Press, 1980), 263-74.

19. The picture survives in its original mahogany frame, which has a gilt, sand-finished fascia and original glazing. On the back, an ink inscription in an eighteenth-century hand reads "Elizabeth Flower November 1765."

20. Ann's picture is in the collections of Winterthur Museum (58.2226).

21. S. Sympson, *A New Book of Cyphers* (London, 1736), 31.

22. A national standard for the Continental forces was not defined until late in the revolutionary war; the flag, with its thirteen stars and thirteen stripes, was first intended for marine use. Land forces were not authorized to carry the Stars and Stripes with their regimental colors until 1834. For information on the use of military flags in the colonial era, see Edward W. Richardson, *Standards and Colors of the American Revolution* (Philadelphia: University of Pennsylvania Press, 1982).

23. As quoted in ibid., 309.

24. Wainwright 1964, 20.

ARCHITECTURE
pp. 17-35.

1. Prime 1929, 276-77. For a review of eighteenth-century American wallpaper, see Lynn 1980, 108-19.

2. Park 1973 documents 119 different titles in pre-Revolutionary America.

3. Ibid., 71-72.

4. Transcribed from the title page of Swan's *British Architect* (London, 1758).

5. For the Vassall house, see Bainbridge Bunting and Robert H. Nylander, *Report Four: Old Cambridge* (Cambridge, Mass.: Cambridge Historical Commission, 1973), 80-81; for the Apthorp house, see Garrett 1960, 62, with a photograph of the Great Chamber taken about 1870-80 that shows the original scenic wallpaper with rococo frames.

6. See Park 1973, 61.

7. The attribution of Apthorp's house to Harrison was made by Fiske Kimball, quoted in Garrett 1960, 29-30; see also ibid., 17, where John Adams declared the house "a splendid edifice...intended for an Episcopal palace."

8. John Perkins Brown, "Christ Church, Cambridge," *Cambridge Historical Society Proceedings* 23 (1937): 21.

9. A pair of carved chimneypiece trusses from the Russell house, in nearby Charlestown, in the collections of the Society for the Preservation of New England Antiquities, are a variant of the Swan-based Apthorp type and look to be by the same hand as those at Elmwood (now the Cambridge residence of Harvard University presidents), one illustrated in *Pencil Points* 23 (September 1937): Fig. 56.

10. Illustrated in Howells 1941, Figs. 23, 24.

11. Chamberlain 1977.

12. For Portsmouth architecture, see Garvin 1983; for illustrations, see Howells 1937.

13. For the Dearing bill, see Garvin 1983, 190; for an illustration of the chimneypieces and staircase, see Howells 1937, Figs. 39, 40.

14. Garvin 1983, 269-70.

15. Other examples of this Portsmouth type of carving are in the Jacob Wendell house (1789) and in the post-Revolutionary remodelings of the Wentworth-Gardner house. For an illustration of the latter, see Howells 1937, Fig. 91.

16. For the history of Philipse Manor, see Stefan Bielinski, *An American Loyalist: The Ordeal of Frederick Philipse III* (Albany: New York State Museum, 1976), 8-11.

17. Compare with the parlor of Hampton Court, built at Elizabeth, New Jersey, about 1761 (now at Winterthur), whose fireplace wall, obviously from the same hand, is nearly identical to that at Philipse Manor, but has a mantel shelf and frieze modeled on the treatment of the adjacent overdoor.

18. The subject is fully explored in Kimerly Rorschach, "Frederick, Prince of Wales (1707-1751), as a Patron of the Visual Arts," Ph.D. diss., Yale University, 1985.

19. Gottesman 1938, 123.

20. The only other New York chimneypiece displaying such ornament is in Van Cortlandt House, constructed in 1748-49 by Jacobus Van Cortlandt and inherited by his son Frederick in the year of its completion. The style of the mantel in the east parlor suggests that it was added sometime in the mid-1760s.

21. See, for example, Plate 9, in Johnson's book of designs.

22. For painted landscape papers, see Lynn 1980, 54-55.

23. First published in 1752, the book was reissued on 1 January 1768, just in time to be regarded as representing the latest fashion.

24. The letter, dated 12 October 1768, is in the files of the American Wing, Metropolitan Museum.

25. For illustrations of Philadelphia architectural carving, see Wallace 1931.

26. For discussions of those carvers, see Beckerdite 1985 and 1987b.

27. Manuscript in Rare Book Collection, Library, University of Pennsylvania.

28. A similar chimneypiece design, but with elaborate frieze carving, is in the parlor (now at Detroit Institute of Arts) of nearby Whitby Hall, a house acquired in 1741 and enlarged in 1754 by James Coultas, High Sheriff of Philadelphia between the years 1755 and 1758.

29. Beckerdite 1985, 500.

30. Bernard and Jugiez are also thought to have carved the pulpit and the organ case at Saint Peter's Church in Philadelphia (1758-63).

31. See Beckerdite 1987b, 1054, 1056, 1058; for the Johnson design, see ibid., Figs. 11, 12.

32. For the Powel house, see Tatum 1976.

33. For workmen engaged on Powel's parlor, see ibid., 52, 54, 90.

See also Fig. 50 for illustrations of the parlor frieze and related engravings in Swan's *Designs in Architecture.* For Clow in Scotland, see Geoffrey Beard, *Decorative Plasterwork in Great Britain* (Oxford: Phaidon, 1975), 88. The only other surviving rococo plasterwork from the Philadelphia area is a ceiling and frieze (now preserved at Winterthur) of about 1762 from Port Royal House, Frankford, on the outskirts of the city.

34. John A. H. Sweeney, *Grandeur on the Appoquinimink: The House of William Corbit at Odessa, Delaware* (Newark, Del.: University of Delaware Press, 1959), 50-56.

35. Beckerdite 1987b, 1052-56.

36. Beckerdite 1982b, 67.

37. For the Chase house, see ibid., 43-52.

38. Ibid., 48-50.

39. For the Hammond house, see ibid., 53-62.

40. Charles Scarlett, Jr., "Governor Horatio Sharpe's Whitehall," *Maryland Historical Magazine* 46 (March 1951): 16, 18.

41. Reiff 1986, 241-44.

42. Beckerdite 1982a, 29-30.

43. Ibid., 7-9.

44. For a full discussion of the table, see ibid., 21-26.

45. For Marmion, see Waterman 1945, 76-81. Mention must also be made of Kenmore, Fielding Lewis's house at Fredericksburg, where splendid chimneypieces and plaster ceilings were installed in 1775. Except for the carved mantel friezes, however, the style was more neoclassical than rococo.

46. For a thorough investigation of carving and carvers in Charleston, see Bivins 1986.

47. Quoted in ibid., 36.

48. Ibid., 15.

49. Ibid., 96-99.

50. See Prime 1929, 275. The only other ornamented ceiling in Charleston is that of the second-story drawing room of the Daniel Huger house (ca. 1760-65) at 34 Meeting Street, which has plaster wreaths of leafage encircling musical trophies. For an illustration, see W. H. Johnston Thomas, "Seven great Charleston houses," *The Magazine Antiques* 97 (April 1970): 559.

51. Illustrated in ibid., 558.

ENGRAVINGS

pp. 37-69.

1. Snodin 1986, 103.

2. For a study of English trade cards, see Ambrose Heal, *The London Furniture Makers* (London: B. T. Batsford, 1953).

3. See Heckscher 1979.

4. Snodin 1986, 86, 93.

5. See Jobe and Kaye 1984, No. 147.

6. On rare occasions, American engravers employed etching to achieve a freer, looser effect. For a good example of that practice, see the Kennedy advertisement by Smither (No. 33).

7. For a complete survey of Johnston as engraver, see Hitchings 1973.

8. See ibid., 126-28, for the inventory of Johnston's estate.

9. Ibid., 95.

10. French 1939, 90.

11. Fales 1973, 212.

12. The portrait (at the Cleveland Museum of Art) is pictured in Ward and Ward 1979, 76.

13. The Day Books, or ledgers, are at the Massachusetts Historical Society. For a discussion of them, see Brigham 1969, 10-12.

14. Ibid., 158-75.

15. For full-length studies of Revere, see Leehey 1988; for his engravings, see Brigham 1969; for his silver, see Buhler 1956; for a discussion of his Masonic activities, see Steblecki 1988.

16. PMA 1976, 64. For a complete biography of Turner, see ibid., 64-65.

17. For Franklin's influence, see Fales 1973, 196-97, 206-7.

18. For Dawkins, see Cole 1966.

19. Wigley, who had been a member of the Clothworker's Company, was working as an engraver on Fleet Street in 1749. We are grateful to D. E. Wickham, archivist of the Clothworker's Company, London, and to the English scholar and author Robert Barker, whose research provided us with this new information on Dawkins.

20. Quoted in PMA 1976, 77.

21. Prime 1929, 18.

22. Cole 1966, 22.

23. Stauffer 1907, 1: 254-55.

24. Prime 1929, 28.

25. Ibid.

BOOKPLATES
pp. 40-45.

26. Logan's bookplate is illustrated in Hornor 1935, Pl. 86.

27. For a full discussion of Hurd's bookplates, see French 1939, 82-137.

28. Ibid., 103.

29. Hitchings 1973, 132.

30. Illustrated in Brigham 1969, Pl. 52.

31. For Revere's bookplates, see ibid., 158-66.

32. The engraving of the Oliver bookplate attributed to Revere, which seems to be more finished in quality than are those he

signed, is possibly of English workmanship and may have been the prototype for his favored bookplate mantling.

33. Brigham 1969, 162.

34. For Gallaudet, see Stauffer 1907, 1: 95-96.

35. Gottesman 1938, 12.

36. As quoted in PMA 1976, 64.

37. For Norris's library, see Marie Elena Korey, *The Books of Isaac Norris (1701–1766) at Dickinson College* (Carlisle, Pa.: Dickinson College, 1976).

38. The volume in which the bookplate illustrated is pasted is *Examen Concilii Tridentini*, published in Dortrecht, the Netherlands, in 1678.

BOOKS, METAL CUTS, AND BOOKBINDINGS
pp. 46-48.

39. See Hitchings 1973, 111, 112, 114, 115.

40. See Brigham 1969, 16-18; Pl. 3.

41. Ibid., 198-212; see 199 for quoted passage.

42. Spawn 1983, 35.

43. Quoted in Spawn 1963, 432.

44. Aitken to Jeremy Belknap, author of *History of New-Hampshire*, which Aitken was then printing, 22 December 1783. This information was kindly provided by Willman Spawn.

45. Spawn 1963, 424-25. The Clarkson copy is now in the Free Library of Philadelphia.

46. For the Thompson provenance, see *Early American Bookbindings from the Collection of Michael Papantonio* (Worcester, Mass.: American Antiquarian Society, 1972), No. 13.

47. For an illustration of that type of English binding, see Dorothy Miner, *The History of Bookbinding, 525–1950* (Baltimore, Md.: Walters Art Gallery, 1957), No. 501.

TRADE CARDS AND OTHER EPHEMERA
pp. 49-58.

48. For Hutt's advertisement, see Gottesman 1938, 12-13; for Norman's, see Prime 1929, 20.

49. For Deblois's newspaper advertisements, see Dow 1927, 76-78, 151, 181.

50. Hitchings 1973, Figs. 42, 43, 45, 46.

51. Dow 1927, 259.

52. Illustrated in ibid., opp. p. 258.

53. As quoted in Brigham 1969, 174.

54. For Revere's Masonic engravings, see ibid., 180-97.

55. As quoted in ibid., 185, 187.

56. Illustrated in ibid., Pl. 63.

57. As quoted in ibid., 146.

58. For Revere's anatomical certificates, see ibid., 146-51.

59. Gottesman 1938, 8.

60. First by I. N. Phelps Stokes, in *The Iconography of Manhattan Island, 1498-1909* (New York: Richard H. Dodd, 1926), 6: 26.

61. Randolph's Account Book, at the New York Public Library, lists a debt of £10-19-1¼ to Smither in 1769 (quoted in PMA 1976, 111), a part of which must have been for engraving and printing the trade card. A faint pencil inscription in what appears to be an eighteenth-century hand at the bottom of Randolph's trade card reads "Engraved / about the year 1770."

62. Kimball 1927, 5-8.

63. For an illustration of the title page, see Hayward 1964, Fig. 136.

64. Prime 1929, 33.

65. Fowble 1987, Nos. 129, 358.

66. The certificate was drawn by J. L. Winn and engraved by "Morrison Sculpte," of Moorfields, London. An impression in the collections of the Metropolitan Museum was presented to Captain William Turner on 11 May 1773.

67. Thomas Earle and Charles T. Congdon, eds., *Annals of the General Society of Mechanics and Tradesmen of the City of New-York, from 1785 to 1880* (New York, 1882), 11-12.

68. The identical certificate of another member, Captain James Magee, was replicated on a Chinese export porcelain punch bowl and a cider jug now at the Boston Marine Society; see MFA 1975, No. 243.

69. For the Portland Marine Society, see Laura Fecych Sprague, ed., *Agreeable Situations, Society, Commerce, and Art in Southern Maine, 1780-1830* (Kennebunk, Maine: The Brick Store Museum, 1987), 48-49.

70. For Buell as engraver, see Wroth 1926.

71. See ibid., 64-66, for the attribution of the certificate to Buell and Rivington.

72. Ibid., 65.

73. Both copies are now at the Connecticut Historical Society, Hartford.

MAPS
pp. 59-65.

74. Quoted in Hitchings 1979, 13.

75. For an illustration, see Brigham 1969, Pl. 24.

76. For Hoeger, see Albert F. Jordan, "Some Early Moravian Builders In America," *Pennsylvania Folklife* (Autumn 1974): 2-17.

77. Ibid., 14, 16 (ills.).

78. The Bethlehem map, not mentioned by Jordan, was published in James H. Lambert, *Pennsylvania at the Jamestown Exposition, Hampton Roads, Va. 1907* (Philadelphia, 1908), 248. The authors are indebted to Christopher P. Monkhouse, Curator of Decorative Arts, Museum of Art, Rhode Island School of Design, for this reference.

79. For the full history of the Fisher map, see Wroth 1950.

80. Ibid., 96.

81. PMA 1976, No. 99.

82. Quoted in Snyder 1975, 62.

83. Quoted in Wroth 1926, 73-74.

CLOCK DIALS
pp. 66-69.

84. Prime 1929, 270.

85. Exceptional among engraved clock dials from Virginia are those of Thomas Walker of Fredericksburg, one of which is at the Museum of Fine Arts, Boston (see Hipkiss 1941, No. 126).

86. The clock is said to have had a history of ownership by the silversmith Thomas Shields, who had a shop on Front Street, Philadelphia, between about 1765 and 1771. See Alexandra W. Rollins, "Furniture in the collection of the Dietrich American Foundation," *The Magazine Antiques* 125 (May 1984): 1110.

87. Prime 1929, 237-38; Brooks Palmer, *The Book of American Clocks* (New York: Macmillan, 1928), 182.

88. For Johnson's images of Father Time, see Hayward 1964, Figs. 120, 170.

89. Quoted in Prime 1929, 20.

90. Quoted in Hoopes 1958, 41. The book contains a full account of Burnap as clockmaker.

91. See ibid., 118-20, for Daniel Burnap's instructions on how to make chime clocks.

92. For an illustration of the clock in its case, see Dean A. Fales, Jr., *The Furniture of Historic Deerfield* (New York: E. P. Dutton, 1976), No. 510.

93. A chime clock with a four-seasons dial by Harland, dated 1776, is at the Department of State (63.10).

SILVER
pp. 71-131.

1. Journeymen having served their apprenticeships were employed by silversmiths and were paid by the day. Outworkers (silversmiths who lacked the resources to establish their own shops) contracted their services to other silversmiths and were paid by the piece. Indentured servants were immigrant craftsmen who were bound in service to master smiths for the period of time required to work off the cost of their passage to the colonies, which their masters had paid.

2. I am grateful to Robert K. Weis, Curator of the Essex Institute, for providing research on the Annesley pot and its ownership.

3. For a thorough discussion of the three pots and an illustration of the Crowninshield example, see Fales 1963.

4. English silver would have been considerably more costly than domestic goods, a consequence of merchant commissions and shipping and insurance rates. I am grateful to the English silver scholar and author Robert Barker for his generous information on this subject.

5. An engraved coat of arms seldom cost more than twice the price of an ounce of silver, which, according to the ledgers of Boston silversmith Paul Revere, was seven shillings or so between 1761 and 1780. During that period, Revere generally charged from nine to thirteen shillings to engrave arms on vessels for which the labor could be three to eight times that much. For example, the expense of engraving arms on the Paine coffee pot (No. 49, detail, p. 97) was sixteen shillings, only about 3.5% of the pot's total price.

6. Philadelphia silversmith Joseph Richardson recorded payments to immigrant carver Hercules Courtenay in 1769; Fales 1974, 87.

7. Revere, for instance, used the same spout pattern for both the Ross and Paine teapots (Nos. 51; 49, detail, p. 85), and another one for both the Paine and Sargent coffee pots (Nos. 49, detail, p. 97; No. 60), although the last two examples date eight years apart.

8. R. Campbell, *The London Tradesman* (1747; reprint, Newton Abbot, Devon: David & Charles, 1969), 141-47.

9. See Clifford 1990, 24-28.

10. Campbell, *The London Tradesman*, 142.

11. Federhen 1988, 73.

12. In one example of the common practice of subcontracting engraving, Providence merchant Moses Brown, placing the order for his wedding silver with Boston silversmith Benjamin Burt in 1763, noted that he would order "marks [initials] & Arms" in due course, whereupon Burt replied: "You'l Please to send Directions for the Engraver soon as is Convenient." The engraver was Nathaniel Hurd, mentioned in Brown's subsequent letter giving engraving instructions and confirmed in turn by Burt: "I have Finish'd Your Plate. Mr Hurd has one piece to Engrave." See Emlen 1984, 41, 43.

13. By the rococo period, the sterling standard was the minimum required in England, an alloy of 92.5% silver and 7.5% copper. Tests of American silver have shown that most American silversmiths tried to abide by that standard despite the lack of regulation.

14. The array of London rococo plate presented to Sir William Pepperrell in appreciation for his victory at Louisburg in 1745 included two covered cups, a large salver, and a pair of smaller salvers, all now at the Portland Museum of Art. For illustrations of some of the plate, see Burton W. F. Trafton, Jr., "Louisburg and the Pepperrell silver," *The Magazine Antiques* 89 (March 1966): 364, 366-67. In Boston, the Faneuils owned a London rococo cruet stand from 1745 and the Apthorps ordered a similar stand two years later; see MFA 1975, No. 59. In Salem, a London rococo covered cup from 1747-48 was owned by John and Martha (Derby) Prince; see Fales 1983, No. 13.

15. Research figures provided by Robert Barker from the CUST 3 series of the Public Record Office, London. These figures must be carefully interpreted. The records were kept in weight in ounces, and the highest amounts exported to New England never exceeded 2,000 ounces, a large part of which probably consisted of small

work. A typical coffee pot, for example, weighed from 30 to 40 ounces. I am extremely grateful to Robert Barker for assisting me with the references to this subject that appear throughout the introduction to the silver chapter.

16. The ratio of silversmiths to Bostonians declined from 1 to 290 in the 1720s to 1 to 430 two decades later; see Ward 1984, 137.

17. Dow 1927, 41-72.

18. For full-length studies of this important silversmith, see Leehey 1988 and Buhler 1956.

19. Gottesman 1938, 51. The "Lion" referred to is an English hallmark.

20. With the exception of one tea caddy still privately owned, all are in the collections of the Metropolitan Museum. The teakettle on stand (40.160a-c) and the coffee pot (42.88) date from 1762-63 and are marked by Benjamin Brewood II. The similarly dated candlesticks (41.130.1a, b) are marked by Samuel Siervent. The tea caddy (59.30a, b), also dating from 1762-63, is marked by Emick Romer and survives with its original chest (40.104).

21. Research figures provided by Robert Barker from the CUST 3 series of the Public Record Office, London.

22. Gottesman 1938, 57. Pinto may have been advertising imported silver, but it would have been odd for him not to indicate so.

23. I am grateful to Ian Quimby, Director, Publications Division, Winterthur Museum, for allowing me access to his research on Fueter, which will be published in a forthcoming catalogue to be titled *American Silver at Winterthur*.

24. Gottesman 1938, 41.

25. A recently auctioned pitcher attributed to Fueter appears to be the most fully developed example of the form in American rococo silver. For an illustration, see *Important Americana*, Sotheby's, sale no. 6132, 30 January–2 February 1991, lot 140.

26. Gottesman 1938, 55. Parisien published similarly worded notices in 1769 and 1774; ibid., 55-56.

27. Ibid., 42-43.

28. Ibid., 57.

29. Ibid., 67-68.

30. In 1760, *The New-York Mercury* advertised for Scots-born John M'Intosh, who "Deserted from His Majesty's 17th Regiment...by Trade a Silver Smith"; ibid., 52.

31. Rosenbaum 1954, 47-48.

32. Gottesman 1938, 53. The servant's name, given as "Meares," was probably misspelled in the advertisement. The Mearses were a prominent New York Jewish family with English and American branches. Myers's servant may have been related to Myers's second wife, Joyce Mears, whose father was English born. I am grateful to Deborah Dependahl Waters, Curator of Decorative Arts, Museum of the City of New York, for graciously sharing her research on the Mears family.

33. Paul Revere's ledgers; Joseph Richardson's letter book.

34. For the Franks family silver, see Dennis 1968.

35. Research figures provided by Robert Barker from the CUST 3 series of the Public Record Office, London.

36. John Anthony Beau, the chaser recorded earlier in New York, announced his services in Philadelphia in 1772, describing himself as ''lately arrived in this city from Geneva,'' and Thomas Beck, of unknown extraction, advertised chasing services in 1774; Prime 1929, 47.

37. For a complete biography of Richardson and an assessment of his silver, see Fales 1974, 33-149.

38. Ibid.; see 210 for reference to Richardson's support of the non-importation agreements.

39. I am grateful to Robert Barker for his assistance in refuting this theory.

40. For a biography of Syng, see PMA 1976, 30.

41. See ibid. Hubert's London apprenticeship with the engraver Paul Garon was recorded in 1735. I am grateful to Robert Barker for sharing this information, gained from the Public Record Office, London, Inland Revenue Department, Apprenticeship Books.

42. Prime 1929, 73.

43. Whereas silver in the amount of 60,723 ounces was exported to the Carolinas, the total to the other three regions was 59,170 ounces. Figures provided by Robert Barker from the CUST 3 series of the Public Record Office, London.

44. Prime 1929, 64, 97-98.

45. Ibid., 63-65, 68, 85, 88.

TEA AND COFFEE FORMS
pp. 79-88.

46. Schroder 1988b, 136; Davis 1976, No. 81; Clayton 1971, 96.

47. Quoted in Christopher Hartop, ''The 'Infusion of that Fragrant Leaf': Tea Drinking in England,'' *Auction News from Christie's* 12 (September 1990): 3.

48. Ibid.

49. For a discussion of tea rituals and equipment in America, see Roth 1961.

50. Federhen 1988, 67.

51. Schroder 1988b, 136.

52. Roth 1961, 68. The period quotes that follow are from this extremely valuable treatise, as is the information on social customs.

53. The Lloyd-Cadwalader set consists of a tea urn, a teapot, a chocolate pot (all privately owned), and a coffee pot (Philadelphia Museum of Art, 1988-35-1). A teakettle on stand, a basket, and a waste bowl from the Franks service are at the Metropolitan Museum and are described in Dennis 1968.

54. Fales 1974, 78; see also 292, n. 6.

55. Ibid., 225, 230.

56. Ibid., 225.

57. The order, dated 15 December 1764, also included pairs of canns, casters, and salts.

58. Although not fully rococo, the earliest surviving American tea sets would seem to be two marked by John Coburn of a purported four thought to have been wedding silver for the daughters of Thomas Welles. The sets, consisting of a teapot (see No. 50), a cream pot, and a sugar caster, date about 1753. See Flynt and Fales 1968, No. 118 (ill.); Wadsworth Atheneum 1985, 288-89.

59. I am grateful to Deborah Dependahl Waters, Curator of Decorative Arts, Museum of the City of New York, for this theory and interpretation.

60. For more information on Riemer, see Miller 1937, 9.

61. For a biography of Paine, see Sabine 1864, s.v. ''Paine, William.''

62. The surviving pieces are in the collections of the Worcester Art Museum. For a complete description and history of the service, see Buhler 1979, 42-47.

63. Fales 1974, 244.

64. Federhen 1988, 67-68.

65. Ibid., 68.

66. An earlier, two-handled covered cup by the same maker is engraved on the seldom illustrated reverse side with a cartouche that displays nascent rococo tendencies. I am grateful to Michael Brown for calling my attention to this feature on what is known as the Comet-Bomb cup, discussed in Warren, Howe, and Brown 1987, No. 57.

67. For a detailed discussion of the teapot, see Buhler 1965, 57-60.

68. Turner did a lot of work for Boston silversmiths. I am grateful to Martha Gandy Fales for this information and for suggesting Turner as the possible engraver of the Hurd pot.

69. Casters are cylindrical vessels with pierced lids for ''casting'' (sprinkling) spices and condiments, such as sugar, mustard, or pepper. For a complete discussion of the Welles set and its provenance, see Flynt and Fales 1968, No. 118. For a discussion of a related set and information on Welles, see Wadsworth Atheneum 1985, 288-89.

70. Flynt and Fales 1968, 185-86.

71. The motto over the engraved crest appears to have been added later; Buhler 1972, 2: 396. The provenance of the pot, as recorded by the last owner/descendant in 1935, traces it to a John Ross of Philadelphia, who married Clementina Plumsted; letter from Phoebe Hoffman Bickerton to Pauline Revere Thayer, files of the Museum of Fine Arts, Boston. A study of family genealogies suggests that Bickerton confused Ross's wife, Clementina Cruikshank, whom he married in 1768, with his granddaughter Clementina Ross Plumsted (1798-1884), but was correct in ascribing original ownership to Ross.

72. Fales 1974, Fig. 55.

73. See Goldsborough 1984, 164.

74. See ibid., 191, 231.

SUGAR DISHES AND CREAM POTS
pp. 89–94.

75. Between 1761 and 1785, Revere recorded five single sugar dishes, one of which is known to have a cream pot en suite (No. 58), and twenty-five single cream pots.

76. Fales 1974, 221–60.

77. For American examples, see Hood 1971, Figs. 6, 7, 11, and 47; for English examples, see Wenham 1931, frontispiece, Pls. VIIa-b, VIII, and IX.

78. See Joan D. Dolmetsch, *Rebellion and Reconciliation: Satirical Prints on the Revolution at Williamsburg* (Williamsburg: The Colonial Williamsburg Foundation, 1976), 9, and illustrations throughout; see also Honour 1975, 4; Nos. 111–123, 147.

79. Schroder 1988b, 250 (ill.).

80. See Alice Baldwin Beer, *Trade Goods: A Study of Indian Chintz* (Washington, D.C.: Smithsonian Institution Press, 1970), 116–19. I am grateful to Amelia Peck, Assistant Curator, Department of American Decorative Arts, The Metropolitan Museum of Art, for her assistance with this idea.

81. For a complete biography of Hulbeart, see PMA 1976, 78–79.

82. Fales 1974, 203–4.

83. Two other New York sets are similar to the Riemer examples. One, marked by William Gilbert, is in the collections of the Currier Gallery of Art (1974.37a, b); the other, marked by Myer Myers, was recently sold at auction (*Important Americana*, Sotheby's, sale no. 6132, 30 January–2 February 1991, lot 115).

84. Schroder 1988a, 197. For examples, see 198–99, 219; see also Grimwade 1974, No. 6.

85. Goldsborough 1984, No. 161. For other examples of these English sets, see Wenham 1931, Pl. LXXVIII; Clayton 1985, 157, No. 13. For information on Charles Carroll, Esq. (always referred to as "Barrister"), see Michael F. Trostel, *Mount Clare: Being an Account of the Seat built by Charles Carroll, Barrister, upon his Lands at Patapsco* (Baltimore: National Society of Colonial Dames of America in the State of Maryland, 1981).

86. For illustrations and a discussion of the portraits, see John Devereux Kernan, Jr., and Remsen Brinckerhoff, "Family Treasure: Some Brinckerhoff Silver and Portraits," *The Magazine Antiques* 54 (October 1948): 248.

87. For an illustration of the Peaston pot, see ibid., 249. Four Albany sugar bowls with bird finials are known. In addition to No. 57, marked by Lansing, another, unchased, is by the same maker (Rice 1964, 27); two chased examples have marks assigned to Abraham Schuyler, one at the Museum of the City of New York (42.469.21a, b), the other at the Albany Institute (1983.22a, b). A fifth, at the Metropolitan Museum, formerly assigned to Jacob Boelen II (Safford 1983, 52; Fig. 69), has recently been reassigned by Safford to John Bayly of Philadelphia.

88. I am grateful to Deborah Dependahl Waters, Curator of Decorative Arts, Museum of the City of New York, for this information. For an illustration, see Blackburn 1976, 101.

89. Revere ledgers, 11 March 1762.

90. See Buhler 1972, 2: Nos. 339, 341.

91. A "Chased Sugar Dish" for Samuel Minott on 5 October 1762; two "Chased Cream Pots" for John Coburn in November 1762.

92. I know of only four other rococo cream pots with claw-and-ball feet, all unchased; one, marked by Bancroft Woodcock, in the Garvan Collection of the Yale University Art Gallery (Buhler and Hood 1970, 2: 242); one, marked by George Christopher Dowig, in the collections of Girard College, Philadelphia; one, marked by Samuel Tingley, unlocated (the last two are recorded in the Decorative Arts Photographic Collection at Winterthur); and one, marked by Thomas Sparrow, in a private collection.

93. See Buhler 1972, 2: No. 492.

94. As quoted in Flynt and Fales 1968, 178.

COFFEE POTS
pp. 95–104.

95. Roth 1961, 68.

96. As quoted in ibid., 67.

97. Federhen 1988, 67–68.

98. As quoted in Roth 1961, 66.

99. Ibid., 64.

100. As quoted in ibid., 72.

101. Revere's ledger entry of 2 September 1773.

102. The earliest documented example of American neoclassical silver is a tea urn marked by Richard Humphreys. For illustrations and further discussion, see PMA 1976, No. 102; Warren, Howe, and Brown 1987, 60–61.

103. A drum-shaped teapot from 1782, marked by Revere, is considered one of his shop's earliest essays in neoclassical hollow-ware. See Skerry 1988, 52.

104. The cartouche is the only rococo element on the neoclassical urn; see PMA 1976, No. 102.

105. For examples made in New York in the shop of Myer Myers, see Rosenbaum 1954, Pls. 12, 14.

106. Fales 1974, 219–60.

107. Wainwright 1964, 52.

108. Warren 1976, unpaged [p. 2].

109. Prime 1929, 73.

110. For a complete biography of Humphreys, see PMA 1976, 128–29.

111. The exception is the Crowninshield pot (see p. 71), illustrated in Flynt and Fales 1968, Fig. 108.

112. Fales 1974, 231, 233.

113. See Clayton 1985, 149, Fig. 7; 150, Fig. 1.

114. The Growden family owned a London coffee pot of 1753–54, of similar shape to the one Syng supplied the Galloways but with-

out rococo ornament; see Fales 1974, Fig. 34. For biographies of the Growden and the Galloway families, see PMA 1976, 55; see also Wolfe 1966, 44.

115. See Clayton 1985, 149, Fig. 7, for a British example similar to the Syng pot; see ibid., Fig. 11, for one similar to the Hall pot; see ibid., 150, Fig. 1, for one similar in profile to the Inch pot.

116. For a biography of Hall, see Gerstell 1972, 37–44.

117. For the tureen, marked by Peter Getz and now at the Wadsworth Atheneum, see Hammerslough 1960, 14–15.

118. The three other pots, which are without chased ornament, are at the Museum of Early Southern Decorative Arts (2507), the Charleston Museum (1971.34.1), and the Minneapolis Institute of Arts (75.6).

119. As quoted in an entry on the Petrie coffee pot to be included in John Bivins, Jr., and Forsyth Alexander, *The Regional Arts of the Early South: A Sampling from the Collection of the Museum of Early Southern Decorative Arts* (Winston-Salem, No. Car.: Museum of Early Southern Decorative Arts, forthcoming). I am grateful to Mr. Bivins for sharing with me his information on the pot and on the Petrie inventory.

120. Prime 1929, 64, 97–98.

121. Ibid., 85.

122. E. Milby Burton, *South Carolina Silversmiths, 1690–1860* (Charleston, So. Car.: Charleston Museum, 1942), 146–49.

123. Prime 1929, 80.

124. Goldsborough 1984, 231. The pot, owned by Judith and Samuel Verplanck and marked by Benjamin Brewood II, of London, is in the collections of the Metropolitan Museum (42.88).

125. For English examples, see Schroder 1988a, Nos. 78, 79.

126. For an illustration, see Fales 1974, Fig. 54.

127. I am grateful to David Cassedy, Associate Curator, Historical Society of Pennsylvania, for providing me with information on Penington.

DRINKING AND SERVING FORMS
pp. 105–14.

128. Clayton 1971, s.v. "Tankard."

129. Exceptions are two tankards with flat chasing by Richard Van Dyck, one in the Garvan Collection at Yale University Art Gallery (Buhler and Hood 1970, 2: No. 647); the other in the Watson Collection at Historic Deerfield (Flynt and Fales 1968, 63–64; ill., 64).

130. See Skerry 1984, Fig. 14.

131. I am grateful to Janine Skerry, Assistant Curator, Historic Deerfield, for providing me with this information.

132. Charles F. Montgomery, *A History of American Pewter*, rev. ed. (New York: E. P. Dutton, 1978), 46; see also Ledlie Irwin Laughlin, *Pewter in America: Its Makers and Their Marks*, 3 vols., reprint (Barre, Mass.: Barre Publishers, 1969–71), 3: 8–9; Pl. LXIX, Figs. 581–84.

133. Fales 1974, 59; Prime 1929, 19 (where Hubert's name is spelled "Herbert").

134. Donald L. Fennimore, "A John Bayly Tankard & Cann," *Silver* 19 (May–June 1986): 18–19.

135. An exception, a double-bellied bowl marked by Myer Myers, is in the collections of the Detroit Institute of Arts; see Hood 1971, Fig. 159.

136. I am grateful to Karie Diethorn, Associate Curator, Independence National Historical Park, for supplying me with information on the families and on the canns, one of which is in the collections of her institution (INDE 9965); the other, currently on loan to the Philadelphia Museum of Art.

137. Buhler and Hood 1970, 2: No. 648, made this discovery and document the Irish example referred to as one in Charles James Jackson, *An Illustrated History of English Plate* (London, 1911), 288, Fig. 310.

138. Davis 1976, No. 36.

139. James Beekman's Account Book, 19 February 1768.

140. Gottesman 1938, 37.

141. For illustrations, see Buhler and Hood 1970, 2: No. 647; Flynt and Fales 1968, Fig. 39.

142. Mrs. Russel Hastings, "Peter Van Dyck of New York, Goldsmith, 1684–1750, Part II," *The Magazine Antiques* 31 (June 1937): 302–5, reprinted in Kolter 1979, 115–18; see 117.

143. Mrs. Russel Hastings, "Two Chafing Dishes by Peter Van Dyck," *The Magazine Antiques* 30 (October 1936): 152–55, reprinted in Kolter 1979, 111–14; see 112.

144. For a complete description of the Van Wyck salver, see Warren, Howe, and Brown 1987, No. 724.

145. See Fales 1963, 83.

146. Gottesman 1938, 50.

147. For more information on the bowl and a transcription of the account, see Buhler and Hood 1970, 2: No. 724.

148. The two salvers are the Syng salver discussed and one marked by Thomas Shields. For the latter, see PMAB 1956, No. 469.

RARE FORMS
pp. 115–31.

149. For a discussion and depictions of the form, see Berenice Ball, "Whistles with coral and bells," *The Magazine Antiques* 80 (December 1961): 552–55; for a whistle and bells depicted in an American painting, see Warren, Howe, and Brown 1987, No. 73.

150. See Ball, "Whistles," 554; see also Bohan 1963, 11.

151. See Fales 1974, 219–60; in particular, see 221, 223, 226–27, and 244.

152. For Revere, see his ledger entry of 18 July 1762 (in 1764 and 1773, he recorded mending whistles); for Syng, see Wainwright 1964, 53.

153. Bohan 1963, Nos. 22–25.

154. For example, a gold whistle from the shop of Daniel Christian Fueter is inscribed "The gift of Mrs Mary Livingston to her grand daughter Mary Duane"; ibid., No. 24; see also Buhler and Hood 1970, 2: No. 716.

155. As quoted in J.M.P., "Mary Duane's Coral and Bells," *Bulletin of the Associates in Fine Arts at Yale University* 12 (February 1943): 3.

156. Gottesman 1938, 59–60.

157. Fales 1974, 237.

158. Buhler and Hood 1970, No. 657.

159. Bohan 1963, 8.

160. Ibid., where see also No. 15.

161. See Fales 1974, 132–33; 223.

162. The Fueter whistle and bells is in the Garvan Collection, Yale University Art Gallery (1942.91) and is illustrated in Buhler and Hood 1970, 2: No. 716. Other examples include a cream pot at the Museum of Fine Arts, Boston, marked by Massachusetts silversmith Daniel Parker (54.658); two pairs of sauceboats from Paul Revere's shop, one pair at the Museum of Fine Arts, Boston (35.1771–1772), the other pair, separated, one sauceboat at the Addison Gallery (1946.88), the other in a private collection; and a cream pot marked by Samuel Tingley, recorded in the Decorative Arts Photographic Collection, Winterthur. Tankards having mask handle terminals, though made during the rococo period, represent a continuation of baroque practice and are excluded from this list.

163. See Dennis 1968.

164. For the Hancock basket, see MFA 1975, 99; for the Byrd family basket, see Davis 1976, 117. I am grateful to William Voss Elder III, Consultant Curator, Decorative Arts, Baltimore Museum of Art, and to Gregory Weidman, Curator, Maryland Historical Society, for bringing to my attention the Lloyd family basket, ordered by Edward Lloyd III about 1753 and still in the family's possession.

165. The dish ring is at Yale University Art Gallery (1936.136); the coffee pot is at the Museum of the City of New York (80.137); the cann is at the Wadsworth Atheneum (1983.155); and the coasters are in a private collection.

166. For another example of that sort of commission, see Emlen 1984.

167. In addition to the Fueter basket (No. 81), the remaining two-thirds of American pierced rococo silver consists of two pairs of Myers coasters, one made for the Schuyler family and now at The New-York Historical Society (1915.18a, b), the other made for the Pierpont family and now on loan to the Museum of the City of New York; a pair of pierced salts marked by John Heath, made for the Van Alstyne family and now at the Wadsworth Atheneum (1983.191–192); a Heath mustard pot at Historic Deerfield (64–231); all the foregoing made in New York. The balance, made in Philadelphia, consists of a pair of salts marked by Thomas Shields now in a private collection (illustrated in *Royal Province New Jersey: 1738–1776* [Trenton: New Jersey State Museum, 1973], 109) and a pair of coasters by William Ball, also privately owned.

168. Sabine 1864, s.v. "Cornell, Samuel."

169. Rosenbaum 1954, 111.

170. The form consisted of a spirit lamp supported by two centrally hinged telescoping arms that, when fully open, served as a cross-shaped stand.

171. Rosenbaum 1954, 112.

172. Davis 1976, 190.

173. See Singleton 1902, 137; 138 (ill.).

174. A cruet stand by Myer Myers is at the Metropolitan Museum (1987.143); two by John David are at Winterthur (59.3362) and at the Museum of Fine Arts, Houston (B.82.1), respectively; one by William Hollingshead is at the Philadelphia Museum of Art (56-84-24, 25, 26); one by Jeremiah Elfreth (D56.59; stolen in 1983, documented in the Decorative Arts Photograph Collection, Winterthur) and one by Bancroft Woodcock (60.62) are in the collections of the Delaware State Museum; one by William Hollingshead, in a private collection, is documented in the Decorative Arts Photographic Collection, Winterthur.

175. Davis 1976, 154; MFA 1975, No. 59; Fales 1983, No. 15 (ill.); Boles 1976, No. 28.

176. Davis 1976, 154.

177. For mention of the cruet frame, see Fales 1974, 229.

178. Entry of 24 May 1781.

179. The second, marked by Myer Myers and now in the collections of the Yale University Art Gallery, survives with its snuffers. See Buhler and Hood 1970, 2: No. 656.

180. Revere's ledger entry of 25 December 1762 (the patron was Zachariah Johonot); for the Cadwalader inventory, see Wainwright 1964, 53.

181. For an illustration, see PMAB 1956, Fig. 514.

182. See *Important American Furniture and Related Decorative Arts*, Sotheby's, sale no. 4478Y, 19–22 November 1980, lot 179.

183. For an illustration, see Hood 1971, 143, Fig. 147.

184. In addition to the two discussed, another surviving rococo example is a New York teakettle on stand assigned to Nicholas Roosevelt, now unlocated but documented in the Decorative Arts Photographic Collection, Winterthur. An earlier, Queen Anne-style kettle on stand marked by Jacob Hurd survives from Boston and is now at the Museum of Fine Arts, Boston (1971.347a, b).

185. James Beekman's Account Book, entries of 4 April 1766 and 6 May 1773.

186. For an English example of the form, see Murdoch 1986, 68; Fig. 4.

187. The pot is at The New-York Historical Society (1964.9).

188. The cock handles of the spigots are replacements.

189. Fales 1974, 34.

190. For an extensive discussion of the Franks family silver, see Dennis 1968. Another English kettle on stand (1750–51), by George Wickes of London, was owned in Philadelphia by the Stocker family; see Fales 1974, 293, n. 14. Another (1749–50), marked by

William Grundy, London, of rococo form but without chased ornament, is believed to have belonged originally to the Carter family of Virginia; see Davis 1976, 94. A third (1762–63), marked by Benjamin Brewood II and having chased decoration, belonged to Judith and Samuel Verplanck of New York, who were married in 1761; it is now at the Metropolitan Museum (40.160a–c).

FURNITURE
pp. 133–217.

BOSTON

pp. 134–52.

1. For a thorough discussion on the subject of tariffs, see pp. 9–10 of this publication.

2. Charles M. Andrews, ed., *Some Cursory Remarks Made by James Birket in His Voyage to North America 1750–1751* (New Haven, 1916), 24.

3. Jobe and Kaye 1984, 7.

4. Mabel M. Swan, in "Newburyport Furnituremakers," *The Magazine Antiques* 47 (April 1945), 225, lists none before 1800; Henry Wyckoff Belknap, *Artists and Craftsmen of Essex County, Massachusetts* (Salem: Essex Institute, 1927), 19, 20, lists only Skillin and, later, McIntire.

5. Jobe and Kaye 1984, 15.

6. Ibid., 11.

7. Samuel Grant, Petty Ledgers, book one, 26, 42; book two, 37; Boston Public Library. I am indebted to Brock Jobe for providing me with these references. (For the only known example of a New England bedstead having pierced cornices, see Heckscher 1985a, No. 90.)

8. Dow 1927, 113, 115.

9. Randall 1964, 136.

10. For Boston carvers, see Swan 1948; Yehia 1974; Beckerdite 1987a.

11. Swan 1948, 199, 281.

12. Ward 1988, No. 82.

13. See Kimball 1940, 8, 11–12.

14. *Diary and Autobiography of John Adams*, 1: 294, quoted in Lovell 1974, 77.

15. Surviving from the period is the basically uncarved middle-class furniture commissioned by Jonathan Sayward about 1760–70, half of it made in Boston, half made locally, which remains in the Sayward House, York, Maine. For examples, see Jobe and Kaye 1984, Nos. 4, 62.

16. For a full discussion of Frothingham, see Randall 1974.

17. See ibid., Fig. 1, for the only exception, a chest-on-chest having pierced and carved finials and a superb shell drawer.

18. For the Bright desk and bookcase, see Randall 1965, No. 64.

19. Heckscher 1985b, 283.

20. With the possible exception of a splat design (Plate XII, 1st edition, 1754), copied once for a side chair. For an illustration of the chair, see Jobe and Kaye 1984, Fig. I-20.

21. John Crunden, *The Joyner and Cabinet-maker's Darling, or Pocket Director* (1760 and 1765); *The Carpenter's Companion... Designs for all Sorts of Chinese Railings and Gates* (1765); and P. Baretti's *New Book of Ornaments for the Year* 1766. Those books and Manwaring's *Cabinet and Chair-Maker's Friend* were all published in London. For Cox and Berry's advertisements, see Dow 1927, 222–23.

22. Dawes's copy is now at the Boston Athenaeum.

23. Eleven are listed at Beckerdite 1987a, 161–62, n. 29. I have determined the others by wood analysis.

24. A number of Blackburn's portraits have rococo frames. Those I have examined are of red pine and so are probably of English manufacture.

25. The standard work on Copley is Prown 1966.

26. Hitchings 1973, 116. (On 8 September 1764, Johnston billed for an identical frame for Copley's recently completed portrait of Savage.)

27. Copley's portrait of John Spooner (1763; Reynolda House) has what looks to be its original carved rococo frame; see Beckerdite 1987, Figs. 32–35, but there dated 1769.

28. Quoted in Ward and Ward 1976, 18.

29. For the Whiting advertisement, see *Boston News-Letter*, 24 February 1757 and 12 November 1767, quoted in Dow 1927, 23, 129.

30. From a list of omissions in "The late Treasurer Hancock's Acct.," about 1780, Harvard University Archives:

Occasional Expenses, viz.	
Boylston's Frame	11. 8.0
J. Copley Do picture	56.18.0
J. Welch carvg. Do.	8. 8.0
	76.14.0

I am grateful to Louise Todd Ambler, Curator, Harvard University Portrait Collection, for this and other references at Harvard.

31. Bunting 1985, 30, n. 31.

32. Letterbook of President Edward Holyoke, 1766–67, Harvard University Archives.

33. Copley's portraits of Rebecca Boylston (1767; Museum of Fine Arts, Boston) and John Winthrop (ca. 1773; Harvard University) have matching frames.

34. Copley's portrait of Samuel Winthrop (ca. 1773; Harvard University) has a matching frame.

35. The bill (quoted in Beckerdite 1987a, 162, n. 30), marked paid on 1 July 1771, is in the files of the Museum of Fine Arts, Boston, where the portraits (41.84; 41.85) now hang.

36. Beckerdite 1987a, 151. The Smith portraits are at Yale University Art Gallery (1941.73; 1941.74).

37. According to a tradition in the Williams family (Bolton 1927, 181), the needlework was made by a daughter of Henry Howell Williams of Noodles Island (East Boston). The coat of arms of the Greene family of Boston, dated 1745, has a carved-and-gilded frame that looks like New York work. For an illustration, see Hipkiss 1941, No. 208.

38. Wadsworth Atheneum 1985, Nos. 267, 271, 272.

39. Woodcock and Robinson 1988, 161-62.

40. The chest's brasses are replacements; the carved streamers depending from the pediment rosettes are now truncated.

41. Vincent 1974, 150; Fig. 102.

42. Downs 1952b.

43. Ibid., 324; Kimball 1940, 56.

44. For a chest of almost identical design, see Hipkiss 1941, No. 34 (incorrectly ascribed to Philadelphia).

45. Cooper 1980, 31; see Fig. 36 for illustration of the inscription.

46. See Randall 1965, No. 42.

47. As quoted in Sack 1981-86: 6, 1466-67.

48. The other set is on a similarly shaped chest at the Department of State (69.103) that descended in the family of Ebenezer Storer, Jr. (1730-1807).

49. For the most complete discussion of this group, see Hayward Yehia 1974.

50. See *The American Heritage Society Auction of Americana*, Sotheby's, sale no. 4048, 17 November 1977, lot 1187.

51. During a recent re-covering of the settee, fragments of a brilliant yellow worsted were found, in accordance with which the new cover of yellow stamped moreen was chosen. Brass nails follow the placement of the originals. See Kathryn Gill, "Minimally Intrusive Upholstery Treatments—A Case History Concerning an Eighteenth-Century American Settee," in Ann French, ed., *Conservation of Furnishing Textiles* (Glasgow: The Burrell Collection, 1990), 7-13.

52. Rodriguez Roque 1984, No. 58.

53. See MFA 1975, No. 53. For an analysis of the two chairs, see Beckerdite 1987a, 123-33.

54. Rhoads 1972, 41.

55. Oedel 1974, 9.

NEW YORK
pp. 153-65.

56. Count based on Price 1977, 146-56, the most complete listing of New York craftsmen of the period.

57. Unless otherwise noted, all New York newspaper advertisements quoted in this section are to be found in Gottesman 1938 and Gottesman 1954.

58. Delaplaine Papers, Manuscript Library, New-York Historical Society.

59. Quoted in Johnson 1964, 21, n. 1.

60. As quoted in Price 1977, 9.

61. Heckscher 1985a, No. 81.

62. Price 1977, 157. One of Hardcastle's apprentices in New York ran away in June 1755 (Gottesman 1938, 127). Hardcastle's death is recorded in the Register of Saint Philip's Church, Charleston, 20 October 1756 (information kindly supplied by Bradford L. Rauschenberg).

63. *New-York Mercury*, 21 July 1755.

64. Ibid., 31 May 1762.

65. *New-York Gazette and the Weekly Mercury*, 30 September 1771.

66. *Rivington's New-York Gazetteer*, 10 March 1774.

67. *New-York Packet*, 24 January 1785.

68. Gottesman 1938, 110-11; Gottesman 1954, 111-12.

69. For the book's publishing history, see Introduction, reprint, *Houshold Furniture*.

70. *New-York Mercury*, 6 October 1760, quoted in Lockwood 1913, 1: 19.

71. *A Catalogue of Books, sold by Rivington and Brown, Booksellers and Stationers from London* (New York and Philadelphia, 1762), 67; Garett Noel, *A Catalogue of Books* (New York, 1762), 27.

72. *A Catalogue of books sold by Noel & Hazard, publishers* (New York, 1771), 81.

73. Heckscher 1979: 17-18; Pl. 30.

74. *Rivington's New-York Gazetteer*, 2 September 1774. For an illustration, see Rita Susswein, "Pre-Revolutionary Furniture Makers of New York City," *The Magazine Antiques* 25 (January 1934): 10.

75. Joy 1960, 72.

76. "Notes: New York Furniture," *Bulletin of the Metropolitan Museum of Art* (June 1934): 110.

77. Gilbert 1978, 1: 165.

78. In James Beekman's Account Book, Personal Affairs, 1761-1796, Beekman Family Papers, New-York Historical Society.

79. For a thorough account of James Beekman, see White 1956, 335-530.

80. Heckscher 1990.

81. *New-York Mercury*, 21 July 1755.

82. See "Accounts of Repairs of my Dwelling House" and "Household Furniture Accounts," both in Beekman's Account Book.

83. See "Portraits of the Philipse Family in the Museum," *Bulletin of the Museum of the City of New York* 1 (March 1938): 45.

84. Beekman's Account Book.

85. Prime 1929, 225.

86. *New-York Gazette or the Weekly Post-Boy*, 24 October 1765.

87. See "The Gifts and Bequests of Gherardi Davis," *Bulletin of the Museum of the City of New York* 5 (January 1942): 27-28.

88. Singleton 1902, 378. For a thorough discussion of the subject, see p. 79 of this publication.

89. *New-York Gazette Revived in the Weekly Post-Boy*, 26 August 1751.

90. The table was presumably part of the furnishings of Dirck Van Vechten's house, situated on the Raritan, near Finderne, New Jersey, which was used during the Revolution for the headquarters of General Nathaniel Greene. See James Brown Van Vechten, comp., *The Van Vechten Genealogy* (Detroit: Privately printed, 1954), 360-61.

91. Playing cards were imported into New York in vast quantities. See Singleton 1902, 265.

92. See "Furniture of Joseph Haynes," *New-York Mercury*, 10 March 1766.

93. For reference to Cox, see *Rivington's New-York Gazetteer*, 7 October 1773; to Prince, see *New-York Gazette and the Weekly Mercury*, 6 February 1775; to Willett, then a partner in the firm of Willett & Pearsee, see *Rivington's New-York Gazetteer*, 22 April 1773.

94. Heckscher 1973.

95. I am indebted to Luke Beckerdite for this observation.

WILLIAMSBURG AND CHARLESTON
pp. 166-81.

96. For the carved chairs, see John Bivins, Jr., *The Furniture of Coastal North Carolina, 1700-1820* (Winston-Salem, No. Car.: Museum of Early Southern Decorative Arts, 1988), 396-97.

97. After further study, Annapolis and Baltimore in Maryland and Norfolk in Virginia may also deserve inclusion.

98. British government records list £2,966 worth of exports in furnishings, including upholstery, to Maryland and Virginia in 1772, a value greater even than to New York. Cited in Joy 1960, 72.

99. For an admirable reconstruction of the history of Williamsburg as a furnituremaking center, see Gusler 1979.

100. Ibid., 63.

101. Ibid., 2-3.

102. See ibid., 25-57, for a discussion of the Scott shop.

103. See ibid., 61-113, for an extensive account of the Hay shop.

104. Ibid., 59.

105. Ibid., 61.

106. Ibid., 13.

107. Ibid., 63, quoting *Virginia Gazette*, 6 January 1767.

108. Ibid., 66.

109. Ibid., 182.

110. A pair of carved candlestands at Mount Vernon, having a tradition of Washington ownership (and copied exactly from Plate 72 of *Houshold Furniture*), has also been attributed to the Hay shop; ibid., 125-26.

111. From Bull's "Representation of the Colony," 1770, quoted in Bivins 1986, 3.

112. Burton 1955, 4, 5.

113. Quoted in ibid., 5.

114. "Journal of Josiah Quincy, Junior, 1773," as quoted in Bivins 1986, 2.

115. Burton 1955, 6, refers to upward of 250 cabinetmakers alone between 1700 and 1825. Bradford Rauschenberg, senior research fellow at the Museum of Early Southern Decorative Arts, who is preparing a comprehensive study of the arts and crafts in Charleston, has compiled biographies of more than five hundred furniture craftsmen who worked in the city prior to 1825.

116. Prime 1929, 158-226. Unless otherwise noted, Prime 1929 is the source of all newspaper advertisements quoted in this section.

117. Thomas Lining, cabinetmaker from London, in *South Carolina Gazette*, 4 July 1754, quoted in Burton 1955, 101.

118. See ibid., 84-89, for a summary treatment of Elfe.

119. Ibid., 84, 85.

120. Rauschenberg 1980.

121. For all references to Elfe's ledgers, see Mabel L. Webber, ed., "The Thomas Elfe Account Book, 1768-1775," *The South Carolina Historical and Genealogical Magazine* 35-42 (January 1934-January 1941), where the account book is reproduced in its entirety.

122. Burton 1955, 91.

123. Bivins 1986, 53.

124. Quoted in ibid., 56.

125. Ibid., 57.

126. Prime 1929, 176.

127. For *The Director* in Charleston, see Heckscher 1985b, 284.

128. For Waite, who also owned *A New Book of Ornaments...for the Year 1762*, P. Baretti's booklet of designs for rococo carvers, see Bivins 1986, 36-40.

129. For what may be an Elfe mahogany frame, see Theus's *Mrs. William Lee* (ca. 1770; Museum of Early Southern Decorative Arts). For an illustration, see Adair 1983, 17.

130. Prime 1929, 10.

131. For Wollaston in Charleston, see Carolyn J. Weekley, "John Wollaston, Portrait Painter: His Career in Virginia 1754-1758," master's thesis, University of Delaware, 1976, 20-21.

132. For a discussion of the monument, see Bivins 1986, 106-11.

133. Rauschenberg 1980, 12.

134. Bivins 1986, 106, 121-22. The second carver was John Lord.

135. For this attribution, see Gusler 1989, 1246-49.

136. Davis 1976, No. 136.

137. Gusler 1979, Figs. 18-22.

138. There may originally have been turned colonettes behind the pierced work of the legs; see Gusler 1989, 1240.

139. Pls. XXVI–XXVIII, CXXIII, CXXXII–CXXXVII; for quoted text, see Pl. LIX.

140. The gallery is a replacement modeled on that of the Lewis-Byrd table (No. 119).

141. Gusler 1979, 66.

142. Gusler 1989, 1241–42.

143. The pediment has been restored based on the engraving.

144. Heckscher 1985a, No. 79.

145. For a discussion of the chair, see Gusler 1979, 75–79.

146. Rauschenberg 1976, 20.

147. See Gusler 1979, Figs. 47, 59.

PHILADELPHIA
pp. 182–217.

148. Gary B. Nash and Billy G. Smith, "The Population of Eighteenth-Century Philadelphia," *Pennsylvania Magazine of History and Biography* 99 (July 1975): 367.

149. Leibundguth 1964, 132–36.

150. See Prime 1929, 158–226.

151. As transcribed in Hornor 1935, 317–21.

152. Heckscher 1989, 94–96.

153. Hayward 1971, 21.

154. Joy 1960, 72.

155. For *The Director* in Philadelphia, see Heckscher 1985b, 284–85.

156. Affleck has long been known to have owned a copy of *The Director*, but a copy of the second edition with the signature of Benjamin Randolph on the title page has only recently been discovered. The book is now in a private collection.

157. Illustrated in Hornor 1935, 189, and Pls. 95, 97.

158. Heckscher 1985b, 285–87.

159. Kimball 1927.

160. For a biographical sketch of Randolph, see PMA 1976, 110–11. His ledgers consist of a receipt book (1763–77), Winterthur Library, and his account book (1768–86), New York Public Library.

161. For the architectural carving, see Wainwright 1964, 20–21; for the furniture, see ibid., 38–39.

162. For a biographical sketch of Affleck, see PMA 1976, 98–99.

163. For Affleck's possible connection to Penn, see Hornor 1935, 184.

164. In the Occupational Tax list for 1783, Affleck was assessed £250, £50 more than any other woodworker in the city. See ibid., 317.

165. Quoted in Beckerdite 1985 (the standard reference for Bernard and Jugiez), 498–99.

166. For Bernard in Charleston, see ibid., 510; in New York, see Gottesman 1938, 126–27.

167. Payment of £73-10-0 for "the King's Arms in the Council Chamber" was approved in February 1768; see Rauschenberg 1980, 12. Payment of £8 for the fireback pattern was received 20 December 1770; see Bivins 1985, 43–45.

168. Goyne 1963, 43–44; for Courtenay, see Beckerdite 1987b.

169. Public Record Office, London, Inland Revenue Department, Apprenticeship Books, 1710–62, 22: 88. Johnson owed the premium rate because of his dilatory payment. I am indebted to Robert Barker for confirming this record.

170. Hayward 1964, 16, 23, 32.

171. As quoted in PMA 1976, 112.

172. For Reynolds, see Beckerdite 1984.

173. Ibid., 23, 32.

174. No printed copy is known. A manuscript version of the 1772 booklet is reproduced in Weil 1979 (unless otherwise noted, the source of the quotations from the book in this chapter). Another manuscript copy, dated 1786, made by lumber merchant Benjamin Lehman, Germantown, Pennsylvania, is transcribed in Gillingham 1930.

175. The drawing is at the Philadelphia Museum of Art; for Mickle, see PMA 1976, 87.

176. For a comprehensive study of Cadwalader as patron, see Wainwright 1964.

177. Robert F. Oaks, "Big Wheels in Philadelphia: Du Simitière's List of Carriage Owners," *Pennsylvania Magazine of History and Biography* 95 (July 1971): 359, 361.

178. Quoted in Wainwright 1964, 1.

179. Prime 1929, 215.

180. Wainwright 1964, 38, 20.

181. For an illustration of the receipted bill, see ibid., 46.

182. See ibid., 45, where Courtenay is credited with the last two frames on the basis of a payment to him on 22 March 1774 by Cadwalader's agent "for 2 Picture Frames @ £14 – £28." But see Beckerdite 1984, 1132, n. 9, where that argument is rejected on the grounds that all five frames are identical and that the bill was altogether too late in date to be relevant.

183. William Williams, Matthew Pratt, and Henry Benbridge were active portrait painters in Philadelphia at different times during the height of the rococo, but none had the talent to rise to a commission such as Cadwalader's. Their works have yet to be surveyed for original frames in the rococo style.

184. Prime 1929, 226.

185. As quoted in Hayward 1971, 113.

186. Ibid., 29.

187. Prime 1929, 195.

188. For a comprehensive examination of John Elliott and ninety-one of his standard-type labeled looking glasses, see Hayward 1971.

189. See ibid., 40–41, for an explanation of why the variant label must be later.

190. Of ninety-one looking glasses studied, only two, both having the variant Walnut Street label, are identified as being of white pine; ibid., 150.

191. See Carl M. Williams, "Thomas Tufft and His Furniture for Richard Edwards," *The Magazine Antiques* 54 (October 1948): 246–47, where the commission is given as 1779; but see also idem, "Richard Edwards," *Important Philadelphia Chippendale Furniture from The Edwards–Harrison Family*, Christie's, sale no. 6400A, 28 May 1987, 12 (lot 201), where the commission is redated to 1775–76. For the Edwards pier table and looking glass, see *Highly Important American Furniture*, Christie's, sale no. 7000, 19 January 1990, lots 689, 690.

192. The account book, now missing, is referred to in Williams, "Thomas Tufft," 247.

193. Greenish bronze overpaint was removed in 1990–91; see conservation report by Mark Minor, Metropolitan Museum, 1991. Carving losses, particularly noticeable at the bottom, had not been restored at the time the photograph was taken (No. 126).

194. Prime 1929, 225.

195. For illustrations of bills, see Wainwright 1964, 46, 124; for an illustration of one of the looking glasses (now at Winterthur), see ibid., 125.

196. For the looking glasses, see Shepherd 1976, 11.

197. Prime 1929, 225.

198. The frames' original white-painted surfaces were restored by John Melody in 1975. His report, on file at Cliveden, notes that some of the floral designs are not of carved wood but of composition material.

199. Overpaint has recently been removed from the bracket. See conservation report by M. S. Podmaniczky, Winterthur Museum, 15 May 1989.

200. Beckerdite 1984, 1125.

201. Quoted in Wainwright 1964, 122.

202. See Monkhouse and Michie 1986, No. 49, where the table is fully described.

203. Wainwright 1964, 122.

204. See Hornor 1935, Pl. 235; Hummel 1976, Fig. 103.

205. The carved motifs match those of a marble slab table (Hipkiss 1941, No. 53), but look to be by a different carver.

206. Gillingham 1936, Fig. 2.

207. J. F. Watson, *Annals of Philadelphia and Pennsylvania* (Philadelphia, 1870), 203–4.

208. Beckerdite 1985, 505–6.

209. For the mate to this table, see PMA 1976, No. 57.

210. Under the iron is a wooden subtop, visible in Sack 1986, 8: 2311.

211. Quoted in Boyer 1931, 134. The advertisement gives the name as Maybery.

212. For a pair of chests of related design at Winterthur said to have been made for Michael Gratz of Philadelphia in 1769, at the time of his marriage to Miriam Simon, see Downs 1952a, Nos. 198, 333.

213. The high chest and the table are fully catalogued in Ward 1988, Nos. 147, 116.

214. Downs 1952a, No. 195; Hummel 1976, Fig. 83. The cartouche, of a type also found on No. 140, is a recent replacement.

215. See Heckscher 1985b, 286.

216. For a full description of the construction of the chest, see Heckscher 1985a, No. 168.

217. For examples, see PMA 1976, No. 104a, b; Hipkiss 1941, No. 55.

218. Except for its uppermost leaf frond, the finial is intact and has never been refinished. The high chest for which it is the crowning ornament is inscribed "Samuel Appleton Joiner," an otherwise unrecorded maker.

219. See PMA 1976, No. 84.

220. See *Important Philadelphia Chippendale Furniture*, Christie's, 28 May 1987, lot 201.

221. For the Logan double chest, see Heckscher 1985a, No. 147.

222. For a thorough examination of Philadelphia finial busts, see Smith 1971.

223. See, for example, Gilbert 1978, 2: Figs. 66–71, 73.

224. Hornor 1935, 119, 189.

225. *Pennsylvania Gazette*, 10 January 1765 and 3 September 1767, as quoted in Wainwright 1964, 35.

226. Goyne 1963, 62.

227. See Terry Friedman and Timothy Clifford, *The Man at Hyde Park Corner: Sculpture by John Cheere 1709–1787* (Leeds: Temple Newsam House, 1974).

228. Robin Reilly, *Wedgwood: Volume I* (London: Macmillan, 1989), 448–56.

229. For an illustration of the desk-and-bookcase pediment, see Hornor 1935, Pl. 94.

230. For the Library Company, see Edwin Wolf 2nd, "A Parcel of Books for the Province in 1700," *Pennsylvania Magazine of History and Biography* 189 (October 1965): 428–46.

231. Smith 1971, Figs. 8, 11, 13, 14, illustrates four of the Locke busts; the fifth is at Stratford Hall, Virginia. In 1775, Wedgwood depended on the same, as yet unidentified, design source for his "basalte" bust of Locke.

232. For another bust of Milton, on the Samuel Nicholas family desk and bookcase, see *The Magazine Antiques* 126 (November 1984): 1031.

233. The bust is after a plaster cast, which Wedgwood was also to copy. For such a cast, see *The Contents of Littlecote, Hungerford, Wiltshire*, Sotheby's (London), 20–22 November 1985, lot 333; for Wedgwood's copy, see *Estate of James R. Herbert Boone*, Sotheby's, 16–17 September 1988, lot 709.

234. The bust is lacking a plinth.

235. Beckerdite 1985, Fig. 17.

236. See Beckerdite 1987b, 1052 and Fig. 2.

237. Woodhouse 1927, 369.

238. The original list of "Donations to the Asylum" is at Haverford College, Pennsylvania.

239. PMA 1976, No. 79.

240. The chair was commissioned by William Hollingshead and Charles Willson Peale, members of the Pennsylvania Assembly Committee for Fitting up the Assembly Room. See Goyne 1963, 161, n. 48.

241. Two pairs of the same model, differing only in the handling of the carving, are known. See Heckscher 1985a, No. 69.

242. For an illustration of the bill, see Wainwright 1964, 44.

243. For one of the seven known, see Heckscher 1985a, No. 59.

244. For Fleeson's bill, see Wainwright 1964, 40.

245. Ibid., 41.

246. Ibid., 69.

247. Ibid., 51.

248. For the fire screens, see Heckscher 1985a, No. 132.

249. For the inventories of 1778 and 1786, see Wainwright 1964, 66–67, 72–73.

250. For the tables, see Downs 1952a, No. 345; for the chairs, see Hummel 1976, Fig. 53.

251. Beckerdite 1984, 1126–28.

CAST IRON, GLASS, AND PORCELAIN

pp. 219–39

CAST IRON

pp. 219–28.

1. Forty such coal-burning fireplace inserts are illustrated in W. & J. Welldon, *The Smith's Right Hand, or A Complete Guide to the Various Branches of all Sorts of Iron Work* (London, 1765).

2. According to Dr. Shoep, a German traveler, quoted in Mercer 1961, 34.

3. In England, cast-iron rococo ornament is found only on two survivals of the closed stoves patented in 1765 by Abraham Buzaglo (1716–1788): one sent to Williamsburg in 1770 to Lord Botetourt, Royal Governor of the colony of Virginia; the other, known only in its end plate, dated 1765; see Snodin 1984, 151 (K5).

4. Gottesman 1938, 208.

5. Bivins 1985, 43.

6. Goyne 1963, 71.

7. All four chimneybacks are shown in situ in photographs of the Lee house interior contained in a late-nineteenth-century album; American Wing files, Metropolitan Museum.

8. A later casting of the Webb chimneyback (now at Winterthur) is identical except for the addition of the date 1781 under the arch; for an illustration, see Schiffer 1979, 155.

9. For an illustration in situ, see Chamberlain 1977, 1167, Pl. IV.

10. The other known casting (now at the Bucks County Historical Society) was made earlier. Though more pitted by rust, it preserves intact the part of the scrollwork missing from the upper right corner of No. 158. For an illustration, see Mercer 1961, Pl. 382.

11. See ibid., Pl. 383, for an illustration of the chimneyback, in the collections of the Metropolitan Museum (36.32).

12. For Aetna Furnace, see Boyer 1931, 164–67.

13. Ibid., 164.

14. Ibid., 165.

15. For illustrations of the two, see Mercer 1961, Pls. 291, 293.

16. Ibid., Pls. 8, 9.

17. Ibid., 86–87.

18. Walter Hugins, "The Story of a 19th-Century Ironmaking Community," *Hopewell Furnace, A Guide to Hopewell Village National Historic Site, Pennsylvania* (Washington, D.C.: National Park Service, 1983), 29.

19. The original Franklin stove had an arched and decorated front plate at the top and a projecting hearth at the bottom. It was inserted into a fireplace and vented through its flue.

20. Quoted in Leonard W. Labaree, ed., *The Papers of Benjamin Franklin*, 1–14 (New Haven: Yale University Press, 1959–70), 12: 236. "Our Friend Grace" was Robert Grace (1709–1766), manager of Warwick Furnace, not far from Hopewell, and the man to whom Franklin presented the model of his Pennsylvania stove; see Mercer 1961, 109.

21. For Marlboro Furnace, see Bivins 1985.

22. Ibid., 45–54; see also Figs. 14–18.

23. For Elizabeth Furnace, see Mercer 1961, 111.

24. See ibid., Pls. 173, 174; 193–99; 222–25.

25. Ibid., Pls. 300, 301.

26. For an illustration, see ibid., Pl. 297.

27. See ibid., Pls. 313, 314, for the Thomas Maybury (Mayberry) stove of 1767 (now at the Henry Ford Museum), the only other version of a rococo-decorated ten-plate stove from the 1760s.

28. Tatum 1976, Figs. 46, 47.

29. For Reading Furnace, see Mercer 1961, 106–8.

30. Illustrated in Beatrice B. Garvan, *The Pennsylvania German Collection* (Philadelphia: Philadelphia Museum of Art, 1982), 107, No. 24.

31. A number of similarly decorated stove plates from the Redwell works in the Shenandoah Valley are dated between 1787 and 1805. See H. E. Comstock, "The Redwell Ironworks," *Journal of Early Southern Decorative Arts* 7 (May 1981): 41–80.

GLASS
pp. 229–33.

32. For a concise summary of the history of early American glass, see Palmer 1984.

33. As quoted in Palmer 1989, 204. The information on Stiegel and his production is entirely derived from this thorough and informative treatise.

34. As quoted in ibid., 208–9.

35. Palmer 1984, 162.

36. Palmer 1989, 216.

37. As quoted in ibid., 212.

38. As quoted in Palmer 1984, 183.

39. Arlene Palmer Schwind is credited with the research and attribution of this pivotal example of Stiegel's English-style production.

40. Palmer 1989, 212–13, 216, 219.

41. As quoted in Dwight P. Lanmon and Arlene M. Palmer, "John Frederick Amelung and the New Bremen Glassmanufactory," *Journal of Glass Studies* 18 (1976): 26. This issue of the journal, the source of information for the Amelung entries, contains a thorough study of Amelung and his manufactory, as well as a catalogue of his signed and attributed glass.

42. As quoted in ibid., 32.

43. As quoted in ibid., 44.

44. As quoted in ibid., 33.

45. Ibid., 76.

PORCELAIN
pp. 234–39.

46. Porcelain is composed of a fine white clay called kaolin and a feldspathic stone known as petuntse. When fired at a temperature of from twelve hundred to fifteen hundred degrees Celsius (2,192–2,732 degrees Fahrenheit), porcelain vitrifies, becoming extremely hard and translucent.

47. For the history of American porcelain in general, see Frelinghuysen 1989; for Duché, see ibid., 6; for a history of eighteenth-century porcelain, see ibid., 6–11 and Nos. 1–3.

48. As quoted in ibid., 8, where additional information on Franklin's interest in American porcelain is recorded.

49. See ibid. for more on Rush and for quotations from his letters.

50. As quoted in ibid.

51. Hood 1972, 13.

52. English soft-paste porcelain manufacturers substituted bone ash for petuntse, as did Bonnin and Morris.

53. As quoted and described in Hood 1972 (the most complete study of Bonnin and Morris), 15, 17. The data used in the preparation of the discussions of the partnership's examples were drawn from Hood 1972 and Frelinghuysen 1989.

54. Advertisements for enamel painters and surviving shards with iron red underglaze decoration suggest that the factory attempted polychrome decoration, at least in the blue-and-red Imari style. For more information, see Frelinghuysen 1989, 9.

55. Hood 1972, 30–31.

56. See ibid., Fig. 24, for an illustration of a similar scene.

57. A similar border decoration, without the blurring, is illustrated in Frelinghuysen 1989, No. 1.

58. Ibid., 72, and Hood 1972, 55.

59. Other six-inch examples are illustrated in Hood 1972, Figs. 1, 30, and 33; for the eight-inch variety, see ibid., Fig. 5, and Frelinghuysen 1989, No. 1.

60. Frelinghuysen 1989, 77.

61. The other two with blue floral decoration in the bowls are in the collections of the National Museum of American Art, Smithsonian Institution (70.597), and the Brooklyn Museum (45.174).

62. For examples, see Snodin 1984, 114 (G17), 115 (G19), 245 (O6, O7), and 247 (O12).

63. Frelinghuysen 1989, 77.

64. For a transcription of both bills with prices, see Hood 1972, 55.

65. I am grateful to Alice Cooney Frelinghuysen, Associate Curator, Department of American Decorative Arts, The Metropolitan Museum of Art, for sharing this theory.

66. Hood 1989, 243.

Bibliography

Adair 1983
William Adair. *The Frame in America, 1700–1900: A Survey of Fabrication Techniques and Styles.* Washington, D.C.: The American Institute of Architects Foundation, 1983.

Beckerdite 1982a
Luke Beckerdite. "William Buckland and William Bernard Sears: The Designer and the Carver." *Journal of Early Southern Decorative Arts* 8 (November 1982): 7–41.

Beckerdite 1982b
Luke Beckerdite. "William Buckland Reconsidered: Architectural Carving in Chesapeake Maryland, 1771–1774." *Journal of Early Southern Decorative Arts* 8 (November 1982): 42–88.

Beckerdite 1984
Luke Beckerdite. "Philadelphia carving shops. Part I: James Reynolds." *The Magazine Antiques* 125 (May 1984): 1120–33.

Beckerdite 1985
Luke Beckerdite. "Philadelphia carving shops. Part II: Bernard and Jugiez." *The Magazine Antiques* 128 (September 1985): 498–513.

Beckerdite 1986
Luke Beckerdite. "A Problem of Identification: Philadelphia and Baltimore Furniture Styles in the Eighteenth Century." *Journal of Early Southern Decorative Arts* 12 (May 1986): 20–65.

Beckerdite 1987a
Luke Beckerdite. "Carving Practices in Eighteenth-Century Boston." In Brock Jobe, ed. *Old-Time New England: New England Furniture: Essays in Memory of Benno M. Forman.* Boston: Society for the Preservation of New England Antiquities, 1987, 123–62.

Beckerdite 1987b
Luke Beckerdite. "Philadelphia carving shops. Part III: Hercules Courtenay and his school." *The Magazine Antiques* 131 (May 1987): 1044–63.

Belden 1980
Louise Conway Belden. *Marks of American Silversmiths in the Ineson-Bissell Collection.* Charlottesville: University Press of Virginia for The Henry Francis du Pont Winterthur Museum, 1980.

Belknap 1927
Henry Wyckoff Belknap. *Artists and Craftsmen of Essex County, Massachusetts.* Salem: Essex Institute, 1927.

Bivins 1985
John Bivins, Jr. "Isaac Zane and the Products of Marlboro Furnace." *Journal of Early Southern Decorative Arts* 11 (May 1985): 14–65.

Bivins 1986
John Bivins, Jr. "Charleston Rococo Interiors, 1765–1775: The 'Sommers' Carver." *Journal of Early Southern Decorative Arts* 12 (November 1986): 1–129.

Blackburn 1976
Roderic H. Blackburn. *Cherry Hill: The History and Collections of a Van Rensselaer Family.* Albany, N.Y.: Historic Cherry Hill, 1976.

Bohan 1963
Peter J. Bohan. *American Gold: 1700–1860.* New Haven: Yale University Art Gallery, 1963.

Boles 1976
John B. Boles, ed. *Maryland Heritage: Five Baltimore Institutions Celebrate the American Bicentennial.* Baltimore: Maryland Historical Society, 1976.

Bolton 1927
Charles Knowles Bolton. *Bolton's American Armory.* Boston: F. W. Faxon, 1927.

Boyer 1931
Charles S. Boyer. *Early Forges & Furnaces in New Jersey.* Philadelphia: University of Pennsylvania Press, 1931.

Brigham 1969
Clarence S. Brigham. *Paul Revere's Engravings.* New York: Atheneum, 1969.

The British Architect
See Swan.

Buhler 1956
Kathryn C. Buhler. *Paul Revere, Goldsmith, 1735–1818.* Boston: Museum of Fine Arts, Boston, 1956.

Buhler 1965
Kathryn C. Buhler. *Massachusetts Silver in the Frank L. and Louise C. Harrington Collection.* Worcester, Mass., 1965.

Buhler 1972
Kathryn C. Buhler. *American Silver, 1655–1825, in the Museum of Fine Arts, Boston.* 2 vols. Boston: Museum of Fine Arts, Boston, 1972.

Buhler 1979
Kathryn C. Buhler. *American Silver: From the Colonial Period through the Early Republic in the Worcester Art Museum.* Worcester, Mass.: Worcester Art Museum, 1979.

Buhler and Hood 1970
Kathryn C. Buhler and Graham Hood. *American Silver: Garvan and Other Collections in the Yale University Art Gallery.* 2 vols. New Haven: Yale University Press, 1970.

Bunting 1969
Bainbridge Bunting. *Early Science at Harvard: Innovators and Their*

Instruments. Cambridge: Fogg Art Museum, Harvard University, 1969.

Bunting 1985
Bainbridge Bunting. *Harvard: An Architectural History*. Completed and edited by Margaret Henderson Floyd. Cambridge: Belknap Press of Harvard University Press, 1985.

Burton 1955
E. Milby Burton. *Charleston Furniture: 1700–1825*. Charleston, S.C.: The Charleston Museum, 1955.

Chamberlain 1977
Narcissa G. Chamberlain. "History in houses." *The Magazine Antiques* 112 (December 1977): 1164–72.

Chippendale
Thomas Chippendale. *The Gentleman and Cabinet-Maker's Director*. 1754. Reprint, 3rd ed., 1762. New York: Dover Publications, 1966.

Clayton 1971
Michael Clayton. *The Collector's Dictionary of the Silver and Gold of Great Britain and North America*. Woodbridge, England: Antique Collectors' Club, 1971.

Clayton 1985
Michael Clayton. *Christie's Pictorial History of English and American Silver*. Oxford: Phaidon-Christie's, 1985.

Clifford 1990
Helen Clifford. "Paul de Lamerie and the Organization of the London Goldsmiths' Trade in the First Half of the Eighteenth Century." In Susan Hare, ed. *Paul de Lamerie: At the Sign of The Golden Ball*. London: Goldsmiths' Company, 1990, 24–25.

Cole 1966
Wilford P. Cole. "Henry Dawkins, Engraver." Master's thesis, University of Delaware, 1966.

Cooper 1980
Wendy A. Cooper. *In Praise of America: American Decorative Arts, 1650–1830*. New York: Alfred A. Knopf, 1980.

Davis 1976
John D. Davis. *English Silver at Williamsburg*. Williamsburg, Va.: The Colonial Williamsburg Foundation, 1976.

Dennis 1968
Jessie McNab Dennis. "Franks family silver by Lamerie." *The Magazine Antiques* 93 (May 1968): 636–41.

The Director
See Chippendale.

Dow 1927
George Francis Dow. *The Arts & Crafts in New England, 1704–1775*. 1927. Reprint. New York: Da Capo Press, 1967.

Downs 1952a
Joseph Downs. *American Furniture: Queen Anne and Chippendale Periods in the Henry Francis du Pont Winterthur Museum*. New York: Macmillan, 1952.

Downs 1952b
Joseph Downs. "John Cogswell, cabinetmaker." *The Magazine Antiques* 61 (April 1952): 322–24.

Thomas Elfe's Account Book
Mabel L. Webber, ed. "The Thomas Elfe Account Book, 1768–1775." The account book is reproduced in its entirety in successive issues of *The South Carolina Historical and Genealogical Magazine* 35–42 (January 1934–January 1941).

Emlen 1984
Robert P. Emlen. "Wedding Silver for the Browns." *American Art Journal* 16 (Spring 1984): 39–50.

Fales 1963
Martha Gandy Fales. "English design sources of American silver." *The Magazine Antiques* 83 (January 1963): 82–85.

Fales 1970
Martha Gandy Fales. *Early American Silver*. Rev. ed. New York: Funk and Wagnalls, 1970.

Fales 1973
Martha Gandy Fales. "Heraldic Emblematic Engravers of Colonial Boston." In Walter Muir Whitehill and Sinclair H. Hitchings, eds. *Boston Prints and Printmakers: 1670–1775*. Boston: The Colonial Society of Massachusetts, 1973, 185–220.

Fales 1974
Martha Gandy Fales. *Joseph Richardson and Family: Philadelphia Silversmiths*. Middletown, Conn.: Wesleyan University Press for The Historical Society of Pennsylvania, 1974.

Fales 1983
Martha Gandy Fales. *Silver at the Essex Institute*. Salem, Mass.: Essex Institute, 1983.

Federhen 1988
Deborah A. Federhen. "From Artisan to Entrepreneur: Paul Revere's Silver Shop Operation." In Patrick M. Leehey et al. *Paul Revere—Artisan, Businessman, and Patriot: The Man Behind the Myth*. Boston: The Paul Revere Memorial Association, 1988, 65–93.

Flynt and Fales 1968
Henry N. Flynt and Martha Gandy Fales. *The Heritage Foundation Collection of Silver*. Old Deerfield, Mass.: The Heritage Foundation, 1968.

Fowble 1987
E. McSherry Fowble. *Two Centuries of Prints in America, 1680–1880: A Selective Catalogue of the Winterthur Museum Collections*. Charlottesville: University Press of Virginia, 1987.

Frelinghuysen 1989
Alice Cooney Frelinghuysen. *American Porcelain: 1770–1920*. New York: The Metropolitan Museum of Art, 1989.

French 1939
Hollis French. *Jacob Hurd and His Sons Nathaniel & Benjamin, Silversmiths, 1702–1781*. Cambridge, Mass.: Riverside Press, 1939.

Garrett 1960
Wendell D. Garrett. *Apthorp House, 1760–1790*. Cambridge: Adams House, Harvard University, 1960.

Garvin 1983
James L. Garvin. *Academic Architecture and the Building Trades in the Piscataqua Region of New Hampshire and Maine*. Ann Arbor, Mich.: University Microfilms, 1983.

Gerstell 1972
Vivian S. Gerstell. *Silversmiths of Lancaster, Pennsylvania, 1730–1850*. Lancaster: Lancaster County Historical Society, 1972.

Gilbert 1978
Christopher Gilbert. *The Life and Works of Thomas Chippendale*. 2 vols. New York: Macmillan, 1978.

Gillingham 1930
Harrold E. Gillingham. "Benjamin Lehman, A Germantown Cabinet-Maker." *The Pennsylvania Magazine of History and Biography* 54 (1930): 289–306.

Gillingham 1936
Harrold E. Gillingham. "James Gillingham, Philadelphia Cabinet-maker." *The Magazine Antiques* 29 (May 1936): 200–201.

Goldsborough 1984
Jennifer Faulds Goldsborough. *Silver in Maryland*. Baltimore: Museum and Library of Maryland History, Maryland Historical Society, 1984.

Gottesman 1938
Rita Susswein Gottesman, comp. *The Arts and Crafts in New York: 1726–1776*. New York: The New-York Historical Society, 1938.

Gottesman 1954
Rita Susswein Gottesman, comp. *The Arts and Crafts in New York: 1777–1799*. New York: The New-York Historical Society, 1954.

Goyne 1963
Nancy Ann Goyne. "Furniture Craftsmen in Philadelphia, 1760–1780: Their Role in a Mercantile Society." Master's thesis, University of Delaware, 1963.

Grimwade 1974
Arthur Grimwade. *Rococo Silver: 1727–1765*. London: Faber and Faber, 1974.

Gusler 1979
Wallace B. Gusler. *Furniture of Williamsburg and Eastern Virginia, 1710–1790*. Richmond, Va.: Virginia Museum, 1979.

Gusler 1989
Wallace B. Gusler. "The tea tables of eastern Virginia." *The Magazine Antiques* 135 (May 1989): 1238–57.

Hammerslough 1958
Philip H. Hammerslough. *American Silver Collected by Philip H. Hammerslough*. Hartford, Conn.: Privately printed, 1958.

Hammerslough 1960
Philip H. Hammerslough. *American Silver Collected by Philip H. Hammerslough*. Vol. II. Hartford, Conn.: Privately printed, 1960.

Hartop 1990
Christopher Hartop. "The 'Infusion of that Fragrant Leaf': Tea Drinking in England." *Auction News from Christie's* 12 (September 1990): 3, 10.

Hayward 1964
Helena Hayward. *Thomas Johnson and English Rococo*. London: Alex Tiranti, 1964.

Hayward 1971
Mary Ellen Hayward. "The Elliotts of Philadelphia: Emphasis on the Looking Glass Trade, 1755–1810." Master's thesis, University of Delaware, 1971.

Hayward Yehia 1974
Mary Ellen Hayward Yehia. "Ornamental Carving on Boston Furniture of the Chippendale Style." In Walter Muir Whitehill, Brock Jobe, and Jonathan Fairbanks, eds. *Boston Furniture of the Eighteenth Century*. Boston: Colonial Society of Massachusetts, 1974, 197–222.

Heckscher 1973
Morrison H. Heckscher. "The New York serpentine card table." *The Magazine Antiques* 103 (May 1973): 974–83.

Heckscher 1979
Morrison H. Heckscher. "Lock and Copland: A Catalogue of the Engraved Ornament." *Furniture History* 15 (1979): 1–23; Pls. 1–67.

Heckscher 1985a
Morrison H. Heckscher. *American Furniture in The Metropolitan Museum of Art. II. Late Colonial Period: The Queen Anne and Chippendale Styles*. Edited by Mary-Alice Rogers. New York: The Metropolitan Museum of Art, 1985.

Heckscher 1985b
Morrison H. Heckscher. "Philadelphia Chippendale: The Influence of the *Director* in America." *Furniture History* 21 (1985): 283–95.

Heckscher 1989
Morrison H. Heckscher. "Philadelphia Furniture, 1760–90: Native-Born and London-Trained Craftsmen." In Francis J. Puig and Michael Conforti, eds. *The American Craftsman and the European Tradition: 1620–1820*. Minneapolis, Minn.: The Minneapolis Institute of Arts, 1989, 92–111.

Heckscher 1990
Morrison H. Heckscher. "The Beekman Family Portraits and Their Eighteenth-Century New York Frames." *Furniture History* 26 (1990): 114–20.

Hipkiss 1941
Edwin J. Hipkiss. *Eighteenth-Century American Arts: The M. and M. Karolik Collection*. Cambridge: Harvard University Press for the Museum of Fine Arts, Boston, 1941.

Hitchings 1973
Sinclair Hitchings. "Thomas Johnston." In Walter Muir Whitehill and Sinclair H. Hitchings, eds. *Boston Prints and Printmakers: 1670–1775*. Boston: The Colonial Society of Massachusetts, 1973, 83–132.

Hitchings 1979
Sinclair Hitchings. "London's Images of Colonial America." In

Joan D. Dolmetsch, ed. *Eighteenth-Century Prints in Colonial America: To Educate and Decorate*. Williamsburg, Va.: The Colonial Williamsburg Foundation, 1979, 11–31.

Honour 1975
Hugh Honour. *The European Vision of America*. Cleveland: Cleveland Museum of Art, 1975.

Hood 1971
Graham Hood. *American Silver: A History of Style, 1650–1900*. New York: Praeger Publishers, 1971.

Hood 1972
Graham Hood. *Bonnin and Morris of Philadelphia: The First American Porcelain Factory, 1770–1772*. Williamsburg, Va.: Institute of Early American History and Culture, 1972.

Hood 1989
Graham Hood. "The American China." In Francis J. Puig and Michael Conforti, eds. *The American Craftsman and the European Tradition: 1620–1820*. Minneapolis, Minn.: The Minneapolis Institute of Arts, 1989, 240–55.

Hoopes 1958
Penrose R. Hoopes. *Shop Records of Daniel Burnap, Clockmaker*. Hartford, Conn.: The Connecticut Historical Society, 1958.

Hornor 1935
William MacPherson Hornor, Jr. *Blue Book: Philadelphia Furniture*. 1935. Reprint. Washington, D.C.: Highland House, 1977.

Houshold Furniture
Genteel Houshold Furniture in the Present Taste by A Society of Upholsterers, Cabinet-Makers, etc. 1762. Reprint, with an introduction by Christopher Gilbert. East Ardsley, West Yorkshire: EP Publishing, 1978.

Howells 1937
John Mead Howells. *The Architectural Heritage of the Piscataqua: Houses and Gardens of the Portsmouth District of Maine and New Hampshire*. New York: Architectural Book Publishing, 1937.

Howells 1941
John Mead Howells. *The Architectural Heritage of the Merrimack*. New York: Architectural Book Publishing, 1941.

Hummel 1970–71
Charles F. Hummel. "Queen Anne and Chippendale furniture in the Henry Francis du Pont Winterthur Museum, Part I." *The Magazine Antiques* 97 (June 1970): 896–903. "Part II." 98 (December 1970): 900–909. "Part III." 99 (January 1971): 98–107.

Hummel 1976
Charles F. Hummel. *A Winterthur Guide to American Chippendale Furniture*. New York: Crown Publishers, 1976.

Ince and Mayhew
See *Universal System*

Jobe and Kaye 1984
Brock Jobe and Myrna Kaye. *New England Furniture, the Colonial Era: Selections from the Society for the Preservation of New England Antiquities*. Boston: Houghton Mifflin, 1984.

Johnson 1964
J. Stewart Johnson. "The Cabinetmakers of New York." Master's thesis, University of Delaware, 1964.

Johnson's book of designs
Thomas Johnson. *One Hundred and Fifty New Designs*. 1761. The book has been reprinted in its entirety in Hayward 1964, following p. 45.

Joy 1960
E. T. Joy. "English Furniture in America in the Georgian Period and some hitherto unpublished Trading Figures." *The Connoisseur* 146 (September 1960): 68–73.

Kane 1976
Patricia E. Kane. *300 Years of American Seating Furniture: Chairs and Beds from the Mabel Brady Garvan and Other Collections at Yale University*. Boston: New York Graphic Society, 1976.

Kauffman 1969
Henry J. Kauffman. *The Colonial Silversmith: His Techniques & His Products*. New York: Galahad Books, 1969

Kaye 1974
Myrna Kaye. "Eighteenth-Century Furniture Craftsmen." In Walter Muir Whitehill, Brock Jobe, and Jonathan Fairbanks, eds. *Boston Furniture of the Eighteenth Century*. Boston: The Colonial Society of Massachusetts, 1974, 267–302.

Kimball 1927
Fiske Kimball. "The Sources of the Philadelphia Chippendale: II. Benjamin Randolph's Trade Card." *Pennsylvania Museum Bulletin* 115 (October 1927): 5–8.

Kimball 1940
Fiske Kimball. *Mr. Samuel McIntire, Carver: The Architect of Salem*. Salem, Mass.: Essex Institute, 1940.

Kimball 1943
Fiske Kimball. *The Creation of the Rococo*. 1943. Reprint. New York: Dover Publications, 1980.

Kindig 1978
Joseph K. Kindig III. *The Philadelphia Chair, 1685–1785*. York, Pa.: Historical Society of York County, 1978.

Kolter 1979
Jane Bentley Kolter, ed. *Early American Silver and Its Makers*. New York: Mayflower Books, 1979.

Leehey 1988
Patrick M. Leehey et al. *Paul Revere—Artisan, Businessman, and Patriot: The Man Behind the Myth*. Boston: The Paul Revere Memorial Association, 1988.

Leibundguth 1964
Arthur W. Leibundguth. "The Furniture-Making Crafts in Philadelphia, c. 1730–c. 1760." Master's thesis, University of Delaware, 1964.

Lockwood 1913
Luke Vincent Lockwood. *Colonial Furniture in America*. 2 vols. New York: Charles Scribner's Sons, 1913.

Lovell 1974
Margaretta Markle Lovell. "Boston Blockfront Furniture." In Walter Muir Whitehill, Brock Jobe, and Jonathan Fairbanks, eds. *Boston Furniture of the Eighteenth Century*. Boston: The Colonial Society of Massachusetts, 1974, 77-135.

Lynn 1980
Catherine Lynn. *Wallpaper in America from the Seventeenth Century to World War I*. New York: W. W. Norton, 1980.

Manwaring
Robert Manwaring. *The Cabinet and Chair-Maker's Real Friend and Companion*. 1765. Reprint. London: Alec Tiranti, 1970.

Means 1958
Mary Elizabeth Means. "Early American Trade Cards." Master's thesis, University of Delaware, 1958.

Mercer 1961
Henry C. Mercer. *The Bible in Iron: Pictured Stoves and Stoveplates of the Pennsylvania Germans*. 3rd rev. ed. Doylestown, Pa.: The Bucks County Historical Society, 1961.

MFA 1975
Museum of Fine Arts, Boston. *Paul Revere's Boston*. Boston: Museum of Fine Arts, Boston, 1975.

Miller 1937
V. Isabelle Miller. *Silver by New York Makers*. New York: Museum of the City of New York, 1937.

Monkhouse and Michie 1986
Christopher P. Monkhouse and Thomas S. Michie, with the assistance of John M. Carpenter. *American Furniture in Pendleton House*. Providence: Rhode Island School of Design, 1986.

Montgomery 1984
Florence M. Montgomery. *Textiles in America, 1650-1870*. New York: W. W. Norton, 1984.

Montgomery and Kane 1976
Charles F. Montgomery and Patricia E. Kane, eds. *American Art: 1750-1800, Towards Independence*. Boston: New York Graphic Society, 1976.

Murdoch 1986
Tessa Murdoch. "The Huguenots and English Rococo." In Charles Hind, ed. *The Rococo in England: A Symposium*. London: Victoria and Albert Museum, 1986, 60-81.

Oedel 1974
William Oedel. "The Francis Borland Tea Table." Research paper, Yale University, 1974.

Palmer 1984
Arlene Palmer Schwind. "The Glassmakers of Early America." In Ian M. G. Quimby, ed. *The Craftsman in Early America*. Winterthur, Del.: The Henry Francis du Pont Winterthur Museum, 1984, 158-89.

Palmer 1989
Arlene Palmer. " 'To the Good of Province and Country': Henry William Stiegel and American Flint Glass." In Francis J. Puig and

Michael Conforti, eds. *The American Craftsman and the European Tradition*. Minneapolis, Minn.: Minneapolis Institute of Arts, 1989, 202-39.

Park 1973
Helen Park. *A List of Architectural Books Available in America before the Revolution*. Rev. ed. Los Angeles: Hennessey & Ingalls, 1973.

Patterson 1978
Jerry E. Patterson. *The City of New York: A History Illustrated from the Collections of The Museum of the City of New York*. New York: Harry N. Abrams, 1978.

Piwonka 1986
Ruth Piwonka. *A Portrait of Livingston Manor*. New York: Friends of Clermont, 1986.

Pleasants and Sill 1930
J. Hall Pleasants and Howard Sill. *Maryland Silversmiths, 1715-1830*. 1930. Reprint. Harrison, N.Y.: Robert Alan Green, 1972.

PMA 1976
Philadelphia Museum of Art. *Philadelphia: Three Centuries of American Art*. Philadelphia: Philadelphia Museum of Art, 1976.

PMAB 1956
"Philadelphia Silver: 1682-1800." *The Philadelphia Museum Bulletin* 51 (Spring 1956), unpaged.

Price 1977
Lois Olcott Price. "Furniture Craftsmen and the Queen Anne Style in Eighteenth Century New York." Master's thesis, University of Delaware, 1977.

Prime 1929
Alfred Coxe Prime, comp. *The Arts & Crafts in Philadelphia, Maryland, and South Carolina, 1721-1785*. 1929. Reprint. New York: Da Capo Press, 1969.

Prown 1966
Jules David Prown. *John Singleton Copley*. 2 vols. Cambridge: Harvard University Press, 1966.

Randall 1964
Richard H. Randall, Jr. "George Bright, Cabinetmaker." *Art Quarterly* 27 (1964): 134-49.

Randall 1965
Richard H. Randall, Jr. *American Furniture in the Museum of Fine Arts, Boston*. Boston: Museum of Fine Arts, Boston, 1965.

Randall 1974
Richard H. Randall, Jr. "Benjamin Frothingham." In Walter Muir Whitehill, Brock Jobe, and Jonathan Fairbanks, eds. *Boston Furniture of the Eighteenth Century*. Boston: The Colonial Society of Massachusetts, 1974, 223-49.

Rauschenberg 1976
Bradford L. Rauschenberg. "Two Outstanding Virginia Chairs." *Journal of Early Southern Decorative Arts* 2 (November 1976): 1-23.

Rauschenberg 1980
Bradford L. Rauschenberg. "The Royal Governor's Chair: Evi-

dence of the Furnishing of South Carolina's First State House."
Journal of Early Southern Decorative Arts 6 (November 1980): 1–32.

Reiff 1986
Daniel D. Reiff. *Small Georgian Houses in England and Virginia.*
Cranbury, N.J.: Associated University Presses, 1986.

Paul Revere's ledgers
Two Day Books. The first, for the years 1761–83; the second, 1784–
97. Massachusetts Historical Society, Boston.

Rhoads 1972
Elizabeth Adams Rhoads. "Household Furnishings in Portsmouth,
New Hampshire, 1750–1775." Master's thesis, University of Dela-
ware, 1972.

Rice 1964
Norman S. Rice. *Albany Silver: 1652–1825.* Albany, N.Y.: Albany
Institute of History and Art, 1964.

Joseph Richardson's letter book
The Letter Book of Joseph Richardson, Sr., which covers the years
1758–74, is in the Downs Manuscript and Microfilm Collection,
Winterthur Museum, and is transcribed in full in Fales 1974, 219–59.

Rodriguez Roque 1984
Oswaldo Rodriguez Roque. *American Furniture at Chipstone.* Madison, Wisc.: University of Wisconsin Press, 1984.

Rosenbaum 1954
Jeanette W. Rosenbaum. *Myer Myers, Goldsmith, 1723–1795.*
Philadelphia: Jewish Publication Society of America, 1954.

Roth 1961
Rodris Roth. "Tea Drinking in 18th-Century America: Its Etiquette
and Equipage." Contributions from the Museum of History and
Technology, Paper 14. *United States National Museum Bulletin* 225
(1961): 61–91.

Sabine 1864
Lorenzo Sabine. *Biographical Sketches of Loyalists of the American Revolution.* 2nd ed., 1864. Reprint. Baltimore, Md.: Genealogical Publishing, 1979.

Sack 1981–86
American Antiques from Israel Sack Collection. 8 vols. Washington,
D.C.: Highland House Publishers, 1981–86.

Safford 1983
Frances Gruber Safford. "Colonial Silver in The American Wing."
The Metropolitan Museum of Art Bulletin 41 (Summer 1983): 3–56.

Schiffer 1979
Herbert, Peter, and Nancy Schiffer. *Antique Iron: Survey of American
and English Forms, Fifteenth through Nineteenth Centuries.* Exton, Pa.:
Schiffer Publishing, 1979.

Schroder 1988a
Timothy Schroder. *The Gilbert Collection of Gold and Silver.* Los
Angeles: Los Angeles County Museum of Art, 1988.

Schroder 1988b
Timothy Schroder. *The National Trust Book of English Domestic*

Silver, 1500–1900. Harmondsworth, England, and New York: Vik-
ing Press, in association with the National Trust, 1988.

Shepherd 1976
Raymond V. Shepherd, Jr. "Cliveden and Its Philadelphia-Chippen-
dale Furniture: A Documented History." *The American Art Journal* 8
(November 1976): 2–16.

Singleton 1902
Esther Singleton. *Social New York under the Georges: 1714–1776.* New
York: D. Appleton, 1902.

Skerry 1984
Janine E. Skerry. "The Philip H. Hammerslough Collection of
American silver at the Wadsworth Atheneum, Hartford, Connect-
icut." *The Magazine Antiques* 126 (October 1984): 852–59.

Skerry 1988
Janine E. Skerry. "The Revolutionary Revere: A Critical Assess-
ment of the Silver of Paul Revere." In Patrick M. Leehey et al. *Paul
Revere—Artisan, Businessman, and Patriot: The Man Behind the Myth.*
Boston: The Paul Revere Memorial Association, 1988, 41–63.

Smith 1971
Robert C. Smith. "Finial busts on eighteenth-century Philadelphia
furniture." *The Magazine Antiques* 100 (December 1971): 900–905.

Smith 1973
Robert C. Smith. "A Philadelphia Desk-and-Bookcase from Chippendale's *Director.*" *The Magazine Antiques* 103 (January 1973): 128–35.

Snodin 1984
Michael Snodin, ed. *Rococo: Art and Design in Hogarth's England.*
London: Victoria and Albert Museum, 1984.

Snodin 1986
Michael Snodin. "Trade Cards and English Rococo." In Charles
Hind, ed. *The Rococo in England: A Symposium.* London: Victoria
and Albert Museum, 1986, 82–103.

Snodin 1990
Michael Snodin. "Paul de Lamerie's Rococo." In Susan Hare, ed. *Paul
de Lamerie: At the Sign of The Golden Ball.* London: Goldsmiths'
Company, 1990, 16–23.

Snyder 1975
Martin P. Snyder. *City of Independence: Views of Philadelphia Before
1800.* New York: Praeger Publishers, 1975.

Spawn 1963
Willman and Carol Spawn. "The Aitken Shop: Identification of an
Eighteenth-century Bindery and Its Tools." *Papers of the Biblio-
graphical Society of America* 57 (1963): 422–37.

Spawn 1983
Willman Spawn. "The Evolution of American Binding Styles in the
Eighteenth Century." In *Bookbinding in America, 1680–1910: From the
Collection of Frederick E. Maser.* Bryn Mawr, Pa.: Bryn Mawr Col-
lege Library, 1983, 29–36.

Stauffer 1907
David McNeely Stauffer, comp. *American Engravers upon Copper and
Steel.* 2 vols. New York: Grolier Club, 1907.

Steblecki 1988
Edith J. Steblecki. "Fraternity, Philanthropy, and Revolution: Paul Revere and Freemasonry." In Patrick M. Leehey et al. *Paul Revere—Artisan, Businessman, and Patriot: The Man Behind the Myth.* Boston: The Paul Revere Memorial Association, 1988, 117-47.

Swan
Abraham Swan. *The British Architect: Or, the Builder's Treasury of Stair-Cases.* 1745. Reprint, 1758 ed. New York: Da Capo Press, 1967.

Swan 1948
Mabel M. Swan. "Boston Carvers and Joiners. Part I. Pre-Revolutionary." *The Magazine Antiques* 53 (March 1948): 198-201. "Part II. Post-Revolutionary." (April 1948): 281-85.

Tatum 1976
George B. Tatum. *Philadelphia Georgian: The City House of Samuel Powel and Some of Its Eighteenth-Century Neighbors.* Middletown, Conn.: Wesleyan University Press, 1976.

Universal System
[William] Ince and [John] Mayhew. *The Universal System of Houshold Furniture.* 1762. Reprint. London: Alec Tiranti, 1960.

Van Rensselaer 1949
Florence Van Rensselaer, comp. *The Livingston Family in America and Its Scottish Origins.* Richmond, Va.: William Byrd Press, 1949.

Vincent 1974
Gilbert T. Vincent. "The Bombé Furniture of Boston." In Walter Muir Whitehill, Brock Jobe, and Jonathan Fairbanks, eds. *Boston Furniture of the Eighteenth Century.* Boston: The Colonial Society of Massachusetts, 1974, 137-96.

Wadsworth Atheneum 1985
The Great River: Art & Society of the Connecticut Valley, 1635-1820. Hartford, Conn.: Wadsworth Atheneum, 1985.

Wainwright 1964
Nicholas B. Wainwright. *Colonial Grandeur: The House and Furniture of General John Cadwalader.* Philadelphia: Historical Society of Pennsylvania, 1964.

Wallace 1931
Philip B. Wallace. *Colonial Houses, Philadelphia, Pre-Revolutionary Period.* New York: Architectural Book Publishing, 1931.

Ward 1984
Barbara McLean Ward. "Boston Goldsmiths, 1690-1730." In Ian M. G. Quimby, ed. *The Craftsman in Early America.* New York: W. W. Norton for the Henry Francis du Pont Winterthur Museum, 1984, 126-57.

Ward 1988
Gerald W. R. Ward. *American Case Furniture in the Mabel Brady Garvan and Other Collections at Yale University.* New Haven: Yale University Art Gallery, 1988.

Ward and Ward 1976
Barbara M. Ward and Gerald W. R. Ward. "The Makers of Cop-ley's Picture Frames: A Clue." *Old-Time New England* 67 (Summer-Fall 1976): 16-20.

Ward and Ward 1979
Barbara M. Ward and Gerald W. R. Ward, eds. *Silver in American Life: Selections from the Mabel Brady Garvan and Other Collections at Yale University.* New York: American Federation of Arts, 1979.

Warren 1976
David B. Warren. *Bancroft Woodcock: Silversmith.* Wilmington: Historical Society of Delaware, 1976.

Warren, Howe, and Brown 1987
David B. Warren, Katherine S. Howe, and Michael K. Brown. *Marks of Achievement: Four Centuries of American Presentation Silver.* Houston: Museum of Fine Arts, Houston, 1987.

Waterman 1945
Thomas Tileston Waterman. *The Mansions of Virginia, 1706-1776.* Chapel Hill: University of North Carolina Press, 1945.

Weil 1979
Martin Eli Weil. "A Cabinetmaker's Price Book." In Ian M. G. Quimby, ed. *American Furniture and Its Makers.* Winterthur Portfolio 13. Chicago: University of Chicago Press for The Henry Francis du Pont Winterthur Museum, 1979, 175-79.

Wenham 1931
Edward Wenham. *Domestic Silver of Great Britain and Ireland.* London: Oxford University Press, 1931.

White 1956
Philip L. White. *The Beekmans of New York in Politics and Commerce: 1647-1877.* New York: The New-York Historical Society, 1956.

Wolfe 1966
Beatrice Bancroft Wolfe. "A Coffee Pot Made by Philip Syng, Junior." *Philadelphia Museum of Art Bulletin* 41 (Spring 1966): 40-44.

Woodcock and Robinson 1988
Thomas Woodcock and John Martin Robinson. *The Oxford Guide to Heraldry.* Oxford: Oxford University Press, 1988.

Woodhouse 1927
S. W. Woodhouse, Jr. "Benjamin Randolph of Philadelphia." *The Magazine Antiques* 11 (May 1927): 366-71.

Wroth 1926
Lawrence C. Wroth. *Abel Buell of Connecticut: Silversmith, Type Founder, & Engraver.* 1926. Reprint. Middletown, Conn.: Wesleyan University Press, 1958.

Wroth 1950
Lawrence C. Wroth. "Joshua Fisher's 'Chart of Delaware Bay and River.'" *Pennsylvania Magazine of History & Biography* 74 (June 1950): 90-109.

Zimmerman 1979
Philip D. Zimmerman. "A Methodological Study in the Identification of Some Important Philadelphia Chippendale Furniture." In Ian M. G. Quimby, ed. *American Furniture and Its Makers.* Winterthur Portfolio 13. Chicago: University of Chicago Press for The Henry Francis du Pont Winterthur Museum, 1979, 193-205.

Exhibition Checklist

The Metropolitan Museum of Art, 26 January–17 May 1992

Los Angeles County Museum of Art, 5 July–27 September 1992

1

Thomas Chippendale, *The Gentleman and Cabinet-Maker's Director*
(London, 1754), open to Plate XII, chair designs
Engraving on paper, 13½ x 8¾ in. (34.3 x 22.2 cm.)
The Metropolitan Museum of Art, Rogers Fund, 1952 (52.519.94)

2

M. Lock and H. Copland, *A New Book of Ornaments with Twelve
Leaves* (London, 1752), open to a chimneypiece design
Engraving on paper, 9⅞ x 7 in. (25.1 x 17.8 cm.)
The Metropolitan Museum of Art, Harris Brisbane Dick Fund,
1928 (28.88.7)

3

Abraham Swan, *The British Architect* (London, 1745),
open to Plate LI, a chimneypiece design
Engraving on paper, 13¾ x 8½ in. (34.9 x 21.6 cm.)
The Metropolitan Museum of Art, Gift of W. Gedney Beatty,
1941 (41.100.30)

4

John Norman, after Abraham Swan, *The British Architect*
(Philadelphia, 1775), open to Plate LI, a chimneypiece design
Engraving on paper, 13⅞ x 8⅛ in. (35.2 x 20.6 cm.)
The Metropolitan Museum of Art, Harris Brisbane Dick Fund,
1943 (43.26.1)

5

*Proposals for Printing by Subscription The Gentleman and
Cabinet-Maker's Assistant* (Philadelphia, 1775)
Bound into John Norman's edition of *The British Architect*
Printed paper, 16½ x 9½ in. (41.9 x 24.1 cm.)
Avery Architectural and Fine Arts Library, Columbia University

6

Thomas Chippendale, *The Gentleman and Cabinet-Maker's Director*
(London, 1754), open to the title page
Printed paper, 17¼ x 11⅛ in. (43.8 x 28.3 cm.)
The Thomas J. Watson Library, The Metropolitan Museum of Art

7

Flintlock rifle, 1812–20
Jacob Kuntz, Philadelphia
Maple, iron, brass, silver, bone, and horn
L.: 59¼ in. (150.5 cm.)
The Metropolitan Museum of Art,
Gift of Wilfrid Wood, 1956 (42.22)

8

Pair of flintlock pistols, 1812–20
Jacob Kuntz, Philadelphia
Maple, iron, brass, silver, and pearl
L.: 14¼ in. (36.2 cm.)
Private collection

9

Flintlock rifle, ca. 1790
Simon Lauck, Winchester, Virginia
Maple, iron, brass, and silver
L.: 60½ in. (153.7 cm.)
Private collection

10

Arms of the Flower family, 1765
Elizabeth Flower, Philadelphia
Embroidery on silk, mahogany frame
11½ x 12¾ in. (29.2 x 32.4 cm.)
Collection of Mr. and Mrs. Edward J. Nusrala

11

Parlor chimney breast, New York, 1763–64
From Mount Pleasant, the James Beekman house
White pine, painted, 115 x 101 x 25 in.
(292.1 x 256.5 x 63.5 cm.)
The New-York Historical Society, New York;
Gift of James W. Beekman (1874.8)

12

Trade card of Joseph Welch, London, 1760–65
Engraving on paper, 6⅝ x 5⅜ in. (16.8 x 13.7 cm.)
The Metropolitan Museum of Art,
Gift of Mrs. Morris Hawkes, 1927 (27.100 [3])

13

Trade card of William Jackson, 1765–70
Attributed to Paul Revere, Boston
Engraving on paper
7⅝ x 6¼ in. (19.4 x 15.9 cm.)
American Antiquarian Society

14

Bookplate of Thomas Dering
Nathaniel Hurd, Boston, 1749
Engraving on paper
2⅞ x 2½ in. (7.3 x 6.4 cm.)
The Metropolitan Museum of Art,
Gift of William E. Baillie, 1920

15

Bookplate with Oliver family arms
Thomas Johnston, Boston, 1755–65
Engraving on paper
3⅞ x 3⅛ in. (9.8 x 7.9 cm.)
American Antiquarian Society

16

Bookplate of Epes Sargent
Paul Revere, Boston, 1764
Engraving on paper
3¼ x 2½ in. (8.3 x 6.4 cm.)
American Antiquarian Society

17

Bookplate of Gardiner Chandler
Paul Revere, Boston, ca. 1765
Engraving on paper
3⅜ x 2¾ in. (8.6 x 7 cm.)
American Antiquarian Society

18

Bookplate of John Burnet
Henry Dawkins, New York, 1754
Engraving on paper
3⅞ x 3 in. (9.8 x 7.6 cm.)
The Metropolitan Museum of Art,
Gift of William E. Baillie, 1920

19

Plate for Philip Van Rensselaer bookplate
Andrew Billings, Poughkeepsie, New York, 1768–86
Engraving on copper, 3⅞ x 2⅞ in. (9.8 x 7.3 cm.)
Historic Cherry Hill (12976.1)

With recent impression of *Philip Van Rensselaer bookplate*
Engraving on paper, 3¾ x 2¾ in. (9.5 x 7 cm.)
Historic Cherry Hill (12978)

20

Bookplate of Jeremias Van Rensselaer
Elisha Gallaudet, New York, 1761
Engraving on paper, 3½ x 2⅝ in. (8.9 x 6.7 cm.)
Historic Cherry Hill (12977)

21

Bookplate of Isaac Norris
James Turner, Philadelphia, ca. 1757
Engraving on paper, 3⅛ x 2⅜ in. (7.9 x 6 cm.)
On inside cover of *Examen Concilii Tridentini* (Dortrecht, 1678)
Dickinson College Special Collections (Norris/270/G338/c.2)

22

Bookplate of Francis Hopkinson
Henry Dawkins, Philadelphia, ca. 1768
Engraving on paper, 3½ x 3 in. (8.9 x 7.6 cm.)
American Antiquarian Society

23

James Lyon, *Urania* (Philadelphia, 1761)
Open to title page, by Henry Dawkins
Engraving on paper, 4 x 8½ in. (10.2 x 21.6 cm.)
American Antiquarian Society

24

Hugh Blair, *Lectures on Rhetoric and Belles Lettres*
(Philadelphia, 1784), showing back cover
Robert Aitkin, binder and publisher
Red morocco, gold tooled
10⅝ x 8⅝ x 1⅞ in. (27 x 22 x 4.8 cm.)
American Antiquarian Society

25

Trade card of Lewis Deblois
Thomas Johnston, Boston, 1757
Engraving on paper
6⅜ x 7⅝ in. (16.2 x 19.4 cm.)
The Winterthur Library: Joseph Downs Collection
of Manuscripts & Printed Ephemera (66x152)

26

Trade card of Nicholas Brown & Company
Nathaniel Hurd, Boston, ca. 1762
Engraving on paper, 6¼ x 7⅞ in. (15.9 x 20 cm.)
The John Carter Brown Library at Brown University (08643)

27

Trade card of Joseph Webb
Paul Revere, Boston, 1765
Engraving on paper
7½ x 6 in. (19.1 x 15.2 cm.)
American Antiquarian Society

28

Notification of meeting, Saint Peter's Lodge, Newburyport
Paul Revere, Boston, 1772
Engraving on paper, 7¾ x 6½ in. (19.7 x 16.5 cm.)
American Antiquarian Society

29

*Certificate of attendance at Dr. John Warren's
anatomical lectures*
Paul Revere, Boston, 1780
Engraving on paper, 9¼ x 7⅝ in. (23.5 x 19.4 cm.)
American Antiquarian Society

30

Trade card of Anthony Lamb
Henry Dawkins, New York, ca. 1755
Engraving on paper
11 x 7½ in. (27.9 x 19.1 cm.)
The New-York Historical Society, New York

31

Invitation for the Hand-in-Hand Fire Company
Possibly by Henry Dawkins, New York, ca. 1755
Engraving on paper, 7⅞ x 6½ in. (20 x 16.5 cm.)
I. N. Phelps Stokes Collection, Miriam and Ira D. Wallach
Division of Art, Prints and Photographs, The New York Public
Library, Astor, Lenox and Tilden Foundations (C. 1750-C-16)

32

Trade card of Benjamin Randolph
James Smither, Philadelphia, 1769
Engraving on paper, 9 x 7 in. (22.9 x 17.8 cm.)
The Library Company of Philadelphia (P.9178.6)

33

Trade card of Robert Kennedy
James Smither, Philadelphia, ca. 1769
Engraving on paper, 10 x 7¼ in. (25.4 x 18.4 cm.)
Winterthur Museum (60.729)

34

Certificate of membership, New York Mechanick Society
Abraham Godwin, New York, 1786
Engraving on paper, 8½ x 11⅛ in. (21.6 x 28.3 cm.)
Winterthur Museum (58.1797)

35

Certificate of membership, Boston Marine Society
Joseph Callender, Boston, 1789
Engraving on paper, 9¼ x 15 in. (23.5 x 38.1 cm.)
Boston Marine Society

36

Writing certificate
Attributed to Abel Buell, in association
with James Rivington, New Haven, ca. 1775
Engraving on paper, 15¾ x 12½ in. (40 x 31.8 cm.)
With lines penned by Susanna Darling, aged eight
The New-York Historical Society, New York
(Shown only in New York)

36a

Writing certificate
Attributed to Abel Buell, in association
with James Rivington, New Haven, ca. 1775
Engraving on paper, 15¾ x 12½ in. (40 x 31.8 cm.)
With lines penned by Matthew Talcott 2nd, 1793
Connecticut Historical Society, Hartford (1982-110-1)
(Shown only in Los Angeles)

37

Plan of Bethlehem Tract with all the adjacent Land
Attributed to Andreas Hoeger, Bethlehem, Pennsylvania, 1755
Ink and wash on paper, 24½ x 31¾ in. (62.2 x 80.7 cm.)
Moravian Historical Society

38

Chart of Delaware Bay
Drawn by Joshua Fisher; engraved by James Turner
Philadelphia, 1756
Engraving on paper, 23⅝ x 45⅛ in. (60 x 114.6 cm.)
The John Carter Brown Library at Brown University

39

Chart of Delaware Bay and River
Probably by Joshua Fisher, Philadelphia, ca. 1775
Ink and watercolor on paper
17⅛ x 27¼ in. (43.5 x 69.2 cm.)
The Historical Society of Pennsylvania (OF 381* 1756)

40

Plan of the Improved Part of the City
After Nicholas Scull, possibly by
Henry Dawkins, Philadelphia, 1762
Engraving on paper, 20⅛ x 26¾ in. (51.1 x 68 cm.)
I.N. Phelps Stokes Collection, Miriam and Ira D. Wallach
Division of Art, Prints and Photographs, The New York Public
Library, Astor, Lenox and Tilden Foundations (P. 1761-B-57)

41

A General Chart of all the Coast of the Province of Louisiana
Henry Dawkins, Philadelphia, 1760–65
Engraving on paper, 14½ x 40½ in. (36.8 x 102.9 cm.)
Map Division, The New York Public Library,
Astor, Lenox and Tilden Foundations

42

Map of the United States of America
Abel Buell, New Haven, 1784
Engraving on paper, 42¾ x 48 in. (108.6 x 121.9 cm.)
The New Jersey Historical Society, Newark, New Jersey

43

Dial of clock by Burrows Dowdney, Philadelphia, ca. 1770
Brass, silvered, 16⅜ x 12 in. (41.6 x 30.5 cm.)
The Dietrich American Foundation

44

Dial of a musical clock
Daniel Burnap, maker and engraver
East Windsor, Connecticut, 1790–94
Brass, silvered, 16⅝ x 12 in. (42.2 x 30.5 cm.)
Historic Deerfield, Inc., Deerfield, Massachusetts (#78-144)

45

Dial of clock by Reuben Ingraham
Engraved by John Avery, Plainfield, Connecticut, 1785–94
Brass, silvered, 16 x 12 in. (40.6 x 30.5 cm.)
Collection of Mr. and Mrs. Frank A. Mauri

46

Coffee pot, 1759–60
Arthur Annesley, London
Silver, H.: 11½ in. (29.2 cm.)
Essex Institute, Salem, Massachusetts (#137,360)

47

Coffee pot, 1772
Paul Revere, Boston
Silver, H.: 12 in. (30.5 cm.)
Private collection

48

Tea set, ca. 1765–75
Pieter de Riemer, New York
Silver, H.: teapot, 6¾ in. (17.2 cm.),
sugar bowl, 4¾ in. (12.1 cm.),
cream pot, 5½ in. (14 cm.)
Museum of the City of New York,
Gift of Mrs. Francis P. Garvan (51.304A-D)

49

Selections from a wedding service, 1773
Paul Revere, Boston
Silver, H.: coffee pot, 13½ in. (34.3 cm.), teapot, 6⅝ in.
(16.8 cm.), cann, 5 in. (12.7 cm.), butter boat, 4⅜ in.
(11.1 cm.); L.: dessert spoon, 8¾ in. (22.2 cm.), teaspoon,
5⅜ in. (13.7 cm.), tea tongs, 5⅜ in. (13.7 cm.)
Worcester Art Museum, Worcester, Massachusetts,
dessert spoon (1937.56), coffee pot (1937.58), cann (1937.59),
Gift of Frances Thomas and Eliza Sturgis Paine in memory of
Frederick William Paine; butter boat (1965.335), tea tongs
(1965.336), teaspoon (1965.337), Gift of the Paine Charitable
Trust; teapot (1967.57), Gift of Richard K. Thorndike

50

Teapot, ca. 1753
John Coburn, Boston
Silver, H.: 6½ in. (16.5 cm.)
Historic Deerfield, Inc.,
Deerfield, Massachusetts (#75-494)

51

Teapot, ca. 1765–70
Paul Revere, Boston
Silver, H.: 5⅞ in. (14.9 cm.)
Museum of Fine Arts, Boston,
Pauline Revere Thayer Collection (35.1775)

52

Teapot, ca. 1755–60
Joseph Richardson, Philadelphia
Silver, H.: 6 in. (15.2 cm.)
The Historical Society of Pennsylvania,
Gift of Edward C. Gardiner, 1945 (S-8-179)

53

Teapot, 1760–70
Philip Syng, Jr., Philadelphia
Silver, H.: 5½ in. (14 cm.)
Diplomatic Reception Rooms, Department of State.
Gift of Alice Harrison Warwick, Virginia Henley Ameche,
and John Edward Warwick in memory of their mother,
Mrs. Alice Harrison-Smith Warwick (66.97.1)

54

Teapot, 1760–70
Gabriel Lewyn, Baltimore
Silver, H.: 6 in. (15.2 cm.)
Yale University Art Gallery,
John Marshall Phillips Collection (1955.10.4)

55

Cream pot, ca. 1760
Philip Hulbeart, Philadelphia
Silver, H.: 4¼ in. (10.8 cm.)
Philadelphia Museum of Art,
Given by Walter M. Jeffords ('58-115-1)

56

Sugar dish and cream pot, 1760–75
Myer Myers, New York
Silver, H.: sugar dish, 6¾ in. (17.2 cm.),
cream pot, 6¾ in. (17.2 cm.)
Collection of David M. Brinckerhoff,
Nelson F. Brinckerhoff, Peter R. Brinckerhoff,
and Robert W. Brinckerhoff, and their families

57

Sugar dish, 1760–75
Attributed to Jacob Gerritse Lansing, Albany, New York
Silver, H.: 4⅝ in. (11.8 cm.)
Albany Institute of History and Art (1949.34.3 a, b)

58

Sugar dish and cream pot, 1761–62
Paul Revere, Boston
Silver, H.: sugar dish, 6½ in. (16.5 cm.),
cream pot, 4⅜ in. (11.1 cm.)
Museum of Fine Arts, Boston,
Pauline Revere Thayer Collection (35.1781; 35.1782)

59

Cream pot, 1755–70
Samuel Casey, Rhode Island
Silver, H.: 4 in. (10.2 cm.)
Museum of Fine Arts, Boston,
Gift of Mrs. Charles Gaston Smith's Group (39.765)

60

Coffee pot, 1781
Paul Revere, Boston
Silver, H.: 12⅞ in. (32.7 cm.)
Museum of Fine Arts, Boston,
Gift of Mrs. Nathaniel Thayer (31.139)

61

Coffee pot on stand, 1770–80
Richard Humphreys, Philadelphia
Silver, H.: pot, 13⅝ in. (34.6 cm.);
Diam.: stand, 6¾ in. (17.2 cm.)
Museum of Fine Arts, Boston, Gift in Memory of
Dr. George Clymer by his wife, Mrs. Clymer (56.589; 56.590)

62

Coffee pot, ca. 1753
Philip Syng, Jr., Philadelphia
Silver, H.: 11⅞ in. (30.2 cm.)
Philadelphia Museum of Art, Purchased:
John D. McIlhenny Fund (66-20-1)

63

Coffee pot, 1760–75
Charles Hall, Lancaster, Pennsylvania
Silver, H.: 10¾ in. (27.3 cm.)
From the Collections of Henry Ford Museum
& Greenfield Village (58.81.2)

64

Coffee pot, 1755–65
Alexander Petrie, Charleston
Silver, H.: 10⅜ in. (26.4 cm.)
Museum of Early Southern Decorative Arts (3996)

65

Coffee pot, ca. 1754
Joseph Richardson, Philadelphia
Silver, H.: 11 in. (27.9 cm.)
The Historical Society of Pennsylvania,
Gift of Edward C. Gardiner, 1945 (S-6-22)

66

Tankard, ca. 1770
Myer Myers, New York
Silver, H.: 6¾ in. (17.2 cm.)
Wadsworth Atheneum, Hartford, Connecticut,
Philip H. Hammerslough Collection (1983.154)

67

Tankard, 1750–58
Attributed to William Bradford, Jr., New York
Pewter, H.: 7⅛ in. (18.1 cm.)
Winterthur Museum (59.34)

68

Tankard, 1760–75
John Bayly, Philadelphia
Silver, H.: 8 in. (20.3 cm.)
Wadsworth Atheneum, Hartford, Connecticut,
Philip H. Hammerslough Collection (1983.497)

69

Bowl, 1750–70
Philip Syng, Jr., Philadelphia
Silver, Diam.: 9 in. (22.9 cm.)
Philadelphia Museum of Art, Given by
Mr. and Mrs. Walter M. Jeffords ('59-2-16)

70

Bowl, 1755–70
Richard Van Dyck, New York
Silver, Diam.: 7⅜ in. (18.7 cm.)
Yale University Art Gallery,
The Mabel Brady Garvan Collection (1930.1068)

71

Salver, ca. 1761
Paul Revere, Boston
Silver, Diam.: 13⅛ in. (33.3 cm.)
Museum of Fine Arts, Boston, Gift of
Henry Davis Sleeper in memory of his mother,
Maria Westcote Sleeper (25.592)

72

Salver, ca. 1768
Myer Myers, New York
Silver, Diam.: 12 in. (30.5 cm.)
Collection of Philip Van Rensselaer Van Wyck

73

Salver, 1765–70
John Heath, New York
Silver, Diam.: 15⅛ in. (38.4 cm.)
Winterthur Museum (59.2301)

74

Salver, 1754–69
Daniel Christian Fueter, New York
Silver, Diam.: 15⅝ in. (39.7 cm.)
The Metropolitan Museum of Art,
Bequest of Charles Allen Munn, 1924 (24.109.37)

75

Salver, ca. 1754
Philip Syng, Jr., Philadelphia
Silver, Diam.: 8½ in. (21.6 cm.)
The Historical Society of Pennsylvania,
Gift of Edward C. Gardiner, 1945 (S-6-21)

76

Pair of sauceboats, 1770–80
Richard Humphreys, Philadelphia
Silver, H.: 6¾ in. (17.2 cm.)
Private collection, courtesy of the
Philadelphia Museum of Art

77

Whistle and bells, 1755–68
Nicholas Roosevelt, New York
Gold; coral, H.: 6⅛ in. (15.6 cm.)
The Metropolitan Museum of Art,
Rogers Fund, 1947 (47.70)

78

Shoe buckle, 1755–75
Myer Myers, New York
Gold; steel, L.: 2⅜ in. (6 cm.); W.: 1¾ in. (4.5 cm.)
Yale University Art Gallery, The Mabel Brady Garvan Collection
(1936.166)

79

Snuff box, 1755–75
Myer Myers, New York
Gold, Diam.: 2⅜ in. (6 cm.)
The Metropolitan Museum of Art, Purchase,
Mr. and Mrs. Marshall P. Blankarn Gift, 1966 (66.102)

80

Snuff box, 1755–70
Joseph Richardson, Philadelphia
Silver, L.: 3 in. (7.6 cm.); W.: 2⅜ in. (6 cm.)
Private collection, courtesy of the
Sterling and Francine Clark Art Institute (TR 314/85)

81

Basket, 1754–69
Daniel Christian Fueter, New York
Silver, L.: 14⅞ in. (37.8 cm.)
Museum of Fine Arts, Boston,
Decorative Arts Special Fund (54.857)

82

Basket, ca. 1756
Myer Myers, New York
Silver, L.: 14½ in. (36.8 cm.)
The Metropolitan Museum of Art,
Morris K. Jesup Fund, 1954 (54.167)

83

Fish slice, 1755–75
Myer Myers, New York
Silver, L.: 14⅛ in. (35.9 cm.)
Wadsworth Atheneum, Hartford, Connecticut,
Philip H. Hammerslough Collection (1983.181)

84

Ladle, ca. 1763
Pieter de Riemer, New York
Silver, L.: 13⅝ in. (34.6 cm.)
Private collection

85

Cruet stand, 1754–69
Daniel Christian Fueter, New York
Silver, H.: 10 in. (25.4 cm.)
With silver casters marked by Samuel Wood,
London, 1752–53, and English glass cruets
Historic Deerfield, Inc.,
Deerfield, Massachusetts (#61-273)

86

Snuffer stand, 1750–70
Philip Syng, Jr., Philadelphia
Silver, L.: 7⅜ in. (18.7 cm.)
The Metropolitan Museum of Art,
Bequest of Charles Allen Munn, 1924 (24.109.39)

87

Ale jug, 1755–75
Myer Myers, New York
Silver, H.: 11¾ in. (29.9 cm.)
Private collection

88

Teakettle on stand, 1745–55
Joseph Richardson, Philadelphia
Silver, H.: 14¾ in. (37.5 cm.)
Yale University Art Gallery,
The Mabel Brady Garvan Collection (1932.93)

89

Picture frame, Boston, ca. 1765
White pine, gilded, 29½ x 24½ in. (74.9 x 62.2 cm.)
With portrait of Mrs. Edward Green by John Singleton Copley
The Metropolitan Museum of Art,
Purchase, Curtis Fund, 1908 (08.1)
(Shown only in New York)

90

Picture frame, Boston, ca. 1767
White pine, gilded, 66¾ x 47⅜ in. (169.6 x 120.3 cm.)
With portrait of Nicholas Boylston by John Singleton Copley
The Harvard University Portrait Collection,
Harvard University, Cambridge, Massachusetts,
Bequest of Ward Nicholas Boylston, 1828 (H 90)

91

Picture frame, Boston, ca. 1770
White pine, gilded, 65¾ x 60½ in. (167 x 153.7 cm.)
With portrait of Richard Dana by John Singleton Copley
Collection of the Richard Henry Dana family

92

Frame, Boston, ca. 1767
White pine, gilded, 24 x 24 in. (61 x 61 cm.)
With the Williams family arms embroidered on satin
Collection of Mr. and Mrs. George M. Kaufman

93

Chest-on-chest, 1782
Signed and dated by John Cogswell, Boston
Mahogany; white pine, 89½ x 44¾ x 23½ in.
(227.3 x 113.7 x 59.7 cm.)
Museum of Fine Arts, Boston,
William Francis Warden Fund (1973.289)

94

Chest of drawers, Salem, ca. 1780
Mahogany; white pine, cedar
35 x 45¼ x 21 in. (88.9 x 114.9 x 53.3 cm.)
Collection of Erving and Joyce Wolf
(Shown only in New York)

95

Chest of drawers, Boston, 1775–85
Mahogany; white pine, 31½ x 35¾ x 20¼ in.
(80 x 90.8 x 51.4 cm.)
The Dietrich American Foundation

96

Side chair, Boston, 1765–85
Mahogany; maple, white pine
38¾ x 23⅝ x 21 in. (98.4 x 60 x 53.3 cm.)
The Metropolitan Museum of Art,
Gift of Mrs. Paul Moore, 1939 (39.88.1)

97

Side chair, Boston, 1765–85
Mahogany; maple, 38 x 23¾ x 22 in.
(96.5 x 60.3 x 55.9 cm.)
The Metropolitan Museum of Art,
Rogers Fund, 1944 (44.55)

98

Card table, Boston, 1765–85
Mahogany; maple, 28 x 35½ x 18 in.
(71.1 x 90.2 x 45.7 cm.)
Collection of Erving and Joyce Wolf
(Shown only in New York)

99

Settee, Boston, 1765–85
Mahogany; maple, cedar, birch, white pine
36⅜ x 57½ x 26 in. (92.4 x 146.1 x 66 cm.)
The Metropolitan Museum of Art, The Sylmaris Collection,
Gift of George Coe Graves, 1930 (30.120.59)

100

Side chair, Boston, 1765–85
Mahogany; maple, white pine
37½ x 25¼ x 24 in. (95.3 x 64.1 x 61 cm.)
The Chipstone Foundation (1976.4)

101

Side chair, England, ca. 1750
Mahogany; beech, 37¼ x 23¼ x 19¼ in.
(94.6 x 59.1 x 48.9 cm.)
Museum of Fine Arts, Boston, Gift of Mrs. Joshua Crane Sr.
in memory of her husband (30.726)

102

China table, Portsmouth, New Hampshire, 1762–80
Mahogany; white pine, 28¼ x 36½ x 22⅜ in.
(71.8 x 92.7 x 56.8 cm.)
The Carnegie Museum of Art, Pittsburgh, Gift of
Richard King Mellon Foundation, 1972 (72.55.2)

103

Picture frame, 1761–62
Stephen Dwight, New York
White pine, gilded, 52¾ x 40 in. (134 x 101.6 cm.)
With portrait of James Beekman by Lawrence Kilburn
The New-York Historical Society, New York;
Gift of the Beekman Family Association (1962.64)

103a

Picture frame, 1761–62
Stephen Dwight, New York
White pine, gilded, 52¾ x 39⅞ in. (134 x 101.3 cm.)
With portrait of Jane Beekman by Lawrence Kilburn
The New-York Historical Society, New York;
Gift of the Beekman Family Association (1962.65)

104

Picture frame, England, ca. 1760
Red pine, gilded, 54¼ x 45¾ in. (137.8 x 116.2 cm.)
With portrait of Abraham Beekman attributed
to Lawrence Kilburn
The New-York Historical Society, New York;
Gift of the Beekman Family Association (1962.66)

105

Picture frame, 1767
James Strachan, New York
White pine, gilded, 43½ x 35½ in. (110.5 x 90.2 cm.)
With portrait of James Beekman, Jr., by John Durand
The New-York Historical Society, New York;
Gift of the Beekman Family Association (1962.71)

106

Tea table, New York, 1760–75
Mahogany, H.: 29 in. (73.7 cm.);
Diam.: 29 in. (73.7 cm.)
The Chipstone Foundation (1968.3)

107

Tea table, New York, 1760–75
Mahogany, H.: 29 in. (73.7 cm.); Diam.: 45⅜ in. (115.3 cm.)
The National Society of Colonial Dames in the State of
New York; Van Cortlandt House (VC 1988.6)

108

Card table, New York, 1765–75
Mahogany; tulip poplar, pine
26¾ x 34⅛ x 33¼ in. (68 x 86.7 x 84.5 cm.)
Collection of Mrs. Murray Braunfeld,
Courtesy of the Los Angeles County Museum of Art
(Shown only in Los Angeles)

108a

Card table, New York, 1765–75
Mahogany; tulip poplar, pine
26¾ x 34 x 33⅜ in. (68 x 86.4 x 84.8 cm.)
The New-York Historical Society, New York;
Gift of the Beekman Family Association (1962.61a)
(Shown only in New York)

109

Card table, New York, 1765–70
Mahogany; tulip poplar, white oak, white pine
27⅞ x 35 x 17¾ in. (70.8 x 88.9 x 45.1 cm.)
The Metropolitan Museum of Art, Purchase,
Joseph Pulitzer Bequest, 1947 (47.35)

110

Desk and bookcase, New York, 1755–60
Mahogany; tulip poplar, 99½ x 45½ x 25 in.
(252.7 x 115.6 x 63.5 cm.)
The Chipstone Foundation (1991.5)

111

Chest of drawers, New York, 1755–65
Mahogany; tulip poplar, 33 x 35½ x 20¾ in.
(83.8 x 90.2 x 52.7 cm.)
Winterthur Museum (54.86)

112

Side chair, New York, 1765–75
Mahogany; sweet gum, 38⅞ x 24¼ x 22¼ in.
(98.7 x 66.1 x 56.5 cm.)
The Metropolitan Museum of Art, Purchase, The Sylmaris
Collection, Gift of George Coe Graves, by exchange, 1957
(57.158.1)

113

Armchair, New York, ca. 1775
Mahogany; red oak, sweet gum
39½ x 30 x 23½ in. (100.3 x 76.2 x 59.7 cm.)
The Metropolitan Museum of Art, Bequest of
Barbara Bradley Manice, 1984 (1984.287)

114

Picture frame, Charleston, ca. 1766
White pine, gilded and painted
61⅜ x 51⅝ in. (155.9 x 131.1 cm.)
With portrait of Barnard Elliott, Jr., by Jeremiah Theus
Gibbes Museum of Art (30.1.7)

115

Picture frame, Charleston, ca. 1767
Cypress, gilded, 37 x 32 in. (94 x 81.3 cm.)
With portrait of Mrs. John Beale by John Wollaston
Museum of Early Southern Decorative Arts,
Gift of Mrs. Jan Mendall (3050)

116

Memorial to Lady Anne Murray, Charleston, 1768–72
White pine, marbleized
73½ x 51¼ in. (186.7 x 130.2 cm.)
First Scots Presbyterian Church, Charleston

117

Tea table, Williamsburg, 1755–70
Mahogany, H.: 28¾ in. (73 cm.); Diam.: 32⅞ in. (83.5 cm.)
Robert E. Lee Memorial Association, Inc.,
Stratford Hall Plantation (G.1959.1)

118

Tea table, Charleston, 1755–70
Mahogany, H.: 28 in. (71.1 cm.); Diam.: 31¼ in. (79.4 cm.)
Museum of Early Southern Decorative Arts (2181)

119

China table, Williamsburg, 1760–75
Mahogany, 30⅛ x 36⅜ x 23¼ in.
(76.5 x 92.4 x 59.1 cm.)
The Colonial Williamsburg Foundation (G1980-95)

120

China table, Williamsburg, ca. 1775
Mahogany, 31½ x 36 x 22¼ in. (80 x 91.4 x 56.5 cm.)
Collection of Mr. and Mrs. George M. Kaufman

121

Pembroke table, Charleston, 1770–75
Mahogany; ash, 29 x 42 x 26 in. (73.7 x 106.7 x 66 cm.)
The Charleston Museum, Charleston, South Carolina (1952.27)

122

Easy chair, Charleston, 1765–75
Mahogany; cypress, 48½ x 37 x 32¼ in.
(123.2 x 94 x 81.9 cm.)
Winterthur Museum (60.1058)

123

Masonic master's chair, Williamsburg, 1767–75
Stamped with the signature of Benjamin Bucktrout
Mahogany; walnut, 65½ x 31¼ x 29½ in.
(166.4 x 79.4 x 74.9 cm.)
The Colonial Williamsburg Foundation (1983–317)

124

Picture frame, 1770–71
James Reynolds, Philadelphia
White pine, gilded, 60 x 50 in. (152.4 x 127 cm.)
With portrait of Lambert Cadwalader by Charles Willson Peale
Philadelphia Museum of Art, Cadwalader Collection,
Purchased with funds contributed by The Pew Memorial Trust
and gift of an anonymous donor (1983-90-4)

125

Picture frame, 1772
Probably by James Reynolds, Philadelphia
White pine, gilded, 60 x 50 in. (152.4 x 127 cm.)
With portrait of the John Cadwalader family
by Charles Willson Peale
Philadelphia Museum of Art, Cadwalader Collection,
Purchased with funds contributed by The Pew Memorial Trust
and gift of an anonymous donor (1983-90-3)

126

Looking-glass frame, Philadelphia, ca. 1775
With the printed label of John Elliott
White pine, painted; northern white cedar
48 x 26 in. (121.9 x 66 cm.)
The Metropolitan Museum of Art, Purchase, Friends of the
American Wing Fund and Max H. Gluck Foundation Gift, 1990
(1990.18)

127

Looking-glass frame, 1772
Probably by James Reynolds, Philadelphia
White pine, painted, 78 x 42 in. (198.1 x 106.7 cm.)
Collection of Cliveden, a co-stewardship property of the
National Trust for Historic Preservation (NT 73.55.22 [1])
(Shown only in New York)

128

Wall bracket, Philadelphia, 1765–75
White pine, painted, 16¼ x 12⅞ x 5½ in.
(41.3 x 32.7 x 14 cm.)
Winterthur Museum (58.2242)

129

Slab table, Philadelphia, 1765–75
Mahogany, marble; pine
32 x 54 x 27 in. (81.3 x 137.2 x 68.6 cm.)
Museum of Art, Rhode Island School of Design,
Bequest of Charles L. Pendleton (04.008)

130

Slab table, Philadelphia, ca. 1770
Mahogany, marble; yellow pine, walnut
32⅜ x 48¼ x 23¼ in. (82.2 x 122.6 x 59.1 cm.)
The Metropolitan Museum of Art,
John Stewart Kennedy Fund, 1918 (18.110.27)

131

Card table, Philadelphia, 1765–75
Mahogany; northern white cedar, white oak
27⅜ x 34 x 32¾ in. (69.5 x 86.4 x 83.2 cm.)
Winterthur Museum (60.1059)

132

Card table, Philadelphia, 1765–75
Mahogany; yellow poplar
29½ x 34½ x 17 in. (74.9 x 87.6 x 43.2 cm.)
Collection of George G. Meade Easby,
On loan to Diplomatic Reception Rooms, Department of State
(Shown only in New York)

133

Tea table, Philadelphia, 1765–75
Mahogany, H.: 28¼ in. (71.8 cm.)
Diam.: 35⅜ in. (89.9 cm.)
The Dietrich American Foundation

134

Tea table, Philadelphia, 1765–75
Mahogany, H.: 27½ in. (69.9 cm.)
Diam.: 33⅜ in. (84.8 cm.)
The Metropolitan Museum of Art,
Rogers Fund, 1925 (25.115.31)

135

Tea table, Philadelphia, ca. 1775
Mahogany, painted iron; tulip poplar
27¾ x 30¼ x 20¼ in. (70.5 x 76.8 x 51.4 cm.)
Private collection

136

High chest, Philadelphia, 1765–75
American black walnut; yellow poplar, Atlantic white cedar,
southern yellow pine, 96¾ x 45½ x 23⅝ in.
(245.8 x 115.6 x 60 cm.)
Yale University Art Gallery, The Mabel Brady Garvan Collection
(1930.2000)

137

High chest, Philadelphia, 1765–75
Mahogany; tulip poplar, white cedar, yellow pine
90¼ x 45⅝ x 25½ in. (229.2 x 115.9 x 64.8 cm.)
Winterthur Museum (58.592)

138

High chest, Philadelphia, 1762–75
Mahogany; tulip poplar, white cedar, yellow pine
91¾ x 44⅝ x 24⅝ in. (233.1 x 113.4 x 62.6 cm.)
The Metropolitan Museum of Art,
John Stewart Kennedy Fund, 1918 (18.110.4)

139

Shield finial, Philadelphia, 1760–65
Mahogany, H.: 11⅜ in. (28.9 cm.)
From a high chest
Philadelphia Museum of Art,
Membership Fund from C. Hartman Kuhn ('23-58-1)

140

Scroll finial, Philadelphia, 1760–70
Mahogany, H.: 14¾ in. (37.5 cm.)
From a desk and bookcase
Philadelphia Museum of Art,
Given by George Lorimer ('29-178-1)

141

Basket finial, Philadelphia, 1765–75
Mahogany, H.: 13¾ in. (34.9 cm.)
From a chest-on-chest
Philadelphia Museum of Art, Purchased:
The Elizabeth S. Shippen Fund ('26-19-1)

142

Urn finial, Philadelphia, 1765–75
Mahogany, H.: 9¼ in. (23.5 cm.)
From a desk and bookcase
Winterthur Museum (G.56.103.2)

143

Bird finial, 1770–75
Probably by James Reynolds, Philadelphia
Mahogany, H.: 12½ in. (31.8 cm.)
From a chest-on-chest
The Metropolitan Museum of Art, Purchase,
Friends of the American Wing and Rogers Funds;
Virginia Groomes Gift, in memory of Mary W. Groomes;
and Mr. and Mrs. Frederick M. Danziger, Herman Merkin,
and Anonymous Gifts, 1975 (1975.91)

144

Finial bust of John Locke
Philadelphia, 1765–75
Mahogany, H.: 10½ in. (26.7 cm.)
From a desk and bookcase
Bernard and S. Dean Levy, Inc.

145

Finial bust of John Milton
Philadelphia, 1765–75
Mahogany, H.: 12¼ in. (31.1 cm.)
From a desk and bookcase
Private collection
(Shown only in New York)

146

Finial bust of a young man
Philadelphia, 1765–75
Mahogany, H.: 8½ in. (21.6 cm.)
From a desk and bookcase
Private collection

147

Side chair, Philadelphia, 1760–70
Mahogany; cedar, 39¾ x 25½ x 20½ in.
(101 x 64.8 x 52.1 cm.)
The Dietrich American Foundation

148

Side chair, Philadelphia, 1765–75
Mahogany; Atlantic white cedar, yellow pine
38 x 21⅞ x 21½ in. (96.5 x 55.6 x 54.6 cm.)
The Metropolitan Museum of Art, Bequest of W. Gedney Beatty
and Rogers Fund, by exchange, 1951 (51.140)

149

Easy chair, Philadelphia, 1765–70
Mahogany; white oak, 45¼ x 24⅜ x 28 in.
(114.9 x 61.9 x 71.1 cm.)
Philadelphia Museum of Art,
Purchased, Museum Fund ('29-81-2)

150

Sofa, Philadelphia, 1763–71
Mahogany; tulip poplar, oak
39⅞ x 90⅜ x 31½ in. (101.3 x 229.6 x 80 cm.)
Collection of Cliveden, a co-stewardship property of the
National Trust for Historic Preservation (NT 83.17)

151

Armchair, Philadelphia, 1765–75
Mahogany; white oak, 40¾ x 29¾ x 29½ in.
(103.5 x 75.6 x 74.9 cm.)
Collection of Mrs. Murray Braunfeld,
Promised Gift to the Los Angeles County Museum of Art

152

Armchair, Philadelphia, 1765–75
Mahogany; white oak, 43 x 28¼ x 30 in.
(109.2 x 71.8 x 76.2 cm.)
The Metropolitan Museum of Art, Purchase,
Mrs. Russell Sage and Robert G. Goelet Gifts;
The Sylmaris Collection, Gift of George Coe Graves;
and funds from various donors, 1959 (59.154)

153

Easy chair, 1770
Thomas Affleck, Philadelphia
Mahogany; yellow pine, Atlantic white cedar, black walnut,
tulip poplar, 45 x 36½ x 34 in. (114.3 x 92.7 x 86.4 cm.)
Collection of H. Richard Dietrich, Jr.

154

Pair of card tables, 1771
Thomas Affleck, Philadelphia
Mahogany; yellow pine, white oak, poplar
28¾ x 39¾ x 19¾ in. (73 x 101 x 50.2 cm.)
The Dietrich American Foundation (8.3.2778);
The Philadelphia Museum of Art, The Cadwalader Collection,
Purchased with funds contributed by The Pew Memorial Trust
(1984-6-1)

155

Side chair, ca. 1770
Thomas Affleck, Philadelphia
Mahogany; northern white cedar
37 x 24½ x 23 in. (94 x 62.2 x 58.4 cm.)
The Metropolitan Museum of Art, Purchase,
Sansbury-Mills and Rogers Funds; Emily C. Chadbourne Gift;
Virginia Groomes Gift, in memory of Mary W. Groomes;
Mr. and Mrs. Marshall P. Blankarn; John Bierwith and
Robert G. Goelet Gifts; The Sylmaris Collection, Gift of
George Coe Graves, by exchange; Mrs. Russell Sage,
by exchange; and funds from various donors, 1974 (1974.325)

156

Fire screen, 1771
Thomas Affleck, Philadelphia
Carving probably by Bernard and Jugiez
Mahogany; cross-stitch needlework
62⅞ x 21 in. (159.7 x 53.3 cm.)
The Metropolitan Museum of Art, Gifts and funds
from various donors, by exchange, 1949 (49.51);
English embroidered panel, Rogers Fund, 1952 (52.167)

157

Fireback, Massachusetts, ca. 1768
James Ruseles, retailer
Cast iron, 29 x 26 in. (73.7 x 66 cm.)
Marblehead Historical Society; Jeremiah Lee Mansion

158

Fireback, ca. 1774
Aetna Furnace, Burlington County, New Jersey
Cast iron, 31½ x 30 in. (80 x 76.2 cm.)
Winterthur Museum (58.2750)

159

Fireback, ca. 1770
Batsto Furnace, Burlington County, New Jersey
Cast iron, 26¾ x 22¼ in. (68 x 56.5 cm.)
New Jersey State Museum (75.99.1)

160

Six-plate stove, 1772
Mark Bird, Hopewell Furnace, Berks County, Pennsylvania
Cast iron, 35 x 41 x 18 in. (88.9 x 104.1 x 45.7 cm.)
Birdsboro Community Memorial Center, Birdsboro, Pennsylvania,
on loan to Hopewell Furnace National Historic Site

161

Front plate from a Franklin stove, 1772
Mark Bird, Hopewell Furnace, Berks County, Pennsylvania
Cast iron, 15 x 31¼ in. (38.1 x 79.4 cm.)
The Historical Society of Pennsylvania (X-137)

162

Side plate from a six-plate stove, ca. 1770
Attributed to Marlboro Furnace, Winchester, Virginia
Cast iron, 22 x 27¼ in. (55.9 x 69.2 cm.)
Private collection

163

Ten-plate stove, 1769
Henry William Stiegel, Elizabeth Furnace
Lancaster County, Pennsylvania
Cast iron, 63¼ x 44¼ x 15 in.
(160.7 x 112.4 x 38.1 cm.)
Hershey Museum (757.12)

164

Side plate for a ten-plate stove, ca. 1772
James Old, Reading Furnace, Berks County, Pennsylvania
Cast iron, 23 x 30 in. (58.4 x 76.2 cm.)
The State Museum of Pennsylvania,
Pennsylvania Historical and Museum Commission (09.2.313)

165

Side-plate pattern for a ten-plate stove, 1785-95
Batsto Furnace, Burlington County, New Jersey
Mahogany, 26 x 33 in. (66 x 83.8 cm.)
Burlington County Historical Society (34.6)

166

Goblet, 1773-74
Attributed to Henry William Stiegel
American Flint Glass Manufactory, Manheim, Pennsylvania
Engraving attributed to Lazarus Isaac
Glass, H.: 6¾ in. (17.2 cm.)
The Corning Museum of Glass, Part gift of
Roland C. and Sarah Katheryn Luther, Roland C. Luther III,
Edwin C. Luther III, and Ann Luther Dexter (87.4.55)

167

Covered tumbler, 1788
John Frederick Amelung, New Bremen Glassmanufactory
Frederick County, Maryland
Glass, H.: 11⅞ in. (30.2 cm.)
The Corning Museum of Glass (55.4.37)

168

Goblet, ca. 1792
John Frederick Amelung, New Bremen Glassmanufactory
Frederick County, Maryland
Glass, H.: 6¾ in. (17.2 cm.)
Collection of Mrs. Graham John Barbey,
Courtesy of the Maryland Historical Society (DEP.337)

169

Sauceboat, 1770–72
Gousse Bonnin and George Morris
American China Manufactory, Philadelphia
Porcelain, H.: 4 in. (10.2 cm.)
The Brooklyn Museum, Dick S. Ramsay Fund (42.412)

170

Sauceboat, ca. 1770
Probably Plymouth Factory, Plymouth, England
Porcelain, H.: 4¼ in. (10.8 cm.)
Collection High Museum of Art, Atlanta;
Frances and Emory Cocke Collection (1985.164)

171

Basket, 1770–72
Gousse Bonnin and George Morris
American China Manufactory, Philadelphia
Porcelain, Diam.: 5⅞ in. (14.9 cm.)
Collection of Eric Noah

172

Pickle stand, 1770–72
Gousse Bonnin and George Morris
American China Manufactory, Philadelphia
Porcelain, H.: 5⅝ in. (14.3 cm.)
The Metropolitan Museum of Art,
Friends of the American Wing Fund, 1990 (1990.19)

173

Pickle stand, 1770–72
Gousse Bonnin and George Morris
American China Manufactory, Philadelphia
Porcelain, H.: 5⅛ in. (13 cm.)
Collection of Mr. and Mrs. George M. Kaufman

Index

Italic numerals refer to supplementary illustrations. Question marks after maker's names denote attributions.

A

Adam, Robert, 4

Adams, John, 18, 137

advertisements: as documentation for furnituremakers, 153, 154, 159, 161, 166, 168, 182, 183, 184, 185; as documentation for silversmiths, 9, 74, 76, 77, 78, 91, 104, 107; (Duyckinck), 46; Fig. 24; (Smither), 39, 183; Nos. 32, 33; *see also* broadsides; trade cards

Aetna Furnace, Burlington County, New Jersey, 220, 222; chimneybacks produced by, 220, 222; No. 158

Affleck, Thomas, 183, 184, 205, 214; card tables by, 214; No. 154; easy chair by, 214; No. 153; fire screens by, 197, 217; No. 156; parlor suite by, 184, 191, 214, 217, 239; Nos. 153–156; side chairs by, 214; No. 155; sofas by, 214

Aitken, Robert, 47; *Lectures on Rhetoric and Belles Lettres*: back cover of, No. 24; bookbinding of, 47

Aitken Bible, 47

Albany: architectural decoration from, 22, 23, 25; silver produced in, 73, 88, 92–93

ale jug (Myers), 76, 106, 127; No. 87

Alexander, William (earl of Sterling), 54

Amelung, Carolina Lucia, 232

Amelung, John Frederick, 229, 231, 232, 239; *see also* New Bremen Glassmanufactory

American China Manufactory, Philadelphia, 234, 236, 239; basket produced by, 236, 239; No. 171; pickle stands produced by, 239; *218*; Nos. 172, 173; sauceboat produced by, 7, 236; No. 169

American Flint Glass Manufactory, Philadelphia, 11, 229–30, 231; goblet produced by, 230, 231; No. 166; table glass produced by, 229–31; No. 166

American Revolution, 62, 103; Boston's role in, 134; effect on American rococo

of, 11–12, 78; events leading to, 10, 11, 208; New York's role in, 9; nonimportation agreements preceding, 10–11, 71; Paul Revere and, 39

andirons (King), 185

Annapolis, Maryland, 29; architectural decoration from, 29, 31; silver produced in, 73, 101, 103

Annesley, Arthur, coffee pot by, 7, 71, 99, 129; No. 46

Apthorp, Charles, 18, 143

Apthorp, Charles Ward, 22; house of, New York City, 22

Apthorp, East, 18, 22; house of, Cambridge, 18, 20, 21, 135; Fig. 5

architectural carving, decoration, and ornament, 12, 17–18, 20, 35, 135, 153–54, 156, 214; archways, 17; Fig. 10; ceilings, 17, 23, 28, 29, 35, 175; Fig. 23; chimney breast, 23; No. 11; chimneypieces, 18, 20, 21, 22–23, 26, 28, 29, 31, 35; Figs. 5, 6, 8, 9, 12, 13, 15, 19, 22; in churches, 17, 20, 22, 25, 35, 172; No. 116; Fig. 11; doorframes, 29, 31; Fig. 16; English application of, 18; fireplaces, 17; fireplace wall, 28; Fig. 14; parlor wall, 32; Fig. 21; staircases, 17, 18, 21; Fig. 7; in stucco, 17, 28, 29, 35, 175

Architectural Remembrancer (Morris), 35

architecture, 5, 6, 17–35

archways, 17

armchairs, 165, 167, 213; Nos. 113, 151, 152; Fig. 39; (Willett), 155

arms of the Flower family, embroidery (Flower, E.), 13; No. 10

Atsion Ironworks, New Jersey, 220

Austin, W., 20

Avery, John, 69; clock dial engraved by, 69; No. 45

B

Badlam, Stephen, 136; chest-on-chest by, 136, 137, 144

Baltimore, silver produced in, 73, 87

Bampton, William, 29

Baretti, 137

Bartlett, Levi, 52

basket finial, 204; No. 141

baskets, porcelain, 236; (American China Manufactory), 236, 239; No. 171

baskets, silver, 115, 121; (Fueter), 76, 121, 122, 123, 127; *121*; No. 81; (Lamerie), 121; (Myers), 4, 75, 122–23, 124; No. 82

Batsto Furnace, New Jersey, 222, 228; chimneyback produced by, 222; No. 159; stove plates produced by, 222;

wooden pattern, used for stove-plate casting by, 228; No. 165

Bayard, John Bubenheim, 87

Bayly, John, 107; tankard marked by, 107; No. 68

Beale, John, 172; portrait of (Wollaston), 170, 172

Beale, Mrs. John, 172; portrait of (Wollaston), 170, 172; No. 115

Beau, John Anthony, 76

bedsteads, 159, 165; Fig. 38; (Elfe), 169

Beekman, Abraham, 156; portrait of (Kilburn), 7, 156; No. 104

Beekman, James, 23, 155, 156; carriages owned by, 155; furniture owned by, 155, 161; Nos. 103, 105; houses of, New York City, 22, 23, 155, 156; No. 11; portrait of (Kilburn), 155, 156; No. 103; portraits of the children of (Durand), 156; silver owned by, 109, 129, 155

Beekman, James, Jr., portrait of (Durand), 156; No. 105

Beekman, James William, 161

Beekman, Jane, 155; portrait of (Kilburn), 155, 156

Beekman family, 9; portraits of, 155, 156

Bell, Robert, 6, 183

Bennett and Dixon, New York City, 76

Bernard, Nicholas, 184; *see also* Bernard and Jugiez

Bernard and Jugiez, Philadelphia, 26–28, 183–84, 185, 220; architectural carving by, 214; chimneyback pattern by, 220, 225; fire screens by, 197; No. 156; looking-glass frames by, 187; portrait busts by, 205; side chair by (?), 209; No. 147; tea table by (?), 196–97; No. 133

Bethlehem, Pennsylvania, 59; plan for the tract of (Hoeger?), 59; No. 37

Biddle, Mary, 63

bill heads, 5, 37, 49, 52, 84; Fig. 25

Billings, Andrew, 42, 57; copper plate for bookplate by, 5, 42; No. 19

Bird, Mark, Jr., 223, 227; *see also* Hopewell Furnace

bird finials, 190, 204–5; No. 143

Blackburn, Joseph, 137

Blackwell, Robert, 28; house of, Philadelphia, 28; Fig. 13

Blair, Hugh, book by: *Lectures on Rhetoric and Belles Lettres*, 47

Blott, John, 35

blue-and-white oriental porcelain, 236

Bonnin, Gousse, 234, 236, 239; *see also* American China Manufactory

Bonnin and Morris, Philadelphia, 11, 234, 236, 239; *see also* American China Manufactory

bookbindings, 47; No. 24

bookcases, 183; (Bright), 137; (Elfe), 169

Book of Shields (Lock), 37, 204

bookplates, 5, 37, 40, 42, 45, 84, 96, 110; (Billings), copper plate for, 5, 42; No. 19; (Dawkins), 39, 40, 42, 45; Nos. 18, 22; (Gallaudet), 42, 45; No. 20; (Hurd, N.), 38, 40, 42, 50; No. 14; (Johnston), 38, 40; No. 15; (Revere), 39, 40; Nos. 16, 17; (Turner), 7, 40, 45; No. 21

Boston, 9, 18, 153; case furniture from, 136, 137, 143-45, 147; chairs from, 133, 135, 147, 151; commercial ties to Philadelphia of, 182; declining prosperity of, 74-75, 134; dominance of, 134; engraving in, 37-39, 40, 42, 46, 49-52, 59; furniture carvers immigrating to, 134; furniture imported to, 135; furniture produced in, 9, 134-52; nonimportation agreements passed in, 10-11, 134; picture frames produced in, 135, 137-38, 142; population of, 182; role in American Revolution of, 134; silver produced in, 71, 73, 74-75, 77, 84-85, 87, 96, 105, 106

Boston Marine Society, 57; certificate of membership in (Callender), 57-58; No. 35

Boston Tea Party, 11, 95

Bouquet, Henry, 64

Bow, England, porcelain produced at, 234, 236, 239

Bowen, Nathan, 136

bowls, 108-9; (Syng), 108; No. 69; (Van Dyck), 109; No. 70

Bowman, Jonathan, 135

Boylston, Mrs. Thomas, portrait of (Copley), 138; Fig. 34

Boylston, Nicholas, 137; portrait of (Copley), 138; No. 90

Bradford, Andrew, 46

Bradford, William, 46

Bradford, William, Jr., 107; tankard attributed to, 107; No. 67

Brasher, Ephraim, 76, 129, 131; tea urn marked by, 129; Fig. 31

breakfast tables, *see* pembroke tables

Breck, William, 37; trade card of (Revere), 37

Brewood, Benjamin, II, coffee pot marked by, 75, 99, 104; Fig. 26

Brewton, Miles, house of, Charleston, 35; Fig. 23

Brice, James, 29; house of, Annapolis, 29; Fig. 15

Bright, George, 136; chairs by, 135

Brinckerhoff, Abraham, 92; portrait of (Stuart), 91

Brinckerhoff, Dorothea Remsen, 92; portrait of (Trumbull), 92

Brinner, John, 154

British Architect: Or, the Builder's Treasury of Stair-Cases, The (Swan), 6, 18, 21, 29, 31, 32, 183; engraving from, No. 3; copy after (Norman), 6, 68; No. 4

broadsides, 6, 46, 89, 183; No. 5

Brooks, Peter Chardon, 57-58

Brown, Nicholas, & Company, Providence, 50; order blank of (Hurd, N.), 50; No. 26

Buckland, William, 18, 29, 31, 32

Bucktrout, Benjamin, 166, 167, 180; Masonic master's chair by, 31, 166, 180-81; No. 123

Buell, Abel, 58, 64; map of United States engraved by, 59, 64; No. 42; writing certificate engraved by, 58, 64; *36*; No. 36

Burbeck, Edward, 20

Burling, Thomas, 154, 155; chests by, 162; linen presses by, 162; tea tables by, 159

Burnap, Daniel, 68; dial of chime clock by, 66, 68; No. 44

Burnet, John, 42; bookplate of (Dawkins), 39, 42; No. 18

Burnett, Henry, 35

butter boats (Revere), 83; No. 49

buttons, 115, 119

Byrd, William, 31, 124; plantation of, Westover, near Williamsburg, 31, 175

Byrd, William, III, 175; table of, No. 119

Byrd family, 121, 175

C

Cabinet and Chair-Maker's Real Friend and Companion, The (Manwaring), 3, 135, 137, 147, 165; design for a "Parlour" chair from, Fig. 36

cabinetmaking, *see* furniture (furnituremaking)

Cadwalader, Anne, portrait of (Peale), 186; No. 125

Cadwalader, Elizabeth Lloyd, 80, 185; portrait of (Peale), 186; No. 125

Cadwalader, John: account books of, 15; furniture of, 28, 183, 184, 185, 189, 191-92, 197, 214, 217; *132*; Nos. 124, 125, 130, 153-156; furniture of, secured, during the Revolution, 9; house of, Philadelphia, 214, 217 (architectural carving for, 183, 214, 239; renovations to, 28, 184, 185); inventory taken after the death of, 217; marriage of, 80; orders from London placed by, 185; parlor suite ordered by, 184, 185, 191, 214, 217, 239; Nos. 153-156; as patron, 185; porcelain owned by, 239; portrait

of (Peale), 186, 217; No. 125; portraits of family commissioned by (Peale), 186, 217; Nos. 124, 125; silver owned by, 80, 99, 104, 117, 126

Cadwalader, Lambert, 186; portrait of (Peale), 186; No. 124

Cadwalader, Martha, 186; portrait of (Peale), 186

Cadwalader, Mrs. Thomas, 186; portrait of (Peale), 186

Cadwalader, Thomas, 186; portrait of (Peale), 186

cake baskets, *see* baskets, silver

Callender, Joseph, 58; certificate engraved by, 57-58; No. 35

Cambridge, Massachusetts, architectural decoration from, 17, 18, 20

canns, 105, 106, 127; (Myers), 122; (Revere), 83, 106; No. 49; (Syng), 109

capitol chair (Wilson?), 167, 168; Fig. 39

card tables, 147, 155, 161, 165, 194-95, 217; Nos. 98, 108, 109, 131, 132; (Affleck), 214; No. 154; (Cox), 161; (Prince), 161; (Willett), 161

Carroll, Charles, Barrister, 88, 92, 104

Carter, Robert, 95, 166

cartouches: on bookplates, 40, 42, 45; on book title page, 47; in clock dial, 69; design for (Copland), 2, 45; Fig. 3; on finials, 204; on firearms, 12, 13; on gold, 119; on maps, 37, 38, 50, 59, 61, 62, 63, 64; on pewter, 107; on printed ephemera, 37, 54; as signature motif of rococo style in America, 84; on silver objects, 72, 84, 85, 91, 96, 101, 106, 108, 109, 110, 113, 114, 119, 121, 124, 126, 127, 129; on trade cards, 37, 49, 54; on wooden frames, 172; *see also* furniture (furnituremaking)

case furniture, 136, 137, 143-45, 147, 162, 178, 199, 202, 204, 220, 222; Nos. 94, 95, 110, 111, 136-138; Figs. 42, 43, 47; (Cogswell), 11, 136, 137, 143, 144; No. 93; (Elfe), 168; (Needham), 143-44; Fig. 35

Casey, Samuel, 94; cream pot marked by, 94; No. 59

cast iron, 12, 219-28; chimneybacks, 220, 222, 225, 227; Nos. 157-159; stove plates, 220, 222, 223, 225, 227-28; Nos. 161, 162, 164; stoves, 5, 223, 225, 227; Nos. 160, 163; stoves, wooden pattern for side plate of, 228; No. 165

certificates, 37, 49, 57-58; (Buell?), 58, 64; *36*; No. 36; (Callender), 57-58; No. 35; (Godwin), 57, 89; No. 34; (Revere), 39, 52; No. 29

chairs, 7, 9, 133, 135, 136, 147, 151, 165, 166, 167, 168, 180-81, 182, 183, 185,

209-10, 217; Nos. 96, 97, 100, 101, 112, 113, 122, 123, 147-149, 151, 152; Figs. 39, 40; (Chippendale), designs for, 5; No. 1; Fig. 36; (Elfe), 169; (Elliott), 182; (Folwell), 183; (Magrath), 169; (Prince), 155; (Scott), 167

Chandler, Gardiner, 42, 110; bookplate of (Revere), 42, 110; No. 17

Chandler, Lucretia, 42; *see also* Murray, Lucretia Chandler

Charleston, South Carolina, 9, 153, 168; architectural decoration from, 17-18, 26, 35, 172; economic ties of, with London, 78; exports from, 78, 168; furniture carvers immigrating to, 134; furniture produced in, 134, 159, 166, 168-69, 170, 172, 174, 175, 177, 178, 180; nonimportation agreements passed in, 10-11; picture frames produced in, 170, 172; prosperity of, 168; silver produced in, 71, 73, 75, 78, 101, 103-4

Chase, Samuel, 29

Chase, Stephen, 152

Chase-Lloyd house, Annapolis, 29, 31; Fig. 16

Cheere, John, 205; portrait busts by, 205

Cherry Hill, Albany, 42, 92

chests, 135, 162; (Burling), 162; (Prince), 162

chests-on-chests, 162, 199, 204; (Badlam), 136, 137, 144; (Bowen and Martin), 136; (Cogswell), 11, 136, 137, 143; No. 93; (Elfe), 169; (Elfe?), 178; Fig. 42; (Skillin, J., and S., Jr.), 136

chests of drawers, 11, 136, 143-45, 153, 162; Nos. 94, 95, 111; (Needham), 136, 137, 143-44; Fig. 35

Chew, Benjamin, 26, 45, 189; house of, Germantown, 26, 28, 184, 189, 211

chime (musical) clocks, 68; dial of, 68; No. 44

chimneybacks, 21, 220, 222, 225; No. 157; (Aetna Furnace), 220, 222; No. 158; (Batsto Furnace), 222; No. 159; (Courtenay), 227

chimney breast, 23; No. 11

chimneypieces, 18, 20, 21, 22-23, 26, 28, 29, 31, 35, 155, 162, 165, 202; Figs. 5, 6, 8, 9, 12, 13, 15, 19, 22; designs for: (Lock and Copland), 5; No. 2; (Norman, after Swan), No. 4; (Swan), No. 3

chimneypiece tablet, design for (Johnson), 202; Fig. 48

china tables, 4, 135, 152, 167, 174-75; Nos. 102, 119, 120

Chippendale, Thomas, 3, 4, 32; descriptions of furniture by, 174-75; designs favored by, 183; engravings by, 4, 5, 6,

183; Nos. 1, 6; furniture made in the shop of, 155; illustrations by, 192; influence of, 6, 153, 183, 202, 209; see also *The Gentleman and Cabinet-Maker's Director*

city views and plans, 59, 63; Nos. 37, 40

Clarkson, David, 127

Clarkson, Gerardus, 47

Clarkson, Matthew, 59, 63, 64

Claypoole, James, 15; fire buckets painted by, 15, 185; painted standard on silk by, 6, 15, 89; Fig. 4

Clifton, Henry, 184; high chest by, 182, 199, 204; Fig. 47

Cliveden, Germantown, 26, 28, 184, 189, 211

clock dials, engraving on, 3, 37, 66, 68-69; No. 43; (Avery), 69; No. 45; (Burnap), 66, 68; No. 44; (Dawkins?), 68; (Harland), 68

clocks, 66, 68, 69; (Dowdney), 66, 68; No. 43

Cloverfields, Queen Annes County, Maryland, 28

Clow, James, 28

coasters, 121; (Myers), 122

coats of arms: carved (Bernard and Jugiez), 184; embroidered, 142; No. 92

Coburn, John, 85; cream pot marked by, 85; sugar caster marked by, 85; teapot marked by, 84-85; No. 50

coffee pots, 72, 80, 91-92, 96, 104, 129; (Annesley), 7, 71, 99, 129; No. 46; (Brewood II), 75, 99, 104; Fig. 26; (Hall, C.), 103, 104; No. 63; (Humphreys), 94, 96, 99; *99*; No. 61; (Inch), 103, 104; Fig. 29; (Myers), 122; (Petrie), 78, 103, 104; No. 64; (Revere), 7, 11, 71, 83, 96, 99; *97*; Nos. 47, 49, 60; (Richardson), 78, 88, 104, 113; No. 65; (Syng), 78, 101, 103, 104, 113; No. 62

Cogswell, John, 143; chest-on-chest by, 11, 136, 137, 143, 144; No. 93

Collection of Designs in Architecture (Swan), 6, 28

Collection of The best Psalm Tunes, in two, three, and four parts, A (Flagg), 46

Coney, John, 75

Connecticut, engraving in, 37, 58, 66, 68, 69

Continental Congress, 47, 101, 106; silver tea urn commissioned by, 96, 99

Coolley, Simon, 109

Coombs, William, 20

Copland, Henry, 2-3, 6, 18, 40, 45; engravings by, 2, 5, 39, 45, 225; No. 2; Fig. 3; pattern books by: *A New Book of Ornaments*, 2, 37, 155; Fig. 3; *A New Book of Ornaments with Twelve*

Leaves (with Lock), 2-3, 5, 25, 37, 155, 225; No. 2; trade cards by, 37

Copley, John Singleton, 137; frames for portraits by, 136, 137, 138, 142, 186; (Johnston), 137; (Welch), 136, 137, 138; portraits by, 39, 135, 137, 138, 142, 156; Nos. 89-91; Figs. 33, 34

Corbit house, Odessa, Delaware, 28

Cornell, Samuel, 75-76, 122, 123

Cornell, Susannah Mabson, 75-76, 122, 123

Courtenay, Hercules, 26, 28, 184, 202; architectural carving by, 214; chimneyback carved by, 227; easy chair by, 180, 210; No. 149; tea table by (?), 197; No. 134

covered tumbler (New Bremen Glassmanufactory), 232; No. 167

Cox, Joseph, 153; card tables by, 161; settee upholstered by, 153

Cox and Berry booksellers, Boston, 137

cream pots, 80, 89, 229; (Casey), 94; No. 59; (Coburn), 85; (Hulbeart), 15, 89, 91, 94, 121; No. 55; (Myers), 91-92; No. 56; (Revere), 80, 83, 93, 110; No. 58; (Riemer), 87, 91, 92, 131; No. 48

cruet stands, 124, 126; (Daniel), 126; (Fueter), 76, 124, 126; No. 85

D

Dana, Richard, 142; portrait of (Copley), 142; No. 91

Daniel, Jabez, 126; cruet stand by, 126

Dart, John, 178

Davis, Richard, 154

Dawes, Thomas, 137

Dawkins, Henry, 39, 40, 42, 52; bookplates engraved by, 39, 40, 42, 45; Nos. 18, 22; chart of the coast of Louisiana engraved by, 59, 64; No. 41; clock dial engraved by (?), 68; invitation engraved by (?), 52, 54; No. 31; music book engraved by, 46; title page of, No. 23; plan of Philadelphia engraved by (?) (after Scull), 59, 63; No. 40; trade card engraved by, 52, 54; No. 30

Dawson, Roper, 23

Dearing, Ebenezer, 21; architectural carving by, 135

Dearing, William, 21

Deas, John, 178

Deblois, Lewis, 49-50; trade card of (Johnston), 49-50; No. 25

Delaplaine, Joshua, 153, 159

Delaware Bay, chart of, engraving (Turner, after Fisher), 59, 61, 62; No. 38

Delaware Bay and River, chart of, water-
    color (Fisher), 62; No. 39
delftware, 234, 236
Derby, England, porcelain produced
    at, 234
Derby, Elias Hasket, 71, 136, 143; furni-
    ture owned by, 136-37, 143, 144, 151;
    Nos. 93, 100; Fig. 35; houses of, Salem,
    136, 143
Derby, Elizabeth Crowninshield, 71
Derby, Richard, 71, 136
Derby family, 9, 71, 136, 143
Dering, Thomas, 40; bookplate of (Hurd,
    N.), 40, 42; No. 14
Designs in Architecture (Swan), see *Collec-
    tion of Designs in Architecture*
desks, 135, 162, 183; (Bright), 137;
    (Elfe), 169
desks and bookcases, 162, 199, 202, 204,
    205, 208; No. 110
Dickinson, Edmund, 167
Dickinson, John, 45, 184, 186; portrait of
    (Peale), 186
Dickinson, Mary Norris, 45
Dickinson College, Carlisle, Pennsyl-
    vania, 40, 45
Director, The (Chippendale), see *The
    Gentleman and Cabinet-Maker's Director*
dish rings, 115, 121, 123; (Myers), 75, 122,
    123; Fig. 30
Display of Heraldry (Guillim), 38, 40
doorframes, 29, 31; Fig. 16
double chests, see chests-on-chests
Dowdney, Burrows, 66; clock by, 66, 68;
    No. 43
dressing tables (lowboys), 135, 162, 199
Duché, Andrew, 234
Durand, John, 156; portraits by, 156;
    No. 105
Duyckinck, Gerardus, 46; newspaper
    advertisement by, 46; Fig. 24
Dwight, Stephen, 154, 156; picture frames
    by, 7, 155, 156; No. 103

E

earthenware, 234
easy chairs, 210; (Affleck), 214; No. 153;
    (Courtenay), 180, 210; No. 149; (Elfe?),
    159, 180; No. 122; (Elliott), 182
Edwards, Richard, 187, 204
Edwards, Thomas, 75, 85
Elfe, Thomas, 35, 168, 169, 180; case
    furniture by, 168; chest-on-chest by (?),
    178; Fig. 42; china tables by, 175; easy
    chair by (?), 159, 180; No. 122; library
    bookcase by (?), 169, 175, 178; Fig. 43;
    pembroke tables by (?), 83, 177; No.

121; picture frames by, 169, 170; royal
    governor's chair by, 165, 168; Fig. 40;
    tea tables by, 169, 175
Elizabeth Furnace, Lancaster County,
    Pennsylvania, 225, 227, 229; stove
    plates produced by, 225, 227; stoves
    produced by, 5, 223, 225, 227; No. 163
Elliott, Barnard, 170; portrait of (Theus), 170
Elliott, Barnard, Jr., 170; portraits of
    (Theus), 170, 172; No. 114
Elliott, John, 182, 187; chairs by, 182; easy
    chair frame by, 182; furniture label of,
    187; looking glasses supplied by, 182,
    187, 189; No. 126
Elliott, Mary Elizabeth Bellinger, 170;
    portrait of (Theus), 170
embroidery, of coats of arms, 142; No. 92
Emlen, George, 114
Emlen, Sarah Fishbourne, 114
engravings, 12, 37-69, 219; advertise-
    ments, 39, 183; Nos. 32, 33; almanacs,
    46; armorial, 106, 108, 109; bill heads,
    5, 37, 49, 52, 84; Fig. 25; bookbind-
    ings, 47; No. 24; bookplates, 37, 38,
    39, 40, 42, 45, 84, 110; Nos. 14-18, 20-
    22; British prototypes for, 37, 85;
    broadsides, 6, 46, 89, 183; No. 5; cer-
    tificates, 37, 39, 49, 52, 57-58; Nos. 29,
    34-36; city views and plans, 59, 63;
    No. 40; on clock dials, 3, 37, 66, 68-69;
    Nos. 43-45; copper plate for bookplate,
    No. 19; earliest rococo indications in, 5;
    economic considerations in the
    development of, 37; English, 2; Figs. 2,
    3; by English-trained craftsmen, 7, 9;
    on firearms, 3, 12-13, 37; furniture
    labels, 50, 52, 137, 154-55, 162, 182,
    184, 187; Figs. 32, 37, 44; on glass, 230,
    231, 232; Nos. 166-168; invitations, 37,
    49, 52, 54; No. 31; magazine illustra-
    tions, 39; maps, 37, 38, 39, 50, 59, 61-
    64; Nos. 38-42; music books, 46; No.
    23; newspaper illustrations, 46; order
    blanks, 50-51; No. 26; ornamental
    prints, 3; pamphlets, 46; on pewter, 3,
    107; printed ephemera, 3, 5, 37, 39, 49-
    52, 54, 84; on silver, 3, 37, 72, 74, 76,
    84, 85, 87, 96, 99, 101, 105, 106, 107,
    108, 110, 113, 115, 123, 127, 129, 131,
    230; suitability for rococo style of, 3;
    techniques of, 37; trade cards, 5, 37, 38,
    39, 49-51, 52, 54, 57, 84, 220; Nos. 12,
    13, 25-27, 30, 32, 33; Fig. 25; urban
    centers for, 37; as widespread manifes-
    tation of rococo ornament, 37; see also
    pattern books
ephemera, see printed ephemera
Etna Furnace, New Jersey, see Aetna
    Furnace

Evans, Lewis, 39; engraving of map by
    (Turner), 39
ewer (Lamerie), 91

F

Fairfax chimneyback (Bernard and
    Jugiez), 220, 225
Faneuil, Benjamin, 126
finials, 190, 204-5, 208; Nos. 139-146
firearms, 3, 5, 12-13, 37; Nos. 7-9
firebacks, see chimneybacks
fire buckets, painted (Claypoole), 15, 185
fireplaces, 17
fireplace wall, 28; Fig. 14
fire screens: (Affleck), 197, 217; No. 156;
    (Bernard and Jugiez), 197; No. 156;
    (Prince), 155
Fisher, John, 168, 169
Fisher, Joshua, 39, 59, 61; chart of
    Delaware Bay by, engraving after first
    edition (Turner), 39, 59, 61-62; No. 38;
    chart of Delaware Bay and River by,
    watercolor of second edition, 62;
    No. 39
fish slices, 121; (Myers), 123-24; No. 83
Fitzhugh, John, house of, near
    Fredericksburg, 32; Fig. 21
Fleeson, Plunket, 11, 17, 185; upholstery
    by, 185, 214
flintlock pistols, 12-13; No. 8
flintlock rifles, 5, 12, 13; Nos. 7, 9
Flower, Elizabeth, 13; embroidered silk
    needlework picture by, 13; No. 10
Folwell, John, 6, 15, 183, 220; painted
    standard designed by, 6, 15, 89; Fig. 4;
    portrait busts by, 205; Speaker's Chair
    by, 183, 213; stove patterns carved by,
    220
frame for memorial plaque (Woodin?),
    172; No. 116
frames, see looking-glass frames; picture
    frames
Franklin, Benjamin, 7, 39, 101, 225, 229;
    correspondence of, 9, 225, 234; instruc-
    tions for the building and furnishing of
    his house given by, 9; interest in porce-
    lain of, 234, 239; as magazine dis-
    tributor, 39; stove invented by, 220
Franklin, James, 220
Franklin stoves, 220, 223; (Hopewell
    Furnace): 225; front plate from,
    No. 161
Franks, David, 77, 80, 121, 131
Frazar, Thomas, 147
Frederick (Prince of Wales), 23
French and Indian War (1754-63), 10, 38,
    59, 62, 64, 77, 78, 153

"French Chairs," 210, 213

Frothingham, Benjamin, Jr., 137; furniture label engraved for (Hurd, N.), 50, 137; Fig. 32

Fueter, Daniel Christian, 45, 76, 121; basket marked by, 76, 121, 122, 123, 127; *121*; No. 81; cruet stand marked by, 76, 124, 126; No. 85; salver marked by, 76, 113; No. 74; whistle and bells marked by, 121

furniture (furnituremaking), 3, 12, 83, 133–217, 219; advertisements, as documentation for the makers of, 153, 154, 159, 161, 166, 168, 182, 183, 184, 185; armchairs, 155, 165, 167, 213; Nos. 113, 151, 152; Fig. 39; bedsteads, 159, 165, 169; Fig. 38; block-front treatment of, 135, 136; bombé-front treatment of, 135, 136, 143, 145; bookcases, 137, 169, 183; cabriole legs, 135, 147, 161, 182, 185, 194, 210; capitol chair, 167, 168; Fig. 39; card tables, 147, 155, 161, 165, 194–95, 214, 217; Nos. 98, 108, 109, 131, 132, 154; carving of, 3, 133, 134, 135, 136, 137, 153–54, 182, 183, 191–92, 202, 204; case furniture, 136, 137, 143–45, 147, 162, 168, 178, 199, 202, 204, 220, 222; Nos. 93–95, 110, 111, 136–138; Figs. 35, 42, 43, 47; chairs, 7, 9, 133, 135, 136, 147, 151, 155, 165, 166, 167, 168, 169, 180–81, 182, 183, 185, 209–10, 217; Nos. 96, 97, 100, 101, 112, 113, 122, 123, 147–149, 151, 152, 153, 155; Figs. 39, 40; chests, 135, 162; chests of drawers, 11, 136, 137, 143–44, 153, 162; Nos. 94, 95, 111; Fig. 35; chests-on-chests, 136, 137, 143, 144, 162, 169, 178, 199, 204; No. 93; Fig. 42; china tables, 4, 135, 152, 167, 174–75; Nos. 102, 119, 120; desks, 135, 137, 162, 169, 183; desks and bookcases, 162, 199, 202, 204, 205, 208; No. 110; double chests, *see* chests-on-chests; dressing tables (lowboys), 135, 162, 199; earliest indications of rococo style in, 5; easy chairs, 159, 180, 182, 210, 214; Nos. 122, 149, 153; English, 4, 7, 9, 151, 156, 213; Nos. 101, 104; English prototypes for, 144, 153, 155, 156, 165, 174, 204; by English- or foreign-trained craftsmen, 7, 9, 153, 154, 166–67, 168, 169, 182, 183, 184, 185, 192, 202; finials, 190, 204–5, 208; Nos. 139–146; fire screens, 155, 197, 217; No. 156; frame for memorial plaque, 172; No. 116; gilding and, 133, 138, 156; height of rococo style in, 133; high chests (highboys), 5, 135, 162, 191, 199, 202, 204, 205; Nos. 136–138; Fig. 47; imported from England, 135, 143, 145, 151, 155, 156, 165, 166, 169, 170, 182,

185, 187; joinery techniques used for, 133; library bookcase, 169, 175, 178; Fig. 43; linen presses, 162; looking-glass frames, 133, 155, 156, 187, 189, 198; Nos. 126, 127; Fig. 45; lowboys, *see* dressing tables; Marlborough legs, 185, 191, 194; Masonic chairs, 31, 166, 168, 180–81; No. 123; method of construction for, in America, 133; naturalistic carving of, 133, 182; neoclassical elements of, 137, 175, 178; nonimportation agreements, effect on, 134, 153, 184, 187; painting of, 133; parlor suite, 184, 185, 191, 214, 217, 239; Nos. 153–156; patrons of, 134, 136–37, 143; pattern books, as design sources for, 134, 135, 137, 147, 152, 154–55, 166, 167, 168, 169, 182–83, 190, 192, 202, 204, 205, 209, 210; pembroke tables, 83, 177; No. 121; picture frames, 7, 133, 135, 137–38, 142, 155, 156, 169, 170, 172, 186; Nos. 89–92, 103–105, 114, 115, 124, 125; Figs. 33, 34, 41; pierced work on, 133, 135, 175, 204; pier table, 187; Queen Anne style of, 135, 184–85; regional styles of, 134, 135, 159, 161, 162, 165, 166, 182, 183, 185, 202, 211; royal governor's chair, 165, 168; Fig. 40; in rural areas, 133, 166; serpentine fronts of, 136, 137, 143, 145, 161, 162, 191, 194, 214; settees, 147, 153, 155, 217; No. 99; side chairs, 5, 7, 9, 135, 136, 147, 151, 155, 165, 183, 209; Nos. 96, 97, 100, 101, 112, 147, 148; slab tables, 4, 133, 183, 191–92, 202, 217; Nos. 129, 130; sofas, 4, 155, 185, 211, 214; No. 150; Speaker's Chair, 183, 213; tables, 4, 135, 147, 152, 155, 159, 161, 167, 174–75, 177, 185, 187, 191–92, 194–98, 217; Nos. 98, 102, 106–109, 117–121, 129–135; tall clocks, 199, 204; tassel-back chairs, 165; No. 112; tea tables, 159, 161, 169, 174, 175, 196–98; Nos. 106, 107, 117, 118, 133–135; upholstered, 147, 153, 168, 180, 185, 211, 213, 214; Nos. 99, 122, 149–153, 155; in urban centers, 133, 166; wall brackets, 190; No. 128; Fig. 46; window cornices, 155; wood used for, 5, 133, 156, 180; writing tables, 183

furniture labels, 52, 154–55, 182, 184, 187; Figs. 37, 44; (Hurd, N.), 50, 137; Fig. 32

G

Gallaudet, Elisha, 42, 45; bookplates engraved by, 42, 45; No. 20

Galloway, Grace Growden, 101

Galloway, Joseph, 101, 103

Galloway family, 9, 78, 113

"Garvan Carver," 202; high chest by, 202, 204; No. 136

General Society of Mechanics and Tradesmen, New York, 57

Genteel Houshold Furniture in the Present Taste ("Society of Upholsterers"), 3, 154–55

Gentleman and Cabinet-Maker's Assistant, The, 6, 183; proposals for the printing by subscription of, 6, 183; No. 5

Gentleman and Cabinet-Maker's Director, The (Chippendale), 3–4, 5, 143, 152; Chinese aspect of rococo represented in, 168, 175; copies of, in American colonies, 137, 167, 169, 182–83; designs in, related to silver work, 83; engravings from, 5; Nos. 1, 6; "French Chairs" illustrated in, 210, 213; furniture designs, based on or copied from engravings in, 32, 54, 155, 166, 169, 174–75, 178, 181, 183, 184, 192, 202, 205, 209, 210, 213; inexpensive version of, 154; influence of, 182–83, 202; modes of design covered by, 4, 123, 133; third, enlarged edition of, 182–83; title page of, 4, 6, 183; No. 6; *see also* Chippendale, Thomas

Gillingham, James, 184, 198; tea tables by, 196

glass, 5, 9, 12, 219, 229–32; Nos. 166–168; goblets, 231; (American Flint Glass Manufactory), 230, 231; No. 166; (New Bremen Glassmanufactory), 5, 232; No. 168

Goddard, John, 94, 137

Godwin, Abraham, 57; certificate of membership engraved by, 15, 57, 89; No. 34

gold, 115; buttons, 115, 119; shoe buckles, 115, 117, 119; No. 78; snuff boxes, 115, 119; No. 79; whistle and bells, 115, 117; No. 77

Gold and Silver Smith's Society, New York City, 76, 131

Goldthwait, Ezekiel, portrait of (Copley), 138

Goldthwait, Mrs. Ezekiel, portrait of (Copley), 138

Gould, Nathaniel, 137

Grant, Samuel, 135, 136

Gravelot, Hubert, 2

Green, Mrs. Edward, portrait of (Copley), 138; No. 89

Greene, Benjamin, 93

Greene, Gardiner, 145

Greenwood, John, 38

Grimke, John Paul, 78, 104

Guillim, John, book by: *Display of Heraldry*, 38, 40

Gunston Hall, Virginia, 32

H

Hainsdorff, Henry, 169

Hall, Charles, 103; coffee pot marked by, 103, 104; No. 63

Hall, Peter, 168–69

Hall, Thomas, 29, 31

Hamilton, George, 167, 175

Hammond, Matthias, 29, 31; house of, Annapolis, 31

Hancock, Thomas, 138; portrait of (Copley), 138

Hand-in-Hand Fire Company, New York, invitation for meetings of (Dawkins), 52, 54; No. 31

Hardcastle, Henry, 153, 154, 159, 165, 168; architectural carving by, 153–54

Harison, Richard, 121

Harland, Thomas, 68, 69

Harrison, Peter, 18

Harvard College, Cambridge, 138

Hay, Anthony, 166–67; china tables by, 174–75; Nos. 119, 120; Masonic chairs by, 168

Heath, John, 76, 113; punch bowl marked by, 113; salver marked by, 94, 113; No. 73

Hensley, William, 28; house of, Queen Annes County, Maryland, 28

Hewson, John, 11

Heyward, Daniel, house of, Charleston, 35

high chests (highboys), 5, 135, 162, 182, 191, 199, 202, 204, 205; Nos. 136–138; (Clifton), 182, 199, 204; Fig. 47; (Garvan type), 202, 204; No. 136; (Tufft), 204

Hoeger, Andreas, 59; plan of Bethlehem Tract by (?), 59; No. 37

Hollis, Thomas, 138; portrait of (Copley), 138; Fig. 33

Holmes, Nathaniel, 135

Holyoke, Edward, 138

Holyoke, Edward A., 71

Holyoke, Mary Vial, 71

Hopewell Furnace, Berks County, Pennsylvania, 223, 227; Franklin stove produced by, 225; front plate from, No. 161; stoves produced by, 5, 45, 223; No. 160

Hopkinson, Francis, 45; bookplate of (Dawkins), 45; No. 22

Houshold Furniture, see *The Universal System of Houshold Furniture* (Ince and Mayhew)

Huber, John Jacob, 225

Hubert, Lawrence, 78, 107

Hulbeart, Philip, 77, 78, 89, 91; cream pot marked by, 15, 89, 94, 121; No. 55

Humphreys, Richard, 77, 78, 99, 101; coffee pot on stand marked by, 94, 96, 99; *99*; No. 61; sauceboats marked by, 114, 236; No. 76

Hurd, Jacob, 38, 94; teapot marked by, 84, 85; Fig. 28

Hurd, Nathaniel, 37–38, 40; bookplates engraved by, 38, 40, 42, 50; No. 14; furniture label engraved by, 50, 137; Fig. 32; order blanks engraved by, 50–51; No. 26; portrait of (Copley), 38; printed ephemera engraved by, 50; as silversmith, 75; trade cards engraved by, 38, 50–51; No. 26

Hutchinson, Thomas, 168; royal governor's chair by, 165, 168; Fig. 40

Hutt, John, 49; trade card engraved by, 52; Fig. 25

I

Ince, William, 3; pattern book by: *The Universal System of Houshold Furniture* (with Mayhew), 3, 54, 152, 169, 183, 192

Inch, John, 101; coffee pot marked by, 101–3, 104; Fig. 29

Ingraham, Reuben, 69; dial of a clock by (engraved by Avery), 69; No. 45

inkstand (Syng), 126–27

invitations, 37, 49; (Dawkins?), 52, 54; No. 31

Isaac, Lazarus, 230; glass engraving by, 230, 231; No. 166

J

Jackson, William, 37; trade card of (Revere), 37; No. 13

Jefferson, Thomas, 106, 166, 181, 183

Johnson, Thomas, 3, 23, 197; copies after engravings of, 28; engravings by, 39, 184, 190, 202, 225; Figs. 46, 48; influence of the designs of, 202, 205; pattern books by: *A New Book of Ornaments*, 3, 202; Fig. 48; *One Hundred and Fifty New Designs*, 3, 54, 68, 183, 190; Fig. 46

Johnston, Thomas, 37–38; bookplates by, 38, 40; No. 15; map cartouches engraved by, 50, 59; music books engraved by, 46; picture frame by, 137; trade cards engraved by, 38, 49–50; No. 25

Jugiez, Martin, 184; *see also* Bernard and Jugiez

jugs, 127; (Myers), 127; No. 87

K

Kennedy, Robert, 54, 57; advertisement done for (Smither), 39; No. 33; trade card of (Smither), 54, 57; No. 33

Kentucky rifles, *see* flintlock rifles

Kilburn, James, 155; portraits by, 155, 156; Nos. 103, 104

King, Daniel, 185; andirons by, 185

King George's War (1744–48), 109, 134

Kip, Richard, 52; trade card of (Hutt), 52; Fig. 25

Kuntz, Jacob, 12–13; flintlock pistols by, 12–13; No. 8; flintlock rifle by, 5, 12; No. 7

L

ladle (Riemer), 124; No. 84

Lamb, Anthony, 52; trade card of (Dawkins), 52, 54; No. 30

Lamerie, Paul de, 2, 92; basket marked by, 121; ewer marked by, 91; tea service marked by, 77, 80, 131; Fig. 27

Lancaster, Pennsylvania, silver produced in, 73, 101, 103

Langdon, John, 21; house of, Portsmouth, 21; Fig. 8

Lansing, Jacob Gerritse (1736–1803), 93; sugar dish by (?), 5, 88, 92–93, 131; No. 57

Lardner, Elizabeth Branson, 108–9

Lardner, Lynford, 108–9; house of, near Tacony, Pennsylvania, 108

Lauck, Simon, 13; flintlock rifle by, 13; No. 9

Lectures on Rhetoric and Belles Lettres (Blair), 47; back cover of, No. 24; binding of (Aitken), 47

Lee, Jeremiah, 20, 135, 137; house of, Marblehead, 20–21, 25, 51, 137, 220; Figs. 6, 7

Lewyn, Gabriel, 88; teapot marked by, 87–88; No. 54

library bookcase (Elfe?), 169, 175, 178; Fig. 43

Library Company of Philadelphia, 40, 78, 108–9, 183, 208

linen presses, 162; (Burling), 162; (Prince), 162

Liverpool, England, porcelain produced at, 234, 236

Livingston, Christina Ten Broek, 80

Livingston, Mary Stevens, 106

Livingston, Philip, 25, 80

Livingston, Robert, 106

Lloyd, Edward, IV, 29; house of, Annapolis, 29, 31; Fig. 16

Lock, Matthias, 2–3, 6, 18, 40, 45, 225; engravings by, 2, 5, 39; No. 2; Fig. 2; pattern books by: *Book of Shields*, 37, 204; *A New Book of Ornaments with Twelve Leaves* (with Copland), 2–3, 5, 25, 37, 155, 225; No. 2; *The Principles of*

Ornament, or the Youth's Guide to Drawing of Foliage, 2; Fig. 2
Locke, John, 205, 208; finial busts of, 205, 208; No. 144
Logan, James, 40, 182
Logan, William, 204–5
looking-glass frames, 133, 156, 187, 189, 198; No. 126; (Bernard and Jugiez), 187; (Elliott), 182, 187, 189; No. 126; (Reynolds), 187, 189, 217; No. 127; Fig. 45; (Strachan), 155
Lord, John, 35, 169
Louisiana, chart of the coast of, engraving (Dawkins), 59, 64; No. 41
lowboys, *see* dressing tables
Lowestoft, England, porcelain produced at, 236
Lyon, James, music book by: *Urania*, 46

M

McCormick, Daniel, 119
McElroy, Archibald, 239
McIlworth, Thomas, 156
McIntire, Samuel, 136, 144
MacPherson, John, 26; house of, near Philadelphia, 26, 28; Fig. 12
Magrath, Richard, 169
Manigault, Peter, 169
Manwaring, Robert, 3, 137; *The Cabinet and Chair-Maker's Real Friend and Companion*, 3, 135, 137, 147, 165; engraving from, Fig. 36
maps, 39, 59, 61–64; (Buell), 59, 64; No. 42; (Dawkins), 59, 64; No. 41; (Dawkins?, after Scull), 59, 63; No. 40; (Fisher), 62; No. 39; (Turner, after Fisher), 39, 61, 62, 63; No. 38
Marblehead, Massachusetts: architectural decoration from, 20, 135; furniture produced in, 135
Marlboro Furnace, Virginia, 220, 225; stove plate produced by, 5, 225; No. 162
Marlborough style, 185, 211
Marmion, near Fredericksburg, 32; Fig. 21
Martin, Ebenezer, 136
Maryland: architectural decoration from, 28; engraved clock dials from, 66
Mason, George, 32; house of, Virginia, 32
Masonic chairs: (Bucktrout), 31, 166, 180–81; No. 123; (Hay), 168
Mayberry, Thomas, 198
Mayhew, John, 3; *The Universal System of Houshold Furniture* (with Ince), 3, 54, 152, 169, 183, 192
Mears, Lewis, 76, 106, 110
Meissonnier, Juste-Aurèle, 1–2; ornamental design engraved by, 2; Fig. 1

Mickle, Samuel, 185
Middleton, Arthur, 177
Middleton, Mary Izard, 177
Middleton Place, outside Charleston, 177
military flags, 6, 15; (Folwell and Claypoole), 6, 15, 89; Fig. 4
milk pots, 76
Milne, Edmund, 77, 104
Milton, John, 205, 208; finial busts of, 205, 208; No. 145
Minshull, Mr., 154
Moffatt, John, 21; house of, Portsmouth, 21
Morris, George, 234, 236, 239; *see also* American China Manufactory
Morris, Robert Hunter, 61
Morris-Jumel house, New York City, 22
Mount Airy, Warsaw, Virginia, 32
Mount Pleasant, near Philadelphia, 26, 28; Fig. 12
Mount Pleasant, New York City, 23, 155; architectural decoration in, 23, 155; No. 11
Mount Vernon, Virginia, 31, 175; Fig. 19
mugs, 106
Murray, John, 93, 110
Murray, Lady Anne, memorial to, 172; No. 116
Murray, Lucretia Chandler, 93, 110
music books, title pages of, 46; (Dawkins), 46; No. 23
Myers, Myer, 76, 119, 121; ale jugs marked by, 76, 106, 127; No. 87; basket marked by, 4, 75, 122–23, 124; No. 82; cann marked by, 122; coasters marked by, 122; coffee pot marked by, 122; cream pot from the shop of, 91–92; No. 56; dish ring marked by, 75, 122, 123; Fig. 30; fish slices marked by, 123–24; No. 83; gold objects marked by, 117, 119; Nos. 78, 79; salver marked by, 76, 110; No. 72; shoe buckle marked by, 117, 119; No. 78; snuff box marked by, 119; No. 79; snuffer stand marked by, 126; sugar dish marked by, 91–92; No. 56; tankard marked by, 76, 106, 107; No. 66

N

Nagle, George, 13
Needham, Thomas, Jr., 136, 144; chest of drawers by (?), 136, 137, 143–44; Fig. 35
needlework, 13; No. 10
neoclassicism, 4, 5, 12, 78, 136; in engraving, 154; furniture made in the style of, 137, 175, 178; in portraiture, 186; in silver work, 96
Nevell, Thomas, 26
New Book of Cyphers, A, 13

New Book of Ornaments, A (Copland), 2, 37, 155; Fig. 3
New Book of Ornaments, A (Johnson), 3; engraving from, 202; Fig. 48
New Book of Ornaments with Twelve Leaves, A (Lock and Copland), 2–3, 5, 25, 37, 45, 155, 225; engraving from, No. 2
New Bremen Glassmanufactory, Frederick County, Maryland, 231; covered tumbler produced by, 232; No. 167; goblet produced by, 5, 232; No. 168
Newburyport, Massachusetts: architectural decoration from, 18, 20, 135; furniture produced in, 135
New England: cast iron work produced in, 219, 220; exports to England from, 168; furniture produced in, 133, 162, 182; silver produced in, 85
New Jersey, cast iron work produced in, 219
Newport, Rhode Island, 94; furniture produced in, 94, 135; silver produced in, 94
newspapers: advertisements for, 46; (Duyckinck), 46; Fig. 24; engraved illustrations for, 46
New York, 9, 153; architectural decoration from, 17–18, 22, 23, 25, 153–54, 156; case furniture produced in, 162; commercial ties to England of, 75, 153; earliest appearance of rococo style in, 153; engraving in, 37, 42, 45, 52, 54; furniture carvers immigrating to, 134; furniture produced in, 134, 153–65, 168; nonimportation agreements passed in, 10–11, 153; paper hangings from, 17; population of, 182; prominence of, 134; prosperous period of, 76, 77, 153; silver exported to, 75, 122; silver produced in, 71, 73, 74, 75–76, 87, 91–92, 99, 105, 106, 109, 110, 113, 121, 122, 124, 127
New-York Gazette and the Weekly Mercury, The, advertisement in (Duyckinck), 46; Fig. 24
New York Marine Society, 57; certificate of membership of, 57
New York Mechanick Society, 57; certificate of membership of (Godwin), 15, 57, 89; No. 34
New York State: cast iron work produced in, 219; engraving in, 42
Noel, Garett, 154
Noel and Hazard, New York, 155
Nomini Hall, Virginia, 95, 166
nonimportation agreements, 10–11, 15, 71, 134, 153, 184, 187, 219, 227, 229, 234
Norman, John, 6, 49, 68, 183; engraving by (after Swan), 6, 68; No. 4

Norris, Issac, 40, 45, 47, 101; bookplate
of (Turner), 7, 40, 45; No. 21
North Carolina, furniture produced in, 166

O

Oeuvre de Juste-Aurèle Meissonnier,
ornamental design from, 2; Fig. 1
Old, Elizabeth Stiegel, 230
Old, James, 227, 228, 230; *see also*
Reading (Redding) Furnace
Old, William, 230
Oliver, Andrew, 40; bookplate of
(Revere), 40
Oliver family, 40; bookplate with family
arms of (Johnston), 40; No. 15
One Hundred and Fifty New Designs
(Johnson), 3, 54, 68, 183, 190; engrav-
ing from, Fig. 46
order blanks (Hurd, N.), 50-51; No. 26

P

Paine, Lois Orne, 83
Paine, William, 83; tea service ordered by
(Revere), 83, 85, 96, 106, 114, 122; 97;
No. 49
Palmer, Joseph, 50; order blank of (Hurd,
N.), 50-51
paper hangings (wallpaper), 17, 20-21, 25,
35; Fig. 10
papier-mâché, 17, 23, 31, 35
Parisien, Otto, 76
Parkinson, Joseph, 169
parlor suite, for Cadwalader (Affleck,
Bernard and Jugiez, Reynolds), 184,
185, 191, 214, 217, 239; Nos. 153-156
pattern books, 59; (Copland), 2, 37, 155;
Fig. 3; (Ince and Mayhew), 3, 54, 152,
169, 183, 192; (Johnson), 3, 54, 68, 183,
190, 202; Figs. 46, 48; (Lock), 2, 37,
204; Fig. 2; (Lock and Copland), 2-3,
5, 25, 37, 45, 155, 225; No. 2; (Manwaring), 3, 135, 137, 147, 165; Fig. 36;
(Meissonnier), 1-2; Fig. 1; (Swan), 6,
18, 21, 28, 183; No. 3; see also *The
Gentleman and Cabinet-Maker's Director*
Peale, Charles Willson, 186; portraits by,
186, 217; Nos. 124, 125
Pearce, Abraham, 168, 169
Peaston, William, 174; salver by, 174
Peaston, William and Robert, London,
91; coffee pot assayed by, 91-92
pembroke tables, 177; (Elfe?), 83, 177;
No. 121
Penington, Edward, 78, 101, 104, 113
Penington, Sarah Shoemaker, 78, 101,
104, 113

Penn, Ann Allen, 213
Penn, John, 183, 185, 189, 205, 211, 213,
229, 239; house of, near Philadelphia,
184, 213
Pennsylvania: architectural decoration
from, 26, 28; cast iron work produced
in, 219, 223, 225, 227; firearms from,
12-13; Nos. 7, 8; furniture produced in,
133, 162
Pennsylvania-German community, 5, 59,
223, 227, 229
Petrie, Alexander, 104; coffee pots
marked by, 78, 103, 104; No. 64
pewter, 3, 107; tankard, 107; No. 67
Philadelphia, 9, 153, 182; architectural
decoration from, 17-18, 26, 28; Figs.
12-14; case furniture produced in, 182,
199, 202, 204, 220, 222; cast iron work
produced in or near, 219, 220, 223;
commercial ties to Boston of, 182; early
history of, 182; engraving in, 37, 39,
45, 46, 59, 62-63; furniture carvers
immigrating to, 134, 182, 183, 202; furniture produced in, 7, 9, 133, 134, 153,
182-217; glass produced in, 219, 229-31;
high chest, as symbol of rococo in, 5,
182, 199; influence of furniture produced in, 182; maps and plans of, 63;
(Dawkins?, after Scull), 59, 63; No. 40;
(Turner), 63; nonimportation agreements passed in, 10-11, 227, 229, 234;
pattern books recorded in, 182-83, 202;
population of, 182; porcelain produced
in, 219, 234, 236, 239; prominence of,
77, 134, 219; prosperous period of, 77,
182, 219; silver exported to, 77, 80, 91,
99, 101, 104; silver produced in, 71, 73,
74, 75, 77-78, 87, 89, 91, 96, 99, 101,
103-8, 113, 124, 127, 131
Philadelphia Chippendale style, 182,
183, 202
Philipse, Frederick, 22; manor house of,
Yonkers, 22-23, 35, 154, 162, 165; Fig. 9
Philipse family, 76; portraits of (Wollaston),
156
Philipse Manor, Yonkers, 22; architectural
decoration in, 22-23, 35, 154, 162, 165;
Fig. 9
pickle stands, 239; (American China Manufactory), 239; *218*; Nos. 172, 173
Pickman, Clark Gayton, 147
picture frames, 133, 137-38, 142, 155, 156,
170, 172; Nos. 89-92, 103-105, 114, 115;
Figs. 33, 34, 41; for Copley's portraits,
135, 137, 138, 142, 186; (Dwight), 7,
155, 156; No. 103; (Elfe), 169, 170;
imported from England, 138, 156; No.
104; (Johnston), 137; (Reynolds), 186,
217; Nos. 124, 125; (Strachan), 155, 156,
170; No. 105; (Welch), 135, 136, 137, 138

pier tables, 32; Fig. 20; (Tufft), 187
Pinto, Joseph, 76
Plumsted, Clement, 131; teakettle on
stand owned by (Richardson), 78, 119,
131; No. 88
Plumsted, Mary Curry, 131
Plymouth, England, porcelain produced
at, 7, 234, 236, 239; No. 170
Pompadour highboy, 202, 205; No. 138
porcelain, 9, 12, 234, 236, 239; Nos. 169-173
portrait-bust finials, 205, 208; Nos. 144-146
portrait busts, 205, 208; (Bernard and
Jugiez), 205; (Cheere), 205; (Folwell),
205; (Wedgwood), 205, 208
portraits: (Copley), 39, 135, 137, 138, 142,
156; Nos. 89-91; Figs. 33, 34; (Durand),
156; No. 105; (Kilburn), 7, 155, 156;
Nos. 103, 104; (McIlworth), 156;
(Peale), 186, 217; Nos. 124, 125;
(Stuart), 92; (Theus), 170, 172; No. 114;
Fig. 41; (Trumbull), 92; (Wollaston),
156, 170, 172; No. 115
Portsmouth, New Hampshire, 21; architectural decoration from, 18, 21;
furniture produced in, 135, 152, 174
Powel, Elizabeth Willing, 28
Powel, Samuel, 28; house of, Philadelphia, 28, 184, 227; Fig. 14
*Prices of Cabinet & Chair Work (Price
Book)*, 133-34, 184-85, 190, 191, 194,
196, 198, 199, 211, 213
Prince, Samuel, 154, 155; card tables by,
161; chests by, 162; furniture label of, 52,
154-55, 162; Fig. 37; linen presses by, 162
*Principles of Ornament, or the Youth's Guide
to Drawing of Foliage, The* (Lock), 2;
title page of, Fig. 2
printed ephemera, 3, 5, 37, 39, 49-52, 54,
84; *see also* bill heads; bookplates; certificates; furniture labels; invitations;
order blanks; trade cards
Prior, Matthew, 181
punch bowl (Heath), 113

Q

Quaï, Maurice, 1
Queen Anne style, 189; in furniture, 135,
184-85; in silver work, 77, 78, 84, 91,
103, 105
Queen Anne's War (1702-13), 134
Quincy, Josiah, Jr., 135, 168

R

Randolph, Benjamin, 54, 183, 184, 210;
advertisement done for (Smither), 39,
183; No. 32; architectural carving by,

214; ledgers of, 183; trade card of (Smither), 7, 54, 183; No. 32

Randolph, Mary W. Fennimore, 210

Randolph, Peyton, 174

Ray, Cornelius, 124

Ray, Richard, 124; portraits of the family of (Durand), 156

Ray, Sarah Bogart, 124

Read, Charles, 220, 222

Read, Charles, Jr., 222

Reading (Redding) Furnace, Schuylkill Valley, Pennsylvania, 227, 230; stove plates produced by, 227–28; No. 164

Remsen, Dorothea, 92

Remsen, Peter, 92

Revere, Paul, 38; account books (Day Books) of, 39, 40, 46, 49, 51, 74, 75, 80, 83, 89, 93, 95, 99, 117, 126; bookplates engraved by, 39, 40, 42, 96, 110; Nos. 16, 17; butter boats, 83; No. 49; canns, 83, 106; No. 49; certificates engraved by, 39, 52; No. 29; coffee pots marked by, 7, 11, 71, 83, 95–96, 99; 97; Nos. 47, 49, 60; copies of engravings by, 46, 85; cream pots marked by, 80, 83, 93, 110; No. 58; as engraver, 37–38, 39, 49, 51, 74, 75, 85, 93; as Freemason, 39, 51; as goldsmith, 75; map cartouches engraved by, 59; maturity in the rococo style of, 51; music book engraved by, 46; newspaper illustrations by, 46; notifications of meetings engraved by, 51; No. 28; porringers, 83; printed ephemera engraved by, 51–52; Nos. 27–29; Revolutionary activities of, 39; salver marked by, 42, 110, 174; No. 71; sauceboats marked by, 114; No. 49; as silversmith, 37, 39, 74, 75, 85; snuffers marked by, 126; snuffer "dish" marked by, 126; spoons marked by, 83; No. 49; sugar dishes marked by, 80, 93, 110; No. 58; tankard marked by, 83; teapot engraved by (?), 85; No. 50; teapots marked by, 4, 77, 80, 83, 85, 87, 96, 131; Nos. 49, 51; tea service marked by, 83, 85, 96, 114, 122; 97; No. 49; tea tongs marked by, 83; No. 49; trade cards engraved by, 5, 37, 39, 51, 220; Nos. 13, 27; training of, 39, 75; whistle recorded by, 117

Reynolds, James, 28, 184, 185, 205; looking-glass frames by, 187, 189, 217; No. 127; Fig. 45; picture frames by, 186, 217; Nos. 124, 125; wall bracket by (?), 190; No. 128

Rhett, William, house of, Charleston, 35

Rhode Island, silver produced in, 73

Richard, William, 228

Richardson, Joseph, 77–78, 107, 131; account books of, 80, 104; coffee pot marked by, 78, 88, 104, 113; No. 65; as executor of Hulbeart's estate, 91; shoe buckles made in the shop of, 117, 119; silver imported from England by, 80, 89, 91, 99, 101, 104, 115, 117, 119, 126; snuff boxes marked by, 119; No. 80; sugar dish marked by, 87, 88, 104; teakettle on stand marked by, 4, 78, 119, 131; 70; No. 88; teapot marked by, 87; No. 52

Richey, George, 155

Riemer, Pieter de, 76, 83; cream pot marked by, 87, 91, 92, 131; No. 48; ladle marked by, 124; No. 84; sugar dish marked by, 87, 91; No. 48; teapot marked by, 87, 91; No. 48; tea set marked by, 80, 91, 92; No. 48

rifles, see firearms

Ringgold, Thomas, 28; house of, Chestertown, Maryland, 28

Rittenhouse, David, 183, 205

Rivington, James, 58, 154

Rivington & Brown, New York and Philadelphia, 154, 183

Rivoire, Apollos, 39, 75

rococo style: characteristics of, 1, 37; Chinese mode of, 4, 123, 133, 168–69, 175; in England, 2–4, 7, 54, 71; fantasy and whimsy of, 37, 239; in France, 1–2; French, or Modern, mode of, 4, 123; Gothic mode of, 4, 123, 133; in Ireland, 123; maturity of, in Europe, 76; naturalism and, 37; origins of, 1; ornamental nature of, 3, 4, 12, 72; patrons of, 4; penchant for flouting convention of, 84; supplanted by neoclassicism, 5, 175, 178

rococo style, in America, 4–7, 9–13, 15; animal allusions, as motif in, 91, 131; as approximation of London rococo, 66; cartouches, as signature motif of, 84; colonial modifications of, as reaction against England's domination, 59, 64; economic considerations in the development of, 37, 71, 78; effect of Revolution on, 11–12, 15, 78; English prototypes as influence on, 5, 7, 9, 15, 18, 37, 38, 40, 42, 47, 49, 52, 54, 234, 236, 239; European influence on, 12; human allusions, as motif in, 42, 89–91, 121, 131, 202, 205, 210; importance of immigrant artisans to, 5, 7, 9, 26, 39, 49, 71, 229; imported goods, influence on, 6–7, 9, 71, 219; introduction of, from England, 5–7; late flowering of, in rural areas, 68; nonimportation agreements, effect on, 10–11, 15, 71,

134, 153, 184, 187, 219, 227, 229, 234; patronage for, 9, 17, 71, 78, 234; political climate, as context for development of, 9–12, 83, 183; post-Revolutionary motifs in, 64; regional character of, 9; supplanted by neoclassicism, 12, 78, 96; urban environment necessary to the development of, 9, 15, 42, 71; see also architectural carving, decoration, and ornament; cast iron; engravings; furniture (furnituremaking); glass; porcelain; silver

Roosevelt, Nicholas, 76, 83, 117; whistle and bells marked by, 117; No. 77

Ross, John, 85, 184; teapot of (Revere), 85, 87; No. 51

royal governor's chair (Elfe and Hutchinson), 165, 168; Fig. 40

Ruseles, James, 220

Rush, Benjamin, 234

Russell, Walter, 169

Ryves and Fletcher, Philadelphia, 17

S

Saint Andrew's Lodges, Boston, 51; notification of meeting for (Revere), 51

Saint Martin's Lane Academy, London, 2, 5

Saint Michael's Church, Charleston, 35

Saint Paul's Chapel, New York City, 22, 25; interior of, Fig. 11

Saint Peter's Lodge, Newburyport, 51; notification of meeting for (Revere), 51; No. 28

Salem: furniture produced in, 135, 147, 152; silver produced in, 71, 99

salvers, 94, 110, 113, 174; (Fueter), 76, 113; No. 74; (Heath), 94, 113; No. 73; (Myers), 76, 110; No. 72; (Peaston), 174; (Revere), 42, 110, 174; No. 71; (Syng), 78, 101, 113; No. 75

Sargent, Epes, 40; bookplate of (Revere), 40, 42; No. 16

Sargent, Paul Dudley, 96

sauceboats, porcelain: (American China Manufactory), 7, 236; No. 169; (Liverpool, England), 236; (Plymouth Factory, England), 7, 236; No. 170

sauceboats, silver, 114; (Humphreys), 114, 236; No. 76; (Revere), 114; No. 49

Savage, Mrs. Samuel P., portrait of (Copley), 137

Savage, Samuel P., 137

Savery, William, 185

Schuyler, Philip, 113

Schuyler family, 9, 76, 110, 113

Schuyler Mansion, Albany, 22

Scott, Peter, 166, 167; chairs by, 167; tables by, 167; tea table from the shop of, 174; No. 117

scroll finials, 204; No. 140

Scull, Nicholas, 63; maps of Pennsylvania by, 39, 63; plan of Philadelphia, engraving after (Dawkins?), 59, 63; No. 40

Sears, William Bernard, 31, 32

settees, 147, 153; (Prince), 155; 217; No. 99

Sharpe, Horatio, 31; house of, near Annapolis, 31; Figs, 17, 18

shield finials, 204; No. 139

shipbuilding, 135, 136

shoe buckles, 115, 117, 119; (Myers), 117, 119; No. 78

side chairs, 5, 7, 9, 135, 136, 147, 151, 165, 183, 209; Nos. 96, 97, 100, 101, 112, 148; (Affleck), 214; No. 155; (Bernard and Jugiez?), 209; No. 147; (Willett), 155

silver, 12, 71–131, 210, 219; absence of government regulation in the production of, 74; advertisements, as documentation for the makers of, 9, 74, 76, 77, 78, 91, 104, 107; apprenticeship, journeyman system and, 74; baluster shape used in, 105, 107, 127; baskets, 115, 121–23, 127; Nos. 81, 82; bird finials used in, 92; bowls, 108–9; Nos. 69, 70; butter boats, 83; No. 49; canns, 83, 105, 106, 109, 127; No. 49; cartouches on, 72, 84, 85, 91, 96, 101, 106, 108, 109, 110, 113, 114, 119, 121, 124, 126, 127, 129; casting on, 72, 84, 92, 93, 96, 101, 103, 106, 113, 114, 115, 117, 121, 123, 124, 126, 127, 129, 131; chasing on, 72, 73, 74, 76, 77, 78, 84, 85, 87, 89, 91, 92, 93, 94, 96, 101, 103, 104, 109, 113, 115, 117, 119, 127, 131; coasters, 121; coffee pots, 71, 72, 75, 78, 80, 83, 88, 91–92, 95–96, 99, 101, 103–4, 113, 129; 97, 99; Nos. 46, 47, 49, 60–65; Figs. 26, 29; cream pots, 80, 83, 85, 87, 89, 91–92, 93, 94, 110, 121, 131, 229; Nos. 48, 55, 56, 58, 59; cruet stands, 124, 126; No. 85; dish rings, 115, 121, 123; Fig. 30; double-bellied shape used in, 72, 84, 89, 91, 93, 96, 104, 127, 131; earliest indications of rococo style in, 5, 71, 75, 78, 121; economic factors in production of, 121; English, 2, 71, 73, 74, 77, 99, 115, 121, 127, 129, 131; No. 46; Figs. 26, 27; engraving on, 3, 37, 72, 74, 76, 84, 85, 87, 96, 99, 101, 105–8, 110, 113, 115, 123, 127, 129, 131, 230; ewer, 91; fish slices, 121, 123–24; No. 83; foreign-trained specialists, importance in the production of, 9, 71, 74–78, 92, 101, 104, 123, 131; imported from England,

75, 77, 78, 80, 88, 92, 99, 101, 103, 104, 115, 117, 119, 121, 122, 126, 142; imported from Ireland, 123; influenced by English prototypes, 85, 88, 99, 101, 103–6, 109, 113, 114, 119, 121, 123, 124, 131; jugs, 76, 106, 127; No. 87; ladle, 124; No. 84; makers' marks on, 73, 74, 76; mugs, 106; neoclassical elements of, 96; nonimportation agreements, effect on production of, 71, 78; patronage for, 71–72, 75–78, 85, 115, 121, 122; piercing on, 72, 73, 76, 115, 119, 121–23, 127, 236; pineapple finials used in, 93, 96, 103; political climate, effect on production of, 83, 95–96; porringers, 83; procedures and methods of producing, 73–74; punch bowl, 113; Queen Anne style of, 77, 78, 84, 91, 103, 105; repoussé decoration on, see chasing on; salts, 121; salvers, 94, 110, 113, 174; Nos. 71–75; sauceboats, 114; No. 76; shapes of, in rococo style, 72, 84, 85, 87, 89, 91, 93, 96, 99, 101, 103–5, 108, 127; shoe buckles, 115, 117, 119; snuff boxes, 115, 119; No. 80; snuffer stands, 126; No. 86; spoons, 83, 121; No. 49; sugar caster, 85; sugar dishes, 80, 87, 88, 89, 91–93, 110, 131; Nos. 56–58; tankards, 83, 105–7, 108, 109, 127; Nos. 66–68; teakettles, 75, 115, 127, 129; teakettles on stands, 77, 78, 80, 119, 129, 131; 70; No. 88; Figs. 26, 27; teapots, 72, 77, 80, 83, 84–85, 87–88, 91, 92, 99, 101, 103, 104, 127, 131; Nos. 49–54; Fig. 28; tea sets and services, 77, 80, 83, 85, 91, 92, 96, 114, 122, 131; 97; Nos. 48, 49; Fig. 27; tea tongs, 83; No. 49; tea urns, 101, 127, 129; Fig. 31; as urban luxury, 71, 99; whistle, 117; whistles and bells, 115, 117

six-plate stoves: (Elizabeth Furnace), 227; (Hopewell Furnace), 5, 45, 223; No. 160

Skillin, John, 136; chest-on-chest by, 136

Skillin, Simeon, 135, 136

Skillin, Simeon, Jr., 136; chest-on-chest by, 136

slab tables, 4, 133, 183, 191–92, 202, 217; Nos. 129, 130

Smith, Isaac, portrait of (Copley), 142

Smith, Mrs. Isaac, portrait of (Copley), 142

Smither, James, 39, 54, 96; advertisements by, 39, 47, 183; Nos. 32, 33; trade cards engraved by, 7, 54, 57, 183; Nos. 32, 33

snuff boxes, 115, 119; (Myers), 119; No. 79; (Richardson), 119; No. 80

snuffers, 126

snuffer stands, 126; (Myers), 126; (Revere), 126; (Syng), 126; No. 86

sofas, 211; No. 150; (Affleck), 214; (Fleeson), 185; (Prince), 155

Sommers, Humphrey, house of, Charleston, 35; Fig. 22

Speaker's Chair (Folwell), 183, 213

spoons (Revere), 83; No. 49

staircases, 17, 18, 21; Fig. 7

Stamp Act (1765), 10, 153

Stamper, John, 28; house of, Philadelphia, 28; Fig. 13

standard of the Philadelphia Light Horse troop (Folwell and Claypoole), 6, 15, 89; Fig. 4

Stedman, Charles, 28, 225, 227; house of, Philadelphia, 28

Stevenson, Cornelius, 195

Stevenson, Hamilton, 170

Stevenson, John, 170

Stiegel, Henry William, 11, 225, 227, 230, 231; table glass by, 229–31; see also American Flint Glass Manufactory; Elizabeth Furnace

stoneware, 234, 236

stove plates, 220, 223, 225, 227; (Batsto Furnace), 222; (Elizabeth Furnace), 225, 227; (Hopewell Furnace), 225; No. 161; (Marlboro Furnace), 5, 225; No. 162; (Reading Furnace), 227–28; No. 164

stoves, 5, 223, 225; (Batsto Furnace), wooden pattern for casting side plate of, 228; No. 165; (Elizabeth Furnace), 5, 223, 225, 227; No. 163; (Hopewell Furnace), 5, 45, 223, 225; No. 160; front plate from, No. 161; (Marlboro Furnace), plate from, 5, 225; No. 162

Strachan, James, 154, 156; looking-glass frames by, 155; picture frames by, 155, 156, 170; No. 105

Stratford Hall, Stratford, Virginia, 174

Stuart, Gilbert, 92

stucco work, 17, 28, 29, 35, 175

Sugar Act (1764), 10, 153

sugar-and-cream sets: (Myers), 91–92; No. 56; (Revere), 93, 110; No. 58

sugar caster (Coburn), 85

sugar dishes, 80, 89; (Lansing), 5, 88, 92–93, 131; No. 57; (Myers), 91–92; No. 56; (Revere), 80, 93, 110; No. 58; (Richardson), 78, 87, 88, 104; (Riemer), 87, 91; No. 48

Swan, Abraham, 6, 18, 21, 26, 28; pattern books by: The British Architect: Or, the Builder's Treasury of Stair-Cases, 6, 18, 21, 29, 31, 32, 183; copy after (Norman), 6, 68; No. 4; engraving from, No. 3; Collection of Designs in Architecture, 6, 28

Sympson, Samuel, 94

Syng, Philip, Jr., 77, 78, 99, 107, 108–9;

bowl marked by, 108; No. 69; canns marked by, 109; coffee pot marked by, 78, 101, 103, 104, 113; No. 62; as executor of Hulbeart's estate, 91; inkstand marked by, 126–27; salver marked by, 78, 101, 113; No. 75; snuffer stand marked by, 126; No. 86; teapot marked by, 87; No. 53; whistle and bells sold by, 117

T

table glass, 229–30, 231; (American Flint Glass Manufactory), 229–30; No. 166; (New Bremen Glassmanufactory), 231–32; Nos. 167, 168
tables, 4, 32, 135, 147, 152, 155, 159, 161, 167, 174–75, 177, 185, 217; Nos. 98, 102, 106–109, 117–121; Fig. 20
tableware, 234, 236
tall clocks, 66, 199, 204
tankards, 105, 106, 108, 127; (Bayly), 107; No. 68; (Bradford, W., Jr.), 107; No. 67; (Myers), 76, 106–7; No. 66; (Revere), 83; (Van Dyck), 109
tassel-back chairs, 165; No. 112
Tayloe, John, 32; house of, Warsaw, Virginia, 32; table from, 32; Fig. 20
Tea Act (1773), 83, 95
teakettles, 75, 115, 127, 129
teakettles on stands, 129; (Lamerie), 77, 80, 131; Fig. 27; (Richardson), 4, 78, 119, 131; 70; No. 88
teapots, 5, 72, 80, 84–85, 87–88, 92, 99, 101, 103–4, 127; (Coburn), 84–85, 87; No. 50; (Hurd, J.), 5, 84, 85; Fig. 28; (Lewyn), 87–88; No. 54; (Revere), 4, 77, 80, 83, 85, 87, 96, 131; 85; Nos. 49, 51; (Richardson), 87; No. 52; (Riemer), 87, 91; No. 48; (Syng), 87; No. 53
tea sets and services, 80, 83; (Lamerie), 77, 80, 131; Fig. 27; (Revere), 83, 85, 96, 114, 122; 97; No. 49; (Riemer), 80, 91, 92; No. 48
tea tables, 159, 161, 174, 196–98; Nos. 106, 107, 118, 135; (Bernard and Jugiez?), 196–97; No. 133; (Burling), 159; (Courtenay?), 197; No. 134; (Elfe), 169, 175; (Gillingham), 196; (Scott), 174; No. 117; (Tremain), 159
tea tongs (Revere), 83; No. 49
tea urns, 96, 101, 127, 129; (Brasher), 129; Fig. 31
ten-plate stove, 5, 223, 227; No. 163; (Batsto Furnace), wooden pattern for casting side plate of, 228; No. 165; (Reading Furnace), stove plate for, 227–28; No. 164

textiles, 12, 13, 15; No. 10; Fig. 4
Theus, Jeremiah, 170; portraits by, 170, 172; No. 114; Fig. 41
Thomson, Charles, 47, 96, 99–101
Tolman, Farr, 84
Tolman, Hannah Fayerweather, 84
Townsend, Peter, 155
Townshend Acts (1767), 10, 11, 83, 95
trade cards, 5, 37, 49–51, 54, 84; No. 12; (Copland), 37; (Dawkins), 52, 54; No. 30; (Hurd, N.), 38, 50–51; No. 26; (Hutt), 52; Fig. 25; (Johnston), 38, 49–50; No. 25; (Revere), 5, 37, 39, 51, 220; Nos. 13, 27; (Smither), 7, 54, 57, 183; Nos. 32, 33
Treasury of Designs (Langley), 18
Tremain, John, 159; tea tables by, 159
Trumbull, John, 92
Tufft, Thomas, 184, 198; furniture label of, 184; Fig. 44; high chest by, 204; pier table by, 187
Turner, James, 39, 45, 61; bookplates engraved by, 7, 40, 45; No. 21; maps engraved by, 39, 59, 61, 62, 63; No. 38; teapot engraved by (?), 84; Fig. 28
Turner, Mary King, 202
Turner, William, 202

U

United States of America, engraved map of (Buell), 59, 64; No. 42
Universal System of Houshold Furniture, The (Ince and Mayhew), 3, 54, 152, 169, 183, 192
upholstery (upholstered furniture), 17, 135, 147, 153, 168, 180, 211, 213, 214; Nos. 99, 122, 149–153, 155; (Fleeson), 185, 214; (Webster), 185, 214
Urania, or A Choice Collection of Psalm-Tunes, Anthems, and Hymns (Lyon), 46; engravings in (Dawkins), 46; title page of, 46; No. 23
urn finials (vase finials), 204; No. 142

V

Valois, Gabriel, 186
Van Cortlandt, Pierre, 113
Van Cortlandt House, Bronx, 22
Van Dyck, Richard, 76, 109; bowl marked by, 109; No. 70; tankards marked by, 109
Van Pelt family, 191, 202
Van Rensselaer, Catherine Livingston, 25
Van Rensselaer, Jeremias, 42; bookplate of (Gallaudet), 42, 45; No. 20

Van Rensselaer, Philip, 42; bookplate of (Billings), 5, 42; copper plate for, No. 19; house of, near Albany, 42
Van Rensselaer, Philip Schuyler, 80
Van Rensselaer, Stephen, II, 23, 25, 161; manor house of, Albany: 22, 23, 25, 155, 161; entrance hall, 5, 25; Fig. 10
Van Rensselaer family, 9, 42, 92, 161, 162, 165
Van Vechten family, 159
Van Voorhis family, 124, 126
Vassall, John, house of, Cambridge, 18, 21, 135
Verplanck, Judith Crommelin, 75, 104
Verplanck, Samuel, 75, 104, 165
Virginia: architecture in, 31–32; cast iron work produced in, 219, 225; engraved clock dials from, 66; firearms from, 12, 13; No. 9; furniture produced in, 133

W

Waite, Ezra, 35, 169
wall brackets, 190; (Reynolds?), 190; No. 128; design for (Johnson), 190; Fig. 46
wallpaper, *see* paper hangings (wallpaper)
Warren, John, 52; certificate of attendance at lectures by (Revere), 52; No. 29
Washington, George, 32, 106, 121, 183; engraved glass goblets given to, 231; as Freemason, 181; furniture owned by, 175; gold box presented to, 93; house of, Mount Vernon, 31; Fig. 19; silver cruet stand acquired by, 126; visit to John Cadwalader by, 185
Webb, Joseph, 51, 220; trade card of (Revere), 51, 220; No. 27
Webster, John, 185; upholstery covers by, 185, 214
Wedgwood, Josiah, "basalte" busts by, 205, 208
Welch, John, 135, 136; picture frames by, 135, 136, 137, 138
Welch, Joseph, 37; trade card of, 5, 37; No. 12
Welles, Thomas, 84–85; teapot of (Coburn), 85, 87; No. 50
Wentworth-Gardner house, Portsmouth, 21
Westover, near Williamsburg, 31, 175
Wharton, Thomas, 239
Whidden, Michael, III, 21
Whipham and Wright, London, 80, 104
Whipple, William, 152
whistle (Revere), 117
whistles and bells, 115, 117; (Fueter), 121; (Roosevelt), 117; No. 77; (Syng), 117
Whitehall, near Annapolis, 31; entrance hall of, 31; Fig. 18; plan and elevations of, 31; Fig. 17

Whiting, Stephen, 137–38
Willett, Marinus, 161; armchairs by, 155; card tables by, 161; side chairs by, 155; window cornices by, 155
Williams, John, 142
Williamsburg, Virginia, 31, 166; furniture carvers immigrating to, 134; furniture produced in, 134, 166–68, 174–75, 180–81
Williams family, frame for the coat of arms of, 142; No. 92
Wilson, James, 167; capitol chair attributed to, 167, 168; Fig. 39
Wilson, Mrs. Algernon, portrait of (Theus), 170; Fig. 41
Winckler, John, 78, 104
window cornices (Willett), 155
Wistar, Caspar, 204
Wistar, Mary Franklin, 204
Wollaston, John, 156, 170; portraits by, 156, 170, 172; No. 115
Wood, John, 66
Wood, Samuel, 126
Woodcock, Bancroft, 99
Woodin, Thomas, 35, 169, 172; frame carved by (?), 172; No. 116
Worcester, England, porcelain produced at, 234, 236

Y

Yale College, New Haven, 58
Yeates, Jasper, 9

Z

Zane, Isaac, 225

Photograph Acknowledgments

The following photographs are reproduced through the courtesy of these institutions: Fig. 5, Massachusetts Institute of Technology, Rotch Library Visual Collections; Fig. 8, Society for the Preservation of New England Antiquities; Fig. 9, Yonkers Historical Society; Figs. 12, 14, Philadelphia Museum of Art; Fig. 19, The Mount Vernon Ladies' Association; Fig. 20, Museum of Early Southern Decorative Arts; Fig. 24, American Antiquarian Society; Figs. 25, 44, The Winterthur Library. Fig. 23 originally appeared in Edward A. Crane and E. E. Soderholtz, *Examples of Colonial Architecture in South Carolina and Georgia* (New York: Bruno Hessling, n.d.), Plate 12.

Photograph Credits

All photographs are by David Allison, except for those acknowledged above and the following: Nos. 13, 15–17, 22–24, 27–29, American Antiquarian Society; Fig. 8, Douglas Armsden; Nos. 100, 106, Gavin Ashworth; No. 5, Avery Library; Nos. 92, 110, Luke Beckerdite; Nos. 26, 38, The John Carter Brown Library; No. 132, Will Brown; No. 102, The Carnegie Museum of Art; Nos. 130, 138, 150, 155, Fig. 38, Richard Cheek; Nos. 117, 119, 123, Figs. 39, 42, 47, Colonial Williamsburg; Nos. 166, 167, The Corning Museum of Glass; Figs. 6, 7, Frank Cousins; No. 159, Joseph Crilley; Fig. 4, First Troop Philadelphia City Cavalry; No. 9, George Fistrovich; No. 90, Figs. 33, 34, Harvard University Art Museums; Nos. 80, 129, Helga Photo Studio; No. 170, High Museum of Art; No. 39, The Historical Society of Pennsylvania; Fig. 28, Hood Museum of Art; Nos. 169, 173, Schecter Lee; No. 32, Library Company of Philadelphia; No. 45, Nathan Liverant and Son; Nos. 120, 162, Hans E. Lorenz; No. 108, Los Angeles County Museum of Art; Fig. 40, McKissick Museum; No. 168, Maryland Historical Society; Nos. 44, 50, 85, Amanda Merullo; Nos. 1–4, 6, 12, 14, 18–21, 35, 37, 41, 157, 165, 172, Figs. 1–3, 10, 21, 23, 26, 27, 36, 46, 48, Photo Studio, The Metropolitan Museum of Art; Fig. 37, Museum of the City of New York; Nos. 64, 115, 118, Figs. 41, 43, Museum of Early Southern Decorative Arts; Nos. 47, 51, 58–61, 71, 81, 93, 101, Museum of Fine Arts, Boston; No. 72, The Museum of Fine Arts, Houston; No. 42, National Geographic Society; Nos. 11, 30, 36, The New-York Historical Society; Nos. 31, 40, The New York Public Library; No. 48, John Parnell; Nos. 43, 124, 125, Fig. 45, Philadelphia Museum of Art; Fig. 15, 16, Pickering Studio; Nos. 116, 121, Terry Richardson; Fig. 35, Israel Sack, Inc., N.Y.C.; Fig. 31, Terry Schank; No. 46, Mark Sexton; No. 164, The State Museum of Pennsylvania; Fig. 32, Taylor and Dull; Fig. 22, Tebbs and Knell, Inc.; Fig. 29, Virginia Museum of Fine Arts; Figs. 17, 18, M. E. Warren; No. 25, The Winterthur Library; Nos. 33, 34, 111, 128, 137, Fig. 13, Winterthur Museum; Fig. 11, Wurts Bros.; No. 136, Fig. 30, Yale University Art Gallery. Frontispieces: engravings, The New-York Historical Society; furniture, Philadelphia Museum of Art.